Mapping the Management Journey

Mapping the Management Journey

Practice, Theory, and Context

Edited by

SUE DOPSON
MICHAEL EARL
and
PETER SNOW

OXFORD
UNIVERSITY PRESS

OXFORD
UNIVERSITY PRESS

Great Clarendon Street, Oxford OX2 6DP

Oxford University Press is a department of the University of Oxford.
It furthers the University's objective of excellence in research, scholarship,
and education by publishing worldwide in

Oxford New York

Auckland Cape Town Dar es Salaam Hong Kong Karachi
Kuala Lumpur Madrid Melbourne Mexico City Nairobi
New Delhi Shanghai Taipei Toronto

With offices in

Argentina Austria Brazil Chile Czech Republic France Greece
Guatemala Hungary Italy Japan Poland Portugal Singapore
South Korea Switzerland Thailand Turkey Ukraine Vietnam

Oxford is a registered trademark of Oxford University Press
in the UK and in certain other countries

Published in the United States
by Oxford University Press Inc., New York

British Library Cataloguing in Publication Data

Data available

Library of Congress Cataloging in Publication Data

Mapping the management journey : practice, theory, and context / edited by
Sue Dopson, Michael Earl and Peter Snow.

p. cm.

Includes bibliographical references and index.

ISBN 978–0–19–921535–5

1. Industrial management. 2. International business enterprises–Management.
I. Dopson, Sue. II. Earl, Michael J. III. Snow, Peter, 1947–
HD31.M37 2007

658–dc22   2007029898

Typeset by SPI Publisher Services, Pondicherry, India
Printed in Great Britain
on acid-free paper by
Biddles Ltd., King's Lynn, Norfolk

ISBN 978–0–19–921535–5

1 3 5 7 9 10 8 6 4 2

CONTENTS

List of Figures   vii

List of Tables   ix

List of Boxes   x

A Note on the Referencing System   xi

Notes on Contributors   xii

Introduction: When the Map Changed?   1
Sue Dopson, Michael Earl, and Peter Snow

PART I   A WORLD OF CHANGE

1 **Globalization's Regional Reality**   21
   Alan M. Rugman

2 **A Tougher World: Managerial Work and Behaviour**   49
   Rosemary Stewart

3 **The Technology of the Possible: IT, Innovation, Capitalism,
   and Globalization**   63
   Chris Sauer

4 **There and Back Again? Organization Studies 1965–2006** 80
   Janine Nahapiet

5 **Forward to the Past or Back to the Future? Leadership,
   1965–2006**   104
   Keith Grint

PART II   A BROADER LENS

6 **Public Management: Shifting Challenges and Issues** 121
   Ian Kessler and Sue Dopson

7 **Professional Service Firms: The Challenges of Innovation** 144
   Tim Morris

Contents

8   **Insights into the Management of Major Projects**   164
Peter Morris

9   **The Retailing Sector: Barrow Boys, Big Business,
and New Technology**   182
Jonathan Reynolds

PART III   MANAGEMENT FUNCTIONS: TOWARDS
A NEW SYNTHESIS

10   **Information Management: A New Age, A New Subject**   211
Michael J. Earl

11   **Corporate Strategy and Structure: The Rise and ?Fall of the
Conglomerate**   233
John McGee and Paul Simmonds

12   **Employment Relations: From Industrial Relations to
Human Resource Management**   257
Roger Undy

13   **Operations Management: Realizing Its Strategic Role**   271
Alex Hill and Terry Hill

14   **The Brave New World of Business Marketing**   289
Keith Blois

PART IV   MAPPING THE FUTURE

15   **Forty Years of Scenarios: Retrospect and Prospect**   307
Rafael Ramírez

16   **In Pursuit of Agility: Reflections on one Practitioner's
Journey Undertaking, Researching, and Teaching the
Leadership of Change**   320
Keith Ruddle

About the Editors   341
Index   343

LIST OF FIGURES

1.1	Multinational enterprise strategies and civil society	42
2.1	Demands, constraints, and choices in jobs	53
5.1	A typology of problems, power, and authority	113
6.1	Models of public-service delivery and the stakeholder consequences	137
8.1	The anatomy of major projects 'management of projects' model	168
8.2	PMBOK Guide (2004)	171
8.3	APM BOK (2005)	172
9.1	Relationship between market cap/value-added ratio and wealth creation efficiency—European General Retailers 2006	186
9.2	'Horses for courses'	188
9.3	The major elements of retail business models	190
9.4	Generic spider web chart for out-of-town discount clothing	190
9.5	Generic spider web chart for a shopping centre jeweller	190
9.6	The differences between particular types of convenience store	191
9.7	High street stores' similarities	191
9.8	The 'wheel of retailing'	192
9.9	The 'retail accordion'	193
9.10	The concept of the 'big middle'	194
9.11	A framework for considering selected ICT applications in retailing	195
9.12	Risks and opportunities in international retail development	203
10.1	A virtuous circle	215
10.2	IT as 'ambiguous technology'	224
11.1	Diversification in post-war France, Germany, and the UK	235
11.2	The rise of focused firms	235
11.3	Life cycle of conglomerate corporate strategy	252
13.1	Ideal strategy-making process	277
13.2	Real-life strategy-making process	277
13.3	Strategy debate stops at the interface	278
13.4	Result of post-assignment market review	279

13.5 Functional contributions to meeting corporate objectives
with markets at the centre of strategic development 283
13.6 Checking what customers say they want will show how
they behave 286
13.7 Markets at the centre of strategy development 287
15.1 Increased interest in scenarios since 9/11 310
15.2 Number of peer reviewed articles since 1972 313
16.1 A journey at SmithKline Beecham: Merger,
transformation, and Simply Better Way 326
16.2 The transformation journey at BP 326
16.3 Journey patterns: The redesign/reinvention journeys
show how companies moved through distinct stages and
sequences 328
16.4 Contrasting styles for radical change 328
16.5 A view of the O2 journey 330

LIST OF TABLES

1.1	World trade, 2004	23
1.2	Comparative differences in the study of international business, 1950–2010	25
1.3	Intra-regional trade in the triad, 1980–2004	31
1.4	Classification of the top 500 MNEs	33
1.5	The top home region-based companies	35
1.6	Global MNEs	36
1.7	Intra-regional sales of the 500 firms over time	36
9.1	Measuring the elements of a business model	192
9.2	The IGD global market index	204
9.3	'Top of Mind' issues amongst global food retail CEOs, 2002–6	205
11.1	FTSE100 survivors 1984–2004	237
11.2	Percentage of proposed mergers classified by type of integration	239
11.3	*Business Week* Survey of Business Profits	243
11.4	Reasons for divestitures	247
11.5	Acquisitions and divestments in the UK, 1988–93	247
13.1	Levels of strategy and their distinctive tasks	276
13.2	Current problems and retention rates	280
13.3	Trends in annual profit per customer	280
15.1	Causal textures: environments and organizations	314
16.1	Leading change—four eras of theory and practice	322

LIST OF BOXES

1.1 Offshoring: A red herring in the globalization debate   39
1.2 Globalization hits the brick wall: Microsoft and the
     European Commission   44
9.1 Key performance indicators identified by OXIRM   189
13.1 Operations development at Benetton   282

A NOTE ON THE REFERENCING SYSTEM

Full references to books, chapters, articles and papers are provided at the end of each chapter. They are listed in sequential order according to their appearance in the text, keyed to the text by superscript numbers. Where a further general reference is made to a previously referenced item, it is cited under the original superscript number. However, where further *specific* pages are cited, the reference is repeated in full identifying the relevant pages under a new superscript number.

NOTES ON CONTRIBUTORS

Keith Blois is an Emeritus Fellow of Templeton College, Oxford, and a Visiting Professor at Lancaster University. His research interests include business-to-business marketing, the marketing of services, and industrial economics. The editor of *The Oxford Textbook of Marketing*, he has published widely in the *Strategic Management Journal*, the *Quarterly Journal of Economics*, and the *Journal of Management Studies*.

Alex Hill is a Senior Lecturer at Kingston Business School and a Visiting Fellow at the Saïd Business School and at the Gordon Institute of Business Science in Pretoria. He spent ten years working in various divisions of the Smiths Group, a large engineering multinational, before entering academe.

Terry Hill is a noted international figure in the field of Operations and Manufacturing Management and runs an active consultancy practice alongside his academic role. Formerly Fellow in Operations Management at Templeton College, he has also held positions at London Business School and at the Universities of Warwick and Bath.

Keith Grint is the Professor of Defence Leadership at Cranfield University. Previously, he was Director of Research at the Saïd Business School and Fellow in Organizational Behaviour at Templeton College before joining Lancaster University Management School, then Professor of Leadership Studies and Director of the Lancaster Leadership Centre.

Ian Kessler is Fellow in Human Resource Management (HRM) and Reader in Management Studies at Templeton College. He has been involved in research projects on performance pay, ACAS, and HRM in the public-service sector. Currently conducting research on public-service modernization, funded by ESRC and Department of Health, he has advised the National Audit Office, Audit Commission, Local Government Management Board and Police Federation and was a member of the Local Government Pay Commission.

John McGee, previously Fellow in Strategic Management and Dean at Templeton, is Professor of Strategic Management and Associate Dean for Corporate Relations at Warwick Business School. Past president of the Strategic Management Society and a former associate editor of the

Strategic Management Journal and the *British Journal of Management*, he pursues research in long-term industrial change and new industries, the deconstruction of corporations and emergence of new corporate forms, international strategic alliances, and the impact of the Information Revolution on corporate headquarters and of stakeholder theories on corporate strategy.

Peter Morris, previously Professor of Engineering Project Management at UMIST and a director of Bovis Ltd, is Professor of Construction and Project Management at UCL. The author of *The Management of Projects* and *The Wiley Guide to Managing Projects*, he originated the 'management of projects' approach in this field.

Tim Morris, Fellow and Professor of Management Studies at Templeton College, has widely published in scholarly journals research on innovation in professional service firms. Over the past ten years he has examined human capital development, promotion and reward systems, and patterns of change in fields including law, architecture, and consulting.

Janine Nahapiet is an Associate Fellow of Templeton College. A member of the editorial board of *Organization Studies*, she was until recently Lead Research Fellow of the ESRC/EPSRC Advanced Institute of Management Research. Her co-authored paper 'Social Capital, Intellectual Capital and the Organizational Advantage' won the *Academy of Management Review* Best Paper Award in 1998.

Rafael Ramirez is Fellow in Strategic Management at Templeton College and Professor of Management at HEC, Paris. Formerly Visiting Professor at Shell International, he has worked at Wharton School, CNRS and SMG in Stockholm. The author of five books, he has pioneered work in scenarios, organizational aesthetics, and the revolution in value creation.

Jonathan Reynolds, Director of the Oxford Institute of Retail Management and Fellow in Retail Marketing at Templeton College, is the author of three books and over 100 articles on retailing. His research interests include e-commerce and multichannel retailing, the marketing information systems, retailer decision-making and the development of new retail forms.

Keith Ruddle is Fellow in Leadership, Organization and Change at Templeton College. After a Harvard MBA and a 25-year career in industry and as a senior partner in Andersen Consulting, he came to Oxford to undertake a thesis on transformational change. He advises and coaches senior teams and boards in government and the public and private sectors on the leadership of change.

Alan M. Rugman is L. Leslie Waters Chair of International Business at the Kelley School of Business, Indiana University, and also Professor of International Business and Professor of Business Economics and Public Policy. Thames Water Fellow in Strategic Management at Templeton College, 1998–2001, he remains an Associate Fellow of the College.

Chris Sauer is Fellow in Information Management at Templeton College. Before working as an academic in Australia and the UK on the challenges of IT projects Chris designed, built, and managed IT projects. His research has been published in four books and many leading journals. Currently joint Editor-in-Chief of the *Journal of Information Technology*, he serves on several other editorial boards and programme committees.

Paul Simmonds is a doctoral researcher at Warwick Business School, a Fellow of the Association of Chartered Certified Accountants and a Member of the Institute of Management. Before pursuing his current research on corporate structures, Paul spent over twenty years in business and held senior positions in several international companies.

Rosemary Stewart, an Honorary Fellow of Templeton College, was for many years Fellow in Organizational Behaviour at the College. The author of thirteen books including *The Reality of Management* (3rd edn., 1996) and *Evidence-Based Management* (2002), she has particular interests in managerial work and behaviour and in healthcare management.

Roger Undy, Emeritus Reader in Management, joined Templeton in 1972 after working as a fitter at Boots Ltd and studying at Ruskin and Wadham. Formerly Acting President, Dean, and Senior Tutor at the College and Director of the Oxford MSc in Industrial Relations, he chairs the Oxford MBA examination board and has just completed a study of trade union mergers.

Introduction:
When the Map Changed?

Sue Dopson, Michael Earl, and Peter Snow

The essays in this volume present a retrospect and prospect from four decades of senior executive teaching and research at Templeton College, Oxford. Templeton College cannot be said to represent an integrated school of management theory—the equivalent of the Contingency Theory Group at Aston or the Symbolic Interaction School in Chicago. Although there are clear common threads connecting the work of its fellows, their interests are too divergent and varying to be characterized as one movement. This volume, therefore, should be seen as an account of a series of highly individual (if related) journeys of exploration across the diverse terrains of management and organizational studies since the College's beginnings in the mid-1960s rather than the record of a single approach and programme of work.

Above all, it is a collection of *personal* stories and voices—of knowledge and insights resulting from individual experience. Reflecting this, the contributors have by and large eschewed the impersonal, abstract, and often impenetrable jargon of much Management Studies writing in favour of the lived reality of experience. Thus, Chris Sauer and Michael Earl in their respective chapters on technology and on information management bear witness at first hand to the emergence of information technology (IT) and information management in organizations: painfully slow, often ludicrous and Heath Robinsonian, but in retrospect powerfully irresistible. Chris Sauer writes:

How strange today to imagine a childhood in which computers play no part, but in my case my only awareness of them came through the awed respect the grown-ups showed my godfather who was responsible in the late 1950s and early 1960s for the British Army's 'electronic brain'. Towards the end of the 1960s, my first holiday job was with a computer-free Inland Revenue office. I can still smell the stagnant odour of pre- and post-war papers in its registry of cardboard files—the rotting core of this government department. Move on two years and I am in a City life assurance firm. People still use in earnest electrical adding machines and even

Facit mechanical calculators, but the adepts are dying out. Here, the company has time-sharing access to its parent company's mainframe—referred to reverently as 'the machine' as if there could be no other.

By the end of my undergraduate career in the mid-1970s, Oxford University was offering programming courses in Algol. I graduated into a young, progressive institution that had introduced data processing for all its back-office systems from its inception in 1969. Its mainframe was dedicated, not shared, and filled an air-conditioned room the size of an Olympic pool. We fed it cards into which we had hand-punched the holes. I first encountered there the relentless pressure for change that has characterized so much of the subsequent history of IT—we were redeveloping our core systems after just seven years. By the 1980s I was wrestling with the early personal computers, and by the middle of the decade I was using the very first Macintosh computers in my teaching with their radical WIMP (Windows, Icons, Menus, Pointer) interface. How extraordinary then to find just ten years later in a colleague's office in Houston a defunct Fat Mac retained as a nostalgic memory and paperweight—it looked prehistoric. For my part, a brief excursion into artificial intelligence was replaced by a more serious and enduring commitment to the real problem—how to manage investment in IT for business value.

Throughout this journey . . . it seemed as though investment in IT was for the most part an act of faith not a rational, commercial decision. I can therefore still vividly remember a technician installing MOSAIC (the first real browser) and showing me how to use it. This, I felt, was IT! For the first time, I was excited to show others what the technology could offer. . . . Today, a little over ten years on, we see companies innovating to compete on the Internet in a variety of ways. We see them working seamlessly across time zones, and reaching out to new markets and customers.

One feature, however, that Templeton fellows have had in common with a new 'school' is that they have broken new ground, and in the process have had a significant impact beyond the College, especially in the world of practice. In fields as disparate as managerial work, information management, major projects, industrial relations, retailing, and health care, they have pioneered new study. Kevin Lowe, for instance, has paid tribute in *The Leadership Quarterly* to the contribution of Rosemary Stewart in going out into the field and studying managers' actual working practices:

Professor Stewart has broadened our understanding of what managers actually do. Her work, spanning five decades . . . stands as a testimony to the benefits of a truly cumulative and programmatic research program focused on systematically exploring a phenomenon layer-by-layer, nuance-by-nuance. Her research methods were (and remain) innovative, exhaustive, and cutting edge. Using a battery of techniques such as structured interviews, diaries, structured observations, group discussions, case analyses, and critical incidents, Stewart was developing grounded theory work and implementing triangulation method before those approaches had fashionable labels.

While often highly personal, the following essays combine the specific and personal with a much broader representative relevance. This fusion is not accidental: Keith Ruddle, for instance, in his chapter on organizational agility explicitly makes the connection between his own trajectory as a student and then consultant and the larger evolutions in thinking about organizational change:

As we are increasingly assailed by prescriptions for 'leading in a world of constant change', the management dictionary has swung into action with a host of new terms: agility, adaptiveness, resilience, ambidexterity, dynamic capabilities, absorptive capacity, and more. But what should the practising leader and manager make of it all? What can, and should, they do differently to deal with change? That is the world I have lived in. In the course of thirty years of management practice, teaching, and research, my own journey has been one of flux, change, and transformation, working with—and learning from—leadership teams as they grappled with a changing world.

Can past experience help us frame new practices and ideas for the future? My own research in the 1990s on organizational transformation used the metaphor of a journey to help understand, frame, and explain strategic and organizational change—and then applied it with some success in the classroom for many of Templeton's company executive education clients. My approach in this chapter will be to take the reader through my own journey, reflecting on the way on some changing assumptions about organizational change.

The Shock of the New

As you might expect in a volume tracing the history of studies in an embryonic and volatile discipline, a recurrent theme in these chapters is the emergence—one might say, the shock—of the new. Through these forty-year journeys, the emergence of a range of new phenomena can be observed. Most notable, of course, are the rise of globalization—and the consequent need for greater cultural understanding; the accelerating pace of technological advance, especially in IT; the increasing speed and ubiquity of communication and its knock-on effects on organizational and capital structures and on managerial decision-making; above all, the relentless pressure to innovate, to leap—and keep—one step ahead of the competition by speeding up the cycle and reducing the organizational 'turning circle'.

We can also observe the progressive widening of the Management Studies lens to take in new fields such as the public-sector organizations and
professional service firms (PSFs) and project management, the subjects of
the chapters by Ian Kessler and Sue Dopson and by Tim Morris; and Peter
Morris respectively. Part and parcel of this expansion has been the export
of techniques whose home market was traditionally business. But how
appropriate and successful has the fit been? Is there a case for 'exceptional-
ism' in such fields? Or can the necessary adjustments be made to ensure
their successful application? Indeed, should the street not just be one-way
but capable of bearing lessons in both directions?

If it is possible to trace the rise, the colonization, and carving out of
new fields and functions in management studies, in others we see their
converse—subsidence, devaluation, and neglect. Such has been the fate,
concludes Terry Hill in his chapter, of Operations Management—in manufacturing and services alike—and he argues the case for a more positive
and integrated role for the function as part of a broad front combining
marketing and corporate strategy.

Another common theme is the decline of large-scale corporatist solutions imposed from above in favour of smaller-scale, more agile, and
entrepreneurial ground-up approaches. Indeed, John McGee and Paul
Simmonds in their chapter draw a parallel between the rise of management education and the evolution (then degeneration) of a particular
organizational life form: the large business conglomerate:

The business school took off as an idea, then a movement, in the USA in the
late 1950s as a result of the Howell and Gordon reports. In the mid-1960s, a
similar groundswell developed in the UK. But at this time business itself was also
changing rapidly. The period of post-war restrictions had given way to economic
expansion, albeit often fitful and unreliable. Both in the USA and in the UK, the
way in which businesses saw their product markets and organized themselves
began to change. In particular, the diversified corporation, and its sibling the
conglomerate, were beginning to emerge. Since then conglomerates have had
a chequered history, exhibiting growth, crisis, and reinvention but eventually
becoming unfashionable and unwanted.

This seems an appropriate moment, therefore, to take stock of the conglomerate
phenomenon that has so closely paralleled the business school movement over
the past forty years. Unlike conglomerates, business schools have expanded in
number and size and are here to stay. But all of us who have been involved at
Templeton and other centres of executive education remember the many diversified or conglomerate companies that we served as clients. We remember the
debates we had about the logic of the diversified corporation and the struggles
these companies had in establishing new managerial logics in order to conduct

their business effectively. We remember the acquisitions, the rush to reorganize and turnaround, the repeated reorganizations, the cost-cutting, the turnover of management teams. Although memory is distorted by recent biting critiques of the conglomerate, we also remember the many clients who fought seemingly against the odds to create viable businesses and in doing so created a new breed—the conglomerate manager.

The conglomerate was a creature of its time, and it is a strength of chapters such as Roger Undy's on industrial relations and Chris Sauer's on technology that they try to place such developments firmly within their times. Sauer writes of the connection between computers and *zeitgeist*:

These decades [the 1950s, 1960s, and early 1970s] were characterized by a curious mix of post-war-Festival-of-Britain-Swinging-Sixties-style optimism together with major macro-economic discomfort (massive debt, balance of payments problems, and devaluation) and chronic industrial unrest. On the one hand, political leaders told the people 'you've never had it so good' and that the economy would be fired by the 'white heat of technology', offering a brave new world of technology-enabled wealth and comfort. On the other hand was the daily experience of strikes and a disaffected management class constrained from making unlimited profits by the combination of trade unions, taxes on business, and other regulations.

The early 1970s saw optimism ebb, leaving only a residue of economic distress epitomized by the Three Day Week. In those circumstances, the automational capacity of IT had two obvious attractions for managers. First, automating work reduced management's dependence on labour. Second, it promised cost savings, which, for many companies, appeared a lower risk way of improving the bottom line than innovating new products and services. There were of course other benefits such as more accurate and consistent calculation of payroll but as such processes were inward, rather than customer-facing, they were valued more for their contribution to cost saving than for any intrinsic value addition.

The 1970s surge in data processing generated vast banks of information with the potential to inform decision-making and management. In practice, the data were used for little more than to provide adequate controls over the automated processes. It was the era when you found in managers' offices vast piles of green-lined printouts, delivered daily, weekly, or monthly. The recipients either did not know what they were for or did not care. So, although many saw the potential of management information to improve decision-making and shape improved work practices, the potential was rarely realized because there was little incentive by way of performance cultures and associated rewards to encourage innovation.

With the 1980s, we saw Margaret Thatcher successfully revolutionize the economy with a number of policy thrusts: deregulation, the diminution of the power of organized labour, the incentivization of entrepreneurship, support for business, and the shift of much economic activity from the public to private sector. Profit-seeking became more acceptable as the shareholder society was encouraged. Business responded to the improved environment by passing responsibility to lower levels. Now, more individuals stood to gain financially by innovating. IT need no longer be restricted to cost-saving through automation but could focus on delivering differentiated business processes that supported revenue growth. Indeed, the transition from automation to strategic advantage is illustrated by the demise of the expert systems movement, which extended the logic of automating routine labour to automating scarce expertise. With the power of labour already diminished by government reform and the new and much greater strategic poten-tial of the technology, expert systems also lost their attraction.... The ideas of strategic IT and IT for competitive advantage emerged as themes in both prac-titioner and academic thinking at this time.

Roger Undy argues in his chapter that the phoenix-like rise of Human Resource Management (HRM) out of the ashes of industrial relations directly reflected changes not only in business but also in Number Ten, Downing Street. The result, he writes, was that:

by 2006, the term 'human resource management' (HRM) had displaced 'industrial relations' as the dominant focus in employment relations practice. It had also gained popularity in the academic world as posts, departments, and courses in HRM mushroomed, while those in industrial relations declined. Oxford was not exempt from such developments. The Oxford M.Sc. in Industrial Relations and Human Resource Management (introduced in 1983) was suspended in 2004–5 and replaced by a human resources stream in the M.Sc. in Management Research. As noted by Sisson, university courses in 'industrial relations' had become difficult to sell to managers. A survey of practitioners in 2005 reported that 'industrial relations' was a term 'no longer widely used by employers'. Moreover, its replace-ment, HRM, was more than just another name for personnel management. It brought with it from the USA 'a radically different philosophy and approach to the management of people at work'.

HRM in this wider sense was initially recognized as antipathetic to industrial relations. As the 'new orthodoxy', it offered a different lens through which to view the employment relationship, starting from the premise that employees were a resource in the same way that capital was a resource. Further differences were identified distinguishing HRM from industrial relations. Indeed, Storey identified twenty-seven such points of difference. Guest, drawing on empirical evidence, noted that the driving force behind HRM had little to do with industrial relations: rather it was driven by the pursuit of competitive advantage.

Critically, the assumption that industrial relations were inherently pluralist was replaced by HRM's unitarist frame of reference. Hence, conflict—institutionalized in industrial relations—was de-emphasized (or considered deviant) in HRM: it focused on the individual worker and not the collective. Trade unions, which had been central to industrial relations, were thus marginalized in the pursuit of an HR strategy. In addition, while the management of industrial relations had frequently been a specialist's job, HRM was seen as the responsibility of line managers. Managements' authority over employment relations was therefore largely seen as unproblematic. In both its hard form, emphasizing the use of the worker as a resource, and its soft form, emphasizing the human potential for commitment, HRM was thus well suited to the new 'enterprise culture' of the 1980s.

Certainly, the commercial and structural innovations of recent decades—downsizing, the collapsing of hierarchies, and the flattening organizational pyramids, outsourcing, offshoring, and reliance on a sophisticated mesh of supply chains at the expense of the vertically integrated corporation—have of course brought in their wake new 'human resource management' challenges. With these changes have come new challenges or—to be more positive—new opportunities. Rosemary Stewart's chapter on managerial work, Ian Kessler and Sue Dopson's on public sector management, and Tim Morris's on PSFs highlight the increasing salience of gender, lifestyle, and cross-cultural issues.

Many of the developments cited above are of course no more than the commonplaces of Management Studies. What gives their treatment in this collection added value is that they are identified and particularized in relation to a range of specific contexts.

Tension and Ambiguity

A phenomenon to which several of the chapters bear witness is a growing fascination on the part of practitioners with management theory. In part a reflection of the increasing and welcome professionalization of managers and the greater prevalence of MBAs, it has also helped swell a tide of fads and fashions. In the resultant wash of hype and consultant-speak has come an international flotsam and jetsam of 'airport' management books peddling instant formulas, cookie cutter recipes, and off-the-peg solutions. Yet the fashion for superficial panaceas and the authority of the three-bulleted overhead or power point slide has in its turn generated a contrary wave of scepticism. Keith Ruddle in his chapter makes witty and insightful play with management fashions as he traces his own voyage of exploration from McKinsey's 7S model, through the mantras of 'the quest for excellence', 'total quality management', 'business process re-engineering', and 'the manager as heroic leader' to the 'eight steps to transformation' and finally the wilder shores of complexity and chaos theory.

Underlying this scepticism and cynicism, it is possible to detect a deeper malaise—an academic uncertainty about the very validity, direction, and parameters of Management Studies. In her chapter on organization studies, 'There and Back Again', Janine Nahapiet writes:

This is a good time to reflect on the field of Organization Studies. The 1960s are widely regarded as the period in which Organization Studies established itself as a separate and identifiable subject—distinguishable from Management Studies—and with its own body of theorizing. Forty years later, leading organization scholars are in a period of reflection and self-examination about the field, its evolution, and future development. . . . I believe it suggests a sense of unease, even disquiet, about the current status and health of Organization Studies as a subject. Despite its growth in importance and many contributions, there are significant and pressing questions to be addressed . . .

In part, this volume represents a response: an attempt, in the words of Chris Sauer, at 'sense-making'—an effort across the various fields of Management Studies to take stock and find some clear patterns and some new bearings. Hopefully, it will provide some form of health check for the discipline as well as a reality check against the world of practice.

Their conclusions are often uncompromising, indeed sometimes almost dogmatically contrarian. In the opening chapter, for instance, Alan Rugman argues forcefully that the global corporation is a myth. Far from taking place in a single global market, he maintains that most business activity by large international firms takes place within regional blocks. The common perception, he adds, of multinational enterprises (MNEs) as 'big, bad, and ugly' is inaccurate: they improve the well-being of workers internationally while manufacturing goods and providing services that improve the quality of life of consumers around the world. If this is the equivalent of kicking sand in the face of much contemporary PC opinion, it has to be said that the sand kicked—certainly with regard to regionalization—is undeniably hard and firmly grounded in the statistical evidence. Other chapters present a more qualified view, identifying key issues and concluding with an open agenda for future investigation and research.

The forty-year history of Management Studies as revealed in this volume can be interpreted as a series of interrelated tensions between different sets of polarities. The first is between what one might call the 'hard' and the 'soft'. On the one hand, there has been an ever more insistent emphasis on creating shareholder value, the virtues of market alignment, and making ever more efficient and stringent use of resources through developments such as delayering and outsourcing; on the other, an acknowledgement of the need, first, to engage more fully with individual employees and unlock their untapped potential, and, second, to articulate and embed deeper social and environmental values within the organization. Even so hard-nosed an economic realist as Alan Rugman recognizes the importance of corporations entering into a more open and constructive dialogue with the organs of civil society:

The firms that will do best in future will be those that take leadership positions with respect to stakeholder management, capture the concept of 'values-driven' rather than 'profit-driven' capitalism, and respect their most important resource—namely their employees. These policies will be the most effective tools at the microeconomic level against ideology-driven mobilizers.

Another tension—related to if not exactly overlapping with the first—is between quantitative and qualitative approaches. Rosemary Stewart traces the rise of the former over the last four decades at the expense of the latter but emphasizes that the results cannot be taken as gospel truths:

Enthusiasm for in-depth studies of what managers are actually doing is rare today although it is such studies that have contributed most to the understanding of managerial behaviour. Quantitative studies are much more popular, particularly in the USA where most management research takes place. It may seem more scientific to use only quantitative methods, but the danger is of making mistaken assumptions about what the answers that managers give to questionnaires and rating scales really mean. Do the answers represent factual information about what their jobs are actually like, or do they rather reflect the particular way in which the responder sees and does the job? Most managers are too busy to be reflective about their work and by temperament they may be unsuited to doing so as management attracts personalities who are action oriented.

A third tension is between the increasing segmentation and demarcation of fields within Management Studies and the overall need for a more integrated and holistic approach. Terry Hill's insistence that Operations Management, for instance, cannot be seen in isolation from wider market and strategic dimensions has already been noted. Likewise, Tim Morris in his chapter on professional service firms identifies them as a new and discrete area for study, but at the same time notes that they represent an area characterized not only by 'distinctiveness' but also by 'blurring'. As an example, he notes the increasing comfort of younger professionals with the more market-driven approaches and 'corporate' structures being adopted alongside more traditional partnership models.

Michael Earl similarly highlights the debates among IT professionals about the role and value of Information Management:

It is not uncommon when Information Systems, MIS, or Information Management academics come together for them to begin agonizing whether their subject is going to survive. They debate what is their core or heartland. Is it computer science-oriented, concerned with the workings of IT, with databases, systems analysis, and project management? Is it economics-oriented, concerned with electronic markets, the impact of IT on firms' productivity, positioning, and configuration, and the impact on resource allocation and distribution? Is it a subset of decision science, technology management, or operations management, concerned with how better information, new technologies, or ambitious information systems can and are transforming decision-making, supply chains, manufacturing processes, products, service management, and the like? Or can it be seen as part of strategic and general management, where the models, rules, and practice of the industrial age are being rewritten for the information age?

Emphasizing that 'techno-cratic, functionally isolated, and naïve models of the contribution of markets and hierarchies [have been] shown to be dysfunctional', Earl argues that Information Management is part and parcel of General Management and that managers who do not embrace this truth miss out on opportunities to create new value. He concludes that in terms of its boundaries and impact Information Management is of its nature indeterminate: '*all* information technologies are essentially ambiguous'.

This is a crucial insight—and one echoed elsewhere in these chapters. A recurrent theme is the increasing realization over recent decades of the uncertain and ultimately ambiguous nature of management enquiry. The forces driving this realization have been twofold. The first has entered, as it were, from without—in the shape of the increasingly multifaceted, irrefrangible, and often intractable problems confronting managers in the real world. As Keith Grint points out in his chapter, thinkers have called these 'wicked' problems to distinguish them from more run-of-the-mill 'tame' problems. For Grint, the arena of the wicked problem is above all leadership—leadership demands a much more open-minded and non-prescriptive stance:

The leader's approach to a wicked problem should be to ask the right questions rather than provide the right answers because the answers may not be self-evident and require a collaborative process to make any kind of progress.

The second impulse is endogenous: the acceptance within Management Studies itself—in common with other areas of social theory—that to isolate and identify an issue is itself a social and intellectual construct and as such never an independent absolute. To extend Earl's comment: 'all *management* is essentially ambiguous'. Keith Grint argues that this ambiguity is especially true of the exercise of leadership:

the very legitimacy of a form of authority depends on the successful presentation of a phenomenon as a particular kind of problem...it is not the accurate representation of the context that should determine what kind of problem exists or what form of authority is appropriate, but rather what kind of persuasive account of the context results in it being seen as a specific type of problem that, in turn, legitimates a particular form of authority. Second, that leadership may be an appropriate form of authority for coping with wicked problems that are perceived as intractable, but this is often seen as indecisiveness by the leader's opponents. It illustrates what may be the irony of leadership: that openness is so difficult to achieve that even when leaders consider it appropriate and even essential, they may be very unwilling to attempt it.

The implication of the approach outlined in this chapter is that we should spend less time going 'forward to the past' and reigniting old worries about getting the right charismatic figure in charge, and trying to analyse the decision-making of formal decision-makers on the basis of 'rational' or 'scientific' understanding of the situation that faces them—as suggested by conventional contingency theories. Instead, we should go 'back to the future' to see how those futures are constructed by the very same decision-makers and consider the persuasive mechanisms that decision-makers use to make situations more tractable to their own preferred form of authority. To repeat, 'situation' is not a noun but a verb: what takes place is not situational decision-making but situated decision-making.

It is evident that a significant shift has taken place in recent decades from what might be termed 'naive' Management Studies with a narrow functional and technical focus and 'trade-school' prescriptions towards a more intellectually sophisticated recognition that we approach organizational issues like all social phenomena through a series of conceptual and experiential grids or—to change the metaphor—we hack our way towards them through a jungly web of preconceived notions and values. Peter Morris argues exactly this point for the world of project management, where academic enquiry is now increasingly proposing socially constructed models in this traditionally 'instrumentally rational' field in the face of the established tools, techniques and paradigms of professional project management institutions. What perhaps gives this perception particular piquancy in the context of Management Studies is that it is a field that has traditionally seen itself above all as straightforward and down-to-earth and simply concerned with finding realistic solutions to immediate problems.

Relevant Continuities

As well as mapping the changes in Management Studies in recent decades, these essays testify to continuities. As the titles of Janine Nahapiet's chapter, 'There and Back Again', and Keith Grint's chapter, 'Back to the Future', indicate, there are cycles in Management Studies. This may even be true of that now unfashionable life form, the large conglomerate. John McGee and Paul Simmonds close their chapter on its rise and fall by hinting at the possibility of its return to the organizational scene:

Organic growth will always be possible, but growth by acquisition will be limited by regulators where competition is in danger of being compromised. Effectively, therefore, competition regulators will restrict the non-organic growth of focused companies. Therefore, it could be argued that the current fashion for divestment and focusing on core business activities is a transitory phase to be superseded by a reinvention of diversification strategies as companies seek paths to growth. Shareholders demand growth in their dividends as well as capital value and a stagnant company is not attractive. Building on the life cycle concept, the conglomerate strategy may currently be in the decline phase but a new growth phase could be imminent. This may involve 'new' conglomerates created by providers of private equity building portfolios of unrelated businesses through their acquisition of unwanted or undervalued companies and their support of MBO and MBI transactions.

In short, is conglomeration a fundamentally unstable corporate strategy or is it capable of reinvention? It may be that the strategy will survive because it increasingly represents the only way in which large focused companies can grow and maintain returns in the face of the regulatory pressures and interventions limiting growth in core business sectors.

Agendas may change but, on revisiting their earlier articulation, it is surprising how relevant they remain. Rosemary Stewart highlights this paradox:

This book records how radically the world of business has changed. This should mean that managing is now strikingly different from what it was forty years ago. In many ways it is, but the findings from early studies of managerial work and behaviour (MWB) are still applicable.

She adds wryly that this may be particularly true of unfashionable areas like the study of managerial work: 'Fashions come and go, but an unfashionable area of research can have a longer life because it does not run the risk of going out of fashion.'

Michael Earl, itemizing the initial research agenda of the Oxford Institute for Information Management (OXIIM), founded in the College in the mid-1980s, is also struck by its continuing relevance. Over time three principal themes evolved:

1. The planning, organization, and control of IT activities.
2. How and whether IT can be a source of competitive advantage.
3. Managing information as a resource.

Interestingly, or fortunately, these themes have not lost their currency over time. Indeed, they remain as sharp, albeit continuously evolving both theoretically and practically, over twenty years after OXIIM was founded, in what Applegate, McFarlan, and McKenney describe as the Ubiquitous Era of IT and Architecture. Here, portable and mobile intelligence is networked where everyone can access information and knowledge everywhere and where businesses and information age entrepreneurs look to IT and information as a source of value creation.

Similarly, Peter Morris in his chapter on project management highlights how the broader conceptual approach to the management of projects developed under the original agenda of the Major Project Association (founded in the College in the early 1980s) with its emphasis on context and front-end definition is now much more influential in the world of professional project management practice then the traditional more techniques-based approaches which dominates the field since the late 1960s.

Tomorrow's Agenda

Of course, it is also undeniable that there has been—and will continue to be—massive changes in management and in Management Studies. As Rosemary Stewart points out with regard to her own field, managerial work, older research approaches are confronted with new questions:

It is evident that management today is more demanding and that, despite the continuing relevance of old research, we badly need new research that will tell us how the many changes have affected managerial work and managerial behaviour and what are the implications for improving managerial effectiveness. Unfortunately, there seems little interest in doing so ...

So what will constitute the agenda in future? Precise prediction is both impossible and—since it will most likely prove off-the-mark—undesirable. As Chris Sauer comments in his chapter, 'the possibilities are enormous, the details hazy'. But some larger shapes, trends, and directions can nevertheless be discerned. Like Jonathan Reynolds in his chapter on the evolution of retailing, Sauer focuses on the accelerating impact of technological innovation. He begins by predicting an intensification of existing trends:

Increased process integration will extend the logic of e-business up and down the demand and supply chains. Businesses will pursue more effective outcomes through more joined up intra- and inter-organizational processes. They will take out slack at boundaries and they will increase cycle times. In short, customers will get a better job, performed faster and more cheaply. In particular, we can expect to see these kinds of development in more complex products, services, and solutions businesses. For example, nuclear power stations will be built under more streamlined procure, design, and build processes. Likewise, the provision of military capability by defence firms will be the result of integrated processes of manufacture, train, service, repair, and recommission.

But he then proceeds to draw a bow at a venture and look ahead in larger social and economic terms at some of the possible knock-on effects:

More and more premium priced knowledge work will be sent offshore with unpredictable effects on the developed economies. A cadre of highly educated knowledge workers will lose their jobs, but how they will respond is less certain. They could become more politically active in protest, or they could choose the economic route and pursue innovation. So long as a large proportion of the profits from developing nations continue to be reinvested in the developed world, as is the case today, there will be the capital to support innovation. Once the developing world becomes more confident in its own economies and starts to prefer the risk : return ratio at home, locational independence will cease to be merely an economic option and will become the focus for a political contest in the developed world.

One thing we can be reasonably certain of, given the increasing pace, complexity, and interrelatedness of change, is that we shall see a lot more 'wicked' problems in future rather than 'tame' ones. In this regard, Rafael Ramirez in his chapter shows how 'futurizing' in the shape of scenario thinking can help organizations anticipate and adapt in times of 'turbulent' or even 'vortical environmental textures'.

Context—the organizational environment in its broadest sense—will therefore loom even larger in future and increasingly have to be taken into account in management responses. Janine Nahapiet writes:

these links between organization and society are likely to be of increasing importance in the years ahead. The changes referred to earlier—the changing balance of power between nations, the uncertainties over the world's natural resources as well as the growing disparity between the rich and poor both within and between nations and regions—will all demand attention and action in the coming years. These issues are likely to increase our awareness of the particular cultural context in which influential ideas have been developed thus far and at the same time stretch further our ability to understand and deliver effective organization. There is much to do.

What is vital in Nahapiet's view is early acceptance of the fact that the emerging knowledge economy will be 'a relationship economy'. She goes on to stress the role that networks will play in this new world and the challenge they pose both to academics and practitioners:

The network perspective offers the prospect of describing and explaining both formal and informal organization and patterns of connection both within and without formal organizations.... Our task is ... to understand how order is created out of the actions of diverse actors. Formal organizations are one means to do this—but not the only means. The challenge now is to deepen our awareness and appreciation of the alternatives. In many ways, the move to more fluid, horizontal, and virtual organizational forms helps us—since we are already gaining experience of alternative modes of organizing that combine these various elements. These alternatives highlight the importance of establishing shared meaning and identity, creating contexts for productive exchange and collective activity as well as self-organization, and they identify a range of processes and practices that appear to support such processes ...

Other contributors agree. In fields as diverse as health care and public services (Kessler and Dopson) and business-to-business marketing (Blois), the contributors to this volume point to the growing role that networks will play in future. Keith Ruddle emphasizes the same point, drawing an interesting parallel with Oxford itself!

recent research has thrown up some fascinating evidence of how new value is being created between and among enterprises and of new solutions—networks, nodes, and connections, distributed intelligence not constrained by the hierarchical rules of a controlling body. Such viral-style change can be seen in phenomena such as anti-globalization protests, in Lucas developing games with its thousands of customers, and maybe even in eBay running itself more as a movement. The corollary may be that future managerial practice will have to learn how social structures can act as a form of distributed intelligence, blurring the boundaries between management and employees and between companies, suppliers, and customers.

Interestingly, this paradoxical concept of viral, loose, and complexly interconnected change is relevant to my own professional and academic circumstances. Consider Oxford University and its 'family'—a complex amalgam of academics, students, staff, colleges, departments, institutes, collaborations, and partnerships. Governance is diffuse, often characterized as hopelessly bureaucratic and cumbersome. Any major change or decision involves democratic consensus to an extreme degree. Detractors say we need more top-down management. But in spite of this Oxford achieves change, pursues radically new research, and continues to educate the political, academic, and business leaders of the future. It has survived revolution and religious strife and has done so for nearly 900 years. Maybe we should study more closely how its loose connections work in action ...

But where are the theoretical frameworks that will equip us to analyse and understand these new organizational forms and the mutual value to which they could give rise? Nahapiet warns that the essential intellectual underpinning, while likely to emerge from studies of 'social capital', is as yet not in place:

the map is not well drawn for this endeavour and we have much to learn. For example, how can shared purpose be identified and sustained in loosely coupled arrangements? What are the appropriate forms of governance for activities that transcend formal organizational boundaries? How can the costs and benefits be measured and distributed appropriately? How will differences and conflicts be resolved, especially in virtual environments and multicultural teams? Why and when will people trust each other and who has power in such settings? Finally, how should we research such complex, emergent, dynamic, and co-evolutionary processes? Perhaps the hardest part will be to recognize and rethink many of our taken for granted assumptions about doing and researching organizing and to engage in the heedful observation and collective sense making that a deep appreciation of organizing requires.

From another direction, Keith Blois, emphasizing the haziness of concepts like 'networks' and 'value creation', puts forward the suggestive idea that we are likely to see a return to earlier studies of *power*—the relative balances of power participants in these relationships in these networks possess and exercise—or choose to forgo.

The Challenge for Management Studies

Looking back on forty years of Management Studies, Rosemary Stewart identifies a central rift running through the subject and leaves us in no doubt on which side of the divide she takes her stand:

there is a particular danger in management studies of theory building without a concern for the practical applications. The author believes that management studies should be like medicine in its concern for application, a heretical view for those who see themselves as management scientists. There tends to be a sharp divide, particularly in the USA, between those who have a primarily, even wholly, academic focus and those who contribute academically but also seek to draw practical lessons for managers. All those who teach experienced managers should do the latter.

If, as suggested earlier, Management Studies has become more intellectu-ally sophisticated and nuanced in its approaches, the need for relevance remains as strong as ever. Keith Ruddle in his chapter proposes that academics and 'reflective' practitioners work alongside one another in 'learning communities', co-producing high quality, relevantly focused insights in the tradition of 'grounded research'. Endorsing this, Janine Nahapiet argues that practice and theory have an interdependent and mutually reinforcing relationship:

theory and practice frequently influence each other. There is now plenty of evidence that descriptive empirical studies produce findings that subsequently have profound normative consequences. But it is also evident that organizational innovations instigated by practitioners often occur well ahead of our ability to understand and theorize them and they often stimulate theoretical and conceptual advances. It took years before scholars developed coherent theoretical explanations of the multidivisional form of organization adopted by major US corporations in the 1920s and 1930s. Today, they face similar challenges in understanding and explaining recent organizational innovations such as open sourcing and networked innovation.

In my own work, my interest in social capital had its origins in a discussion at Templeton College with executives in a leading insurance company about global relationship management—and their need to respond to global clients seeking coordinated world wide service. Global relationship management is a business practice rooted in the proposition that value can be created through linkage and coordination—both within and between organizations. However, at the time, most extant theories in Organization Studies and microeconomics seemed to provide little insight into value creation through coordination, focusing instead on organizational choices based on minimizing the costs of coordination. The search for an alternative perspective led eventually to work on social capital and the development of a framework that provides a theoretical explanation of the benefits as well as the costs of connections and relationships. The framework has subsequently been taken up and used extensively by both academics and practitioners.

What, then, are the implications for senior management education? Michael Earl describes how in the early days of OXIIM a 'virtuous circle' or feedback loop was created, by which empirical research and case study production led, successively, into executive education programmes, the subsequent refocusing of policy agendas, and then in turn to further research projects. If valid then, such an approach is even more relevant in today's far greater turbulence and faster change. As in management research, co-production, co-design, and co-delivery are key ingredients in executive education if it is to deliver what clients want and also make its fullest contribution to academic enquiry. As Janine Nahapiet comments:

we may be better placed if we regard developments in organization theory and organization practice as reciprocal and co-evolutionary. Practice raises important questions for theory and theories, and their related assumptions, have significant implications for practice and the two co-evolve through time. A commitment to this dialectical view of knowledge creation and sharing, exploration and exploitation, underpins Templeton's distinctive approach to research and pedagogy.

From its beginnings, executive education was the *raison d'etre* of Templeton College, and the interdependence of theory and practice, the close relationship between academics and practitioners, has always been the key to its work. Co-production—the close and constructive union between practice and theory and between practitioners and academics: that is the real living legacy of Templeton, one that it hands on to Oxford to extend and carry forward into our turbulent future.

Part I

A World of Change

1

Globalization's Regional Reality

Alan M. Rugman

Depending on your point of view, globalization is either the best of things or the worst. It is blamed for many of the ills of the modern world but also praised for bringing many of its benefits. Certainly, the accelerating pace of international business is having a profound effect on life in rich and poor countries alike, transforming regions such as Detroit or Bangalore from boom to bust—or vice versa—in a generation.

The internationalization of business is not new. It is a product of the industrial revolution. Britain grew rich in the nineteenth century as the first global economic superpower because of its superior manufacturing technology and improved global communications such as steamships and railroads. But its pace, scope, and scale have accelerated dramatically since the Second World War, especially in the last twenty-five years.

The dizzying pace of international economic change can be alarming. The speed and scale of economic change gives the impression that it is becoming increasingly difficult for governments to keep their economic destiny in their own hands. What is most disturbing for many people is that no one seems to be in charge, or be able to agree to fair rules for the new global economic order. The international institutions meant to deal with the globalizing world appear to be in trouble. The World Trade Organisation (WTO) is under fire for failing to take into account labour standards or the environmental impact of trade. And its efforts to break down global trade barriers are faltering.

Despite this, I feel confident in putting forward three basic propositions:

- The first is that the internationalization of business has played a key role in the unprecedented increase in prosperity in the last fifty years, which is now spreading from the USA and Europe to include many formerly poor countries in Asia, including China and India.
- The second is that the common perception of multinational enterprises (MNEs) as 'big, bad, and ugly' is inaccurate. In general, MNEs improve the well-being of workers across the world while

manufacturing goods and providing services that improve the quality of life of consumers around the world.

• Finally, globalization as it is commonly understood is a myth. Far from taking place in a single global market, most business activity by large international firms takes place within regional blocks. Government regulations, transportation costs, and cultural differences divide the world into the triad of North America, Europe, and the Asia-Pacific—an extension of the three large economic hubs at its core: the USA, the European Union (EU), and Japan. Within these blocks, rival MNEs compete for regional market share and so contribute to economic efficiency.

Globalization, in the sense of increased economic interdependence among nations, may be the issue of our times but, like many sweeping historical phenomena, it is poorly understood. It is necessary to look at the key actors in the globalization process, namely the firms that drive this process. This chapter explains the fundamental impediments that prevent most of these firms from becoming truly 'global' businesses, in the sense of having a broad and deep penetration of foreign markets across the world. This new view on globalization is very different from the conventional, mainstream perspective. The latter perspective focuses primarily on macro-level growth patterns in trade and foreign direct investment (FDI) and compares these data with national growth rates, but without ever analysing the equivalent domestic or home region growth data for the MNEs responsible for the trade and FDI flows.

The Internationalization of Business

Three interconnected factors have acted as the engines of global business: trade, liberalization, and technology. World trade in merchandise goods has grown around 200 times (from $95 billion to $19 trillion) in the past fifty years—much faster than the overall growth of the world economy. Table 1.1 provides a current breakdown of worldwide trade. It shows that the EU is the world's single largest exporter, followed by North America and then Asia. The EU is also the largest importer, followed by Asia and North America. Of course, most of the EU's trade is within the community itself and is therefore not really 'international' trade as it is for truly sovereign nations who can impose their own trade regulations (as against EU-wide ones). The majority of this export and import activity involves manufactured goods, such as industrial machinery, computers, cars, televisions, VCRs, and other electronic goods. However, an increasing

TABLE 1.1 World trade, 2004

Country/Region	Imports		Exports	
	Billions of US$	% of total	Billions of US$	% of total
North America	2,045.8	21.6	1,320.2	14.6
USA	1,525.5	16.1	816.5	9.0
Canada	299.1	3.2	316.0	3.5
Mexico	221.3	2.3	187.8	2.1
European Union (15)	3,695.8	38.9	3,714.7	40.8
Asia including Japan	2,466.2	26.0	2,618.7	28.7
Japan	454.9	4.8	565.8	6.2
Other Asian countries	2,011.3	21.2	2,052.9	22.5
All others	1,280.5	13.5	1,458.5	15.9
Total	9,488.3	100.0	9,112.1	100.0

Source: Adapted from A. M. Rugman and S. Collinson, *International Business*, p. 7.[1]

proportion of world trade is in services. Furthermore, services now account for the great majority of output in the world economy; but most services are not traded.

A related aspect of international business has been the liberalization of trade and investment. Firms in triad countries have prospered in more open markets. Yet, at the same time, triad rivalry has led to some set-backs in trade liberalization. For example, Japan and China have been threatened with trade sanctions by the USA unless they allow US firms to sell products and services freely in their countries. There are also trade conflicts between the EU and the USA over biotech foods and crops, steel, beef hormones, and export subsidies. Despite minor conflicts and disagreements over the role of international bodies such as the WTO and the World Bank, the liberalization of international trade is here to stay and will continue to be a major stimulus to international business transactions.

The third related factor changing the way MNEs do business is new technology. Two factors, in particular, are having a major impact. One is communication technology, which has advanced at such a rapid rate that all businesses now use computers and rely on the Internet to both access and send information. In addition, thanks to cellular technology, individuals can now remain in constant contact with both their customers and their home office. The latest technology reports reveal that there now are more than 300 million mobile phone users in the EU—81 per cent of the population. Indeed in some EU countries, mobile phone users account for

90 per cent of the population. More than 55 per cent of the US population has access to the Internet.

The other major application of technology is in the production of goods and services. Modern factories can now produce goods in a shorter period of time and with fewer defects thanks to production process programmes. One example is the introduction of 'Six Sigma' (a statistical term that refers to an acceptable ceiling of only 3.4 errors per million), which eliminates performance problems in the production process and encourages worker participation and innovation to create products that meet the needs and wants of consumers. Since Motorola engineers introduced the concept into their production process in the 1980s, hundreds of MNEs, including General Electric (GE), Coca-Cola, and Boeing, have adopted the process, thereby reducing defects, lowering costs, and improving quality.

The Study of Globalization

The study of modern international business, now often called globalization, began in the 1950s. At that time, there were not many MNEs, and most were American. The Second World War had ended less than a decade before and many nations, including Japan and the European countries, were more concerned with rebuilding than with overseas investing. Early international business textbooks were often written by American professors, and they offered a general, descriptive approach to the field. There were few international research studies to provide substantive information. International companies that served as teaching examples were often those with international divisions rather than true MNEs. And professors teaching international business were frequently educated in areas such as economics or general business and relied on an interdisciplinary approach to address the varied needs of the course. (Table 1.2 maps in summary form the evolving study of the field.)

During the 1970s and 1980s, the study of international business changed greatly. The economic growth of Europe and Japan, coupled with great strides by newly industrialized countries, resulted in more attention being focused on international business. Professors were becoming much more research oriented, and the number of Ph.D.-granting institutions offering at least a minor in international business began to increase.[2] Articles and books by Canadian, European, and Asian professors started to appear, and US research sophistication grew markedly. International economics and finance became primary areas of interest, and the general research approach of the 1950s and 1960s was supplemented by more rigorous

TABLE 1.2 Comparative differences in the study of international business, 1950–2010

Topic	1950–69	1970–89	1990–2010
Focus of interest	General information	Functional areas of development	Strategic emphasis
Approach to studying international business	Descriptive	Analytical	Integrative
Method of explanation	Heavily historical	Functional	Multidisciplinary
Research emphasis	Interdisciplinary	Some quantitative research methods	Quantitative research methods
Enterprise viewpoint	US enterprises	Multinational enterprises	Multinationals as networks
Countries examined	Industrialized	Industrialized, NICs, and LDCs	Industrialized and emerging economies
Number of journals	Some	Many	Ever increasing
Journal emphasis	General international topics	Functional	Functional and strategic

Source: Adapted from A. M. Rugman and S. Collinson, *International Business*, p. 23.[1]

quantitative and methodological designs. More research studies were conducted, and the number of journals in the field rose sharply. By the late 1980s, efforts began to bring together much of what was happening into a meaningful composite. How could we understand what was going on in the world of international business, when so much seemed to be occurring at the same time? It was becoming evident that many of the developments of the 1970s and 1980s had been studied in too micro a fashion and that a more macro approach was needed.

By the 1990s, a strategic management focus had emerged in the study of international business. The descriptive ideas of the 1950s and 1960s and the analytical ideas of the 1970s and 1980s were integrated. Historical and quantitative research was incorporated into models for describing, explaining, and helping predict what was happening in international business. The earlier interdisciplinary and functional approaches were supplemented by an approach drawing on information from a wide variety of disciplines. New journals in the field were also taking a more strategic management view of developments. This new focus encompassed the formulation, implementation, monitoring, and control of strategy together with the environmental analysis of external and internal conditions and the evaluation of organizational strengths and weaknesses.

The 'Diamond' of Strategic Advantage

In the 1980s, US businesses saw their economic competitiveness eroded by Japanese and European competitors. By the mid-1990s, however, they had bounced back and by 2004 the USA was again the most competitive nation in the world. How had American companies achieved and maintained their international competitive advantage? Largely by continuing to be innovative. In the computer industry for example, Intel's R&D arm created a continuing flow of New Age computer chips, each more powerful than its predecessor. At the upper end of this market, IBM's strength in marketing and service helped it rebrand itself as a service business, allowing it to sell its computer manufacturing business to the Chinese firm Lenovo. In industries from industrial equipment to financial services and from shipping to entertainment, American companies led the way thanks to their ability to innovate.

Looking at these developments, the question arose: why can some firms innovate consistently while others cannot? Michael Porter of Harvard University tried to provide answers to this question. Studying 100 industries in 10 countries, Porter devised a 'diamond' model based on 4 country-specific determinants and 2 external variables.[3] Each determinant affects the others and all in turn are affected by the role of chance and government.

The determinants included the following:

1. Factor conditions, including the quantity, skills, and cost of personnel; the nation's physical resources; its stock of knowledge resources; the capital resources available to finance industry; and the infrastructure, including the nation's transportation system, communications system, health care system, and other factors affecting the nation's quality of life.
2. Demand conditions, including the size, growth, and composition of home market demand and how it could smooth the path to the internationalization of a nation's products and services.

3. The presence of internationally competitive related and supporting industries.
4. Firms' strategy, structure, and competitiveness.

Two other variables also played important roles:

1. *Chance*: It can nullify competitors' advantages and bring about a shift in the overall competitive position through new inventions; political decisions by foreign governments; wars; shifts in world financial markets or exchange rates; discontinuities such as oil shocks; surges in world or regional demand; and major technological breakthroughs.
2. *Governments*: They can influence all four determinants through subsidies, education policies, the regulation or deregulation of capital markets, the establishment of local product standards and regulations, the purchase of goods and services, tax laws, and antitrust regulation.

However, before accepting Porter's 'diamond', a number of qualifications need to be put forward:

- Porter's model was solely based on export shares for ten countries and historical case studies for four industries. In each case, the country was either a member of a regional triad or an industrialized nation. Since most countries of the world are not in this position, his model cannot be applied to them without modification.
- Governments are of critical importance in influencing a home nation's competitive advantage, but their actions can backfire and end up creating a 'sheltered' domestic industry unable to compete in the worldwide market.
- Although chance is a critical influencing factor in international business strategy, it is extremely difficult to predict and guard against.
- In the study of international business, Porter's model should be applied in terms of company-specific and not national advantages. As Porter himself noted: 'Firms, not nations, compete in international markets.'
- Porter identifies four distinct stages of national competitive development: factor driven, investment driven, innovation driven, and wealth driven. Because these stages greatly influence a country's competitive response, the placement of countries is critical. However, not all industries or companies in major economies move at the same rate between different stages.

- Porter contends that only outward FDI is valuable in creating competitive advantage and inward foreign subsidiaries are not sources of competitive advantage. Yet in a country like Canada, the R&D undertaken by foreign-owned firms is not significantly different from that of indigenously owned companies. Moreover, the twenty largest US subsidiaries in Canada export virtually as much as they import (about 25%).
- Reliance on natural resources is judged by Porter to be insufficient to create worldwide competitive stature. However, taking Canada again, that country has developed a number of successful mega-firms that have turned the country's comparative advantage in natural resources into proprietary sources of sustainable advantage in resource processing and further refining.
- Porter's model does not adequately address the role of MNEs. Researchers, such as Dunning,[4] have suggested including multinational activity as the third external variable in addition to chance and government. Certainly there is good reason to question whether MNE activity is covered in his 'firm strategy, structure, and rivalry' determinant. Researchers have asked how the same competitive determinant can include multinationality for global industries and yet exclude it for multidomestic industries. This is true for 95 per cent of the world's MNEs. For example, virtually all of Canada's large multinationals rely on sales in the USA and other triad markets. Indeed, it could be argued that the US diamond is just as relevant for Canada's industrial multinationals as Canada's own diamond since more than 70 per cent of Canadian MNE sales take place in the USA. Thus, a 'double diamond' perspective is required. Other nations with MNEs based on small 'home diamonds' include Australia, New Zealand, Finland, and most, if not all, Asian and Latin-American countries. Even small nations in the EU, such as Denmark, have been able to overcome the problem of a small domestic market by gaining access to one of the triad markets. So, from applying Porter's framework to international business, one conclusion is inescapable: different 'diamonds' need to be constructed and analysed for different countries.

The 'Transnational' Multinational

Bartlett and Ghoshal's 1989 book putting forward a 'transnational solution' was the single most influential study of international business in the 1990s.[5] Their approach, combining the pursuit of global-scale economies, worldwide innovation, and national responsiveness, is widely cited in international business textbooks as the formula for success in the global marketplace. It contains three important insights: that changes in strategy and structure are to some extent conditioned by the MNE's administrative heritage; that a stronger focus on socialization to effect coordination and control can help change a 'multinational', 'international', or 'global' mentality to a 'transnational' one; and that corporate-level management cannot treat all the operating units in an MNE in the same way.

'Administrative heritage' is now widely accepted as a critical factor when an MNE undertakes strategic and structural change, but we must not forget that it may encourage rigidity in host regions. Bartlett and Ghoshal place an overly optimistic emphasis on the use of learning rather than bureaucratic and market-based coordination and control mechanisms inside the MNE. Socialization mechanisms, like any other coordination and control devices, are not without cost. Such internal institutionalization can reduce the effectiveness of subsidiaries in locally embedded host-country clusters.

But what is perhaps the most important limitation of Bartlett and Ghoshal's approach is its division of geographic space into 'national' and 'global' space to differentiate subsidiary roles and responsibilities. It is not clear whether CEOs and senior management in MNEs consistently think in such terms. In contemplating international expansion, investments and plant closures, etc., senior management often adopts a regional rather than a global or national focus. For example, Bayer recently reorganized its European activities into regional groups to improve its competitiveness in Europe. Moreover, worldwide also, the company is split into three regions—Europe, the Middle East, and Africa; the Americas; and the Asia-Pacific. Similarly, Sony Music recently realigned its affiliates in Poland, the Czech Republic, Slovakia, and Hungary into a subregional division called Sony Music Central Europe and has also taken measures to strengthen its regional strategies for East Asia, the Americas, and Europe.

Imagine a group of senior MNE executives looking at a map of the world and trying to formulate strategy. In many cases, these executives will try to identify regions with enough similarities to form the basis for coherent, market-based decisions and actions. Such regions could be subnational or span several countries. Just as with Porter's analysis of the competitive advantage of nations, there is the problem that geographical units of analysis other than the nation may be critical in explaining the competitiveness of particular national firms and industries. Below, the national level knowledge clusters may be very narrow and localized;

above, a 'double' or 'multiple diamond' spanning two or more countries may be needed to understand the international competitiveness of a particular firm or industry.

I argue that for the largest 500 companies, the regional triad constitutes a legitimate starting point for analysis. Indeed, Bartlett and Ghoshal in the preface to the paperback edition of their book[6] acknowledge the increased complexity of the international business environment and the broadening of regionalization of trading blocs, referring to 'a social, political and economic revolution... opening up whole regions of the world for the first time and ... creating political blocks and economic alliances that were radically changing the context for companies' operations'.

The Concept of the 'Triad'

Far from taking place in a single global market, most business activity by large firms takes place within regional blocs. Government regulation and cultural differences have split the world into a 'triad' of three broad regions: North America, the EU, and the Asia-Pacific. Within these, rival MNEs from the triad compete for regional market share and so enhance economic efficiency. Global markets are neither becoming homogenized nor is there a trend towards globalization. Rather, there has been a trend over the last quarter century towards regionalization and increased intra-regional economic activity. As a result, top managers need to design triad-based regional strategies not global ones. Only in a few sectors, such as consumer electronics, is a global strategy of economic integration viable. For most other manufacturing sectors and for all services, regional strategies are required.

The heart of the first of these three trading and investment blocs, North America, is of course the USA, the largest economy in the world with a gross domestic product (GDP) of over $10 trillion. The second segment of the triad is the EU, with twenty-seven members and a collective GDP greater than that of the USA. The third triad group centres on Japan, which like the other two members plays a major role in international business. Japan is the world's sixth largest importer and fourth largest exporter. At market prices, it is the largest economy in Asia and it has by far the highest GDP per capita.

The trade ties of USA to Canada and Mexico are part of the triad effect, as these three countries are members of the North American Free Trade Agreement (NAFTA). Indeed, more than 55 per cent of the exports of the USA, Canada, and Mexico are intra-regional, that is, to each other. A similar picture of regional trade concentrations appears in the EU, where

TABLE 1.3 Intra-regional trade in the triad, 1980–2004

	Intra-regional exports (%)		
Year	EU (15)	NAFTA	Asia
2004	61.5	55.9	54.5
1995	62.3	46.2	52.7
1980	59.6	33.6	41.1
Cumulative average change			
1980–2004	1.9	22.3	13.4
1995–2004	−0.8	9.7	1.8

Source: Adapted A. M. Rugman and Simon Collinson, *International Business*, p. 8.[1]

more than 60 per cent of all the exports of the member states are with each other. Similarly, around 55 per cent of Asian exports are to other Asian countries. Table 1.3 shows how most exports in triad areas are made within each region and that this pattern has increased significantly since 1980.

Over the last few years, a number of emerging economies have become increasingly important in international business. In particular, the BRICs—Brazil, Russia, India, and China—are emerging players in international trade and FDI. However, the triad continues to dominate international business. Each year companies from these three groups account for the majority of the world's trade and FDI. During the twenty-first century, the triad will continue to be of central importance in international business.

The 'Regional' Multinationals

The world's largest 500 companies are often called MNEs in that they produce or distribute products or services across national borders. They have repeatedly been identified as the drivers of globalization. They account for nearly half of all world trade and more than 90 per cent of FDI. Yet very few MNEs are truly 'global' firms, with a 'global' strategy, if we define that as the ability to sell the same products or services all around the world. Instead, nearly all the top 500 firms are based in their home regions of the 'triad' of North America, the EU, and the Asia-Pacific. In 2000, of the world's 500 largest MNEs, 430 were based in these regions.

Inter-bloc business is likely to be restricted by government-imposed barriers to entry. The EU and the USA are now fighting trade wars and are responsive to domestic business lobbies seeking shelter in the form of subsidies and/or protection, as in the case of steel and agricultural sectors. Cultural and political differences between members of the triad will remain, but there will be fewer of these within each triad bloc. Increasingly, there will be European firms, North American firms, and Asian firms, which will continue to have 70 per cent or more of their sales in their home region of the triad.

In my book *The Regional Multinationals*,[7] I showed, using data for 2001, that the world's 500 largest firms average 72 per cent of their sales in their home region. Their assets are even more localized, averaging 75 per cent in their home region. Finally, the strong regional nature of production and assembly in manufacturing reflects the continued existence of localized clusters which are region bound. There is no evidence of the existence of global supply chains. There are only a handful of purely 'global' MNEs in the world's largest firms. Globalization remains a mirage, and regionalism will continue to dominate international business strategy.

Another common misconception is the belief that MNEs are globally monolithic and excessively powerful. The latest research shows that of the 500 largest MNEs, 203 are headquartered in North America, 153 in the EU, and 123 in Japan/Asia. This implies not a dominant MNE culture, rather the interaction of different cultures in the international business arena. Recent research has also shown that the vast majority of MNEs do not try to spread their marketing operations evenly across the world but depend on their own regions of the triad for more than half of their revenue. These companies are engaged not in global but regional triad competition, and this rivalry is so strong that it has effectively eliminated the possibility of their achieving guaranteed long-term profits or building strong, enduring political advantage. In fact, it is now common to find MNEs joining forces with local firms who can help them penetrate local markets. In recent years, the strategic alliance, a business relationship in which two or more companies work together to achieve a collective advantage, has become extremely popular with MNEs, who realize that they need to develop strategies with a regional or local focus to succeed.

Another misconception is the belief that MNEs develop homogeneous products for the world market and through their efficient production techniques dominate local markets everywhere. In fact, multinationals have to adapt their products for the local market. For example, there is no 'global' car. Rather, there are regionally based automobile factories supported by local and regional suppliers who provide steel, plastic, paint, seats, tyres, radios, and other necessary products to make cars for that geographic region. Additionally, the car designs that are popular in one

TABLE 1.4 Classification of the top 500 MNEs

Type of MNE	No. of MNEs	% of 500	% Intra-regional sales
Global	9	1.8	38.3
Bi-regional	25	5.0	42.0
Host-region oriented	11	2.2	30.9
Home-region oriented	320	64.0	80.3
Insufficient data	15	3.0	40.9
No data	120	24.0	na
Total	500	100.0	71.9

Source: Adapted from A. M. Rugman, *The Regional Multinationals*, p. 12.[7]

area of the world are typically rejected by buyers in other geographic areas. The Toyota Camry, which dominates the American auto market, is a poor seller in Japan and even poorer in Europe. The Volkswagen Golf, which does extremely well in Europe, has not made much of an impact in North America. Pharmaceutical firms, which manufacture medicines that are often referred to as 'universal products', have to modify their goods to satisfy national and state regulations, thus making centralized production and worldwide distribution economically difficult.

Three Types of Regional Multinationals

My research shows that there are three types of MNEs:

- 'Home region-oriented' MNEs, which derive at least 50 per cent of their sales in their home region.
- 'Bi-regional' MNEs, which derive less than 50 per cent of their sales from their home region but more than 20 per cent from one other region. This includes firms with at least 20 per cent of their sales in two regions of the triad, including their own, and firms with more than 50 per cent of their sales in a host region (host region-oriented firms).
- Truly 'global' MNEs, with at least 20 per cent of their sales in all three regions of the triad, but less than 50 per cent in any one region.

The overall picture, therefore, is one of regionalization not globalization. As shown in Table 1.4, of the 380 firms for which data are available, as many as 320 are home region oriented, having less than a combined 50 per cent of their sales in the other two regions of the triad. A somewhat larger group—thirty-six—comprises companies with a strong presence in two regions of the triad or deriving more than 50 per cent of their revenues in a host region. But only 9 of the 500, such as IBM, Coca-Cola, and LVMH, qualify as truly global MNEs.

Table 1.5 lists the twenty-five largest home region-based MNEs. They essentially pursue a domestic intra-regional strategy and cannot be considered global MNEs.

There are twenty-five 'bi-regional' MNEs, which include some MNEs that are very nearly global by our definition such as Unilever and McDonald's, both of which have less than 20 per cent of their sales in Asia. There are eleven 'host region-oriented' MNEs. Most of these are attracted by the US economy, and their strategies are market access ones. They include DaimlerChrysler, one of eight European-based MNEs with more than half of their sales in North America. One Asian business, Honda, and the Australian News Corp also have most of their sales in North America. Only one US MNE, Manpower, has more sales in Europe than in its home market. The nine truly 'global' MNEs are identified in Table 1.6. Apart from Coca-Cola and LVMH, seven are in the computer, telecom, and high-tech sectors.

There are also nine MNEs that are 'near miss' global MNEs. Missing data prevented Exxon Mobil, Shell, Nestlé, and others from being formally classified as global. Even when the data were complete, a few MNEs, such as 3M and Kodak, just missed meeting the 20 per cent of their sales criteria for all three regions of the triad.

These data were for the year 2001. I have since extended them to cover 2001–4, as summarized in Table 1.7, broken down into manufacturing and services. I also include data on assets to provide clues about the nature of the 'upstream' or 'back-end' activities of these firms. It has been suggested that asset data might provide confirmation of the existence of a global supply chain. Yet the data on assets essentially support the same conclusion as for sales: most large firms are home region based.

Panel A of Table 1.7 shows that the average intra-regional sales figure for all firms is 75.6 per cent, with a plus or minus variation of only less than 0.5 per cent by year . There is no significant difference over time, and hence no evidence of a trend towards the globalization of international business activity during this later period. Services average 81.1 per cent home region sales as against 65.0 per cent for manufacturing—a statistically significant difference.

Panel B of Table 1.7 again shows no trend towards globalization, but it does highlight a statistically significant difference in the average intra-regional assets of services and manufacturing. The conclusion is that services are even more home region-oriented than manufacturing across

TABLE 1.5 The top home region-based companies

No.	500 Rank	Company	Revenues in billion US$	% Of total sales		
				North America	Europe	Asia-Pacific
1	1	Wal-Mart Stores	219.8	94.1	4.8	0.4
2	3	General Motors	177.3	81.1	14.6	na
3	5	Ford Motor	162.4	66.7	21.9	na
4	9	General Electric	125.9	59.1	19.0	9.1
5	12	Mitsubishi	105.8	5.4	1.7	86.8
6	13	Mitsui	101.2	7.4	11.1	78.9
7	15	Total Fina Elf	94.3	8.4	55.6	na
8	17	Itochu	91.2	5.5	1.7	91.2
9	18	Allianz	85.9	17.6	78.0	4.4
10	21	Volkswagen	79.3	20.1	68.2	5.3
11	22	Siemens	77.4	30.0	52.0	13.0
12	23	Sumitomo	77.1	4.8	na	87.3
13	24	Philip Morris	72.9	57.9	25.8	na
14	25	Marubeni	71.8	11.6	na	74.5
15	26	Verizon Communications	67.2	96.2	na	na
16	27	Deutsche Bank	66.8	29.3	63.1	6.5
17	28	E.ON	66.5	9.4	80.1	na
18	29	US Postal Service	65.8	97.0	na	na
19	30	AXA	65.6	24.1	51.2	19.9
20	31	Credit Suisse	64.2	34.9	60.9	4.1
21	32	Hitachi	63.9	11.0	7.0	80.0
22	34	American International Group	62.4	59.0	na	na
23	35	Carrefour	62.2	na	81.3	6.6
24	36	American Electric Power	61.3	87.7	11.8	na
25	39	Duke Energy	59.5	96.5	na	na

Source: Adapted from A. M. Rugman, *The Regional Multinationals*, p. 17.[7]

Globalization's Regional Reality

TABLE 1.6 Global MNEs

500 Rank	Company	Revenues in billion US$	North America % of total sales	Europe % of total sales	Asia-Pacific % of total sales
19	International Business Machines	85.9	43.5	28.0	20.0
37	Sony	60.6	29.8	20.2	32.8
143	Royal Philips Electronics	29.0	28.7	43.0	21.5
147	Nokia	27.9	25.0	49.0	26.0
162	Intel	26.5	35.4	24.5	40.2
190	Canon	23.9	33.8	20.8	28.5
239	Coca-Cola	20.1	38.4	22.4	24.9
388	Flextronics International	13.1	46.3	30.9	22.4
459	LVMH	11.0	26.0	36.0	32.0
	Weighted average	33.1			
	Total	298.0			

Source: Adapted from A. M. Rugman, *The Regional Multinationals*, p. 14.[7]

TABLE 1.7 Intra-regional sales of the 500 firms over time

Year	Number of firms	Intra-regional sales (%)		
		All industries	Manufacturing	Services
Panel A. Intra-regional sales				
2001	329	75.6	66.5	84.2
2002	325	75.8	65.4	83.7
2003	323	75.8	64.3	84.5
2004	317	75.2	63.6	84.1
Weighted average		75.6	65.0	84.1
Panel B. Intra-regional assets				
2001	261	77.2	70.0	83.8
2002	275	76.9	69.5	83.5
2003	278	76.4	68.3	83.8
2004	276	76.4	68.2	84.2
Weighted average		76.7	69.0	83.8

Source: Annual reports, 2001–4.

both downstream (sales) and upstream (assets) activities. All the evidence therefore is that MNEs, in both services and manufacturing, remain based in their home regions. There is no evidence to support a trend towards globalization, in either the upstream (production end) or downstream (customer end) of MNE activity.

The Implications for Corporate Strategy

The 'global' and 'bi-regional' firms identified earlier do not perform any better than the firms limited to their home region. This suggests the existence of a factor that offsets the advantages of operating globally. There are indeed good business reasons that restrict the activities of the world's largest firms to their home regions and limit the economies of scale, brand, and other FSAs available to large firms. It is difficult to extend the FSAs beyond the borders of the home region. I call these difficulties the 'liability of regional foreignness'.

Given the robust nature of country- and firm-level data that deny the existence of globalization, it is somewhat puzzling that people stress the need for businesses to have a global strategy. Instead, firms need to develop regional strategies. Only in a few sectors, such as consumer electronics, is a global strategy of economic integration viable. For most other manufacturing sectors, such as automobiles, and for all services, strategies of national responsiveness are required.

All the advantages of homogeneity can be achieved within a home region, especially if the governments of that region pursue internal market policies such as social, cultural, and political harmonization (as in the EU) or economic integration (as in NAFTA and in Asia), and there are few additional scale, scope, or differentiation advantages to be gained by going global or even into other regions of the triad. However, there is nothing to stop an MNE pursuing a 'global' strategy within its home region. Through this, an MNE sells the same product or service in the same way across the countries of its home region. This allows the MNE to gain economies of scale and scope and advantages of differentiation within its home region market. Once an MNE exhausts the possibilities for growth in its home region, it makes sense to go into other regions of the triad. But it will then face the barriers of 'foreignness'.

From a strategic management perspective, a key problem in trying to implement the 'transnational' solution is the implicit assumption that every activity in the firm requires careful analysis of its location- and non-location-bound CSAs, and subsequent action to develop and deploy such strengths. The reality is that not all individual activities conducted in the MNE require FSAs instrumental to outperforming rivals, or require location-specific adaptation investments abroad. It is therefore important to identify those activities for which FSAs are critical to success that may require location-specific adaptation investments abroad.

The largest service companies appear even less global than manufacturing companies. In retail, only one of the largest forty-nine retail firms is global (LVMH), and only five are bi-regional. In banking, all but one (Santander Central Hispano Group) of the forty companies have the vast majority of their sales in the home region. Insurance is even more local. Even knowledge-intensive service industries are largely local. For example, professional service firms, such as law firms, consultants, and accountants, are usually embedded in local clusters, with partners being largely immobile and their loose networks being, at best, regionally based.

This situation was anticipated by Campbell and Verbeke, who assessed the validity of the transnational solution for service MNEs.[9] They concluded that the potential for scope economies resulting from the transfer of non-location-bound FSAs is usually lower in service firms because of the impossibility, in many cases, of separating the upstream and customer-end segments of the value chain (inseparability of production and delivery). In this context, this implies that regional-market responsiveness at the customer end is possible only if innovation at the upstream end is also decentralized. In other words, decentralization of decision-making power to the regional level may require that substantial decisions are delegated to that level.

Even in allegedly globalized sectors, such as finance, regional biases need to be taken into account:

- The world financial system is now largely dominated in terms of financial intermediation by the three major currencies: the US dollar, the euro, and the yen.
- Leading stock markets largely serve local companies. For example, 91 per cent of the new issues on the NASDAQ are by US companies. In the German *Neuer Markt*, 83 per cent of new issues are German and most of the remaining ones other EU companies.
- Foreign exchange traders in New York and Tokyo are strongly influenced by home-country patterns of behaviour. Even in a perfect market with instantaneous transmission of information, American foreign exchange traders behave differently from Japanese traders. Hence, even for tasks and functional areas whose non-location-bound nature is widely accepted, it may be necessary to revisit the old assumption of international transferability.

If MNEs face a higher liability of 'foreignness' in their customer-end activities compared to their upstream activities, this has two managerial implications. First, learning—in the sense of lowering the liability of foreignness through location-specific adaptation investments in market knowledge—occurs at a different pace in particular activities of the value chain. Foreign market penetration success ultimately is constrained by the activity area with the lowest rate of learning. Managers wanting to achieve international market growth need to identify the most constraining activities in the critical chain. Second, whereas upstream activities can successfully link an MNE's FSAs to foreign CSAs, this does not appear so simple at the customer end. K. Ohmae may be correct when he suggests that deep market penetration of host-triad regions should be achieved via collaborative instruments (consortia, joint ventures, etc.).[10] These give access to social networks and encourage rapid local 'embeddedness'. However, collaborating with foreign partners and permitting foreign affiliates to develop local network ties can bring problems. There is a danger of FSA dissipation through intentional appropriation by the foreign partner, and also in a broader sense through knowledge diffusion. There is also a danger of reduced coherence within the MNE, if its affiliates become too embedded in host-region networks at the expense of the MNE's overall goals and strategies.

Box 1.1 Offshoring: A red herring in the globalization debate

One of the main arguments advanced to support globalization is the increase in 'offshoring'—outsourcing abroad. But this is not a new phenomenon. For the last fifty years, multinationals have taken advantage of cheaper labour costs abroad, especially in Asia. Such activities have largely been confined to the manufacturing sector and are known in the literature as offshore assembly platforms. In North America, from the late 1980s a considerable amount of offshoring in manufacturing went to Mexico, a process accelerated when NAFTA started in 1994.

Recent data collected by the Duke University CIBER and reported by Lewin and Peeters[8] indicates that US offshoring consists of two elements: offshoring to India, mainly in the information technology (IT) service sectors, and to China and some other Southeast Asian countries in manufacturing. US firms are taking advantage of country factors in these two countries—in the case of China, the relatively cheap labour. These MNEs help speed up Chinese economic development, and over time Chinese MNEs will develop on the basis of country-specific advantages of cheap labour and cheap money. The latter is available since China runs a balance of trade surplus with the USA and many other countries. This

Box 1.1 *Continued*

increases China's foreign exchange reserves and allows it to indirectly provide cheap financing to Chinese firms that then engage in foreign acquisitions.

Most Chinese outward FDI is in the natural resources sector, especially energy and mining. For example, China is now the largest foreign investor in these sectors in Africa. Lenovo's recent acquisition of the PC division of IBM is exceptional in that a Chinese firm is attempting to develop knowledge-based, firm-specific advantages (FSAs). However, it is not yet clear whether knowledge-based FSAs can be sustained through a process of merger and acquisition. Instead, most Chinese FDI in the USA is likely to reflect China's country-specific advantages in cheap labour and cheap money. It is likely to take ten years or more before Chinese multinationals develop managerial skills in systems integration and network coordination such that they rival US knowledge-based firms.

The offshoring of US service jobs to India can be analysed in the same way. While India has more skilled labour than China, the critical point is that offshoring to India is also determined by a country-specific advantage. India's IT workers enjoy a cheap labour advantage compared to their US counterparts. Offshoring from US firms will continue until Indian wages and salaries begin to increase to close the gap with average US salaries in the IT sector. One difference between India and China is that India is further ahead in the ability to develop its own knowledge-based multinationals. The IT service sector should provide India with a faster pace of economic development than is available to China through low-wage manufacturing and assembly.

However, until there is a major growth of new Chinese and Indian MNEs, it is highly unlikely that the robust nature of North American regional business activity will be upset. Indeed, the vast majority of business activity in North America is conducted within manufacturing and services clusters in which locational network advantages remain extremely important. The dynamics of innovation and continued knowledge development are closely linked to these clusters. In future, it is likely that Chinese and Indian MNEs would be attracted to join existing US clusters, in a similar manner to the success that Japanese firms have enjoyed in the automobile, tyre, and related components sectors. In other words, offshoring is likely to reinforce the strengths of the US business system in the long run. Offshoring is a process by which US MNEs remain efficient and are able to develop sustainable FSAs within dynamic local clusters.

Implications for Public Policy and Society

Globalization has opened up a gulf between representatives of 'civil society' such as non-governmental organizations (NGOs) on the one hand and international business such as multinationals (MNEs) on the other. Unfortunately, these differences of opinion have become entrenched, and the result all too often appears to be a 'dialogue of the deaf'.

Paralleling this is the intellectual failure of academic theory to develop explanations of today's global economy and the nature of FDI. In economics, the traditional efficiency-based neoclassical paradigm (with its associated theory of comparative advantages and the overall country gains from free trade) is unsuitable as an explanation of FDI. Despite the efforts by international business writers over the last thirty years to develop a modern theory of the MNE, most economists are unable to accept this explanation of the reasons for FDI. As a consequence, the GATT and WTO have developed institutional frameworks to deal with the 'shallow' integration of tariff cuts, but have failed to deal with the 'deep' integration of FDI.

Related to the out-of-date economics paradigm of free trade is the political science focus on the nation state. Despite minor modifications to nation-state paradigms, there is a limited buy-in to the alternative 'International Political Economy' viewpoint. In the study of the role and power of the MNE, both economics and political science have failed to change out-of-date thinking among most academics, despite abundant evidence of the real relevance of MNEs to the global economic and political systems of today. The NGOs have slipped into this vacuum with their view of MNEs. NGO thinking is now more influential with governments in North America and Europe than the work of scholars.

The issue is also one of process. There is an 'administrative heritage' of ideas. Today's media are poorly trained in economics, politics, and international business. Those few who have any training are usually victims of out-of-date paradigms. The MBAs of business schools, who are now exposed to the new thinking on MNEs, are in business rather than the media. The professional intermediaries, such as management consultants, focus on their business or government clients rather than the media, and their very skills of confidential advice and in-house retraining make them poor advocates compared to the NGOs. Finally, the civil service is basically at sea in dealing publicly with antitrade NGOs as bureaucrats attempt to support and influence ministers and other officials rather than enter into the public forum. The failure of academics, consultants, and bureaucrats to prepare a credible case for initiatives such as the Multilateral Agreement on Investment (MAI) and debate it publicly leaves the field open to NGO activists.

Figure 1.1 categorizes MNE responses to 'civil society' criticisms. The vertical axis distinguishes between a strategy that differentiates between stakeholders with which a dialogue is possible and those with whom it is not and, on the bottom, a strategy of uniform response. The horizontal axis makes a distinction between a broad stakeholder perspective, on the right, whereby goals other than shareholder wealth maximization

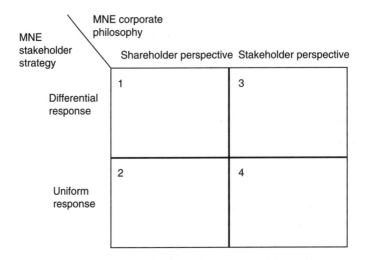

FIG. 1.1 Multinational enterprise strategies and civil society

Source: Adapted by the author with permission from A. M. Rugman, *The Regional Multinationals*.[7]

are considered relevant, and, on the left, a narrower shareholder, profit-maximizing perspective.

Quadrant 2 reflects the outdated perspective on MNEs, paradoxically adopted by most mobilizers. They view MNEs as profit maximizers, who will systematically refuse a constructive dialogue with any stakeholder representing the civil society. Quadrant 1 represents an equally outdated response that is now being rejected by most large MNEs. Management has a shareholder perspective and its differential response is usually a 'public relations' exercise whereby an MNE provides lip service to the goals of 'friendly' stakeholders but in fact is not serious about stakeholder management.

In fact, many MNEs are now positioned in quadrant 3. They pursue a stakeholder management model, perhaps driven by sustainable development environmental considerations. Here MNEs try to identify those salient stakeholders that can contribute to a win–win situation for the firm and society at large. These firms face the challenge of distinguishing between destructive 'mobilizers' and benevolent, 'technical' NGOs.

The main danger is for MNEs to fall in the quadrant 4 trap, whereby their stakeholder management approach can be abused by mobilizers, because the firm has not set up proper screening mechanisms to establish which stakeholder demands are legitimate and which are not. This problem is faced by many companies operating in both developing and advanced countries that are unfairly accused of unethical behaviour, for example, Shell in the disposal of a North Sea oil rig where Greenpeace misrepresented the position in order to win publicity.

A useful alliance could take place between MNEs with a quadrant 1 viewpoint in Figure 1.1 and the technical NGOs of quadrant 2. An example of this is the idea of sustainable development, whereby MNEs are the actors making new and environmentally sensitive investments. In contrast, alliances between the protected and inefficient firms in quadrant 3 and mobilizer NGOs in quadrant 4 are not useful. Yet this was exactly the type of coalition put together in Seattle in 1999 to disrupt the WTO meetings. There, labour, mobilizer NGOs, and even technical NGOs made common cause against business and governments.

Three suggestions might be offered as to how MNEs should proceed:

- The activities of external stakeholders should be discussed at the Board and top management level, and an overall strategy should be developed to deal with them. It is important to make a distinction between technical NGOs and anti-global mobilizers. Initiatives should be developed to work with the former. Clear arguments should be developed to appropriately counter the 'discourse' of the mobilizers, and this should be combined with an effective communication strategy to reach relevant audiences.
- Sustainable development and ethical stakeholder perspectives should be embedded within the organization and its culture.
- The firm should not engage in a debate with NGOs through a small set of public relations people; instead all senior managers should be trained to articulate the concept of stakeholder capitalism, rather than shareholder capitalism and the contribution of the organization to the resulting wealth creation. In other words, all senior managers in the firm should engage with NGOs.

As a result of the above initiatives, firms should experience a dramatic improvement in both profile and performance. The firms that will do best in future will be those that take leadership positions with respect to stakeholder management, capture the concept of 'values-driven' rather than 'profit-driven' capitalism, and respect their most important resource—namely their employees. These policies will be the most effective tools at the microeconomic level against ideology-driven mobilizers.

For their part, NGOs need to understand that anti-global rhetoric is leading to regional integration and bilateral agreements as a politically more feasible—but ultimately less efficient—alternative to global integration. This does not benefit the objectives of civil society. Free trade and investment liberalization have not yet been achieved because of the vested interests and misperceptions of some components of civil society and affected stakeholders. We now need to recognize and correct these misperceptions as a precondition to achieving an overarching increase in world welfare and incomes.

Box 1.2 Globalization hits the brick wall: Microsoft and the European Commission

The dispute between Microsoft and the European Commission (EC) demonstrates that globalization does not exist. Microsoft has ridden the wave of worldwide Internet access and software applications but it has run into a brick wall in Brussels. There the EU Directorate General for Competition and State Aid (DG Comp) has imposed large fines on Microsoft for breaking its competition rules. In March 2004, the DG Comp ruled that Microsoft was abusing its dominant market position with its Windows operating system. Now the DG Comp is threatening to impose large daily fines because it says Microsoft is failing to comply with that ruling.

This case illustrates that even the world's most successful software company does not have unrestricted global market access for its products. Microsoft is simply the latest large multinational enterprise to misread the world marketplace. For US firms, entering a foreign triad market in Europe and Asia is fraught with peril. Firms like Microsoft need to understand that a business model developed for North America will need to be adapted in Europe and Asia.

In the case of Microsoft, the key difference is in the way that the EU regulatory system operates. In Europe, competition policy can be used as a barrier to entry. A single firm (in this case, Sun Microsystems) can trigger an EU-wide investigation. In this process, the deck is stacked against the foreign firm. In 2001, GE also made a similar mistake in its acquisition of Honeywell, which was disallowed by the EU.

While the USA has somewhat similar antitrust provisions, the application of these is more business-friendly than in Europe. Microsoft was able to settle its antitrust case with the Bush Administration, but it has consistently failed to do so with the EU because the regulatory climate in Europe is harsher than in North America. Multinational firms like Microsoft, which assume free trade, worldwide market entry, and the other attributes of globalization, are learning expensive lessons.

Antitrust legislation is but one of an array of market entry barriers. Even stiffer are anti-dumping and countervailing duty laws that are used to keep out foreign rivals. The USA itself administers its anti-dumping and countervailing duty laws in favour of the home team. In 2006, Congress on security grounds overturned the executive branch's decision to allow Dubai Ports International to acquire the US ports owned by the British firm P&O. The Europeans, perceiving that US commitment to free trade is weak, have stiffened their stance with regard to Microsoft. The end result is typical triad-based economic warfare, where market entry is denied by the local bureaucrats and politicians.

The lessons of the Microsoft case are that it is unlikely that the regulatory standards across the triad will be harmonized. Multinationals must be prepared to adapt their business models when they enter foreign regions of the triad. Even in high-tech areas such as software, the technology does not guarantee worldwide market access. The surface of our new 'global' world is not even: there are strong regional fault lines.

A New Research Agenda

The implications of MNE activity have been the subject of a large and varied literature. Four contradictory approaches have emerged:

1. An emphasis on the economic inferiority of regional vis-à-vis multi-lateral integration outcomes.
2. The view that regionalism is an efficient substitute for ill-functioning multilateral institutions in terms of economic outcomes.
3. A focus on the comparative ease of conducting a regional integration process (with only a limited number of participants that are geographically close) vis-à-vis a multilateral integration process that could involve all the 144 countries in the WTO.
4. A focus on the organic nature of economic integration via regional clusters. Here, regional integration is not seen as being primarily driven by the strategic intentions of government agencies, etc., to increase or consolidate economic exchange within a region through new institutions in a top-down fashion but as the result of bottom-up efforts by a multitude of actors wishing to expand their geographical business horizon, guided by immediate opportunities that are geographically close, involve low transaction costs, and have a high potential for economies of scale.

With some exceptions, none of these four perspectives has paid much attention to the MNE as the appropriate unit of analysis. However, this focus can open up fruitful avenues for future research in international business in several areas:

- The role of individual MNEs in the institutional processes of regional integration could be investigated in more depth, not starting from the ideological assumption that all MNEs pursue a narrow and homogenous business agenda. Each firm's preferences and role regarding regional integration will depend upon the configuration of its FSAs, much in line with its preferences regarding trade and investment protection at the national level. These preferences may even vary from business to business within a single firm. As indicated earlier in this chapter, the main question for the MNE is to assess how regional integration reduces the need for location-specific adaptation in the various national markets, when expanding the geographic scope of its activities.

- Rather than simply analysing macroeconomic or sectoral data, there are opportunities for research into the precise firm-level adaptations required in regional integration, focusing particularly on the region-specific adaptations needed to link MNE (location- and non-location-bound) FSAs with the locational advantages of the region, and the nature of MNE investments (internal development vs external acquisition). Such analysis of new knowledge development in MNEs may be critical to understanding fully the social effects of increased regionalization.

- The impact of regional trading agreements has often been interpreted in terms of changes to the entry barriers that insiders and outsiders face at the macro, industry, and strategic-group levels. From a resource-based perspective, however, there is a real need to understand how the processes of regional integration affect the creation or elimination of isolating mechanisms, and thereby economic performance, at the level of the individual MNE and subunits within the MNE.

- In particular, in the academic literature, the type of entry barrier involving the 'liability of regional foreignness' has not been examined. Future work needs to be undertaken to assess the nature and extent of the liability of regional foreignness and the manner in which it may serve to limit the financial performance of MNEs.

- Regional integration also has implications for knowledge exchange, as it is likely to increase the reach of MNE networks and linkages and even the MNEs' broader flagship networks. To the extent that such linkages and networks are associated with spillovers in knowledge diffusion, these should be taken into account in any analysis of the benefits of regional integration.

- Regional integration has an impact on the MNE's own allocation of internal resources. More specifically, firm-level investments in regional adaptation often involve relocating production facilities to the most efficient units. This implies a zero-sum game with 'winning' and 'losing' subsidiaries within the MNE. Interestingly, it has been observed that regional integration may also energize subsidiaries to start new initiatives and to develop new capabilities. This implies the converse—a non-zero-sum game, with overall macro-level benefits.

- Also, will the deepening of regional trading blocs strengthen MNE activities *across* the triad? Or will they, on the contrary, act as an incentive to concentrate resources allocation processes and market expansion plans even more narrowly? The data presented in this chapter indicate that regional integration during the past decade has had little effect on the abilities of MNEs to increase their overall globalization capabilities.

The tools of analytical research should yield new scholarship and insight far beyond this chapter. Further research should be undertaken to test the regional dimension of international strategy. The embeddedness of FSAs at regional level requires new thinking, case studies, data analysis, surveys of managers within MNEs, etc. Specifically, key analytical devices used in international business research will need to be modified. For example, the economic integration–national responsiveness matrix popularized by Bartlett and Ghoshal needs to be complemented with a regional dimension.

The 'big question' for research in international business is: Why do MNEs succeed as regional organizations without becoming global? International business is not just about foreign sales; it matters where those sales occur—if in the home region (as for most large firms), then forget global and focus on regional issues. The regional geographic scope of most MNEs is matched by a regional reach of their FSAs. Large firms have a regional alignment, not a global one. Scholars of international business need to pay less attention to models of 'global' strategy, as it is a special case. There are so few 'global' MNEs as to render the concept of 'globalization' meaningless. Most MNEs are not global, but regional. No longer can globalization be confused with multinationality.

References

1. Alan M. Rugman and Simon Collinson, *International Business* (4th edn.; Englewood Cliffs, NJ: Prentice-Hall, 2006).
2. Alan M. Rugman (ed.), *Leadership in International Business Education and Research* (Oxford: Elsevier, 2002).
3. Michael E. Porter, *The Competitive Advantage of Nations* (New York: Free Press, 1990).

4. John H. Dunning, *The Globalization of Business* (London: Routledge, 1993).
5. Christopher A. Bartlett and Sumantra Ghosal, *Managing across Borders: The Transnational Solution* (Cambridge, MA: Harvard Business School Press, 1989).
6. Christopher A. Bartlett and Sumantra Ghosal, *Managing across Borders: The Transnational Solution* (2nd. edn.; Cambridge, MA: Harvard Business School Press, 1998).
7. Alan M. Rugman, *The Regional Multinationals* (Cambridge: Cambridge University Press, 2005).
8. Arie Y. Lewin and Carine Peeters, 'Offshoring Work: Business Hype or the Onset of Fundamental Transformation?', *Long Range Planning*, 39/3(June 2006): 221–39.
9. Alexandra J. Campbell and Alain Verbeke, 'The Globalization of Service Multinationals', *Long Range Planning*, 27/2(1994): 95–102.
10. Kenichi Ohmae, *Triad Power: The Coming Shape of Global Competition* (New York: Free Press, 1985).

2

A Tougher World: Managerial Work and Behaviour

Rosemary Stewart

This book records how radically the world of business has changed. This should mean that managing is now strikingly different from what it was forty years ago. In many ways it is, but the findings from early studies of managerial work and behaviour (MWB) are still applicable. The chapter will explore this paradox and suggest lessons for managers today. It will also discuss how researchers, taking account of previous work, can fruitfully investigate the nature of MWB in organizations in the modern world.

Research into MWB

There are four remarkable features of this field of social research. The first is its longevity. The first major study, *Executive Behaviour*[1] by the Swedish professor Sune Carlson, appeared in 1951.[2] The second and third are that its researchers have usually sought to draw practical lessons for managers, though doing so did not necessarily enhance their academic status; and that, as stated above, its major findings still remain largely true today despite the radical changes affecting business. The fourth is its unfashionableness, reflected in the very limited number of studies since then compared to those in leadership research.

Although highly important for understanding what managers can do to improve their efficiency and effectiveness, MWB has never been fashionable, even after the stir caused by Henry Mintzberg's popular study, *The Nature of Managerial Work*—often the only one cited by American scholars.[3] Fashions come and go, but an unfashionable area of research can have a longer life because it does not run the risk of going out of fashion.

MWB continues to attract researchers. However, leadership has always been a much more popular subject, as the immense volume of studies over many years shows. One explanation for the longstanding popularity of leadership studies is that the idea of the central role of leaders is particularly appealing to American scholars, who form such a large group of researchers in organizational behaviour. Another explanation for the small number of studies of MWB compared with leadership is the complexity of researching MWB—unless a simplistic quantitative approach is used, which relies too much on what managers say they think or do.

One problem with an unfashionable area of research is that attempts to open up new avenues of research and thinking produce no response, whereas in a fashionable area many people would seek to build on or refute what has been written. One example of the neglect of attempts to encourage new developments in the field is Colin Hales's well-argued criticisms of studies of MWB as atheoretical. He has worried over a long time about what he sees to be this serious defect of researchers in this area. He accepts that the studies have shown common characteristics of managerial work but wants to develop a causal explanation. In an article in the *British Journal of Management* he sets out a model to try to provide such an explanation.[4] Another example is my article 'The Ways Forward' which sought to show the many different ways in which MWB might be usefully studied.[5] I have not found a response to either article.

The major changes affecting managers' jobs *must* have transformed what managers do. In some ways, of course, it is obvious that they have: managers have to work harder and for much longer hours; e-mail and the mobile phone have revolutionized the nature and frequency of communications; the Web has transformed the availability of information and the rapidity of change has complicated managerial work. Yet some generalizations about managing remain applicable. Even Henri Fayol's early theorizing about management[6] that managers plan, organize, motivate, control and coordinate is as true today as when he wrote it, although the ways in which managers do each of these have changed. The drawback to his generalization is that it suggests, as befits a Frenchman, a theoretical and aloof view of what managers do.

Later research into what managers actually do conveys a very different picture of what being a manager is actually like. After Sune Carlson's early research, described below, an early study in 1967 by me, *Managers and their Jobs*,[7] also showed what a different picture of managerial work from that evoked by Fayol emerged after actually examining it. This was a study of 160 managers who kept specially designed diary records for a month. The design of this record had been piloted to discover what format was most convenient and what headings could produce reasonable results. The pilot showed that one could not get comparable results for categories about managers' activities, because of ambiguity, but only about where, how and with whom the manager was working. The volunteers, who kept the diaries, in convenient booklets of individual sheets for each episode, said that they had found it very helpful to do so and resolved to try to use their time more efficiently. They were shocked at how episodic and fragmented was their working day.

Mintzberg in his later observational study of five chief executives, *The Nature of Managerial Work*, identified ten managerial roles.[3] He distinguished between three main roles, which he called 'Interpersonal, Informational and Decisional'. In Interpersonal he distinguished between Figurehead, Leader and Liaison. His emphasis on the first and the third of these should have helped some managers to be more aware of their importance. As he studied chief executives the figurehead role was particularly salient. It is noteworthy, incidentally, given the enthusiasm for leadership studies, that he included only 'leader' as one of his ten roles. He divided the Informational roles into Monitor, Disseminator and Spokesman, and the Decisional roles into: Entrepreneur, Disturbance Handler, Resource Allocator and Negotiator. He, like Carlson and some of the other researchers into MWB, suggested lessons that managers could usefully draw from these studies.

Differences Between Managers' Jobs

Another area of MWB, popular in its early days, sought to identify the differences between management jobs. To do so is obviously relevant for management training, but research has not revealed anything to suggest that the customary divisions by levels, and for some courses by functions, are inappropriate. Nor has the research into differences between managers' jobs identified additional forms of grouping. This may be because only the traditional divisions matter for management training and development, but more likely they reflect the fact that there has been inadequate research into job differences.

The early research may have had some influence on the content of courses. An early article, reprinted in 2005 in a classic article series of The Academy of Management's *Executive*, by Kraut, Pedigo, McKenna and Dunnette on 'The Roles of the Manager: What's Really Important in Different Management Jobs' makes suggestions from their research for relevant course content for different levels.[8]

Studies of differences between management jobs are potentially useful to remind management academics of the limitations to generalizing about management. Studies of differences between jobs at the same level can provide a warning for managers that moving between jobs, even those that carry the same title, such as 'general manager', can pose unexpected difficulties because the demands on the manager may be very different. John Gabarro in his book *The Dynamics of Taking Charge* illuminatingly described the risks in job changes from his study of seventeen managers at different levels who took up new jobs.[9]

Quantitative or Qualitative?

Enthusiasm for in-depth studies of what managers are actually doing is rare today although it is such studies that have contributed most to the understanding of managerial behaviour. Quantitative studies are much more popular, particularly in the USA where most management research takes place. It may seem more scientific to use only quantitative methods, but the danger is of making mistaken assumptions about what the answers that managers give to questionnaires and rating scales really mean. Do the answers represent factual information about what their jobs are actually like, or do they rather reflect the particular way in which the responder sees and does the job? Most managers are too busy to be reflective about their work and by temperament they may be unsuited to doing so as management attracts personalities who are action oriented.

An example of where it is misleading to rely only on quantitative measures is in studies that seek to distinguish differences in job demands by asking questions like 'Do you work under time pressure?' and 'Do you have problems with the workload?' Such questions will be misleading indicators of the nature of the job because managers, even in similar jobs, will differ both in their perceptions of the demands of the job and in their capacity to organize their workload.

I learnt the hard way that the answers that managers give about the nature of their jobs are very personal, when I first sought to distinguish differences between jobs. I believed then that one could discover these differences by asking managers to rate the extent to which particular characteristics applied to their job. I thought to check their answers by comparing those of managers in similar jobs and was startled to find that their replies ranged the whole length of a rating scale. In later studies, I discovered the explanation of this unexpected result: managers in similar jobs can both see and do them very differently. This is explained in the first of the lessons for managers from studies of MWB, which are given below.

This unexpected and unwelcome discovery provided the trigger for a series of studies of mine in MWB. I found that each study produced

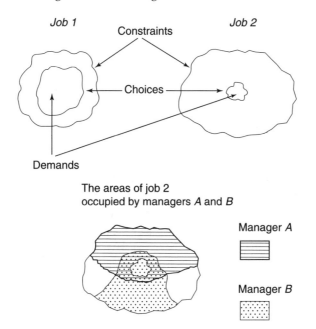

FIG. 2.1 Demands, constraints, and choices in jobs

unexpected results, which I wanted to probe in later studies, and that sometimes the explanation of the findings became apparent only in later studies. This was especially true of the extent to which managers in similar jobs may do them very differently, both because they have a different perception of what needs doing and because of their different previous job experiences. It was this discovery that led to my development of the demands, constraints and choices model, illustrated above, both as a way of explaining this and of helping managers to review the ways they worked (Figure 2.1).

The lessons that I, and other early researchers, drew are still relevant for managers who are interested in improving their effectiveness.

A Blinkered, Highly Personal View of the Job

Few managers are likely to worry about this threat to their effectiveness, but the author's studies[10] suggest that this is a common danger. A major lesson of the intensive studies of managerial behaviour that I have undertaken over the years is that managers both see and do their jobs very differently. They make different assumptions, often implicit rather than explicit, about what matters and hence about what they should be doing.

The model I developed from these studies of Demands, Constraints and Choices[11] provided a way of thinking about the differences between jobs and between how managers see and do their jobs. It also provided a tool that managers have found helpful for reviewing their effectiveness. Demands are defined as the core of the job, what any manager in the job would have to do; constraints as the factors that limit what the manager can do; choices are the opportunities in a job for one manager to do it differently from another. All three are dynamic, that is they change over time, both from changes in circumstances, including the expectations of those with whom the manager works, what the manager does to shape the job, and the length of time that he or she has been in it.

One reason why managers can have a blinkered view of the job is that they may exaggerate both the demands of the job and the constraints upon it and not realize that much of the work that they do may be a choice; someone else in the job may spend his or her time in different ways and focus on different aspects of it.

It can be hard, particularly for less analytical managers, to take a strategic view of the job and of what they can most usefully contribute. It is easier for most managers to have a highly personal view of the job shaped by their personality and by previous experience. This can easily be seen by comparing the amount of time that managers in similar jobs spend with various categories of people. My research shows that this can be very different. Some managers are more focused on their staff and choose—although often not consciously—to devote much of their attention to them. Others are more concerned with working with their peers, and yet others devote more time to people outside the organization. Some are more focused on making a good impression on their boss.

This is a simple illustration of how people can do jobs very differently, often without recognizing that they are doing so. A strategic view of what one should be doing requires both an assessment of what needs doing in the job and of the contribution that one is best equipped to make. Managers may be too busy or temperamentally unsuited to do so without guidance.

A management training course can provide an opportunity for such analysis. I found that a good way of helping managers to review the effectiveness of their work was, after an introduction to examining a job using the author's model of demands, constraints, and choices, to put them in groups of three with two of them acting as consultants to examine what the third thought were the demands, constraints, and choices in his or her job. It was usual for the two consultants to identify, and seek to persuade the third, that many of the demands and constraints that he or she identified were purely personal rather than intrinsic to the job. This discovery can be usefully linked to the advice in Drucker's *The Effective Executive*[12]—that the aim should be to build on an executive's strengths rather than to deplore his or her weaknesses. The same is true for managers seeking to improve their own effectiveness or seeking to help their staff to develop.

Mistaken Beliefs About How One Spends One's Time

Carlson first noticed that the chief executives he studied had mistaken beliefs about how they spent their time.[1] He gave as an example that they regarded personal tours of plants and offices as an important aspect of their job, but they were quite mistaken about the time that they actually spent doing this.

There is no reason to believe that executives today are likely to have more reliable views about how they spend their time. This is why managers can find it illuminating to try to keep an ongoing record of what they do. My study *Managers and Their Jobs* gives examples of the kind of diaries that can be kept.[7] The popularity of courses on the management of time over many years shows that many managers feel a need to learn to use it more efficiently.

Constraints of Brevity, Variety, and Fragmentation

Sune Carlson first highlighted this characteristic of the managing directors whom he studied and I found the same thing in my diary study of 160 middle managers.[7] We both discovered that managers were rarely alone and undisturbed for any length of time. In that and subsequent studies I also found that they frequently switched their attention from one subject or person to another and seemed to find it easier to do so than to focus on a particular task. We do not know what effects new means of communication have had on this, but they are likely to have intensified this behaviour.

Mintzberg suggested that 'superficiality is a prime occupational hazard of the manager'.[3] Put another way, busyness is a major temptation for the manager, and many find that appealing and preferable to working in any other way; responding to whatever comes into their mind, or to the latest call even if it is less important than the work that it interrupted. In many management jobs it is hard, but not impossible, to take time to consider what you are doing.

The pattern of managerial work remains of interest to researchers, though more theoretically, considering how a manager can deal with short-term issues, 'putting out fires', while ensuring time for longer-term projects.[13]

Not in Control?

There seems no reason to think that the changes affecting managers' jobs have made Carlson's memorable conclusion from his study less potentially true:

Before we made the study, I always thought of a chief executive as the conductor of an orchestra, standing aloof on his platform. Now I am in some respects inclined to see him as a puppet in a puppet show with hundreds of people pulling the strings and forcing him to act in one way or another.[1]

Carlson's concern arose from his conclusion that the chief executives he studied were slaves to the engagements in their diaries, which were often determined by others. Probably most executives would reject the idea that they are not in control, though they worry about whether they know what is going on below them.

John Kotter had a more positive view of how the general managers he studied sought to exercise control. He said that they did this—though some were much better than others—by developing what he called 'agendas'.[14] He argued that during the first few months in the job the general managers developed their view of what needed doing, which constituted their agenda for what they wanted to do. This agenda differed from the formal plans by being less about financial objectives and more about broader and longer-term issues that they would seek to follow. The general managers kept their agenda in mind and sought to forward it both in an organized way and opportunistically. The more effective general managers had better developed agendas and were more aware of making use of unexpected opportunities, including chance contacts, to forward them.

Develop a Supportive Network of Contacts

Kotter in his study of general managers argued that they sought to pursue their agendas for doing their job by developing a supportive network of contacts. He also described the different methods that they used to make others feel obliged to them and therefore more willing to reciprocate to further the general manager's agenda—the trading of favours. Leonard

Sayles had earlier, in a pioneering participant observation study of production managers, stressed their dependence on their peers, which they managed by such trading.[15] He argued that good managers should know what their trading counters with particular individuals are.

Enlist the Cooperation of all the Stakeholders

This is a much broader point than the previous one. Tony Watson, in a much later study than Sayles's, was a participant observer in a telecommunications factory where he sought to find out what it was like to be a manager.[16] He, like Sayles, was struck by the need to enlist cooperation from so many different people and concluded that

> Management is essentially a human social craft. It requires the ability to interpret the thoughts and wants of others—be these employees, customers, competitors or whatever—and the facility to shape meanings, values and human commitments.[17]

Here he echoes the views of Dan Gowler, another social anthropologist and a Fellow of Templeton College until his death, who talked of management being the management of meaning.[18] Watson's ethnographic background helped him to observe how the managers behaved, how they sought to adjust to the problems of being a manager in a factory, and what they had to learn to do so. He stressed, like Kotter, the need to develop a sense of shared obligation; it is arguable that it is an even greater need for middle managers in a factory than for general managers. Watson's conclusion suggests the dangers of relying on a technocratic approach to management training, or even more to management development, which can usefully include helping managers to understand themselves and what their strengths and weaknesses are.

Manage Information

Today managing information is likely to be interpreted in terms of information technology because that is one of the major changes over the forty years. But Mintzberg's suggestion[3] that one of the ways in which executives can improve their efficiency is by improving their use of informal information is still true today. He argued that the executives he studied showed a preference for informal information. E-mail is likely to have greatly increased managers' access to informal information and may—though I am not aware of a study about this—have further encouraged a preference for that kind of information.

Mintzberg also stressed the need for managers to think consciously about what information they need to share with others, particularly with their staff, because they have contacts and access to information that differs from them.

Researching MWB Now

It is evident that management today is more demanding and that, despite the continuing relevance of old research, we badly need new research that will tell us how the many changes have affected managerial work and managerial behaviour and what are the implications for improving managerial effectiveness. Unfortunately, there seems little interest in doing so, with two major exceptions. One newer area of research is about the differences in the behaviour of men and women managers, in response to the great increase in the number of women managers. Another is cross-cultural studies of differences in managerial behaviour, which has grown in importance with increasing globalization. A related area of research that is more popular today is that of managerial ethics, perhaps in part because managers in global companies have to deal with those with different ethical backgrounds.

Understanding Cross-Cultural Differences

The need to draw practical lessons for managers is, and for long has been, obvious in cross-cultural studies, even though such studies can be pursued without doing so. Understanding why and how it is different doing business with managers from another country, or working with them in the same company, has become of increasing relevance. It always concerned international companies, such as the oil giants, who needed to prepare their managers to work overseas, but now many more companies need to do so.

Managers, and especially senior executives, need research that will help to identify differences that arise from differences in behaviour, which may come, at least in part, from differences in expectations. The rapid development of China creates a new area for such cross-cultural studies, following on an earlier interest in comparisons with Japan. Comparisons with China are now being actively pursued, not just by Western academics but also by Chinese students and academics. A recent study of Chinese managerial behaviour warned against deceptive managerial practices.[19]

Currently there is also interest in comparative studies of managers from a much wider range of countries, particularly in South Asia.

Unfortunately some of these use Mintzberg's roles as a way of comparing cultures. The popularity of his ten roles as a research tool over the years is in my view unfortunate because it means that the researcher does not have to think about possible differences in their meanings for individual managers, and particularly those working in different countries. It is a convenient tool for ensuring, if no such awkward questions are asked, that a research result will be guaranteed—something particularly useful for doctoral students!

Managers in different countries can have very different conceptions of what a manager should be doing. This can also be true for managers in different Western countries, as shown, for example, by an intensive comparison of how German and British middle managers in similar industries thought about their work and by observation to find out how they did their jobs.[20] Both proved to be very different: the German middle managers saw their jobs as specialist ones in which they used their greater specialist knowledge to guide their subordinates, whereas the British middle managers saw their jobs as managerial ones in which training and delegation to subordinates were important. They differed in many other ways too, for example, in their attitudes to time and punctuality and to socializing with their colleagues and staff. That French managers are also highly distinctive is well brought out by Jean-Louis Barsoux and Peter Lawrence who point out that this makes it hard for those who want to import American management practices.[21] Earlier Peter Lawrence had described the distinctive character of German management.[22]

The differences in managerial expectations and behaviour between countries can be very great, but there can also be unexpected similarities. John Child and Livia Markoczy, for instance, compared reports of managerial behaviour in Chinese and Hungarian joint ventures and intriguingly found close similarities.[23] They attributed this to their common form of industrial governance because Hungary at that time, the early 1990s, had a system of state socialism, as did the Chinese, which shaped managerial behaviour.

The Lessons from MWB Research

The most important lesson from the diverse studies of MWB for managers who wish to improve their effectiveness, or at least who are willing to consider that they could do so, is to ask themselves whether they are doing the right job—right in the sense that it is what needs doing in that job at that time, tempered by recognition of what contribution they can best make.

A useful approach for individual managers is to compare what they are actually doing with what they think is important and also with what they think they are doing. They can do this by keeping an ongoing record of their activities, either in a special diary format or by recording notes. Examples of diaries are given in *Managers and their Jobs*.[7] They should then look at the record of what they do and ask which activities were things they had to do and which were in practice a choice, even if not recognized as such. Once they identify the choices that they made they may decide that other work is really more important, such as the things that they always believed are important but never found time to do.

For academics, three lessons are suggested. One is to be more aware of what can be relevant to their research in adjacent fields. There is always a danger in academic studies of narrow segmentation, so that relevant work from related fields is ignored. The second is to examine the assumptions that they make about managing when deciding what and how they teach. The third is to learn from the early research the value of open, exploratory qualitative studies for seeking to understand what is happening to managerial work in the modern world. Quantify wherever possible, but beware of the dangers of making mistaken assumptions about the validity of what they want to compare.

Above all, there is a particular danger in management studies of theory building without a concern for the practical applications. The author believes that management studies should be like medicine in its concern for application, a heretical view for those who see themselves as management scientists. There tends to be a sharp divide, particularly in the USA, between those who have a primarily, even wholly, academic focus and those who contribute academically but also seek to draw practical lessons for managers. All those who teach experienced managers should do the latter.

Postscript

The author's studies were described in the introduction to a Leadership Classic review of her work by Kevin Lowe in *The Leadership Quarterly*:

From her seminal book *Managers and Their Jobs: A Study of the Similarities and Differences in the Ways Managers Spend Their Time* (1967) through the third edition of *The Reality of Management* (1997), Professor Stewart has broadened our understanding of what managers actually do. Her work, spanning five decades (Stewart 1965, 2002), stands as a testimony to the benefits of a truly cumulative and programmatic research program focused on systematically exploring a phenomenon layer-by-layer, nuance-by-nuance. Her research methods were (and remain) innovative, exhaustive, and cutting edge. Using a battery of techniques such as structured interviews, diaries, structured observations, group discussions, case analyses, and critical incidents, Stewart was developing grounded theory work and implementing triangulation method before those approaches had fashionable labels. Among the many important contributions emerging from this work are the demands–constraints–choices framework and the notion of managerial exposure, useful models for defining differences in managerial work and discretion across jobs.[24]

Notes and References

1. S. Carlson, *Executive Behaviour: A Study of the Workload and Working Methods of Managing Directors* (Stockholm: Strombergs, 1951).
2. The author's work in MWB was recognized by an honorary doctorate by Carlson's old university, Uppsala.
3. H. Mintzberg, *The Nature of Managerial Work* (2nd edn.; Englewood Cliffs, NJ: Prentice-Hall, 1980).
4. C. Hales, 'Why Do Managers Do What They Do? Reconciling Evidence and Theory in Accounts of Managerial Work', *British Journal of Management*, 4/10(1999): 335.
5. R. Stewart, 'Studies of Managerial Jobs and Titles: The Ways Forward', *Journal of Management Studies*, 26/1(January, 1989).
6. G. H. Fayol, *General and Industrial Management* (1st English edn.; London: Pitman, 1949).
7. R. Stewart, *Managers and Their Jobs: A Study of the Similarities and Differences in the Ways Managers Spend their Time* (2nd edn.; London: Macmillan, 1988).
8. A. I. Kraut, P. R. Pedigo, D. D. McKenna, and M. D. Dunnette, 'The Roles of the Manager: What's Really Important in Different Management Jobs', *The Academy of Management Executive*, 3/4(1989): 286–93.
9. J. J. Gabarro, *The Dynamics of Taking Charge* (Boston: Harvard University Press, 1987).
10. R. Stewart, *Choices for the Manager: A Guide to Managerial Work and Behaviour* (London: McGraw-Hill, 1982).
11. R. Stewart, *Managing Today and Tomorrow* (London: Macmillan, 1991). Chapter 1 gives the best account of the demands, constraints, and choices model for a manager.
12. Peter Drucker, *The Effective Executive* (London: Heinemann, 1967).
13. Sridhar Seshadri and Zur Shapiro, 'Managerial Allocation of Time and Effort: The Effects of Interruptions', *Management Science*, 47/5(2001): 647–62.
14. John Kotter, *The General Managers* (New York: Free Press, 1982).
15. L. Sayles, *Managerial Behavior: Administration in Complex Organizations* (New York: McGraw-Hill, 1964).
16. T. J. Watson, *In Search of Management: Culture, Chaos and Control in Managerial Work* (London: Routledge, 1994).

17. Ibid. 223.
18. D. Gowler and K. Legge, 'The Meaning of Management and the Management of Meaning', in M. J. Earl (ed.), *Perspectives on Management: A Multidisciplinary Analysis* (Oxford: Oxford University Press, 1983).
19. D. Ahlstrom, M. Young, and A. Nair, 'Deceptive managerial practices in China: Strategies for foreign firms', *Business Horizons*, 45/6(2002): 49–59.
20. R. Stewart, J.-L. Barsoux, A. Kieser, H.-D. Ganter, and P. Walgenback, *Managing in Britain and Germany* (London: Macmillan, 1994).
21. J.-L. Barsoux and P. Lawrence, *Management in France* (London: Cassell Educational, 1990).
22. P. Lawrence, *Managers and Management in West Germany* (Aldershot: Gower, 1986).
23. J. Child and L. Markoczy, 'Host-Country Managerial Behaviour and Learning in Chinese and Hungarian Joint Ventures', *Journal of Management Studies*, 4/30(1993): 611–32.
24. K. B. Lowe, 'Demands, Constraints, Choices and Discretion: An Introduction to the Work of Rosemary Stewart', *The Leadership Quarterly*, 14(2003): 193.

3

The Technology of the Possible: IT, Innovation, Capitalism, and Globalization

Chris Sauer

I often find myself taking for granted the technological changes that have taken place over the last forty years and the social, political, and economic shifts that have accompanied them. I combat this tendency by reflecting on my own experience. How strange today to imagine a childhood in which computers play no part, but in my case my only awareness of them came through the awed respect the grown-ups showed my godfather who was responsible in the late 1950s and early 1960s for the British Army's 'electronic brain'. Towards the end of the 1960s, my first holiday job was with a computer-free Inland Revenue office. I can still smell the stagnant odour of pre- and post-war papers in its registry of cardboard files—the rotting core of this government department. Move on two years and I am in a City life assurance firm. People still use in earnest electrical adding machines and even Facit mechanical calculators, but the adepts are dying out. Here, the company has time-sharing access to its parent company's mainframe—referred to reverently as 'the machine' as if there could be no other.

By the end of my undergraduate career in the mid-1970s, Oxford University was offering programming courses in Algol. I graduated into a young, progressive institution that had introduced data processing for all its back-office systems from its inception in 1969. Its mainframe was dedicated, not shared, and filled an air-conditioned room the size of an Olympic pool. We fed it cards into which we had hand-punched the holes. I first encountered there the relentless pressure for change that has characterized so much of the subsequent history of information technology (IT)—we were redeveloping our core systems after just seven years. By the 1980s I was wrestling with the early personal computers, and by the middle of the decade I was using the very first Macintosh computers in my teaching with their radical WIMP (Windows, Icons, Menus, Pointer) interface. How extraordinary then to find just ten years later in a colleague's office in Houston a defunct Fat Mac retained as a nostalgic memory and paperweight—it looked prehistoric. For my part, a brief excursion into artificial intelligence was replaced by a more serious and enduring commitment to the real problem—how to manage investment in IT for business value.

Throughout this journey, notwithstanding the emergence in the mid-1980s of a handful of iconic strategic information systems that conferred valuable and lasting competitive advantage—most notably American Airlines' SABRE reservation system and American Hospital Supplies' ordering system—the bulk of the effort in IT had been devoted to cost saving and, to a lesser extent, cycle time reduction through automation. Given the prevalence of IT project failures, it seemed as though investment in IT was for the most part an act of faith not a rational, commercial decision. I can therefore still vividly remember a technician installing MOSAIC (the first real browser) and showing me how to use it. This, I felt, was IT! For the first time, I was excited to show others what the technology could offer.

Today, a little over ten years on, we see companies innovating to compete on the Internet in a variety of ways. We see them working seamlessly across time zones, and reaching out to new markets and customers. It is therefore easy to see a world in which the forces of capitalism are enabled by technology to produce value for shareholders through innovation and globalization. A simplistic judgement would see this as good for the shareholders but bad for those whose jobs have been offshored. But this is just a snapshot and assumes somehow that today represents the endpoint in a historical process.

This chapter, therefore, is intended as an essay in sense-making. It aims to connect some key developments in the past five decades to produce a richer interpretation of the history we have lived through and a better basis for understanding possible futures. While many new technologies, such as bio-tech and materials, have emerged through the past fifty years, the focus is squarely on IT because it has been central to the period, is pervasive in the lives and businesses of citizens in advanced economies, and underpins and enables much development in other technological areas such as imaging and scanning in health, drug targeting in pharmaceuticals, and avionics in aerospace. Like steam and electricity before it, IT is a general-purpose technology[1] and as such enables a wide variety of possibilities. By reflecting on the history of IT, we can see both the paradox of vast investment in a technology that everyone views as underperforming and the cumulative transformation of modern life. In order to understand this transformation, it is necessary to go beyond developments in technology and to consider parallel developments. A mainspring for progress has been the capitalist dynamic. But capitalism is manifested in diverse ways, and these have evolved along with new trends in management. Some of these changes have influenced and will continue to influence the direction and impact of technology. It is the combination and interaction of technology, innovation, globalization, and capitalism that helps us make sense of the past and the future.

I argue that capitalism has motivated the exploitation of IT but for many years this was because of its potential rather than its actual value. This is at some remove from the archetype of the hard-nosed capitalist firm that does nothing that does not immediately contribute to maximizing profits. Capitalism, therefore, proves a different beast from its simplistic characterizations. Innovation has been encouraged but until the late-1990s has generated more by way of learning than profits. But the potential for capital has always been there, and now we see it being realized. But the same conditions that have permitted exploitation—cheaper, more accessible, and more widely diffused technology—have also made the enabling technology available to other companies, thereby often reducing the very competitive advantages that firms have pursued. Short-term advantages accrue to the owners of first-mover companies, but longer-term advantages are secured by the customer. Innovation has been one way to gain advantage. Globalization extends the logic of capitalism to secure returns across national boundaries through access to markets and through increased volumes and cost consolidation. But the capitalist dynamic plays out in paradoxical ways—through offshoring, for example, the pursuit of profit in higher cost countries shifts economic activity and redistributes wealth to lower cost countries. For centuries the West has wanted to sell its goods to China's millions but now they have the money to pay for them.

This is not a covert argument for the predictive power of the 'invisible hand'.[2] It is more to say that while from a historical perspective it is easy to discern the workings of market forces, at any point in time individuals and their companies will be pursuing self-interest in ways that oppose the simple playing out of market forces. What we see is a series of mutual adjustments, not the outputs of a linear model.

Elsewhere in this book, Michael Earl writes about developments in Information Management. I therefore restrict myself to the linkage between macro-level shifts in economics and society and the kinds of work that academics in Information Management and Information Systems have engaged in. It should be viewed as a scene setting for Chapter 10.

Michael Earl has also described IT as an ambiguous technology.[3] The same technology can be interpreted in different ways. Sometimes competing interpretations prove equally valid. The same system that deskills and automates one person can be seen to streamline and improve control from another person's perspective. For that reason, and because history does not unfold in simple steps but advances on a very uneven front, I do not present a neatly tabulated stage model. Rather, I describe the development of IT in the next section as a narrative in roughly chronological order, with the expectation that readers will realize that it is an impressionistic sketch supporting the overall thesis of this chapter.

In the following section, I relate technological innovations and their application in business to developments in capitalism, including globalization. To this, I link references, where possible, to the work of the Oxford Institute of Information Management to the extent that it mirrors the developments I discuss. Because both Templeton College and the Oxford Institute of Information Management are UK based and because of the limits of space, the discussion in this chapter takes a UK perspective. If this thesis is credible, then it should be equally applicable to other developed countries.

The Many Faces of IT

From a historical perspective, I conceive of innovations in IT as having offered organizations benefits in a number of distinct ways. These include task automation, decision support, process re-engineering, organizational change, connection and coordination, and convergence. Each has been more or less important at different times.

The earliest efforts at applying computers to organizational needs focused on automating complex, time-consuming, and error-prone tasks such as calculating payroll. The technologies supporting this included high-level programming languages such as COBOL and report generators. The accumulation of data from such processes then made available the raw material for management to use as input to its own work—decision-making and managing. Starting in the early 1970s this was the era of management information systems and decision-support systems supported by database technology. By the 1980s this had extended into the automation of complex, expert decision-making with the advent of the expert systems and artificial intelligence movement enabled by expert systems' shell technologies. From the mid-1980s process re-engineering came in two forms—purpose-built and 'vanilla'. The purpose-built form largely employed existing technologies to support differentiated business processes. The vanilla form employed ERP (Enterprise Resource Planning) technologies such as those supplied by SAP and Oracle to enable the so-called best practice processes in areas such as procurement, inventory management, manufacturing scheduling, and many others.

From the early 1990s communication and Web technologies combined to endow organizations both with greater scope to deliver richer and more complex goods and services and the means by which to manage this greater complexity. The complexity of services is visible all around us, for example in the integration of services offered through Internet banking. We see greater richness in the convergence of technological media, as voice, data, and graphics are combined into a single device enabling multimedia offerings such as podcasts. Email and browser technologies have permitted organizations to connect internally and externally to larger numbers of employees, customers, and suppliers. This has made it possible to reconfigure organizationally so that internal complexity is requisite to that of the product and service set and the external environment. ERP and the development of architectures have served to provide a uniform platform across large, complex enterprises, which, in turn, has permitted at once greater consistency of offering across locations, greater ability to relocate activities, and greater ability to control performance.

While the development of new technologies has not followed a strictly sequential path, the general trajectory can be viewed as moving from discrete, task-oriented technological systems to organizationally transformational reconfigurations of structures, systems, and processes. Taken together over forty years, the changes enabled by the technology fully justify the cliché, the 'Information Revolution', though we might equally well view it as the 'Organizational Revolution'.

Capitalism, Globalization, and the Management of IT

The UK economy, like technology, has been revolutionized since the mid-1960s. My contention is that the economic and technological changes have, not surprisingly, co-evolved. In some cases, the specific focus on deploying the technology has been encouraged by changes in economic circumstances; in others the potential of the technology has taken economic activity into new territory. As business has shifted its attentions from cost-cutting to strategic advantage to re-engineering to new business models, so IT management has had to change its focus and face up to new challenges. This is the territory that the Oxford Institute of Information Management has pioneered.

The economy of the 1950s, 1960s, and early 1970s was by today's standards heavily state-dominated, with the government active in sectors ranging from banking, telecommunications, and utilities to coal, steel, and oil, and with government regulation in the form of heavy taxes on business and legislation that gave organized labour real power vis-à-vis employers. These decades were characterized by a curious mix of post-war-Festival-of-Britain-Swinging-Sixties-style optimism together with major macro-economic discomfort (massive debt, balance of payments problems, and devaluation) and chronic industrial unrest. On the one hand, political leaders told the people 'you've never had it so good' and that the economy would be fired by the 'white heat of technology', offering a brave new world of technology-enabled wealth and comfort. On the other hand was the daily experience of strikes and a disaffected management class constrained from making unlimited profits by the combination of trade unions, taxes on business, and other regulations.

The early 1970s saw optimism ebb, leaving only a residue of economic distress epitomized by the Three Day Week. In those circumstances, the automational capacity of IT had two obvious attractions for managers. First, automating work reduced management's dependence on labour. Second, it promised cost savings, which, for many companies, appeared a lower risk way of improving the bottom line than innovating new products and services. There were of course other benefits such as more accurate and consistent calculation of payroll but as such processes were inward, rather than customer-facing, they were valued more for their contribution to cost saving than for any intrinsic value addition.

The 1970s surge in data processing generated vast banks of information with the potential to inform decision-making and management. In practice, the data were used for little more than to provide adequate controls over the automated processes. It was the era when you found in managers' offices tall piles of green-lined printouts, delivered daily, weekly, or monthly. The recipients either did not know what they were for or did not care. So, although many saw the potential of management information to improve decision-making and shape improved work practices,[4] the potential was rarely realized because there was little incentive by way of performance cultures and associated rewards to encourage innovation.

With the 1980s, we saw Margaret Thatcher successfully revolutionize the economy with a number of policy thrusts: deregulation, the diminution of the power of organized labour, the incentivization of entrepreneurship, support for business, and the shift of much economic activity from the public to private sector. Profit-seeking became more acceptable as the shareholder society was encouraged. Business responded to the improved environment by passing responsibility to lower levels. Now, more individuals stood to gain financially by innovating. IT need no longer be restricted to cost saving through automation but could focus on delivering differentiated business processes that supported revenue growth. Indeed, the transition from automation to strategic advantage is illustrated by the demise of the expert systems movement, which extended the logic of automating routine labour to automating scarce expertise. With the power of labour already diminished by government reform and the new and much greater strategic potential of the technology, expert systems simply lost their attraction.

The ideas of strategic IT and IT for competitive advantage emerged as themes in both practitioner and academic thinking at this time. Landmark innovations at American Airlines,[5] Merrill Lynch,[6] and American Hospital Supplies[7] encouraged the spread of these ideas. Revisionist commentators have noted that it was only a very few such applications that conferred genuine strategic advantage. In retrospect, this is hardly surprising for, as David Feeny and Blake Ives showed,[8] competitive advantage requires the right conditions to be satisfied, and these conditions are not easy to meet. Nevertheless, the ideas were consistent with the economic mood of the time and were to enjoy fuller consummation in the subsequent periods of business process change and e-business.

Perhaps more important was the organizational impact of the new understanding that such possibilities existed. Combined with the management consultancy-fuelled trend to decentralize, it created the basis for multiple IT units within a single corporation. Thus the strategic potential and the need for corporate-level oversight led many organizations to move IT from under the CFO to become a function in its own right represented at C-level by its own leader, the CIO. This was the genesis of many of the problems of alignment—strategic, structural, and personal—that have made Information Management an enduring topic in management studies.

Michael Earl played a leading part in the development of information systems strategy, which became increasingly a necessary element of the politics by which CIOs sold the activities of their function to their business colleagues and created a plan of execution for their own function.[9,10] As large corporations were divisionalized, the issue of how to structure IT in alignment with the business led to innovations in organizational design such as the federal structure.[11] In the 1990s, Earl and Feeny contributed most of the principal insights into what it takes to be a successful C-level executive responsible for IT.[12–14] Underlying these three streams of work the theme of the split between business and IT was recurrent. One answer from OXIIM was the hybrid manager who could span the knowledge bases and sets of interests in both areas.[10,15] An elegant solution, it never took off because of its in-built tensions. More recently, Sauer and

Willcocks[16] have argued for a liaison role specifically intended to combine technology and strategic execution in an organizational architecture that recognizes and mediates some of the tensions between business's desire for flexibility and IT's inherent constraints.

The revisionist movement referred to earlier was already alive and well in the 1980s. Critics of IT in both business and academia had begun to note what has come to be referred to as the 'Productivity Paradox'— or as Robert Solow[17] put it, 'You can see the computer age everywhere but in the productivity statistics.' This was consistent with the mood of the age, which was to value only that which contributed to profitability and shareholder value. The potential of IT had yet to be proved empirically. This resulted in a stream of academic research championed by Leslie Willcocks and others on IT evaluation.[18,19] Its principal focus has been identifying the cost-benefit of IT investments at the project level. This stream of work has lost prominence with the publication of several influential articles proving the economic benefits of IT at firm level,[20] the continuing generation of handsome profits by signature e-businesses such as e-bay and Google, and the transition into profitability of other pioneers including LastMinute.com and Amazon.

By the late 1980s, though, business executives, spurred on by investors, were seeking not merely to gain market share, sell more product, and gain greater profitability. There was, it was thought, an even quicker route to wealth through the discovery of hidden value in the corporation. This idea underpins several subsequent popular movements in management— namely core capabilities, knowledge management, business process re-engineering, and the more extreme experiments in e-business.

The core capabilities movement redirected strategic thinking beyond industry analysis towards the distinctive capabilities of the individual enterprise. Accompanied by the theoretical development of the Resource-Based View of the Firm, core capabilities thinking gave rise to two agendas. The first was to reframe what made a firm distinctive in terms of capabilities evolved over many years that were not readily replicable. The second was to home in on these distinctive capabilities by a process of elimination. Companies examined their own activities and started to outsource anything they viewed as non-core but readily available on the open market, thus narrowing down what they took to be their core.

IT was immediately affected. A widely reported mega-deal outsourcing IT at Kodak led to the rapid growth of the technology services industry. For reasons both good and bad, companies—and subsequently government—took up this option. Good reasons were access to scale for both cheaper procurement of technology and access to expertise while IT itself genuinely was non-core. Bad reasons included selling the IT function to gain access to capital and getting rid of a problem IT function. And, whether for good or bad reasons, many companies made their lives unnecessarily difficult by negotiating punitive contracts that motivated undesirable behaviour in suppliers and by outsourcing critical staff needed to manage the suppliers. The upshot was that the 1990s were a time of great turmoil. Researchers contributed substantially to the understanding of the outsourcing phenomenon and to bringing some sense to practice. At OXIIM, Leslie Willcocks, David Feeny, and Guy Fitzgerald, in partnership with Institute Associate, Mary Lacity, contributed much by way of analyses of outsourcing practice and numerous frameworks.[21-23]

Where initially so much practice proved dysfunctional, the debates were often over whether IT outsourcing was good or rational. In theoretical terms, much debate centred on whether IT was obtainable on the market without prohibitive transaction costs. Over time the service industry and its customer base have matured. Today, it is easier to spell out under what conditions what types of IT should be outsourced, and to prescribe sensible management practices to ensure a productive customer–supplier relationship. An indicator of how far we have come is the recent Auditor-General's report[24] praising HM Revenue & Customs for the way it re-competed its massive, ten-year outsourced IT contract. In a creative application of core capabilities theory, Feeny and Willcocks[25] identified the minimal capabilities required by an IT function whether or not it has outsourced IT services. More recently, with Mary Lacity, they identified core capabilities for IT suppliers.[26]

In the last five years, outsourcing has developed significantly in two directions. The first has been the shift into business process outsourcing. Companies recognize that not only some of their IT is non-core, but so too are many back-office processes supported by IT, including accounting, HR, and much indirect procurement. Here again, Feeny, Willcocks, and Lacity have been pioneering researchers.[27] The second new direction is to offshoring both IT infrastructure provision and business processes. This is territory that Jeff Sampler has observed throughout its evolution in India.[28]

The whole massive IT outsourcing, business process outsourcing, and offshoring movement was spawned by the desire to focus on core capabilities. It has been the principal focus for researchers, but alongside it there has been the steady development of a stream of research that has taken the alternative RBV (Resource Based View) perspective to the effect that the ability to exploit IT for business advantage is itself a core capability that is difficult to replicate and is competitively significant. At OXIIM, doctoral researcher Tan Yang has found evidence to support this view.

I see the knowledge management movement as an extension of the drive to identify and exploit hidden value in core capabilities, specifically value in the form of dispersed knowledge across a distributed organization or distinctive knowledge not readily available to competitors. For IT functions, this initially meant the assessment and installation of software such as Lotus Notes to store and make available knowledge resources. But as Michael Earl[29] demonstrated, there is more to knowledge management than a simplistic codification of nuggets of knowledge. His taxonomic framework has helped companies to think more analytically about the different kinds of contribution they can make to improve knowledge management. That said, this movement has not taken off in a big way, largely because the research community and practice both lack an adequate conceptualization of the key constructs. In short, we have only an embryonic understanding of what 'knowledge' is and how to manage it.

Core capabilities were rapidly overtaken by the business process re-engineering (BPR) movement. The BPR rhetoric preached revolutionary demolition of the old business practices to be replaced by gleaming new processes that stripped away unnecessary and non-value-adding activity. Reality proved more mixed, with almost any restructuring or reworking of business practice being badged BPR, and it being, in many cases, an opportunistic cover for the crudest downsizing. Stripping away the rhetoric and opportunism, BPR suggested that there was new value to be discovered in reintegrating organizational activities that had previously been separated through intense specialization. It thus brought two changes in mindset—it gave businesses licence to rethink their processes, and it encouraged that rethinking to span functional boundaries.

This development in management thinking once again brought mixed blessings for IT. In principle, it pushed IT to the fore as the means by which the essential tension of organizational design between differentiation and integration[30] could be finessed. In practice, managers often saw the IT function as too lacking in business nous to engage in the executive decision-making leading to BPR. They assumed they could decide on objectives for the redesign of processes in isolation from any consideration of IT's ability to execute. This practice of 'throwing over the wall' has never been smart. In this case it was particularly inappropriate because re-engineering processes across functions disrupted power structures. The politics could not be resolved by the IT function alone. It required heavy senior executive involvement. When the politics required extensive project redesign, the existing technologies proved insufficiently flexible.

Little wonder that many reports quoted 70 per cent or more failure rates for re-engineering.[31]

The publicity attached to these failure rates combined with business recognition of the increasing strategic importance of IT investments fuelled the growing demand for an understanding of risk, reliable delivery, and change management.[32] Critiques of performance and assessments of risk had long been a focus of academic research, but the attention to change was new.[33] The problems companies and governments experience with large projects continue to be a matter of shareholder and citizen concern and an active target of research within OXIIM.[34,35]

The positive side of this initial experience of re-engineering was that it directed executive thinking away from a traditionally incremental approach that responded to problem after problem by layering complexity upon complexity towards organizational design and processes streamlined according to business goals. The emergence in the mid-1990s of Internet technologies with the ability to extend reach and range both internally and externally offered a new opportunity to radically revise organizations and business models.[36] While the e-business bubble of the late-1990s was based on volumes of uncritical hype, it also had a substantial basis in real potential. Since the bubble burst, we have seen continued investment in e-business though not always under that label. To the consumer, e-retail has been most apparent with year-on-year growth in Internet sales. To businesses, the ease with which it is possible to build platforms for collaboration has led to tighter coordination in cross-business activities. The Dell supply chain is but one example that has resulted in a business being able to serve its customers more effectively. And what has been achievable externally has also often been replicated internally, for example, in the adoption of self-service human resource management and purchasing in many organizations. The extension of IT to deliver new value through redesigned customer–supplier interactions continues today so that not only do we buy airline tickets online but check-in and choose our seats from the comfort of our offices as well.

The extension of reach and range through developments in communications and the Internet has facilitated further significant developments— the offshoring of the delivery of IT itself and of business processes to lower-cost locations. Several major corporations, such as InfoSys and Tata in India, have grown rapidly through exploiting both the availability of cheap, highly educated labour and the increasingly global communications infrastructure to undertake software development and IT service delivery for client companies worldwide. Others have exploited the same structural conditions to provide both back-office and call-centre services twenty-four hours a day around the world. Thus we see IT playing a major part in globalization—both supporting and encouraging this extension to the logic of capitalism.

The discussion so far in this section has simplified history by talking as if management discourse had been totally dominated by these popular movements. In practice, they overlaid a solid base of business-as-usual. Thus, businesses pursued continual improvement through either a version of Total Quality Management or the adoption of best practice, and continued to cut costs wherever possible. The pursuit of common infrastructures to support uniformity of process, the rationalization of supplier bases, and the desire for a platform to enable offshoring of IT and business processes have all encouraged the ERP movement and with it the debate about the commoditization of IT.

My argument so far has been that the development of technology has expanded economic possibilities and that as those possibilities have been realized by business, so businesses have learnt to exploit the technology to support them. The resultant economic value has been immense, as is immediately apparent if we try to imagine modern life but without the existence of computers and integrated circuitry. But where has the value been captured? Who has gained?

Of course, almost everyone in developed economies and many in developing economies have enjoyed some of the benefits of cheaper prices, new services, enhanced communication, novel job opportunities, and other similar things. While in the early days of IT, the big winners were the manufacturers of hardware and software, with many businesses doubting the value of their investments, today technology manufacturing is close to a commodity business. The high margins lie more in software and solutions. Business users of IT care about what they can achieve with the technology because increasingly it underlies the competitive frontier where they seek to differentiate themselves from competitors. But, as the debate about the commoditization of IT, promoted by Nicholas Carr,[37] has developed, so the question has become more urgent as to whether any company can differentiate itself sustainably from its competitors. In other words, IT-enabled innovations are rapidly copied, and their competitive value dissipated. The upshot is that, while there are short-term premiums for first movers, in the long term the customer gains all the value.

There are exceptions with certain companies such as eBay, Amazon, and Google securing enduring competitive positions as a kind of category killer in their market. In general, though, I argue that as IT has opened up consumer markets and labour markets, it has increased competition with a resultant downward pressure on prices. We appear therefore to be in the midst of a historical process within which some of the fundamental dynamics of economic competition are being given greater scope than ever before. With the offshoring movement we also see these dynamics leading to some redistribution of wealth globally.

There is also the question of whether my thesis has any applicability to government's use of IT. On the face of things, governments do not function in the same competitive space as the private sector, so they might be expected to march to a different beat. However, part of the changing capitalist dynamic I have identified as an influence on IT has itself derived from government policy. For example, the desire to be seen to preside over a smaller government has led successive administrations to seek to streamline processes through improved application of IT. This has largely been a self-generated dynamic.

However, the increased focus on providing 'joined-up' services—for example Choose and Book for hospital appointments—has been the result of a different dynamic. This has been driven by new expectations among citizens arising from their experiences with the private sector. Nevertheless, government faces some very different issues when it comes to offshoring jobs in the public sector. Here it encounters constraints that do not affect private-sector firms so immediately. We should therefore see government as a special case that is not immune to changes in capitalism but not fully responsive to them either.

Envisioning the Future

Can we predict where technology will lead us from here? What economic possibilities may it engender and what effects may they have? I think we can identify directions but timings are harder to state. I base this on an exercise in what my colleague Rafael Ramirez refers to as 'backcasting'— the exercise of going back in time and asking what of today could have been predicted at an earlier time.[38]

If I cast my mind back twenty or more years, I can remember in the early 1980s teaching an Open University course that discussed EFTPOS (Electronic Fund Transfer/Point of Sale) a decade or more before it became a routine part of retail. At the same time, researchers and lawyers were debating privacy issues that seemed to lay commentators academic in the sense of irrelevant. Today, few would argue that the issue is not real or relevant. In the mid-1980s my colleague Perry Morrison and I started to investigate antisocial behaviour on the Internet including SPAM and viruses. We could not predict when they would emerge as economically significant problems but predictable they were. At the same time, email, though confined to research establishments, was a world-changing innovation waiting to happen. Already researchers were examining the potential of tele-commuting or working from home.

So, in looking forward twenty years, I do not pretend that we can provide a predictable timeline, but I do suggest that much that will occur has visible antecedents today. Business will continue to seek out hidden sources of value. I focus on three: increased process integration, further reduced dependence on geographical location, and greater digitization.

Increased process integration will extend the logic of e-business up and down the demand and supply chains. Businesses will pursue more effective outcomes through more joined up intra- and inter-organizational processes. They will take out slack at boundaries and they will increase cycle times. In short, customers will get a better job, performed faster and more cheaply. In particular, we can expect to see these kinds of development in more complex products, services, and solutions businesses. For example, nuclear power stations will be built under more streamlined procure, design, and build processes. Likewise, the provision of military capability by defence firms will be the result of integrated processes of manufacture, train, service, repair, and recommission.

Similarly, given the current state of world economic development, it is reasonable to assume the continued availability of requisite economic capabilities in low-cost locations that enable business activities to be location-independent. IT infrastructure will only become increasingly more sophisticated and thereby enable more offshoring. We already see City finance houses offshoring financial analysis to Indian MBA graduates. More and more premium priced knowledge work will be sent offshore with unpredictable effects on the developed economies. A cadre of highly educated knowledge workers will lose their jobs, but how they will respond is less certain. They could become more politically active in protest, or they could choose the economic route and pursue innovation. So long as a large proportion of the profits from developing nations continue to be reinvested in the developed world, as is the case today, there will be the capital to support innovation. Once the developing world becomes more confident in its own economies and starts to prefer the risk : return ratio at home, locational independence will cease to be merely an economic option and will become the focus for a political contest in the developed world.

Like the other two trends, greater digitalization is already well established. Just as email has digitized much written or oral communication,

CD and MP3 formats have digitized music, and electronic testing and tuning of vehicles has transformed car repair. We can expect more and more work to be translated into digital form, thereby permitting its easy transfer from one specialist to another and from one location to another. The further digitalization of people and objects will likewise enable the tracking and checking of identity with greater facility. The potential for radically re-engineered logistics and travel systems is considerable. In the future, with a radio frequency identification technology tag on my package or person, I can specify my destination half-way across the world, turn up at a bus stop or logistics depot, and be transported in the most efficient manner without having to specify a carrier. Whoever transports me or my package on each leg automatically gets paid their proportion of my overall fare.

The possibilities are enormous, the details hazy. The ways in which the technology will be applied will continue to be a function both of breakthroughs and of the ways in which the economics of capitalism develops. If current trends lead to political difficulties, we could see regulation and protection reshaping the capitalist economy. This, in turn, will influence which technological and commercial possibilities are realized.

References

1. R. G. Lipsey, K. I. Carlaw, and C. T. Bekar, *Economic Transformations: General Purpose Technologies and Long Term Economic Growth* (Oxford: Oxford University Press, 2005).
2. A. Smith, *An Inquiry into the Nature and Causes of the Wealth of Nations* (1776).
3. M. J. Earl, 'IT: An Ambiguous Technology?', in B. Sundgren, P. Martensson, M. Muhring, and K. Nilsson (eds.), *Exploring Patterns In Information Management* (Stockholm: Stockholm School of Economics, 2003), 39–48.
4. S. Zuboff, *In the Age of the Smart Machine: The Future of Work and Power* (New York: Basic Books, 1988).
5. J. McKenney, R. O. Mason, and D. Copeland, *Waves of Change: Business Evolution through Information Technology* (Boston, MA: Harvard Business School Press, 1995).
6. C. Wiseman, *Strategy and Computers: Information Systems as Competitive Weapons* (Homewood, IL: Irwin, 1985).
7. H. R. Johnston and M. R. Vitale, 'Creating Competitive Advantage with Inter-Organizational Systems', *MIS Quarterly*, 12/2(June 1988): 153–65.
8. D. F. Feeny, B. Edwards, and K. Simpson, 'Understanding the CEO–CIO Relationship', in L. P. Willcocks, D. F. Feeny, and G. Islei (eds.), *Managing IT as a Strategic Resource* (New York: McGraw-Hill, 1997), 22–42.

9. M. J. Earl (ed.), *Information Management: the Strategic Dimension* (Oxford: Clarendon Press, 1988).
10. M. J. Earl, *Management Strategies for Information Technology* (Englewood Cliffs, NJ: Prentice-Hall, 1989).
11. M. J. Earl (ed.), *Information Management: the Organizational Dimension* (Oxford: Clarendon Press, 1996).
12. D. F. Feeny, B. R. Keppel, and M. Simpson, 'Understanding the CEO–CIO Relationship', *MIS Quarterly*, 16/4(1992): 435–48.
13. M. J. Earl and D. F. Feeny, 'Is Your CIO Adding Value?', *Sloan Management Review*, 35/3(1994): 11–20.
14. M. J. Earl and D. F. Feeny, 'Opinion: How To Be a CEO for the Information Age', *Sloan Management Review*, 41/2 (2000): 11–23.
15. M. J. Earl and D. J. Skyrme, 'Hybrid Managers: What Do We Know about Them?', *Journal of Information Systems*, 1/2(1992): 169–87.
16. C. Sauer and L. P. Willcocks, 'The Evolution of the Organizational Architect', *Sloan Management Review*, 43/3(2002): 41–9.
17. Robert Solow, 'We'd Better Watch Out', *New York Review of Books*, 12 July 1987, 36.
18. L. P. Willcocks, 'Evaluating Information Technology Investments: Research Findings and Reappraisal', *Journal of Information Systems*, 2/3(1992): 243–68.
19. L. P. Willcocks and S. Lester, *Beyond the IT Productivity Paradox* (Chichester: Wiley, 1999).
20. E. Brynjolfsson and L. M. Hitt, 'Paradox Lost? Firm-Level Evidence on the Returns to Information Systems', *Management Science*, 42/4(1996): 541–58.
21. L. P. Willcocks and G. Fitzgerald, *A Business Guide to Outsourcing Information Technology: A Study of European Best Practice in the Selection, Management and Use of External IT Services* (London: Business Intelligence, 1994).
22. D. F. Feeny, M. Lacity, and L. P. Willcocks, 'The Value of Selective IT Sourcing', *Sloan Management Review*, 37/3(1996): 13–25.
23. M. Lacity and L. P. Willcocks, *Global IT Outsourcing: In Search of Business Advantage* (Chichester: Wiley, 2001).
24. Comptroller and Auditor General, *HM Revenue and Customs: ASPIRE—the Re-Competition of Outsourced IT Services* (London: HMSO, 2006).
25. D. F. Feeny and L. P. Willcocks, 'Core IS Capabilities for Exploiting IT', *Sloan Management Review*, 39/3(Spring 1998): 9–21.
26. D. F. Feeny, M. Lacity, and L. P. Willcocks, 'Taking the Measure of Outsourcing Providers', *MIT Sloan Management Review*, 46/3(2005): 41–8.
27. M. Lacity, D. F. Feeny, and L. P. Willcocks, 'Transforming a Back-Office Function: Lessons from BAE SYSTEMS' Experience with an Enterprise Partnership', *MIS Quarterly Executive*, 2/2(2003): 86–103.
28. M. J. Earl and J. L. Sampler, 'Market Management to Transform the IT Organization', *Sloan Management Review*, 39/4(1998), 9–17.
29. M. J. Earl, 'Knowledge Management Strategies: Towards a Taxonomy', *Journal of Management Information Systems*, 18/1(2001): 215–33.

30. P. R. Lawrence and J. W. Lorsch, *Organization and Environment: Managing Differentiation and Integration* (Boston, MA: Harvard University Graduate School of Business Administration, 1967).
31. K. Grint, P. Case, and L. P. Willcocks, 'Business Process Re-Engineering Reappraised: The Politics and Technology of Forgetting', in W. J. Orlikowski, G. Walsham, M. R. Jones, and J. I. DeGross (eds.), *Information Technology and Changes in Organisational Work* (London: Chapman & Hall, 1995), 39–61.
32. L. P. Willcocks and C. Griffiths, 'Predicting Risk of Failure in Large Scale Information Technology Projects', *Technological Forecasting and Social Change*, 47 (1996): 205–28.
33. C. Sauer, P. W. Yetton & Associates, *Steps to the Future: Fresh Thinking on the Management of IT-Based Organisational Transformation* (San Francisco, CA: Jossey-Bass, 1997).
34. C. Sauer, A. Gemino, and B. Reich, 'Managing Projects for Success: The Impact of Size and Volatility on IT Project Performance', *Communications of the ACM* (to be published).
35. A. Gemino, B. H. Reich, and C. Sauer, 'Factors Influencing IT Project Performance', in *Proceedings of the Twelfth Americas Conference on Information Systems* (Acapulco, 4–6 Aug. 2006).
36. P. Weill and M. Vitale, *From Place to Space* (Boston, MA: Harvard Business School Press, 2001).
37. N. G. Carr, 'IT Doesn't Matter', *Harvard Business Review*, 81/5(2003): 5–12.
38. M. Hojer and L.-G. Mattsson, 'Determinism and Backcasting in Future Studies', *Futures*, 32/7(Sept. 2000): 613–34.

4

There and Back Again? Organization
Studies 1965–2006

Janine Nahapiet

> What we call the beginning is often the end
> And to make an end is to make a beginning
> The end is where we start from...
> We shall not cease from exploration
> And at the end of all our exploring
> Will be to arrive where we started
> And know the place for the first time
>
> *T. S. Eliot: Four Quartets: Little Gidding*

This is a good time to reflect on the field of Organization Studies. The 1960s are widely regarded as the period in which Organization Studies established itself as a separate and identifiable subject—distinguishable from Management Studies—and with its own body of theorizing. Forty years later, leading organization scholars are in a period of reflection and self-examination about the field, its evolution, and future development. In part, this is a millennial phenomenon as, stimulated by the year 2000, scholars in many disciplines sought to make sense retrospectively and prospectively about their subject and its contribution. It also represents a generational transition, as pioneering researchers in our field are invited to reflect on the study of organizations and the challenges ahead.[1,2]

More fundamentally, I believe it suggests a sense of unease, even disquiet, about the current status and health of Organization Studies as a subject. Despite its growth in importance and many contributions, there are significant and pressing questions to be addressed. Some of these persist through time; for example, what should be the links between theory and practice and how are we to understand and explain organizational change? Others are more recent and include concerns over the consequences of the dominance of economics as a discipline and *homo economicus* as a 'model of man' in Organization Studies,[3,4] the cultural hegemony that results in the field being heavily shaped by Western views of the world, particularly North American[1] and male perspectives,[5] and a growing sense that current theories do not adequately address the fundamental changes in organizations, organizational contexts, and the accompanying practices that occurred during the late twentieth century.[6]

Our ideas about organization and organizations are rooted in a set of assumptions, theories, constructs, language, and methods developed in a particular context and time. Although many of these persist, they no longer serve us well in understanding and theorizing organizations in our own context and time. Cherns suggests: 'At any time, there is a set of topics and problems which are understood to constitute the subject matter of an applied discipline. The set changes over time less because the topics are exhausted and the problems solved than because they are differently perceived; the cultural context has changed.'[7]

In this chapter, I reflect on the evolution of Organization Studies, consider the influences on change, and outline what I regard as the central challenges we face in both theorizing and designing effective organizations at the start of the twenty-first century. In summary, we see a journey in which the field grew from an interest in managing and organizing within the enterprise to a focus on the organization itself as a collective actor and important unit of analysis.

Forty years on, I believe that we are revisiting this important transition in two important respects. First, developments in recent years increasingly suggest that we need to return to a focus on organizing as a central concern for the field. Only now the task requires theorizing and designing productive interaction and exchange both within and without conventional organizational boundaries and in the context of an increasingly relational perspective. Second, important questions are again being asked about the impact of organizations as collective actors. For much of the period under review, organizations were viewed as heavily dependent upon, if not significantly determined by, the environments in which they operate. Today, organizations are again seen as major actors in society, playing a significant role in shaping and influencing the world around them. However, this role is coming under increasing scrutiny from a wide variety of stakeholders. In both these respects, I suggest we are returning to earlier themes but with a far deeper appreciation of their dimensions and significance.

Organization Studies in Context

In line with the core proposition of this volume, this chapter starts from the premise that both particular organizational forms and theories about organizations are rooted in time and a particular social context. My departure point is Stinchcombe's[8] discussion of social structure and organizations. Echoing Weber, Stinchcombe observes that distinct organizational types originate in a relatively short historical period and change relatively slowly after that. These types reflect the resources available to organizations at a particular time and they frequently come to characterize specific industries. A familiar example is the development of factory organization around the new technologies for both transportation and manufacturing afforded by the industrial revolution.

Although the pace of change may have altered in the interim, the connection persists between distinct organizational designs and the time, social context, and resource conditions in which they appear. For example, research has identified three strategies and modes of organization adopted by companies for managing across international borders—the multinational, the international, and the global. Each developed in a different time period and different parts of the world—Europe, North America, and Japan, respectively. In the 1980s, a fourth model emerged—the transnational, an approach made possible by social, political, and technological changes and designed to achieve the combined benefits of all three earlier strategies.[9] However, as companies sought, indeed continue to seek, the benefits of the transnational, they are confronted and limited by the constraints of their administrative heritage. Moving to a new organizational model is a substantial challenge for incumbent firms, as IBM as a case history demonstrates.[10] This is all the more evident today as we witness established firms attempting to replicate aspects of those organizational innovations enabled by the Internet and developed by new arrivals such as Linux.

Just as organizational practice is shaped by contextual factors, so too is Organization Studies as an academic field. Writing about the origins of organization theory and the period up until the 1960s, Starbuck[11] argues that contemporary organization theory owes its existence to the social and technological changes that occurred during the last half of the nineteenth century and the first half of the twentieth century—changes that created both a basis for theorizing and an audience for theories about organizations. He pays particular attention to the role of education alongside technology in making it possible for large organizations to proliferate and to work effectively. Reflecting on the period from 1945, March similarly shows how the history of Organization Studies is embedded in its times and in the way those times affect different regions differently and he too identifies the importance of both resources and of markets for ideas about effective organization.[1] Like Starbuck, March emphasizes the role of education in the development of the subject, highlighting the significance of the rapid expansion of the business schools, initially in the USA, and more generally thereafter—in creating both a demand for and supply of specialist faculty and research in the organizational field. The fact that Organization Studies developed largely with a business school setting has had important and long-term implications for its central themes and evolution over time.[12]

The Importance of Linking Organizational Theory and Practice

The links between ideas, markets for ideas, and resource availability demonstrate the importance of considering both theory and practice in discussing the development of Organization Studies. First, they are subject to the same influences. For example, information technology has shaped both how we think about organizations and how organizations work.[13,14] The technology is a resource available to both the scholar and practitioner communities.

Second, theory and practice frequently influence each other. There is now plenty of evidence that descriptive empirical studies produce findings that subsequently have profound normative consequences. But it is also evident that organizational innovations instigated by practitioners often occur well ahead of our ability to understand and theorize them and they often stimulate theoretical and conceptual advances. It took years before scholars developed coherent theoretical explanations of the multidivisional form of organization adopted by major US corporations in the 1920s and 1930s. Today, they face similar challenges in understanding and explaining recent organizational innovations such as open sourcing and networked innovation.

In my own work, my interest in social capital had its origins in a discussion at Templeton College with executives in a leading insurance company about global relationship management—and their need to respond to global clients seeking coordinated world wide service.[15,16] Global relationship management is a business practice rooted in the proposition that value can be created through linkage and coordination—both within and between organizations. However, at the time, most extant theories in Organization Studies[17] and microeconomics[18] seemed to provide little insight into value creation through coordination, focusing instead on organizational choices based on minimizing the costs of coordination. The search for an alternative perspective led eventually to work on social capital and the development of a framework that provides a theoretical explanation of the benefits as well as the costs of connections and relationships.[19] The framework has subsequently been taken up and used extensively by both academics and practitioners.

Finally, this personal example suggests that we may be better placed if we regard developments in organization theory and organization practice as reciprocal and co-evolutionary. Practice raises important questions for theory, and theories and their related assumptions have significant implications for practice and the two co-evolve through time.

A commitment to this dialectical view of knowledge creation and sharing, exploration and exploitation, underpins Templeton's distinctive approach to research and pedagogy. Since its foundation, it has sought to create a context conducive to conversation and dialogue between those engaged in and with organizing and organizations. Consistent with Oxford's philosophy, politics, and economics (PPE) tradition, both in teaching and in research the College has consistently emphasized the importance of considering managerial and organizational action in its wider context, acknowledging that important practices both shape and are shaped by their social and institutional settings. This approach is evident in the work that first drew me to Templeton—the study of accounting in its social and organizational context.[20,21] It is in this spirit that I now pursue the premise that many of the core ideas about organizations developed in previous times and different places live on—embedded in our thinking and practice—even though the circumstances of our time and the resources available already provide radically different alternative forms of organizing that challenge these core ideas.

Five Decades of Organization Studies

Although Organization Studies had yet to emerge as an identifiable field of research, the foundations on which subsequent work was built were laid during the first half of the century. Three themes stand out that defined the agenda and debates that followed.

- First, those who wrote about organizations did so in universalistic terms and within a largely rational frame of reference. The Weberian concept of bureaucracy in particular provides the core model. Although presented as an ideal type, the properties Weber attributed to modern bureaucracy include a formal division of labour, functional specialization, a clear hierarchy of authority, and administrative actions based on formal rules rather than personal relationships.[22] Though rooted in a very different tradition, the influential engineering perspectives manifest in scientific management placed a similar emphasis on formal aspects of design. Thus, in the first half of the century, ideas about appropriate organizing from both scholars and practitioners converged on the importance of formal structure, hierarchical control, impersonal relations, and a clear division of labour. Both emphasized the importance of rational and universal design principles as the foundation for efficient organization.

- Second, although what many regarded as the classical model was established early as the departure point for any discussion of organization, also from early on there was an alternative story showing that much of what happens in organizations cannot be explained in terms of this formal, structural model. One strand of work highlights the many dysfunctions of bureaucracy.[23] Another argues for regarding organizations as social systems best understood as a combination of formal and informal activities. Barnard[24] and Selznick[25] were among the early writers to focus on organizations per se and both discuss the often paradoxical interrelationship between the formal and informal within organizations. This distinction was taken up and developed by Gouldner[26] who sets out two contrasting models of organization: the 'rational systems' model in which organizations are viewed as formal structures explicitly designed to achieve given ends and the 'natural systems' model in which organizations are seen as adaptive social systems seeking survival through often unspecified, indeterminate processes. This recognition that organizations can be understood from coherent but distinct and often contradictory perspectives highlights a tension and debate that has persisted in Organization Studies ever since. It represents an early expression of the dualisms and dualities that many scholars continue to believe characterize organizational theory and design.[27,28]

- Finally, since the late 1950s, implicitly or explicitly, organizations have been viewed from a systems perspective, that is, as more or less complex combinations of related elements. Systems perspectives were in the ascendancy at the time and have come to be regarded as the *sine qua non* of Organization Studies. The debate since has turned on what type of system model helps us best understand and design organizations—a debate enabled and enhanced by wider discussion of systems theories in the social and physical sciences.

The 1960s: Towards an Open-Systems Perspective

It is rarely possible and perhaps even unwise to attempt to pinpoint the appearance of an idea. The period following the Second World War saw the steady institutionalization of organization as a unit of analysis in its own right, accomplished and manifest through the influential publications of the period. This marked a gradual transition and explication of Organization Studies as a separate field distinguishable from both management studies and organizational behaviour, that is, a shift from a concern with management and behaviour within an organizational setting, to the organization itself as the prime focus and organizations as important and influential collective actors.

Although there was important work in Europe, the rapid expansion of universities and business schools in the USA provided the resources and institutional setting for the early development of the subject. Chandler's[29] work on strategy and structure continued in the tradition of universal forms, identifying the multidivisional structure as a rational solution to the increasing scale and complexity of industrial enterprise. It also established the argument that organization design follows strategy.

Publication of the first *Handbook of Organisations* in 1965 in the USA represents an important mapping of the subject at this transition point. In it we see a focus on the study of both organizations and behaviour within organizations, an agenda rooted in core disciplines and emerging methodologies, and a direction for organizational analysis that examines formal organization in a variety of institutional settings.[30] Nine of the chapters deal with specific institutional domains, including military organizations, unions, hospitals, prisons, and business organizations.

This view of organizations was already changing with the growth of the comparative analysis of organizations. In both Europe and North America, there was a discernible move to empirical studies beyond the rich, case-oriented research that had been so important hitherto. New researchers set out to measure and compare key dimensions of organizations across different settings and to explore their impact. In the UK, the Aston studies specified and developed systematic measures of the several dimensions of bureaucracy and then studied their relationships empirically in a sample of organizations drawn from different industries.[31] In the USA, work at the Harvard Business School took a more aggregated approach, focusing initially on the design principles of differentiation and integration.[32] Together, their findings led to typologies of organization that were no longer defined in terms of institutional context, such as schools or political parties, but rather based on important factors shaping the functioning of organizations across a range of settings. These included internal influences such as technology[33] and size[31] and external factors, particularly environmental change and uncertainty—a theme that was to endure.[32,34]

Though not without its critics, the contingency approach to organizations as it became known was a major influence on the transition from a universalistic and closed system model of organization to an open-system perspective.[35] Moreover, it established the argument for the significance of aligning organizational design to context that persists to this day across a range of topics—from knowledge transfer[36] to project organization[37] and network performance.[38] Finally, the body of research undertaken during this period helped consolidate and validate the importance of organization as a field of study.

The 1970s: New Theories for a New World

Clearly, slicing history neatly into decades is somewhat arbitrary as there are important continuities as well as changes through these temporal boundaries. However, the 1970s did see significant changes in research on organizations—changes that can be linked to three major developments. The first of these was the growing political unrest manifest in the protest movements particularly in Europe in the late 1960s and into the 1970s, unrest that represented a profound questioning of society and action on the basis of recognized conflicts of interest. The second was the 1973 oil embargo and subsequent economic uncertainty and the third was the growing potential and impact of new technologies, particularly computers.

If the 1960s saw the emergence of an interest in the links between organization and environment, the nature of these links became one of the central concerns for both theory and practice in the 1970s. Only now, far from being assumed to be generally munificent if changing, economic and political environments were increasingly viewed as turbulent, complex, and even hostile, a constraint rather than an opportunity to which organizations had to adjust. It is during this period we see the development of several major theories of organization and environment: population ecology,[39] resource dependence,[40] and institutional theory[41]— each presenting a different explanation of how organizations are shaped by their environments. In all these accounts, the concept of the organization as a discrete and bounded entity, separated if heavily influenced by, its environment remains. A view of the organization as a dependent variable shaped by the environment prevailed, notwithstanding those who argued at the time that the boundaries between organization and environment are less clear and more permeable than many presume[42] and that indeed organizations themselves help create and shape their environments.[43,44]

It is during this period we see another development that was to influence Organization Studies in the coming years. While most early twentieth-century thinking about organization was rooted largely in psychology, sociology, and political science, economic perspectives came to increasing prominence in the 1970s, particularly through the work of Oliver Williamson. Williamson's work builds on the economic insight that all transactions are costly but some are more costly than others. Transaction cost analysis influenced thinking about organizations in two significant ways.[18] It provided a strong theoretical explanation both for the multidivisional structure and, more fundamentally, for why organizations exist at all. For Williamson, markets constitute the most efficient institutional arrangement for the exchange of goods and services. However, markets are ill equipped to handle some transactions—specifically those that are uncertain and complex. According to Williamson, organizations constitute a mechanism that can handle these transactions by aligning interests and creating systems to discourage opportunistic behaviour. Transaction cost theory both raises the fundamental question of why organizations exist and provides the answer that they do so when markets fail. The markets and hierarchies debate, and the assumptions built into the theory, particularly bounded rationality and the lack of trust implied by opportunism, came to influence much subsequent work, not only in economics but also in organization theory. For example, Ouchi's discussion of alternative organizational forms—markets, bureaucracies, and clans—takes the market failures framework as its starting point.[45]

If rational economic man was rising in importance in North America as an explicit foundational model for understanding and designing organizations, in Europe scholars were advancing the argument that an understanding of organizations requires not one but multiple perspectives. The diversity within Europe and its more critical approach to dominant ideologies was manifest in a greater emphasis on power and on critiques of positivist approaches. The publication of *Sociological Paradigms and Organisational Analysis* in 1979 brought together these different perspectives on organization, locating them in their wider sociological context.[46] Working from their central premise that all theories of organization are based upon a philosophy of science and a theory of society, the authors set out a comprehensive and theoretically strong framework identifying four distinct paradigms for the study of organizations. These are based upon different assumptions about (*a*) the nature of social science, specifically the distinction between objectivist and subjectivist assumptions about the world, and (*b*) the nature of society, distinguishing between theories of order and regulation and of conflict and radical change.

Whilst most organizational research fall within the functionalist paradigm, with its emphasis on objectivist explanations of social affairs and a concern with problem solving and effective regulation, the framework also identified three alternative spaces. These are the interpretive paradigm, focusing on understanding the social world at the level of meaning and subjective experience; the radical humanist paradigm, concerned with understanding radical change from the subjectivist standpoint; and finally, the radical structuralist paradigm, advocating the study of radical change from an objectivist standpoint. The book stimulated a great deal of debate in Europe—particularly about whether the paradigms were incommensurate or could be combined in some way. It highlighted the importance of a socially constructed world in which the creation and negotiation of meaning is a central endeavour[21] and it brought power centre stage in discussions about organization. In so doing, it raised again in a more radical and complex form the issues raised earlier by Gouldner about theoretical alternatives to rational systems models.

Within the functionalist paradigm, work continued seeking to deepen our understanding of organizational design informed by developments of the day, including the new possibilities afforded by computers. In the contingency tradition, Galbraith[13] developed a view of organizations as information-processing systems arguing that task uncertainty influences organizational design through its impact on the amount of information that must be processed by decision-makers. He uses this framework to explain the increasingly complex structural arrangements that appeared during the 1970s. The matrix organization received particular attention perhaps because it contravened the taken for granted assumption of one person, one boss. The matrix form combines dual lines of authority up the hierarchy with an emphasis on lateral relationships and decision-making processes. Still regarded as a complex organizational form, its popularity has waxed and waned in the subsequent years. However, the question of how to combine and blend different organizational choices remains at the centre of current debates about organizational design.[27,28]

The 1980s: The Challenge of Globalization

The 1980s and the 1990s have been described as a period of rapid structural change characterized by increased competition, significant economic, social, and technological change, and globalization. In this context, competitive strategy emerged as an influential perspective within management studies, particularly through the work of Michael Porter.[47] In competitive environments, organizations sought to align structure to competitive strategy and to achieve increasing efficiency through removing levels of management and streamlining core systems and processes. These enabled them both to reduce costs and speed-up decision-making and information flows, assisted by advances in computers and communication technologies. Over time, 'downsizing', 'rightsizing', and 'reengineering' became the focus for much organizational effort.

In parallel, interest continued in developing multiple lenses for understanding and managing organizations. In the USA while writing for managers, Bolman and Deal set out four perspectives on organizations: the structural, close to the rational systems model of earlier times; the symbolic, emphasizing the importance of subjective sense making and the management of meaning; the political, addressing power, conflict, and coalitions; and the human resource perspective, bringing back people and their management as a central issue.[48] Meanwhile, now in Canada, British scholar Gareth Morgan describes eight different metaphors that represent coherent but alternative perspectives and theories of organization.[49] In so doing, he returns to the word used years earlier by Selznick, 'paradox', to describe the challenge that comes from recognizing that organizations are best understood and managed through multiple lenses.

But the theme that most significantly marks out the 1980s from previous periods is that of internationalization and globalization. Enabled by political change, deregulation, and advances in computer technology, multinationals sought to build stronger connections between their previously autonomous subsidiaries. The new challenge for many firms was how best to manage and create value from a growing array of activities across national borders. The challenge went beyond earlier organizational choices between centralization and decentralization. Research indicated the importance of combining elements of both global integration and local responsiveness alongside the ability to build and leverage learning, increasingly regarded as a crucial activity for companies during this period.[9] Different organizational solutions emerged in different parts of the world and scholars increasingly turned to the idea of networks to provide an alternative perspective on the design and functioning of organizations as they moved towards a new configuration, the transnational organizational form. In doing this, they were able to draw upon the new stream of writing on social networks.[50]

The 1990s: Beyond Boundaries

The late 1980s and 1990s saw another period of major change—in the world at large and within Organization Studies. Economic development outside Europe and North America accelerated, most obviously in Asia. The end of the Cold War, the fall of the Berlin Wall, and the break-up of the Soviet Union constituted major political and social changes and the rise of a renewed commitment to local and regional identities within a more open and free world. For many it signalled the triumph of capitalism and markets over other economic and political models. The period also saw transformational developments in information and communications technologies—with the growing influence of Microsoft and the appearance of Internet. It is hard to remember now that Netscape went public only in 1995—little more than a decade ago. The pace of change continued, accelerating with new technology companies, born global, frequently supplanting old established companies at or near the top of the published lists of top 100 companies. The language moved from competition to hyper-competition and disruptive change as new technologies enabled companies to transform old industries and create new ones by leveraging the new opportunities in creative ways.

These contextual changes were paralleled by transformational change in organizational design. First, there was a significant move to externalize activities previously undertaken within the enterprise. The huge expansion of outsourcing, including international outsourcing, the growing significance of managed connections across the supply chain, and the increase in the number of strategic alliances, including across borders, all began to challenge conventional thinking about organizations. Most fundamentally, they challenged the assumption that ownership is necessary to control or benefit from assets—companies could influence and benefit from the assets of other organizations through their connections and relationships with them. As a consequence, the boundaries of the organization, hitherto regarded as clear and defined, became increasingly blurred and permeable as companies invested in ways of developing and organizing collaborative relationships.

Associated with these developments was another major switch in focus. As companies recognized the opportunities to outsource key activities, from manufacturing to IT, they were faced with a fundamental question—which activities were core to their business, significant contributors to their performance, and potential sources of distinctive advantage? To answer this question, both scholars and executives identified resources and capabilities as major determinants of both their strategy and identity. In the resource-based view as it became known, attention increasingly switched from physical assets to intangible assets—to system level knowledge and capabilities, particularly organizational capabilities.[51] This represented an important step in two respects. First, it raised the profile of organization as a critical factor to be considered by managers and showed that far from following strategy, organization increasingly shaped that strategy. Second, it demonstrated that organization design involves very much more than formal structure.

Organizing for intangible assets, particularly for knowledge and learning, implies a very different approach to design. As a mobile resource, distributed around the organization and embodied in key knowledge workers, the organization of knowledge does not align readily with hierarchical control and formal structure. Moreover, the most valuable knowledge is frequently tacit, deeply embedded in organizational processes and practices and in the dynamic connections and relations between people and groups. Both the exploitation of existing knowledge and the creation of new knowledge through innovation are heavily dependent on social processes, particularly the exchange and combination of ideas. In researching these phenomena, scholars found that theories of social capital provide powerful insights into the links between knowledge and relationships. Social capital perspectives move beyond individual level knowledge and human capital to demonstrate the many and complex ways in which both the structure and quality of relationships shape the creation and exploitation of intellectual capital.[19]

All these developments are associated with a transition towards designing organizations on the basis of principles that focus on ways of encouraging and enabling connections, exchange, combination and multiplication—on networks and designs for emergence. To explain these new forms of organizing, scholars drew on ideas from complex adaptive systems theory,[52] and both executives and researchers began talking of the boundary-less company, drawing attention to the increasingly flexible and porous boundaries both between units within the firm and between the firm and its environment.

The move to the knowledge-based view of the firm had one further impact. With the growing awareness of the importance of organizations as social and knowledge communities, this stream of work provided a strong theoretical basis for challenging the market failures explanation for the existence of organizations.[53] Specifically, Nahapiet and Ghoshal proposed that since organizations as institutional settings are conducive to the development of high levels of social capital, they have an important advantage over markets in creating and sharing intellectual capital.[19]

Enter the Twenty-First Century

If the 1990s opened in a mood of some optimism about social and economic change associated with the end of the Cold War, the decade that followed was very different. Three factors in particular undermined most of the taken for granted assumptions about the world at least as it had appeared to powerful Western eyes: the destruction of the World Trade Center in New York on 9/11, the demise of large corporations, such as Enron, Tyco, and WorldCom, and the mounting evidence for the phenomenon of global warming. The dot-com collapse at the start of the decade provided a further shock to expectations about growth and opportunities.

The fast and highly visible demise of major corporations, particularly Enron, which had been regarded by so many as a successful exemplar of the new ways of organizing business, had a major impact. First, it increased the salience of corporate governance and social responsibility, highlighting again the significant role of organizations as a major force within society. In some ways, it represented a return to the often critical debates of the 1960s about the importance of organizations as powerful actors in the world. Second, it caused those who had been directly or indirectly involved in drawing attention to the success of leading companies such as Enron to reflect on their own roles and social responsibilities. Executives, scholars, and business advisors could all be seen as participants in the Enron phenomenon and felt the need to reflect on their roles, individually and collectively.[54]

Finally, beyond the clear need for integrity for all involved, less obviously Enron highlights another critical issue. As companies move to new models of business, particularly those based on value creation in complex networks of inter-organizational arrangements, they are increasingly difficult to describe and monitor—by both insiders and outsiders—since they fall outside current conventions for reporting. Since what is accounted for is a major influence on what people see as important as well as providing the basis for informed action,[20] one of the challenges ahead will be to recognize these limitations and to develop different ways of representing and accounting for the new economy firm that meet the needs of multiple stakeholders.

The political and economic events of recent years are refocusing attention in important ways—towards greater emphasis not only on the role of organizations within society but also on the need for effective cooperation between organizations, public, private, voluntary and government to address the major challenges of our time. It will take effective collective efforts even to begin addressing such issues as the growing disparity between rich and poor and global warming. It is in this context that we reflect on the journey we have taken over the last forty years or so and consider the way ahead.

Taking Stock

As we look back over the evolution of Organization Studies, what do we see? What are the key themes and areas of contention?

- The common ground across the many constituencies interested in and engaged with Organization Studies is the central role of systems thinking in this applied discipline—a general perspective developed in the years following the Second World War and adapted and extended ever since. The largely unquestioned principle that unites otherwise radically different theories is that organizations are appropriately viewed as complex combinations of interrelated elements.
- Second, the main theme that has defined the field is the relationship between organization and environment. Organization Studies began with little explicit consideration of the environment but with the largely tacit assumption that organizations are bounded units separate from their environments but appropriately viewed as important collective actors—an assumption evident in theories of bureaucracy and reinforced by the legal institution of the corporation. The economic uncertainties triggered by the upheavals of the 1970s led to a series of theories of organization–environment relationships in which the organization was largely viewed as determined by environmental factors. Over time, many researchers have come to accept Weick's early observation that environments do not exist separate from organizations and are largely enacted by them.[43] Increasingly, the relationship between organization and environment is viewed as co-evolutionary, and with the growth of inter-organizational activity across porous and permeable boundaries, the distinction between what is 'inside' and what is 'outside' is often difficult to discern. This is all the more so when we remember how deeply organizations are embedded in the values of wider society.

- Third, Organization Studies is a field that is centrally concerned with design and its consequences. However, from the early and prevalent assumptions of classic bureaucracy, there is now widespread agreement that, stimulated and enabled by both globalization and information and communication technologies, we are seeing the development of new and innovative forms of organization that overturn our previous understanding of core design principles. Many different labels have been used to describe these new models, including heterarchy,[55,56] the networked form,[57] and more recently, the collaborative community.[58] However, most observers are in agreement that new forms of organization represent a series of interrelated changes that move the balance of power from vertical to lateral relations, from structures to processes and practices, from clear to flexible and permeable boundaries, and from command and control to connect and collaborate. Empirically, research shows that the trend towards these new forms of organization is found across different geographic regions but at different speeds. Moreover, and importantly, these changes in forms of organizing are supplementing not supplanting existing forms. In other words, the new is emerging alongside and within the old.[59]

- Fourth, a related issue that has been central to the subject has been and continues to be the nature of the links between strategy and organization. I have outlined how the argument has moved through time from the clear assertion that structure follows strategy through to the situation today when many argue that organization is itself the strategy. This is particularly evident where the key strategic choices centre on where to draw the boundaries of the firm, what is done within the enterprise, and what is outsourced or accomplished through forms of inter-organizational cooperation. This change is moving the emphasis within strategy away from the firm as a portfolio of businesses towards the firm as a portfolio of relationships.

- Finally, while the dominant theoretical perspective within Organization Studies remains structural functionalism, scholars have long argued that organizations need to be understood from several different perspectives. Although alternative theories have been developed on both sides of the Atlantic, there has been an important divergence between North American and European perspectives on organizations. In the former, theories of organization became increasingly dominated by economic reasoning in the last quarter of the century, particularly with the ascendance of transaction cost explanations of organizations and Industrial Organization[47] theories of strategy. Within Europe, Organization Studies is characterized by a much stronger and continuing emphasis on multiple perspectives for understanding organizations, greater questioning of the structural functionalist paradigm, and critique from power and postmodernist perspectives.

For some, this pluralism represents unwanted fragmentation of the subject, undermining its contribution. For others, it is a manifestation of the independence necessary for scholars studying an important social phenomenon of our era in a manner that recognizes but is separate from the interests of particular, and especially powerful, constituencies.[12] However, whatever the starting point, it is now clear that serious questioning is now more widespread as many of those concerned with organization theory and design express their disquiet about the assumptions that underpin both practice and theory, as well as the adequacy of our theories to explain innovative organizational forms.

Looking Forward

On the basis of this review of the evolution of the field and the important questions that we now face, I believe three interrelated themes are likely to occupy the attention and energies of both scholars and practitioners in the coming years. These are the organizational implications of a knowledge economy, the shift from a focus on organizations to organization and organizing, and the challenges associated with an enriched understanding of the social embeddedness of organizations.

A Knowledge Economy Is a Relational Economy

The substantial body of research that has shown the importance of human and social capital in knowledge processes, particularly where that knowledge is novel and complex, demonstrates that we should view our economy not just as a knowledge economy but also as a relational economy. This has profound implications.

Although there is a growing consensus that we are seeing a move towards new and innovative forms of organizing and that these forms place much greater emphasis on social exchange and collaboration, this is accompanied by a concern that we have yet to develop adequate theories that sustain and explain these alternative forms. For example, as managers recognize the importance of making the most of their existing knowledge and encouraging innovation, they increasingly seek to make cooperative relationships the norm in their organizations. However, they are hampered in their attempts to do so by organization designs that institutionalize the dominant assumption about human intentionality, which currently sees people and their relationships as motivated by self-interest. I have argued elsewhere that the self-interest assumption runs counter to the types of cooperation required to leverage fully the potential of the knowledge-based view of the firm since it provides for relatively restricted and largely self-maximizing forms of social exchange.[60] We need now to rethink many of the assumptions about motivation and relationships that have dominated Western practice in recent years. In particular, we need to remember that people are social and emotional beings with bonds, attachments, and affiliations to groups and communities and that these are important influences on them.

As scholars seek to develop theories that explain recent organizational developments, two constructs stand out in current work. First, in the search for an alternative configuration—beyond markets and bureaucracies—many of them are focusing on the concept of community.[58,61] Although there are important differences between them, studies of organizations as community are primarily concerned with the factors shaping cooperation, collaboration, and coordination in interdependent activities. They focus on social values, especially trust, and social ties, particularly shared identity, as important drivers and enablers of the processes and practices involved in innovation and value creation. As a result, they provide a different perspective on dynamics of differentiation and integration, and in doing so, combine both social and economic perspectives on organization.

The second important focus of interest is networks. Over the last twenty years, network approaches have come to prominence—providing a metaphor, language, and robust methods for describing and understanding patterns of connection and social relationships. The network perspective offers the prospect of describing and explaining both formal and informal organization and patterns of connection both within and without formal organizations. However, there is still no general consensus on what constitutes a network theory of organization, though social capital theory is a strong contender. Interest in social capital has flourished in recent years and is likely to continue, not least because the theory provides powerful explanations of creativity and learning, trust and collaboration, power and influence, and social and economic outcomes both within and between organizations.[62-4]

Community and networks are proving attractive concepts to both practitioners and scholars in part because they apply across a wide range of contexts. They can be used to understand organizational design, inter-organizational relations, and relationships beyond organizational boundaries. They also resonate with the emergence of new institutional forms such as communities of practice, virtual teams, social networking, open sourcing, and networked innovation, all of which cut across or stand apart from conventional boundaries. These developments, when taken alongside the growing significance of inter-organizational relationships, are leading many to conclude that it is time to alter the balance of our work away from the study of formal organizations to deepen our understanding of organization and organizing.

From Organizations to Organization and Organizing

In a far-sighted paper on organization theory written over twenty-five years ago, Pondy and Mitroff propose that 'from one point of view, the subject matter is organisation (no "s"), not a collection of people and tasks but a property of that collection having to do with orderliness and patterns.'[65] Our task is thus to understand how order is created out of the actions of diverse actors. Formal organizations are one means to do this— but not the only means. The challenge now is to deepen our awareness and appreciation of the alternatives.

One of the first concepts we need to revisit in understanding social order is the idea of boundaries. Boundaries are central to our understanding of organizations and organization and organizing, and they are becoming an important focus for both scholars and practitioners. The core idea of boundary is a notion of separateness—boundaries set limits on interaction and influence. They define who and what are 'outside' and who and what are 'inside' and they are widely regarded as important shapers of order and stability. Where boundaries are permeable, ideas, information, artefacts, and people flow freely, unhindered by conventional limits and restrictions. So, in a knowledge and relational economy, how do we now think of boundaries?

Beyond legal and regulatory definitions, research has drawn attention to the importance of boundaries of identity, defining and shaping social collectives, and of knowledge, based on shared understandings of the world, as well as temporal boundaries. Santos and Eisenhardt have recently identified four ways of thinking about boundaries in organization theory that underpin important design decisions.[66] These are efficiency boundaries, which focus on choices to minimize costs; power boundaries, chosen to shape the distribution of control, influence, and autonomy in organizations; competence boundaries, which address the development and distribution of key resources and capabilities; and finally, identity boundaries, which focus on the shaping of shared values and understandings and the coherence that constitutes the organization as a social entity. The challenge going forward will be to understand the dynamic interplay between these important but very different influences on organizing.

In many ways, the move to more fluid, horizontal, and virtual organizational forms helps us—since we are already gaining experience of alternative modes of organizing that combine these various elements. These alternatives highlight the importance of establishing shared meaning and identity, creating contexts for productive exchange and collective activity as well as self-organization, and they identify a range of processes and practices that appear to support such processes. These include conversation and dialogue, ways of mapping and visualizing connections and interdependencies, and processes for coordinating work.[58,67]

However, the map is not well drawn for this endeavour and we have much to learn. For example, how can shared purpose be identified and sustained in loosely coupled arrangements? What are the appropriate forms of governance for activities that transcend formal organizational boundaries? How can the costs and benefits be measured and distributed appropriately? How will differences and conflicts be resolved, especially in virtual environments and multicultural teams? Why and when will people trust each other and who has power in such settings? Finally, how should we research such complex, emergent, dynamic, and co-evolutionary processes? Perhaps the hardest part will be to recognize and rethink many of our taken for granted assumptions about doing and researching organizing and to engage in the heedful observation and collective sense making that a deep appreciation of organizing requires.

Organizing in Its Social Context

The central theme of this book and this chapter is management and organization in context. The research reviewed here has highlighted the many ways in which organizations are embedded in wider society—both influenced by and influencing the social, political, and economic environments in which they operate. There are strong reasons to believe that these links between organization and society are likely to be of increasing importance in the years ahead. The changes referred to earlier—the changing balance of power between nations, the uncertainties over the world's natural resources as well the growing disparity between the rich and poor both within and between nations and regions—will all demand attention and action in the coming years. These issues are likely to increase our awareness of the particular cultural context in which influential ideas have been developed thus far and at the same time stretch further our ability to understand and deliver effective organization. There is much to do.

References

1. J. G. March, 'The Study of Organizations and Organising since 1945', *Organization Studies*, 28/1(2007): 9–20.
2. W. R. Scott, 'Reflections on Half a Century of Organizational Sociology', *Annual Review of Sociology*, 30(2004): 1–21.
3. F. Ferraro, J. Pfeffer, and R. Sutton, 'Economics Language and Assumptions: How Theories Can Become Self-Fulfilling Prophecies', *Academy of Management Review*, 30/1(2005): 8–24.
4. S. Ghoshal, 'Bad Management Theories Are Destroying Good Management Practices', *Academy of Management Learning*, 4/1(2005): 75–91.
5. A. Gherhardi, 'Feminist Theory and Organization Theory', in H. Tsoukas and C. Knudsen (eds.), *The Oxford Handbook of Organization Theory* (Oxford: Oxford University Press, 2003), 210–36.
6. J. P. Walsh, A. D. Meyer, and C. B. Schoonhoven, 'A Future for Organization Theory: Living in and Living with Changing Organizations', *Organization Science*, 17/5(2006): 657–71.
7. A. Cherns, 'Culture and Values: The Reciprocal Influence between Applied Social Science and Its Cultural and Historical Context', in Nigel Nicholson and Toby Wall (eds.), *The Theory and Practice of Organizational Psychology* (London: Academic Press, 1982), 25.
8. A. L. Stinchcombe, 'Social Structure and Organizations', in J. G. March (ed.), *Handbook of Organizations* (Chicago: Rand McNally, 1965), 142–93.
9. C. Bartlett and S. Ghoshal, *Managing across Borders: The Transnational Solution* (Boston: Harvard Business School Press, 1989).
10. 'Globalization's Offspring', *The Economist*, 7 April 2007, 11.
11. W. H. Starbuck, 'The Origins of Organization Theory', in Haridimos Tsoukas and Christian Knudsen (eds.), *The Oxford Handbook of Organization Theory* (Oxford: Oxford University Press, 2003), 143–82.
12. C. R. Hinings and R. Greenwood, 'Disconnects and Consequences in Organization Theory?', *Administrative Science Quarterly*, 47(2002): 411–21.
13. J. Galbraith, *Designing Complex Organisations* (Reading, MA: Addison Wesley, 1973).
14. J. Banbury and J. Nahapiet, 'Towards a Framework for the Study of the Antecedents and Consequences of Information Systems in Organizations', *Accounting, Organisations and Society*, 4/3(1979): 163–77.
15. J. Nahapiet, 'Strategies for the Global Service Firm', in *Mastering Global Business* (London: Financial Times; Pitman Publishing, 1999), 52–7.

16. J. Nahapiet, *The Globalization of Professional Service Firms: Are They a Special Case?* (Templeton College Briefing Paper; Oxford: 2000).

17. J. D. Thompson, *Organizations in Action* (New York: McGraw-Hill, 1967).

18. O. E. Williamson, *Markets and Hierarchies: Analysis and Antitrust Implications* (New York: Free Press, 1975).

19. J. Nahapiet and S. Ghoshal, 'Social Capital, Intellectual Capital and the Organizational Advantage, *Academy of Management Review*, 23/2(1998): 242–66.

20. S. Burchell C. Clubb, A. Hopwood, J. Hughes, and J. Nahapiet, 'The Roles of Accounting in Organizations and Society', *Accounting, Organizations and Society*, 5/1(1980), 5–27.

21. J. Nahapiet, 'The Rhetoric and Reality of an Accounting Change: A Study of Resource Allocation in the NHS', *Accounting, Organizations and Society*, 13/4(1988): 333–58.

22. M. Weber, *The Theory of Social and Economic Organization* (Glencoe, IL: Free Press, 1947).

23. P. M. Blau, *The Dynamics of Bureaucracy* (Chicago: Chicago University Press, 1955).

24. C. I. Barnard, *The Functions of the Executive* (Cambridge, MA: Harvard University Press. 1938).

25. P. Selznick, 'Foundations of the Theory of Organizations', *American Sociological Review*, 13(1948): 25–35.

26. A. W. Gouldner, 'Organizational Analysis', in R. K. Merton, L. Broom, and L. S. Cottrell (eds.), *Sociology Today* (New York: Basic Books, 1959), 400–28.

27. A. M. Pettigrew and E. M. Fenton, 'Complexities and Dualities in Innovative Forms of Organizing', in A. M. Pettigrew and E. M. Fenton (eds.), *The Innovating Organization* (London: Sage, 2000).

28. M. L. Tushman and C. A. O'Reilly, 'Ambidextrous Organization: Managing Evolutionary and Revolutionary Change', *Sloan Management Review*, 45/4(1996): 8–30.

29. A. D. Chandler, *Strategy and Structure: Chapters in History of the American Industrial Enterprise* (Cambridge, MA: Harvard University Press, 1962).

30. J. G. March (ed.), *Handbook of Organizations* (Chicago: Rand McNally, 1965).

31. D. S. Pugh, D. J. Hickson, C. R. Hinings, and C. Turner, 'Dimensions of Organizational Structure', *Administrative Science Quarterly*, 13(1968): 65–105; D. S. Pugh, D. J. Hickson, and C. R. Hinings, 'An Empirical Taxonomy of Work Organizations', *Administrative Science Quarterly*, 14(1969): 115–26.

32. P. R. Lawrence and J. W. Lorsch, *Organization and Environment: Managing Differentiation and Integration* (Boston, MA: Division of Research, Graduate School of Business, Harvard University, 1967).

33. J. Woodward, *Industrial Organization: Theory and Practice* (Oxford: Oxford University Press, 1965).

34. T. Burns and G. M. Stalker, *The Management of Innovation* (London: Tavistock, 1961).

35. L. Donaldson, *The Contingency Theory of Organizations* (London: Sage, 2001).

36. M. T. Hansen, 'The Search Transfer Problem: the Role of Weak Ties in Sharing Knowledge across Organizational Sub-Units', *Administrative Science Quarterly*, 44(1999): 82–111.

37. J. Nahapiet and H. Nahapiet, 'A Comparison of Contractual Arrangements for Building Projects', *Construction Management and Economics*, 3/3(1985): 217–31.

38. B. Uzzi, 'Social Structure and Competition in Inter-Firm Networks: The Paradox of Embeddedness', *Administrative Science Quarterly*, 42(1997): 35–67.

39. M. T. Hannan and J. Freeman, 'The Population Ecology of Organizations', *American Journal of Sociology*, 82(1977): 829–64.

40. J. Pfeffer and G. Salancik, *The External Control of Organizations* (New York: Harper and Row, 1978).

41. J. Meyer and B. Rowan, 'Institutionalized Organizations: Formal Structure as Myth and Ceremony', *American Journal of Sociology*, 83(1977): 340–63.

42. W. H. Starbuck, 'Organizations and Their Environments', in M. D. Dunette (ed.), *Handbook of Industrial and Organizational Psychology* (Chicago: Rand McNally, 1976), 1069–123.

43. K. Weick, *The Social Psychology of Organizing* (Reading, MA: Addison Wesley, 1969).

44. J. Child, 'Organizational Structure, Environment and Performance: The Role of Strategic Choice', *Sociology*, 6/1(1972): 1–22.

45. W. Ouchi, 'Markets, Bureaucracies and Clans', *Administrative Science Quarterly*, 25(1980): 120–41.

46. G. Burrell and G. Morgan, *Sociological Paradigms and Organizational Analysis* (London: Heinemann, 1979).

47. M. E. Porter, *Competitive Strategy* (New York: Free Press, 1980).

48. L. G. Bolman and T. E. Deal, *Modern Approaches to Understanding and Managing Organizations* (San Francisco: Jossey Bass, 1984).

49. G. Morgan, *Images of Organization* (Beverley Hills, CA: Sage, 1986).

50. J. R. Lincoln, 'Intra (and Inter) Organizational Networks', in *Research in the Sociology of Organizations*, 1 (Greenwich, CT: JAI Press, 1982), 1–38.

51. K. M. Eisenhardt and F. M. Santos, 'Knowledge-Based View: a New Theory of Strategy?', in Andrew Pettigrew, Howard Thomas, and Richard Whittington (eds.), *Handbook of Strategy* (Oxford: Oxford University Press, 2002), 139–64.

52. S. Brown and K. M. Eisenhardt, *Managing on the Edge: Strategy as Structured Chaos* (Boston, MA: Harvard Business School Press, 1998).

53. B. Kogut and U. Zander, 'What Do Firms Do? Coordination, Identity and Learning', *Organization Science*, 7/5(1995), 502–18.

54. R. Whittington et al., 'Taking Strategy Seriously: Responsibility and Reform for an Important Social Practice', *Journal of Management Inquiry*, 12/2(2003), 396–409.

55. G. Hedlund, 'The Hypermodern MNC: A Heterarchy?', *Human Resource Management*, 25/1(1986): 9–35.

56. G. Fairtlough, *The Three Ways of Getting Things Done* (Bridport: Triarchy Press, 2005).
57. W. W. Powell, 'Neither Market nor Hierarchy: Network Forms of Organization', in B. Staw (ed.), *Research in Organizational Behaviour*, 12 (Greenwich, CT: JAI Press, 1990): 295–336.
58. P. S. Adler and C. Heckshcher, 'Towards Collaborative Community', in C. Heckshcher and P. S. Adler (eds.), *The Firm as a Collaborative Community* (Oxford: Oxford University Press, 2006).
59. A. M. Pettigrew and S. Massini, 'Innovative Forms of Organizing: Trends in Europe, Japan and the USA in the 1990s', in A. M. Pettigrew, R. Whittington, L. Melin, C. Sanchez-Runde, F. Van den Bosch, W. Ruigrok, and T. Numagami (eds.), *Innovative Forms of Organizing: International Perspectives* (London: Sage, 2003), 1–32.
60. J. Nahapiet, L. Gratton, and H. O. Rocha, 'Knowledge and Relationships: When Cooperation Is the Norm', *European Management Review* (Special Issue on Cooperation and Responsible Management), 2/1(2005): 3–14.
61. D. C. Galunic and K. M. Eisenhardt, 'Architectural Innovation and Modular Corporate Forms', *Academy of Management Journal*, 44/6(2001): 1229–49.
62. R. S. Burt, *Brokerage and Closure: An Introduction to Social Capital* (Oxford: Oxford University Press, 2005).
63. J. Nahapiet, 'Social Capital and Interorganizational Relations', in S. Cropper et al. (eds.), *The Oxford Handbook of Interorganizational Relations* (Oxford: Oxford University Press; forthcoming).
64. J. Nahapiet, 'Social Capital, Strategy and Innovation', in V. Bartkus and J. Davis (eds.), *Reaching out, Reaching in: Multidisciplinary Perspectives on Social Capital* (Forthcoming).
65. L. R. Pondy and I. I. Mitroff, 'Beyond Open System Models of Organization', in *Research in Organizational Behaviour*, 1 (Greenwich, CT: JAI Press, 1979), 5.
66. F. M. Santos and K. M. Eisenhardt, 'Organizational Boundaries and Theories of Organisation', *Organization Science*, 16/5(2005): 491–508.
67. J. Nahapiet, 'Knowledge, Learning and Social Relations: the Role of Conversation'. (Paper presented at the Conference on the Microfoundations of Organisational Capabilities and Knowledge Processes, Copenhagen Business School; Oxford: Templeton College Working Paper, 2005.)

5

Forward to the Past or Back to the Future? Leadership, 1965–2006

Keith Grint

To understand the development of leadership—and where we are likely to go in future—we need to go back to the past. In the beginning was God, or rather the godlike creatures that peppered the 1840 lectures of Thomas Carlyle whose fascination with the 'Great Men' of history effectively reduced the role of mere mortals—women and followers—to extras.[1] Despite Carlyle's dislike of the early industrial entrepreneurs of Britain— the 'millocracy' as he called them—the model of individual heroism that he constructed personified a popular assumption about leadership in Victorian times: it was irredeemably masculine, heroic, individualist, and normative in orientation and nature.

That model prevailed throughout the latter half of the nineteenth century and was not really challenged until the first professional managerial group began displacing the original 'heroic' owner-managers towards the end of the century. Then, the argument runs, the context and thus the requirement for leadership shifted from such heroic individuals to rational systems and processes as the scale of industry and the level of integration began to create huge industries (especially in the USA) that needed significant numbers of administrators to retain organizational coherence. Many of the models for this organizational leadership were derived from the army, civil service, post office, and railroads, and most saw leadership in terms of administrative positions within formal hierarchies.

However, as the productive growth unleashed by these giants began to encourage significant market competition and eat into profit margins, attention quickly turned to cost reduction strategies. Two forms led the way: scientific management and Fordism. The former, led by F. W. Taylor, concentrated on the control of knowledge by management at the expense of the workforce and the deskilling of jobs in line with the increasing division of labour at both divisional level in firms and the task level in factories and offices. In this model, leadership was seen as knowledge leadership, with the leaders as repositories of the knowledge that generated power over production—in contrast to the control over production formerly wielded by craft workers. Moreover, Taylor argued that since it was the collectivization of work that generated worker solidarity and what he called 'systematic soldiering' (or work avoidance), the scientific solution—the 'one best way' as he put it—was to isolate workers as individuals with each individual's rewards relating only to that individual's performance.[2]

Fordism, though still rooted in the rational science of production, focused less on embodying the knowledge in the minds of managers than on encasing it in the technologies of production. Indeed, Henry Ford positively disliked scientists and academic experts and much preferred the experience of time-served autodidacts like himself. In effect, leadership at Ford was absorbed into the assembly line so that the disciplining of employees was undertaken by the technology rather than the production-line supervisors. However, Ford soon recognized the limits of this mode of leadership and began to develop an approach that switched from the objective technologies of production to the subjective technologies of control. He introduced a department of sociology rooted in normative strategies of control and tried to ensure that only moral workers (those who did not visit brothels or bars) were given bonuses and loyalty rewards. But these strategies quickly fell by the wayside in the 1920s as the economic downturn began to bite and huge redundancies were announced.[3]

That downturn coincided with the next major shift in leadership models—one that Ford's sociology department had prefigured. For our purposes, it represented a major shift back to the role of normative power and away from the rationality of scientific systems and processes that had dominated the previous two decades. This return to the previous normative model grew out of the Hawthorne experiments in the 1920s and 1930s at the General Electric (GE) plant near Chicago. There, Taylorist scientific experiments to develop optimal working conditions had first generated perplexity, then a realization that work could not be measured objectively because the very act of measurement altered the experience, and thus the behaviour of those being measured.

This 'Hawthorne Effect' as it was called spawned a series of related experiments that eventually persuaded GE and then whole swathes of American management that workers were not rationally motivated and the culture of groups was not individually oriented. In effect, workers could not be motivated by economic rationalism as Taylor had suggested, but only by recognizing their natural and 'non-rational' desire to work in teams led by sympathetic supervisors endowed with what we would now call 'emotional intelligence'. It might be argued that these two embryonic models of leadership—the normative model of Carlyle of the second half of the nineteenth century and the rational model of Taylor and Ford in the first two decades of the twentieth century (which was, in turn, superseded by a return to the normative model of the Hawthorne experiments that formed the basis for the Human Relations approach of the 1930s and 1940s)—reflected two broader phenomena: economic cycles and the political models of the period.

The economic cycles form the basis of Kondratiev's controversial theory of Long Economic Waves or Cycles. However, the political cycles are less controversial and more intriguing, for it seems unlikely that industry could have isolated itself from the global rise of the mass movements of communism and fascism in the late 1920s and 1930s and far more likely that the leadership models embodied in these were mirrored by industry (see Barley and Kunda[4] and Kunda and Ailon-Souday[5] for longer accounts of this approach). In other words, in an era when mass political movements driven by normative adherence to the collective will—but manifested in cult-like loyalty to the party leader—were so prominent, it seemed perfectly natural to assume that the best way to lead an industrial organization was to incorporate their assumptions: work should be normatively rather than rationally organized—in groups led by leaders who embodied the same desires as the masses.

By the time the Second World War ended and the economic boom returned, the model dominant in the West once again shifted back from the normative cult of mass heroic leadership back to one dominated by rational analysis of the situation. This movement away from norms back towards the rational understanding of contexts built on the critiques of traits by Jenkins[6] and Stogdill[7,8] and the work of the University of Michigan and Ohio State University.[9] These provided the framework for a radically new development: Contingency Theory.

Under the general umbrella provided by Fred Fieldler's Contingency Theory,[10] and Robert Blake and Jane Mouton's Managerial Grid,[11] the theoretical fragility of relying upon a potentially endless list of traits and superhuman charismatic figures was dealt a crippling blow. From then on what really mattered was not having the most charismatic leader but having a rational understanding of the situation and responding appropriately. These leadership theories that eschewed the dominant and proactive role of the individual leader in favour of social or structural factors tended to assume that the context or situation should determine how leaders respond. In terms of the early contingency theories,[10,12] situation X required leadership X to ensure an appropriate and rational response.

More recent developments in Contingency Theory, for all their more sophisticated accumulation of significant and independent variables, are still based on the assumption that the 'correct' leadership response is determined by the correct analysis of the situation. For example, Nadler and Tuchman's Congruence Model[13] proposes that the three primary inputs to the system are the environment, the available resources, and the history of the organization. These assumptions are questionable. Taking the last one first, an organization's history is seldom uncontested and is often, as Rowlinson and Hassard[14] suggested in their analysis of the history of Cadbury, a means to reconstruct the past to fit the needs of the present. As to the resources available to an organization, it was clear to the Allies in 1940 that they had more than enough resources to defeat Germany; unfortunately, the latter did not agree with this 'objective' analysis.[15]

Regarding the role of the environment in determining what leaders should do, we have only to consider the different positions taken by leaders on the issue of global warming to see that the environment is not some objective variable but rather an 'issue' to be interpreted in terms of a whole variety of assumptions. In effect, contingency theories, whatever their complexities—and there are few more complex than House's reformulation[16] of his Path-Goal theory with its multiplicity of variables—are premised on the essentialist notion that we can render the context or situation transparent through scientific analysis.

Since the early days of the contingency approach—which, incidentally, coincided with the beginning of Management Studies in Oxford—we have 'progressed' by returning to the importance of leaders working within the normative strong cultures beloved of Peters and Waterman,[17] then to the (rational) pedagogy of the Re-engineering Revolution of the 1990s,[18] and finally to the contemporary developments of transformational and inspirational leadership theory.[9] Coupled with concerns about the importance of emotional intelligence and of inspiring visions and missions, this seems to have ensured the return of the original normative trait approaches: we seem to have gone forward to the past.

At present, we seem to be once again in thrall to inspirational individuals.[19-21] Many political commentators describe the global political situation in terms of the dominant role of individual politicians.[22-4] Others report that politicians are the world's least trusted people—but that again implies that it is the individual leader that matters not the situation.[25] Yet there is considerable support for an approach that accepts that even if individual leaders do make a difference, that difference is only marginal in comparison to the effect of structural features like the economy, religion, political party, social class or gender, or any other of the myriad variables on offer.[26,27]

Patterns of Leadership

The argument for a swing between normative and rational forms of leadership is not universally accepted. Indeed there are other ways to understand the pattern. It could be determined by the binaries of language that can operate only on such dichotomies as night and day, good and bad, black and white—or in this case—rational and normative models.[28] Perhaps the pattern is that of a spiral rather than a pendulum[29]—or more appropriately, the architecture of the nautilus shell that is Templeton's emblem! Although the extreme limits of the swing are the rational and normative approaches to leadership, each return may operate at a higher level than before. Alternatively, we may be witnessing an increasingly rational approach to leadership as we reach the limits of one approach and transcend these in good Hegelian fashion, encompassing its rational elements and shedding its irrational elements. Or there may be no pattern at all, just an accumulation of historical detritus strewn around by academics and consultants hoping, at most, to make sense of a senseless shape or, at least, make a living from constructing different patterns to sell.

The third approach is obviously untrue! But the others also seem overly tidy. We need to question the whole basis of these tidy unilinear and binary models (and there are lots of the former in airport bookshops and of the latter in the leadership literature).[30] What follows briefly considers the limits to the normative approaches, which focus on the leader's character, and also the weakness of their alleged opposite, the contingency approach, which claims the heritage of a more rational approach. In their place, we might usefully draw upon contemporary social constructionist philosophy to consider the extent to which decision-makers themselves construct the context that, in turn, allows them to 'respond' appropriately. In other words, the decision-makers construct the future and then appeal to it as if it were the present. We need to tread sceptically around the whole idea of decision-making and take another look at the way it presents the future: in short, we need to go 'back to the future' not 'forward to the past'.

Situating Situations

A critical weakness of contingency or situational approaches is their tendency to underestimate the extent to which the context is actively created by leaders and decision-makers. In effect, leadership involves the social construction of a context that both represents the world and legitimates a particular course of action. If the presentation of the context is successful— for there are usually competing versions—the new version determines the alternatives available and makes those involved begin to act differently. To put it another way, we might consider not what the situation is but how it is 'situated'. Shifting from noun to verb in this way re-emphasizes the proactive role of leadership, not in the normative sense that individual leaders are independent agents able to manipulate the world at will, as in Carlyle's 'Great Man' theory, but in the sense that they play an active role in interpreting and constructing the context—a context that is not independent of human agency, and can never ultimately be objectively and rationally assessed.

Social constructionist accounts are not new. Their roots stretch back to Kuhn's (1962) work on scientific paradigms to C. Wright Mills's work[31] on the vocabularies of motive and to the seminal work of Berger and Luckman, *The Social Construction of Reality*.[32] However, recent theoretical developments of the work are best approached through the works of Burr[33] and Gergen,[34] and their application to leadership can be seen in the work of Grint.[2,3] The critical element—and there are now many different forms of social constructionism (see Gergen and Gergen[35])—is that what counts as 'true', 'objective', and 'fact' is in fact rooted in competing accounts of reality, and the account that prevails is often both a temporary and a collective phenomenon. In short, the book is never closed but permanently open to reinterpretation, just as assessments of, say, Winston Churchill are never final but always subject to being overturned by different interpretations. The key message of this approach is that knowledge— what counts as 'true'—is the property of particular communities and thus that knowledge is never neutral or divorced from ideology.

To reiterate, contingency theories that are premised on securing rational and objective accounts of the context, the situation, the leader, and the followers are fundamentally flawed, and we should pay much more attention to the role of leaders and decision-makers in constructing contexts that legitimate their actions and interpretations. The next section outlines a typology to illustrate the way this alternative model operates.

Problems, Power, and Uncertainty

Much of leadership research is grounded in a typology that distinguishes between leadership and management as different forms of authority (equating to Weber's concept of legitimate power). Leadership, for instance, tends to involve longer periods of time, a more strategic perspective, and the requirement to resolve new problems.[9,37] But in most cases, the difference relates to the analysis of the situation: management is the equivalent of *déjà vu* (seen this before), whereas leadership is the equivalent of *vu jàdé* (never seen this before).[38] If this interpretation is valid, the manager simply has to engage the same process to solve the problem that he or she applied the last time it emerged. In contrast, the leader has to reduce the anxiety of his or her followers as they face the unknown by providing an innovative response to a new problem rather than rolling out a known solution for a previously experienced problem.

But the division between management and leadership, rooted in this distinction between the known and the unknown, belies the complexity of the relationship between problem and response. Often the *déjà vu* approach does not lend itself to the application of a tried and trusted formula because it is more a case of '*déjà vu* all over again': in effect, the 'certain' process has not solved the uncertain problem. In leadership also, the situation is sometimes seen as too complex and divisive to allow the leader to impose his or her will upon his or her followers.

Perhaps the first thing to do is develop a contextualized typology of problems. Management and leadership, as two forms of authority rooted in the distinction between certainty and uncertainty, can be related to Rittell and Webber's typology of 'tame' and 'wicked' problems.[39] A tame problem may be complicated but is resolvable through a series of actions because there comes a point where the problem is solved, and it is likely to have occurred before. In other words, there is only a limited degree of uncertainty, and thus it falls within the province of management. The manager's role, therefore, is to provide the appropriate processes to solve the problem. Examples might include timetabling railways, building a nuclear plant, training an army, carrying out planned heart surgery, undertaking wage negotiations, or putting into force a tried and trusted policy for eliminating global terrorism.

A wicked problem, in contrast, is complex and often intractable: there is no straightforward solution, no stopping-point—apparent solutions often generate other problems. Often there is no 'right' or 'wrong' answer, only better or worse alternatives. In other words, there is a huge degree of uncertainty involved. Wicked problems, therefore, fall within the province of leadership. The leader's approach to a wicked problem should be to ask the right questions rather than provide the right answers because the answers may not be self-evident and require a collaborative process to make any kind of progress. Examples might include developing a transport strategy, an energy strategy, a defence strategy, a national health system, an industrial relations strategy, or a new strategy for dealing with global terrorism. This kind of issue implies that techniques such as appreciative enquiry may be appropriate in leadership.[40]

However, there is a third set of problems that do not fit any of these criteria and thus fall outside the whole leadership/management dichotomy. These can be termed 'critical problems'. The nature of a critical problem—for instance a crisis—is recognized as self-evident. It allows very little time for decision-making and action, and is often associated with authoritarian forms of command.[41,42] Here, there is virtually no uncertainty about what needs to be done, at least in the behaviour of the 'commander'. The commander's role is to take the necessary decisive action: provide the answer to the problem, not just to engage processes (as in management) or ask questions (as in leadership). Of course, it may be that the commander is privately uncertain whether the action is appropriate or the presentation of the situation as a crisis is persuasive, but that uncertainty will probably not be apparent to the commander's followers. Examples might include the immediate responses to a major train crash, a leak of radioactivity from a nuclear plant, a military attack, an industrial strike, or an unexpected and overwhelming terrorist attack such as 9/11.

That such situations are 'constructed' by the participants rather than being straightforwardly self-evident is best illustrated by considering the way an ill-defined threat becomes a crisis only when it is defined as such. For example, financial losses—even rapid and radical losses—do not constitute a 'crisis' until the shareholders decide to sell in large numbers, and even then the notion of a crisis does not emerge objectively from the activity of selling but at the point at which a 'crisis' is pronounced by someone significant and accepted as such by a significant number of others.

These three forms of authority—command, management, and leadership—suggest in turn that those responsible for decision-making have to find the appropriate answers, processes, and questions for problems, respectively. This analysis is not put forward as a discrete typology but rather as a heuristic device to help us understand why those charged with decision-making seem sometimes to act in ways that others find incomprehensible. It is not that correct decision-making consists solely in correctly analysing situations, but that decision-makers tend to legitimize their actions on the basis of a persuasive account of a situation. In short, the social construction of the problem legitimizes the deployment of a particular form of authority. However, it is often the case that individuals or groups with authority will switch between command, management, and leadership modes as they perceive—and by so doing, construct—the problem as critical, tame, or wicked, or even one that combines all these categories.

It is not being suggested that different ways of constructing problems restrict those in authority in their choice of an appropriate form of power. Commanders, for example, having defined a problem as critical do not need to rely on coercion alone, but their use of coercion will be legitimated by identifying the problem as critical in a way that managers would find more difficult and leaders almost impossible. Conversely, commanders who follow up their identification of the problem as critical by asking their followers questions and seeking to make progress through collaboration (the attributes of leadership) are less likely to be seen as successful commanders than those who provide clear solutions and demand obedience.

That the ability to present a persuasive account of a problem partly springs from decision-makers' access to—and preference for—particular forms of power constitutes the dilemma of leadership. Leadership remains the most difficult of approaches, and one that many decision-makers will try to avoid at all costs because it implies that (a) the leader does not have the answer, (b) the leader's role is to make the followers face up to their responsibilities (often an unpopular task),[43] (c) the 'answer' to the problem is going to take a long time to construct and it will only ever be 'more appropriate' rather than 'the best', and (d) it will require constant effort to maintain. It is far easier either to opt for a management solution—engaging a tried and trusted process—or a command solution—enforcing the answer upon followers, some of whom may prefer to be shown 'the answer' anyway.

The notion of 'enforcement' suggests that we need to consider how different approaches to—and forms of—power fit with this typology of authority. The most useful for our purposes is Etzioni's typology of compliance.[44] Etzioni distinguished between coercive, calculative, and normative compliance. Coercive compliance or compliance due to physical power was related to 'total' institutions, such as prisons or armies, calculative compliance to 'rational' institutions, such as companies, and normative compliance to institutions or organizations based on shared values, such as clubs and professional societies. This typology of compliance fits well with the typology of problems: critical problems are often associated with coercive compliance, tame problems with calculative compliance, and wicked problems with normative compliance.

None of this is to suggest that we can objectively divide the world up into particular kinds of problems and their associated and appropriate

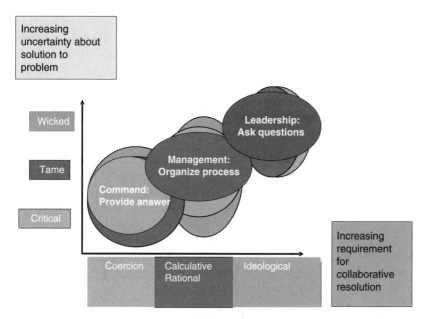

FIG. 5.1 A typology of problems, power, and authority

forms of authority, but rather that the very legitimacy of a form of authority depends on the successful presentation of a phenomenon as a particular kind of problem. While Contingency Theory suggests a precise and objective rational connection between the context (the problem) and the style of leadership (the authority form), what actually constitutes legitimate authority depends upon the persuasive presentation of the context and the persuasive display of the appropriate authority style. In other words, success is rooted in persuading followers to accept that the problem is either critical or tame or wicked, and that therefore the appropriate authority form is either command or management or leadership—forms in which the role of the decision-maker is to provide an answer, organize a process, or ask a question, respectively.

This relationship can be plotted along two axes, as shown above in Figure 5.1, with the vertical axis representing increasing uncertainty about the solution to the problem in those in authority and the horizontal axis the increasing need for collaboration in resolving the problem. Again, it should be borne in mind that the measure of uncertainty used here does not represent an objective aspect of the situation but the way the situation is constructed by those in authority. Of course, the nature of that authority and that problem may be disputed, but the model assumes that the successful identification of a problem as wicked, tame, or critical provides the framework for particular forms of authority. It also indicates the most likely model of authority. But again it should be noted that while commanders may, for example, use approaches more commonly adopted by leaders or managers, their most prevalent form is likely to be that of coercion.

What is also evident from this figure is that the more decision-makers perceive the problem as wicked and interpret their power as essentially normative, the more difficult their task becomes, especially in cultures that associate leadership with the effective and efficient resolution of problems. In other words, for a democratic contender to seek election on the basis of tackling global terrorism as a wicked problem that requires long-term, collaborative leadership processes with no easy solutions in which everyone must participate and share the responsibility, the less likely he or she is to be elected. This is the irony of leadership: it is often avoided where it is most necessary.

Where no one can be certain about what needs to be done to resolve a wicked problem, the more likely they are to seek a collective response. For example, a road traffic accident is usually deemed to call for rapid and categorical authority—command—on the part of those perceived to have the requisite knowledge and authority to resolve the problems: usually the police, the fire service, and the ambulance service. Those who are uncertain about what to do in a road traffic accident should—and usually do—make way for those who seem to know what they are doing, especially if they are in an appropriate uniform. We will, therefore, normally allow ourselves to be commanded by such professionals in a crisis.

However, when the problem is not an emergency but, for instance, the planned phasing of an urban traffic light system, we are more likely to comply with a traffic management expert than a flashing blue light— at least as long as the system works. Even more difficult is rethinking a traffic strategy to balance the needs of the environment with those of rural dwellers, those without private transport, and those whose houses would be demolished if private roads or public railways were to be built. In effect, as the level of uncertainty increases, so does our preference for involvement in the decision-making process. The implication of this is that political leaders do well to construct political scenarios that either increase or decrease assumptions about uncertainty in order to ensure the right levels of political support. For example, it might not be in the interests of political leaders to equivocate about the threat posed by terrorism but to imply that the threat is so obvious and urgent that any necessary measure need be taken, including pre-emptive strikes.

The shift from command through management to leadership also relates to the degree of subtlety necessary for success. For instance, a sergeant with a gun standing over a squad of soldiers facing an attack does not need to be very subtle about his or her command to stand and fight. Similarly, a police officer coming upon a train crash need not spend a lot of time, effort, or rhetorical skill in persuading onlookers to move away; he or she can simply command them to move. However, for that same police officer to operate as a manager in a police training academy would require a much more sophisticated array of skills and behaviours in order to train police cadets in the art of policing. Many of these techniques and processes are known, tried, and tested. But developing a new policing strategy for Iraq might mean more than commanding civilians and simply training cadets using management processes: it might require a whole new framework for constituting a post-Baathist society—and that demands sophisticated leadership.

Back to the Future

This chapter began by suggesting that there are various ways to model developments in leadership theory over time: from rational to normative and from unilinear to dualist—but taking into account the context that, like Frank Ward O'Malley's account of life, is 'just one damn thing after another'! Assumptions about the importance of context rationally determining leadership responses are as traditional as those that focus solely on the normative nature of a leader's traits or character—and they are just as illusory: the appearance of the wooden horse outside the walls of Troy did not mean the Trojans had to bring the horse inside the wall, they chose to do it. This reassertion of the role of choice in decision-making neither implies that the leader, manager, or commander (often the same person at different times) is free to do whatever he or she wants nor that they are totally constrained in their actions by the situations they find themselves in. What this chapter has tried to illustrate is the difficulty of separating the situation from the decision-maker because the former is often a consequence of the latter.

Two critical points stand out. First, it is not the accurate representation of the context that should determine what kind of problem exists or what form of authority is appropriate, but rather what kind of persuasive account of the context results in it being seen as a specific type of problem that, in turn, legitimates a particular form of authority. Second, that leadership may be an appropriate form of authority for coping with wicked problems that are perceived as intractable, but this is often seen as indecisiveness by the leader's opponents. It illustrates what may be the irony of leadership: that openness is so difficult to achieve that even when leaders consider it appropriate and even essential, they may be very unwilling to attempt it.

The implication of the approach outlined in this chapter is that we should spend less time going 'forward to the past' and reigniting old worries about getting the right charismatic figure in charge, and trying to analyse the decision-making of formal decision-makers on the basis of 'rational' or 'scientific' understanding of the situation that faces them—as suggested by conventional contingency theories. Instead, we should go 'back to the future' to see how those futures are constructed by the very same decision-makers and consider the persuasive mechanisms that decision-makers use to make situations more tractable to their own preferred form of authority. To repeat, 'situation' is not a noun but a verb: what takes place is not situational decision-making but situated decision-making.

References

1. T. Carlyle, *On Heroes, Hero-Worship and the Heroic in History* (Lincoln, NB: University of Nebraska Press, 1966).
2. K. Grint, *The Sociology of Work* (3rd edn.; Cambridge: Polity Press, 2005).
3. K. Grint, *Leadership: Limits and Possibilities* (London: Palgrave Macmillan, 2005).
4. S. R Barley and G. Kunda, 'Design and Devotion: Surges of Rational and Normative Ideologies of Control in Managerial Discourse', in K. Grint (ed.), *Work and Society: A Reader* (Cambridge: Polity Press, 2000).
5. G. Kunda and G. Ailon-Souday, 'Managers, Markets and Ideologies', in S. Ackroyd, R. Batt, P. Thompson, and P. S. Tolbert (eds.), *The Oxford Handbook of Work* (Oxford: Oxford University Press, 2005).
6. W. O. Jenkins, 'A Review of Leadership Studies with Particular Reference to Military Problems', *Psychological Bulletin*, 44(1947): 54–79.
7. R. M. Stogdill, 'Personal Factors Associated with Leadership', *Journal of Psychology*, 25(1948): 35–71.
8. R. M. Stogdill, *Handbook of Leadership* (New York: Free Press, 1974).
9. J. Bratton, K. Grint, and D. Nelson, *Organizational Leadership* (Oxford: Oxford University Press, 2004); ibid. 58–89.
10. F. E. Fielder, *A Theory of Leadership Effectiveness* (New York: McGraw Hill, 1967).
11. R. Blake and J. S. Mouton, *The Managerial Grid: Key Orientations for Achieving Production through People* (Houston, TX: Gulf Publication Company, 1964).
12. R. House and G. Dessler, 'The Path-Goal Theory of Leadership', in J. G. Hunt and L. L. Larson (eds.), *Contingency Approaches to Leadership* (Carbondale, IL.: Southern Illinois University Press, 1974).
13. D. Nadler and M. Tuschman, *Competing By Design* (Oxford: Oxford University Press, 1997).

14. M. Rowlinson and J. Hassard, 'The Invention of Corporate Culture', in K. Grint (ed.), *Work and Society* (Cambridge: Polity Press, 2000).

15. E. R. May, *Strange Victory* (London: I. B. Tauris, 2000).

16. R. House, 'Path-Goal Theory of Leadership', *Leadership Quarterly*, 7/3(1996): 323–52.

17. T. Peters and R. Waterman, *In Search of Excellence: Lessons from America's Best-Run Companies* (New York: Harper & Row, 1982).

18. M. Hammer and J. Champy, *Reengineering the Corporation* (London: Nicholas Brealey, 1993).

19. S. Covey, *Principle-Centred Leadership* (New York: Simon & Schuster, 1990).

20. S. A. Kirkpatrick and E. A. Locke, 'Leadership', *The Executive*, 5(1991): 48–60.

21. G. A. Yukl, *Leadership in Organizations* (6th edn.; London: Prentice-Hall, 2005).

22. J. Freedland, 'Ken's One Man Show', *Evening Standard*, 5 December 2005, 21.

23. M. Riddell, 'The Politics of Bob', *Observer*, 1 January 2006, 22.

24. G. Steinem, 'I'm a Hopeaholic. There's Nothing George Bush Can Do about It', *Guardian*, 13 September 2005, 28.

25. B. Whitaker, 'Politicians are Voted the World's Least Trusted People', *Guardian*, 15 September 2005, 17.

26. A. King (ed), *Leaders' Personalities and the Outcome of Democratic Elections* (Oxford: Oxford University Press, 2002).

27. J. Pfeffer and R. I. Sutton, *Hard Facts: Dangerous Half Truths and Total Nonsense* (Boston, MA: Harvard Business Review Press, 2006).

28. K. Grint, *Fuzzy Management* (Oxford: Oxford University Press, 1997).

29. K. Grint, *The Sociology of Work* (2nd edn.; Cambridge: Polity Press, 1998), 320–2.

30. D. Collinson, 'Dialectics of Leadership', *Human Relations*, 58(2005): 1419–42.

31. C. Wright Mills, *The Sociological Imagination* (Oxford: Oxford University Press, 1959).

32. P. Berger and T. Luckman, *The Social Construction of Reality* (Garden City, NY: Doubleday, 1966).

33. V. Burr, *Social Constructionism* (2nd edn.; London: Routledge, 2003).

34. K. Gergen, *An Invitation to Social Construction* (London: Sage, 1999).

35. K. Grint, *The Arts of Leadership* (Oxford: Oxford University Press, 2001).

36. M. Gergen and K. Gergen (eds.), *Social Construction: A Reader* (London: Sage, 2003).

37. A. Zaleznik, 'Managers and Leaders', *Harvard Business Review*, 55/5(1977): 67–80.

38. K. E. Weick, 'The Collapse of Sensemaking in Organizations', *Administrative Science Quarterly*, 38(1993): 628–52.

39. H. Rittell and M. Webber, 'Dilemmas in a General Theory of Planning', *Policy Sciences*, 4(1973): 155–69.

40. D. Cooperrider and D. Whitney, *Collaborating for Change* (San Francisco, CA: Berrett Koehler, 1999).

41. B. Howieson and H. Kahn, 'Leadership, Management and Command', in P. Gray and S. Cox (eds.), *Air Power Leadership* (London: HMSO, 2002).
42. B. Watters, 'Mission Command' (Paper at the Leadership Symposium, RAF Cranwell, 13 May 2004).
43. R. Heifetz, *Leadership without Easy Answers* (Cambridge, Mass.: Harvard University Press, 1998).
44. A. Etzioni, *Modern Organizations* (Englewood Cliffs, NJ: Prentice Hall, 1964).

Part II

A Broader Lens

6

Public Management: Shifting Challenges and Issues

Ian Kessler and Sue Dopson

Public management as a sphere of teaching, research, and practice focuses on the context, techniques, processes, and outcomes associated with the management of public-sector organizations. It has only gradually emerged as a discrete area of study. As an article in volume 6 of the *Journal of Management Studies* noted, 'Theoretical and descriptive work on organisation and management draws too much on manufacturing industry and, at least in the UK, almost ignores the public sector.'[1] Public management has not only taken some time to step out of the shadows of public administration, but it is a step that has been contested along the way. Debate about the distinctiveness of management in the public sector continues, reflecting the fact that interest in the subject is dispersed across a range of academic, practitioner, and policymaking communities and the difficulty of developing shared approaches or paradigms.

In many respects, the slow development of public management is surprising and difficult to justify. As the renowned management commentator Peter Drucker noted almost twenty-five years ago, 'Every citizen in developed, industrialized, urbanized societies depends for his very survival on the performance of public-service institutions.'[2] The importance of the public services is reflected in the fact that the public sector covers a significant part of any developed economy, whether this be in terms of public expenditure, which typically ranges between 30 and 40 per cent of GDP, or employment, with state employees rarely constituting less than 12 per cent of the workforce and, in some countries such as those in Scandinavia, as much as a quarter or even a third.[3]

Since the emergence of modern economies, determining the scope of state activity and ensuring its coordination have been central to public policy debate. The outcomes of these deliberations have been critically related to the configuration of social, political, and economic circumstances and have been seen to revolve around three basic mechanisms: hierarchies, markets, and networks.[4] These mechanisms, often seen as the basis of successive models of public-service provision, are used to structure this chapter. An introductory section, considering the parameters of public management as a subject area, is followed by sections that consider in turn each of these models and their managerial consequences. It is argued that the management issues and challenges confronted by the major stakeholders in public-sector organizations—the state itself, service users, managers, and professionals—have been related to the prevailing model of public-service provision. In short, hierarchies, markets, and networks will be seen to have very different implications for stakeholders and, in particular, for the way in which they combine to manage the resources needed to deliver public services.

Carving Out a Subject

Public management's struggle to emerge as a discrete area of study might be related to a basic uncertainty as to where the divide between the 'public' and the 'private' lies. While most economies might readily agree on a range of services deemed as 'public' by virtue of the fact that they address a fundamental collective need, such as education, health, and defence, it remains much more open to debate whether such services should be provided by privately or publicly owned organizations. Indeed, a consensus that there are certain services only the state is able or willing to sponsor, perhaps because of market failure, still leaves open whether they are provided directly by the government or simply commissioned by it from the private sector. Drucker's reference to 'public-service institutions' is clearly broader than publicly owned organizations and begs the question whether public management covers organizations providing public services or organizations in the public sector or both. It is a question made all the more difficult to answer given that private-sector organizations delivering public services might be doing so on a not-for-profit basis. In such circumstances, the 'not-for-profit' distinction might be viewed as a more legitimate basis for delineating a particular sphere of management activity than ownership.

As implied at the outset, the study of public management in Britain, at least, has tended to concentrate on management in public-owned and run organizations. This is because the British public sector has traditionally been broadly based. Public-sector organizations are typically classified as being nationalized or falling within local government, including primary and secondary education and social services, the National Health Service (NHS), and central government covering the civil service. The precise location of the organization in the public sector has important implications for governance, funding, and service regulation. For example, nationalized industries have tended to operate according to trading principles, while local government, the health service, and the civil service, often seen in combination as the public services, have more usually functioned on a non-trading basis, sheltered from 'product' market pressures and free at the point of delivery. However, these are organizations that share distinctive features, suggesting a particular approach to management.

Just how distinctive these features are in practice and whether they necessitate a particular approach to management has been subject to ongoing debate. As management studies were developing as a field of study, different views emerged on the nature of public-sector organizations and management. Mainly played-out in the US literature, these early debates focused on conceptual differences between the public and the private sectors.[5–7] While few, if any, commentators were prepared to deny such differences, some were inclined to regard them more as a matter of degree than of kind. For example, it was argued by Murray[8] that the political imperative to the fore in public-sector organizations was nothing more than a strong version of the political processes to be found in any organization even if the basis and nature of interest articulation varied; that the need to address multiple stakeholders and their contrasting goals was shared by public- and private-sector organizations even though the character of these stakeholders might differ; and that constraints on activity whether from statutory regulation or from other forces were intrinsic to organizational context regardless of sector.

Others, however, were more forceful in asserting important differences between the sectors and their implications for management practice. As Ring and Perry noted: 'Basic distinctions do exist between public and private sectors and they are critical to understanding differences in strategic management processes.'[9] These authors proposed five major distinctions, so in public-sector organizations:

- Policy directives are less precise
- Decision-making is more open, creating greater constraints on management action
- Policymakers are more exposed to direct and sustained influence from a greater number of interest groups
- Managers must respond to time constraints, which are much more likely to be artificial
- Policy coalitions are less stable and more likely to disintegrate.

Whether these are differences of degree or kind is arguably beside the point; a cluster of differences in a given organizational context, however acute, is more than enough to suggest that management might assume a different form. But such a view is reinforced on a much more grounded basis by features associated with public-sector organizations. Employees, for example, are the key resource to be managed in public-sector organizations. Most organizations in the sector are labour intensive, with public services being delivered on a direct personal, often one-to-one, basis. This is reflected in the fact that in Britain more than 70 per cent of public expenditure comprises labour costs and in most developed countries it rarely falls below 50 per cent.[10] This might apply to many service organizations, but there are a number of particular features associated with the public-sector workforce.[11]

First, the proportion of women employees is high and increasing. In the British public sector, almost two-thirds of employees are women compared to well under half in the private sector. More generally, across Organization for Economic Cooperation and Development (OECD) countries, women make up more than half the public-sector workforce, with a substantial growth in the proportion of women with 'high level responsibilities', which increased from 14 to 24 per cent between 1990 and 2000–1.[12] Second, alongside and related to the gendered nature of the workforce, there is a relatively high proportion of part-time workers in the sector. In Britain, a third of public servants work part-time compared to a quarter in the private sector.

Third, public servants are relatively well qualified. In this country, 44 per cent have a degree or a high-level vocational qualification; this compares to barely a quarter in the private sector.[11] This situation should come as no surprise and relates to a much broader point on the centrality of the professions in the public sector. Clearly, the high proportion of qualified workers is associated with the presence of such professionals as doctors, nurses, social workers, and teachers. These not only comprise a significant part of the workforce but also have become highly organized, ensuring the presence and influence of professional associations in the public sector. Indeed, collective organization amongst public-sector workers in Britain is reflected in the fact that almost 60 per cent are trade union members compared to less than 20 per cent in the private sector.

Finally, public-sector employees have often been seen to have a distinctive set of values, especially in terms of what motivates them. It is a difference that Le Grand highlights in categorizing public servants as 'knaves' or 'knights'.[13] Public choice theorists suggest that public servants engage in bureaucracy, maximizing 'knavish' behaviour to increase their status and remuneration; a situation facilitated by the absence of competitive pressures or systems of performance management and the availability of a steady stream of public funding.[14] Others view public servants as 'knights' with a distinctive public service ethos comprising a strong commitment to the public interest and a willingness to sacrifice immediate personal gain to pursuing broader welfare goals.[15] The latter perspective finds support in the work of Crewson,[16] which suggests that public servants in the USA are driven more by intrinsic than extrinsic rewards. This work finds an echo in Britain where research amongst municipal workers indicates that a social exchange ideology is often complemented by a public-service orientation, which emphasizes the pursuit of communal interests alongside individual, instrumental goals.[17]

The distinctive character of public-sector organizations, in terms of their external environment, internal processes, and outcomes as well as their key resources including employees, should not detract from an appreciation of the choices available to states on how they deliver and coordinate their services. It has been stressed that three mechanisms—hierarchies, markets, and networks—have successively emerged as the means of such delivery and coordination with different managerial implications. However, some care is needed in assessing these implications. The predominance of the three models has been reflected in a shifting discourse apparent in managerial prescriptions and policy pronouncements. It remains a related but analytically distinct issue as to how far such a discourse has been apparent in changes in managerial practice.

Hierarchies

For thirty years post-1945, the state played a central and expansive role in the British economy and in the lives of its population. This was the era of a strong welfare state founded on a political consensus forged in turn by an appreciation of the social, political, and economic consequences of market failure in the interwar years. It was a welfare state that comprised support in the form of not only benefits and care for vulnerable members of the community—the elderly, the unemployed, and children in need—but also the universal right to key services free at the point of receipt, such as health and education. Indeed, the reach of the state went even further as it took on the ownership of key industries, such as steel manufacturing, coal mining, air and rail transport, alongside the provision of the major utilities—water, gas, and electricity. The development of the welfare state was illustrated in the growth of public expenditure: in 1900 general government expenditure was barely 12 per cent of GDP; during the 1950s and

1960s it rose steadily to around 35 per cent, reaching a peacetime peak of close to 50 per cent in the early 1970s.[18]

Despite the broad and inclusive nature of the state, a specific focus on public management was difficult to discern amongst academics and other commentators in the thirty years or so after 1945. This can be related in large part to the predominance of two principles governing the provision of services during this period, identified by Kirkpatrick, Ackroyd, and Walker[19] as bureaucratic regulation and professional expertise. Both principles were founded on notions of hierarchy, the former in relation to organizational authority and the latter to workforce structure. In combination these different forms of hierarchy created a constraint or control over resources that significantly precluded the kinds of discretion and freedom of action needed to manage in a meaningful way.

Bureaucratic regulation emerged in the delivery of public services through monolithic structures, run according to clear and fixed rules dictating how resources were managed and how service users interfaced with the organization. The civil service was founded on a limited number of major government departments, which combined high-level policy-making with its low-level execution. The NHS was created as one of the largest employers in the world with around one million staff and run centrally by the Department of Health. Certainly, the delivery of public services in this way implied 'command and control', but it was predicated on more positive principles.[20] Bureaucratic organizations by virtue of their ordered structure and transparent procedures were viewed as ensuring the accountability essential to the provision of public-funded services and the 'fairness' needed to deal with external stakeholders, such as service users and internal stakeholders, particularly staff, in an equitable way.

Indeed, in the case of staff, the predominance of bureaucratic forms of organization in the public services was mirrored by a system of pay determination based on an equally centralized and rule-bound system known as the Whitley model.[21] Originally developed in the early years of the twentieth century, it became fully established post-1945, with separate national joint councils setting standard terms and conditions, primarily driven by the treatment of comparable staff in the private sector. This system not only provided 'fairness' by ensuring that public-sector workers doing similar jobs in any part of the country would be working under the same employment conditions but also helped account for pay increases by tying them to outside rates. Such a system provided little scope for local discretion in the management of staff, reflected in the fact that personnel or human resource specialists were typically labelled

'Establishment Officers', responsible simply for ensuring that the number of workers required by the organization to deliver the service were in place.

The centrality of professional expertise can be related to the circumstances surrounding the birth of the welfare state, and in particular the NHS in 1948. The settlement needed to bring especially the medical professions into this system not only provided potentially high rewards through the right to private practice in hospital pay beds but also ensured the continuation of a high degree of self-regulation by the professions.[22] This combination of high reward with self-regulation is succinctly captured by a system of performance pay awards for doctors instigated at the birth of the NHS. This was based on a peer review of performance and significantly boosted many doctors' pay.

The importance of expertise helped ensure that one of the strongest research streams at this time amongst those interested in public management focused on professionals. Initially viewed as being founded on socially functional traits,[23] professions increasingly came to be seen as contested and socially constructed. This led to a focus on 'professionalization' or the 'professional project'[24]—a power-driven process by which certain groups sought occupational 'closure' or control over entry, thus ensuring labour market privilege and the associated social status and economic rewards. It was a process heavily reliant on a mandate or licence from the state to undertake particular activities, but at the same time retained a degree of uncertainty as other occupations sought to challenge prevailing occupational jurisdiction.[25]

This interest in the professions has been sensitive to differences in the position of professional groups. For example, Etzioni viewed teachers, nurses, and social workers as 'semi-' or 'quasi-'professionals, unable to secure the same degree of closure as 'purer' professions in medicine and law.[26] More relevant was Johnson's suggestion that 'state professionals' assumed a distinctive form, being subject to a degree of political control and not, therefore, having the same degree of discretion over their activities as professionals elsewhere in society.[27] It was equally clear, however, that in a general sense, the emphasis on professional expertise under this model implied the importance of professional values and standards in determining the level and nature of service delivery. This was not to imply the absence of a management process, but it did suggest a management process where decisions were made on behalf of the service user as judged by the professional. It is an approach labelled by Ackroyd and colleagues as 'custodial management', a process where 'management sees itself primarily as the custodians of standards of service provision'.[28]

Markets

In the late 1970s, Britain's economic performance and circumstances challenged the sustainability of the post-war settlement on the welfare state, with the Callaghan Labour government of the time forced to cut public expenditure as a condition for receiving a loan from the International Monetary Fund.[29] However, to this economic expediency was added a more profound and sustained ideological assault on the welfare state when the Conservative government under Margaret Thatcher came to power in the 1979.

It would be a mistake to see this assault as solely driven by ideological values. These values were informed by a respectable academic school of thought, public choice theory, which, as already noted, viewed public servants as 'knaves' rather than 'knights'. For such theorists, the public-service bureaucracy was less the medium for the fair and transparent delivery of services than the site for 'rent-seeking and budget maximising bureaucrats to conspire to exploit the polity for their own ends'.[30] The Conservatives' ideological values were also underpinned by tangible fiscal and social pressures on public services, arising, for example, from the ageing of the population and advances in medical technology. Not only were demands for welfare services increasing, but there was also growing criticism of the quality of public-service provision and a perceived failure to meet citizens' expectations. Certainly the government was confronted with the difficult challenge of 'squaring the circle' of higher demand in a context of fiscal constraint.[31] This was a challenge shared with many developed countries that were also seeking to respond by reforming their public services.[3]

Nonetheless, there can equally be little doubt that an ideological fervour accounted for the particularly radical attempt to reshape the structure and operation of the public sector in Britain between 1979 and 1997 with significant implications for the nature and process of management. These changes in the management approach were captured by the notion of the New Public Management (NPM), seen by Hood[32] as comprising the following practices:

- Greater competition in service provision
- Disaggregation of units
- Hands-on professional management in the public sector
- Private-sector styles of management
- Tighter and more efficient use of resources
- Explicit standards and measures of performance
- Emphasis on output controls.

The NPM perspective has been viewed in different ways. It has variously been seen to present a set of policy prescriptions, to provide the basis for analysing developments in public-service reform, and to highlight trends in practice. In Britain, it is an approach that has undoubtedly been manifested in the development of public policy, although whether this policy has been 'successfully' implemented remains more of an open question.

The emphasis on competition signalled the emergence of markets as the preferred means of service delivery. It was given effect in various ways. Most dramatically, it saw the wholesale privatization of the nationalized industries and public utilities, effectively spinning them off into competitive product markets. At the end of the period of Conservative rule, more than a million and half jobs had been lost to the private sector, with the Royal Mail left as the only publicly owned national industry.[33] More insidiously, the government under the Local Government Planning and Land Act 1980 and the Local Government Act 1988 instituted a policy that required an increasing range of services to be put up for competitive tender. In-house providers were forced to compete with external, private-sector contractors, placing significant downward pressures on employee terms and conditions, as attempts were made to reduce costs.[34] It was a process that extended to ancillary services in the NHS and found its counterpart in market testing in the civil service. While in many instances contracts were won by in-house teams, this was a process that contributed to the 'hollowing-out' of the state[35] as it became an 'enabler', commissioning services from outside contractors rather than providing them itself. Finally, this reliance on markets was evident in the attempt to set up an internal market in the health service under the NHS and Community Care Act 1990. In the absence of a well-developed market for health care in Britain, competitive forces could be set loose only by establishing an internal purchaser–provider, health authorities and GP fund holders acting as the former, and hospitals, newly created as trusts, the latter.

The structural and operational changes to the public sector sought by the government flowed from this emphasis on markets. For public-sector organizations to compete effectively they needed discretion over their resources. The disaggregation of service units, with the creation of self-governing trusts in the NHS and the break-up of central government departments to establish executive agencies, was designed to provide these freedoms. Seen as better able to respond to discrete product market circumstances than the former monoliths, these units were given responsibility for key resources such as budgets and employees: NHS trusts, for example, became employers of their own staff, while civil service agencies were given delegated authority to determine the pay of their employees.

Disaggregation and devolution could not negate the ongoing need for political control and this in large part accounted for the development of more explicit performance standards and measures. If public-sector organizations were to be given discretion to compete, they still needed to be held to account, encouraging the development of a tighter audit framework.[36]

This framework was not, however, solely related to central control and accountability. The use of performance measures and targets was also associated with attempts to provide the kind of transparency needed for service users, as consumers, to make informed choices. This was apparent, for example, in the Thatcher government's introduction of a league table for mapping school performance. The league table was designed to help parents choose the 'best schools'. In a more general sense, it was reflected in the Citizens' Charter formulated by the Major government in 1991, seeking to safeguard 'customer rights' to quality public services.

This elevation of 'user rights' can, in turn, be seen as part of the government's project to wrest control of the public services from producers. The attempt to develop a cadre of professional managers in the public services was clearly compatible with a market orientation, which called on the management rather than the administration of resources to ensure 'competitive success'. But the emergence of the manager also constituted a threat to the authority of the professional and 'custodial management'. Senior managers were expected to be change agents, recruited on short-term contracts with substantially higher salaries, but required to achieve demanding performance targets.[37] The numbers employed as general managers dramatically rose; between 1985 and 1995 the number of employees categorized as NHS managers, for example, increased from 300 to more than 23,000.[19]

This was accompanied by a vilification of professional groups by the government and a more general attack on the producer interest reflected in attempts to undermine trade union power, apparent in the year-long miners' strike of 1983–4 and the symbolically significant derecognition of the trade unions at GCHQ in 1984. Government hostility towards employees had significant costs in terms of staff attitudes and behaviours. Kirkpatrick, Ackroyd, and Walker[19] have highlighted findings from the UK's 1998 Workplace Employment Relations Survey, which showed that public-sector workers were more likely than employees in the private sector to experience stress and be absent through illness.[38] Equally significant were the detrimental consequences for recruitment and retention, particularly amongst professional groups, such as nurses, social workers, and teachers: between 1995 and 1999, the number of applications to social work fell by 55 per cent.[39]

During this period, the interest shown by the public management research community in professionals was sustained, with particular attention being given to potential tensions between these groups and general managers. The early NPM literature noted the capacity of professional groups, such as medical staff, to resist the budgetary goals associated with NPM, but as these policies became more embedded it was often suggested that professional staff had fared less well in terms of their power, authority, and status.[40] As these developments unfolded, research suggested a more nuanced picture. Senior managers had become increasingly reliant on professionals to deliver on central government targets and professional control of services remained strong.[19] Nonetheless, professional roles had altered and in the NHS professional staff had been required to undertake more managerial work.

The challenge to professional values was reinforced by the weight placed on private-sector management practices. The importance attached to such practices was reflected in the use of high-profile private-sector businessmen to review and recommend on operational changes, for instance the Rayner Reviews in the civil service and the Griffith Report, which in the early 1980s led to the establishment of a general management structure in NHS. It was reflected in attempts to import certain private-sector management techniques, the most obvious being individual performance-related pay (PRP). The British government was not alone in seeking to introduce PRP. Many governments, including those in Canada, the Netherlands, New Zealand, Sweden, and the USA, adopted PRP in some form from the 1980s.[41] It had a number of apparent attractions. First, characterized by standard pay rates and service-related increments, traditional pay systems were perceived as weak tools for the management of employee performance. PRP was viewed as fostering individual motivation by establishing a link between achievement and rewards. Second, PRP was seen as a means to establish tighter control of the pay bill by reducing across-the-board pay increases and annual increments and, instead, targeting pay increases at high performers. Third, PRP had a political objective in demonstrating that public-sector workers were not unaccountable and only receive pay increases linked to performance.[41]

However, the introduction of PRP, particularly in Britain, again proved far from straightforward. While the government was able to introduce PRP into the civil service where it remained the direct employer, its application to the health service and local government was limited. In the civil service, it is questionable whether PRP was effective. In terms of pay bill control, there was such a strong expectation amongst employees of an across-the-board cost-of-living increase that any attempt to use PRP to motivate employees required supplementary funding to the existing pay bill. Research that examined PRP in the UK Inland Revenue Department cast major doubts on the motivational effects of such schemes.[42] Adopting the tenets of expectancy theory, the authors found that PRP was unlikely to motivate public servants. The setting of tangible performance objectives for public servants is difficult given the range of stakeholders they have to serve and the nature of their work; the clarity of the link between such objectives and pay is likely to be poor given various pay constraints; and typically civil servants place less weight on pay relative to other rewards, especially where the amounts of performance pay available are small.

Networks

More recently, the NPM has lost some of its potency and its contradictions have become more visible.[43] This shift of perspective is exemplified in recent OECD publications, which reassert the distinctive character of the public management and by implication suggests that the NPM was not sensitive enough to it:

While it is important to have better goals, targets and measures in government, we must recognise that such a highly formalised approach has severe limitations for complex activities.... There is a danger that the constitutional, legal, cultural and leadership factors which together create what is important and distinctive about public services and the people who work in them, are not considered or, worse, are dismissed as the bureaucratic problem which must be 'reformed'.[44]

If the traditional organizational logic in the public sector was based on bureaucracy and that under NPM was founded on markets, the emergent managerial form is seen as being underpinned by networks. This emphasis represents a shift from 'government' to 'governance', focusing on who makes public decisions and how these decisions are implemented to safeguard constitutional values. Governance signals that a wider range of agencies and stakeholders from within and beyond the public sector are becoming involved in service delivery. In Britain, this approach coincided with the 1997 election of a New Labour government, which has chosen to emphasize three closely related features of public-service reform or 'modernization':

- An emphasis on person-centred services
- The pursuit of a 'partnership' approach
- An increased emphasis on service quality and performance

The emphasis on user- rather than producer-driven services has been strengthened and increasingly pushed to the fore by the government. As the Prime Minister asserted in his introduction to the White Paper on community social and health-care services, *Our Health, Our Care, Our Say*:

These proposals . . . will allow us to accelerate the move into a new era where the service is designed around the patient rather than the needs of the patient being forced to fit around the service already provided.[45]

In seeking to give effect to this notion of person-centred services, the government has emphasized such principles as 'choice', 'independence', and 'voice'. There has been considerable debate about whether genuine choice is possible in the public services given finite capacity and underdeveloped markets or indeed whether users, preferring universal access to a high standard of localized state provision, really want it. However, the government has sought to give some substance to the notion of 'choice' through such mechanisms as direct payments and individual budgets, which provide users with the funds to purchase their own care. 'Independence' is designed to allow those with long-term conditions and the elderly to remain within their communities, an approach facilitated by helping users manage their own conditions and by the growing public policy emphasis on intermediate and primary care. While 'voice' is geared towards involving service users in the delivery of care, taking the form of user participation in and the development of effective user networks and interest groups and their inclusion in the selection and training of professionals.[46]

This person-centred approach has been founded on various sorts of partnership arrangements with or bargains between different sort of stakeholders. The first of these bargains has been that between the state and the service users. While under NPM the emphasis was on individual consumer entitlement to services, there has been a shift in emphasis within service charters towards collective, civic obligations.[47] In other words, users as citizens rather than consumers have responsibilities (e.g. for their health) as well as rights, perhaps reducing a concern that aggrieved 'customers' will take out their dissatisfaction directly on public-sector workers, a justifiable worry taking account of increases in violence against front-line public-sector workers.

The second has been a bargain between the service user and the professional. The public suspicion of professional expertise has arguably continued with high-profile examples coming to light of what often appear to be professional failure, such as at Alder Hay where a medical practitioner retained children's organs without parental permission and as in the Victoria Climbié case, where a child in need was let down by so many public agencies with tragic consequences.[48] However, policymakers have been seeking a new relationship between users and professionals based on a shared interest in the user's well-being. The government has sought to reinforce the position of the professional as a means of increasing user confidence and trust. This has been apparent in a strengthening of professional regulation. Regulatory bodies such as the General Teaching Council and the General Social Care Council have been set up, requiring teachers and social workers to register on gaining approved graduate qualifications and committing them to formal codes of practice. Moreover, a 'new professionalism' has been promoted with the professional less of an 'expert' telling the user what is 'best' for him or her and more as 'advocate' or 'navigator' helping him or her to make the 'right' decisions on care.[49,50]

The third bargain has been between the state and its employees. The government has moved away from crude attempts to weaken professional and employee interests in the public services as means of wresting control from producers, recognizing that staff might better serve users if they are well treated rather than vilified. On its website the NHS now proudly proclaims itself a 'model employer'; as it notes, 'A management style that is both involving and facilitating will result in NHS staff feeling more valued, which benefits patients in turn.' It is an approach that also has a practical rationale: ongoing professional shortages have required an attractive public-sector employment package to recruit and retain them. Such an approach has, for example, been reflected in the NHS's new pay and grading arrangements as set out in Agenda for Change, which involves a re-evaluation of jobs, addressing equal pay concerns, while providing new earnings and career opportunities. The more supportive treatment of staff, however, comes at a 'price', typically in the form of employee commitment to work in new and more flexibly ways. This bargain is neatly captured by the title of the NHS's human resources plan, 'More Staff Working Differently'.[51] It is further reflected in the education sector where the Workload Agreement was reached between government, local government employers, and the trade unions in 2003. This has reduced administrative 'burdens' on teachers by delegating them to teaching assistants, but only on the condition that they accept the introduction of a new grade, the Higher Level Teaching Assistant, an 'unqualified' post that breaks the teachers' monopoly over whole class responsibilities.[52]

The fourth bargain is between organizations in the provision of public services. Within the public sector, this inter-organizational working has been equated with a 'joined-up' approach within government, but it has also embraced joint working between organizations in the public, independent, and private sectors.[53] These forms of partnership mark a retreat from key elements of the NPM approach with a reliance on dis-aggregated service units, giving way to a greater emphasis on integrated working. Moreover, the privileging of market forces and private-sector practices now succumbs to a more pragmatic, mixed approach where 'What works best is used.' Various examples are available of these dif-ferent forms of partnership. The most controversial is the Public Finance Initiative. Introduced by the Major government in 1992 but embraced on a grander scale by New Labour, this initiative provides a way of funding major capital investment through the involvement of private-sector consortia without immediate recourse to the public purse. While these projects are typically delivered on time,[54] they are viewed as more expensive, creating medium- and longer-term budgetary pressures. Part-nerships within the public sector also appear to be widespread. Sullivan and Skelcher[55] have identified some 5,500 individual partnership bodies at local and regional level across Britain clustering around sixty types of policy area, including health improvement, regeneration, community safety, and child development.

Inter-organizational working, whether within the public sector or between the public, private, and voluntary sectors, creates a new range of managerial issues and challenges. Inevitably different, often conflicting, organizational cultures need to be managed. A contrast is often drawn between the 'medical' and the 'social care' models of welfare provision, the former top-down, based on authoritative decisions by senior practi-tioners, the latter bottom-up, more inclusive and consensual. As health–social care partnerships have developed, particularly with the growth of community-based care, clashes between these contrasting cultures have had to be addressed.[56] More practical problems have arisen in dealing with different working procedures. Health and social care organizations again often vary in their referral and assessment criteria, necessitating alignment to ensure agreement on who is to be seen and how they are to be treated. Such procedural difficulties have extended to the treatment of workers, with staff from across the public services working jointly, but covered by a range of collective agreement and therefore on varied terms and conditions of employment.[46]

If the partnership principle, manifest in this range of bargains between different stakeholders, represents the novel and distinctive feature of the network model, then the emphasis on organizational performance and service quality represents 'the most significant line of continuity with New

Public Management'.[57] Certainly, there has been a move away from a reliance on the discipline of the market to manage performance. But this has been countered by the development of a much stronger regulatory framework to ensure efficiency and effectiveness. This is illustrated in the case of local government where CCT has largely been replaced by a Best Value regime where authorities benchmark the cost and quality of their services and are assessed accordingly by the Audit Commission. In 2002 this was complemented by the Comprehensive Performance Assessment (CPA), a more integrated, structured, and systematic evaluation of service delivery in local government again managed by the Audit Commission. This process finds its counterpart in the rating system in the NHS, which until recently saw the Healthcare Commission awarding trusts stars on the basis of performance against a range of targets.

The reinforcement of the regulatory framework has again affected the management agenda, in particular causing some tensions with other elements of New Labour's modernization programme.[57] The pursuit of a wide range of performance targets and the preparation for regular inspections have been extremely resource intensive in terms of time and energy. The administrative burden associated with servicing this performance culture has increased employee workload, weakened morale, and created recruitment and retention difficulties, outcomes that have undermined the attempt to develop a more positive relationship with staff. The Audit Commission found that 'half of the former public-sector workers we surveyed said that too much bureaucracy and paperwork was the most important reason why they left',[11] with employees often 'citing too many targets' as a key contributory factor. Indeed, Guest and Conway[58] have confirmed that 'levels of satisfaction, trust and commitment are all lower in the public than the private sector.' More generally, such targets have also been seen as distorting organizational priorities, sometimes to the detriment of service users, while complicating arrangements for inter-organizational working in not being sensitive enough to partnership outcomes.[57]

Summary and Conclusions

Despite early debates on whether the context, processes, techniques, and outcomes of management in public sector were distinctive, public management has over the last forty years developed strongly as a field of study. Certainly, interest in the management of public-sector organizations remains diffuse, engaging academics, policymakers, and practitioners from a range of different communities. However, interest has tended

	Hierarchies	Markets	Networks
Professionals	*Controller*	*Defender*	*Supporter*
Service Users	*Recipient*	*Consumer*	*Citizen*
The State	*Provider*	*Contractor*	*Regulator*
Managers	*Administrator*	*Leader*	*Facilitator*

FIG. 6.1 Models of public-service delivery and the stakeholder consequences

to coalesce around the management issues and challenges generated by three successive models of public coordination and delivery based on hierarchies, markets, and networks. This chapter has mapped those issues and challenges, highlighting the consequences for the main stakeholders in public-sector organizations: the state, managers, professionals, and service users. Figure 6.1 summarizes the different ways these stakeholders have been conceived under these models and, by implication, how they have been treated and acted.

As can be seen, a model founded on hierarchy recognized the state as a major provider of services, ensuring organizational performance through conformity to well-established procedural rules and, therefore, restricting the manager to an administrator and the user to a passive recipient of universal benefits and services. In such circumstances, the control of resources lay with the professional who relied on his or her expertise to act as 'custodian' of the users' interest. A market-driven model saw the emergence of the New Public Management, which relied on the discipline of the market to guarantee performance. Here the role of the state narrowed to one of contracting services from in-house and external providers, elevating the public-sector manager to a leader able to inspire efficiency and effectiveness in response to the demands of a more active consumer and at the expense of the 'self-serving' professional. The contemporary network model has involved a much more inclusive approach, which recognizes the range of agencies and stakeholders required to deliver public services. It sees the state as providing the regulatory framework needed to ensure high-quality service performance and is founded on mutuality between different parties, so allowing professionals to support users, ensuring that citizens recognize their civil responsibilities as well as their rights to services, and helping managers facilitate inter-organizational working. The form taken by the next model of public service remains open to debate, but it will no doubt generate a new set of management issues and necessitate an ongoing interest in public management.

In conclusion, nine issues can be identified as candidates for future research:

1. *Context*: A more sophisticated notion of the role of context on action is required. A great deal of the work in this area views context as a set of static and independent variables. There are three difficulties with such a unidirectional view of context. First, organizations, groups, and individuals are portrayed as passive recipients subject to aspects of context that shape behaviour, but with no leeway in choosing which aspects of context to bring into the organization and with no influence with which they could reshape context. Second, these contexts are somehow separated out rather than treated as an 'integrated configuration'. Third, such a view implies a static view of context, that is, context is seen as a particular setting at a particular point in time, rather than as evolving and changing over time. A final general observation is that the ways in which actors interact with and mobilize aspects of context is underplayed and is often not treated in a sustained way.

2. *Collaboration*: Inter-organizational collaboration, partnership, and integration are dominant themes of the new arrangements for the public sector. Understanding how collaborative arrangements form, hold together, and perform in whatever policy context exists is critical.

3. *Multiple Actors*: The public sector is a crowded field with a wide range of organizations and interest groups within it, often with different priorities and agendas. The research 'spotlight' has fallen rather unevenly on these different groups and actors, although the future development of the public services raises key issues for all of them.

   • *Professionals*: The most sustained attention has been given to professionals; however, as a 'user-centred' reform agenda challenging their expertise gathers pace, research will be needed on how and whether professionals have managed to retain their values, identity, working practices, and associated labour market privileges.

   • *Other Types of Worker*: The concentration on professionals has often been at the expense of research on other groups of employees. One such group, assuming increasing importance in the public services over recent years, has been support workers. A recent estimate suggested that around a million employees could be classified as support workers in social and health care alone.[59] Some research has been undertaken to further explore the structure and consequences of these roles in education and social care.[60,61] Ongoing work on other support roles, for example a study on health-care assistants being undertaken by the authors, suggests the value of further work on the non-qualified public-service employees.

- *Service Users*: The development of 'person-centred' services also encourages future research on another neglected group, service users themselves. Clarke et al.'s notion of the 'citizen-consumer' has sought to capture public policy assumptions on how customers might engage with public services, with its emphasis on the balance between user rights and responsibilities.[62] However, future user involvement in service delivery and design, ranging from a strengthening of user voice with the development of more powerful consumer networks to users acting as direct employers in their own right (see ref. 46), is worthy of further study.

4. *New Ways of Working*: Many public-sector innovations seek to disturb divisions of labour traditionally agreed across occupational groups. The boundaries between these groups are often very difficult to cross in practice. Attending to such inter-group issues and studying what organizational capabilities need to be developed for improved multi-occupational working could yield important insights.

5. *Regulation and the Management of Risk*: Public servants have always worked with the most needy and vulnerable members of the community—the sick, the elderly, and the young. However, shifting job boundaries combined with high-profile, often tragic instances of failure to protect such groups encourages a public policy and research focus on managing risk. It is striking, for example, that the use of non-qualified workers in social care, education, and health has been unregulated beyond basic (and sometimes flawed) attempts to make criminal checks[60,59] At the time of writing, a pilot scheme to regulate health-care support workers in Scotland is in progress. There is considerable scope for research on how service and work-force regulation unfolds.

6. *Improved Understanding of What Makes a Receptive Context for Change*: A better understanding of the core participating influences in achieving change is critical. This agenda has probably been best tackled in heath care where the following factors have been identified:

- The availability and engagement of local, credible, and skilled opinion leaders
- The foundation of prior relationships, especially between different clinical groups and between different clinicians and managers

- The historical development of the services that influence current organization
- The structural characteristics of the location; the complexity, volume, and configuration of the various organizational components; the skills available; the change management and project management capacity within the stakeholder groups
- The support of the senior management, though this may be at a distance.

Identifying factors for other areas of the public sector would also be useful.

7. *Emergent Outcomes*: Given the developing complexity of the public sector, it is likely that there will be a number of unplanned and unanticipated outcomes. Such outcomes and the processes that lead up to them are potentially fruitful areas for further research.

8. *New Organizational Forms*: Researchers will eagerly be seeking to identify and perhaps contribute to debates on the organizational principles likely to succeed 'networks' as the means of coordinating the delivery of public services. The 'best bet' for the next key organizational form is perhaps a 'social enterprise', a not-for-profit form of organization operating on business lines, but with social objectives and based on the assumption that any surplus will be ploughed back into the endeavour. It is a business model that could be readily transferred to the delivery of certain public services with some interesting implications for governance and future funding.

9. *Longitudinal Studies*: A reading of the issues for further research indicates the need for longer-term research strategies. This is not to say that research with shorter timescales is not of value but that there is an absence of longer-term research that might more adequately inform thinking about these complicated areas.

References

1. R. Baker, 'Organization Theory and the Public Sector', *Journal of Management Studies*, 6/1(1969): 15–32.
2. P. Drucker, 'Managing the Public Service Institution', *Public Interest*, 33(Autumn 1973): 43–55.
3. C. Pollitt and G. Bouckaert, *Public Management Reform* (Oxford: Oxford University Press, 2004).
4. G. Stoker (ed.), *The New Management of British Local Governance* (Basingstoke, UK: Palgrave, 1999).

5. M. D. Fottler, 'Is Management Really Generic?', *Academy of Management Review*, 6/1(Jan.1981): 1–12.

6. J. Whorton and J. Worthley, 'A Perspective on the Challenge of Public Management', *Academy of Management Review*, 6/3(1981): 257–361.

7. J. Perry and H. Rainey, 'The Public–Private Distinction in Organisation Theory: A Critique and Research Strategy', *Academy of Management Review*, 13/2(1988): 182–201.

8. M. Murray, 'Comparing Public and Private Management: An Exploratory Essay', *Public Administration Review*, 35/4(1975): 364–71.

9. P. Ring and J. Perry, 'Strategic Management in Public and Private Organizations: Implications of Distinctive Contexts and Constraints', *Academy of Management Review*, 10/2(1985): 276–86.

10. P. Ingraham et al., 'Public Employment and the Future of Public Service', in G. Peters and D. Savoie (eds.), *Governance in the Twenty-First Century* (Montreal: Canadian Centre for Management Development, 2000).

11. Audit Commission, *Recruitment and Retention* (London: Audit Commission, 2002); ibid. 22–3.

12. OECD, *Highlights of Public Sector Pay and Employment Trends: 2002 Update* (Paris: OECD, 2002), 5–6.

13. J. Le Grand, *Motivation, Agency, and Public Policy* (Oxford: Oxford University Press, 2003).

14. W. Niskanen, *Bureaucracy and Representative Government* (Chicago, IL: Aldine-Atherton, 1971).

15. J. Perry and L. Porter, 'Factors Affecting the Context for Motivation in Public Organizations', *Academy of Management Review*, 7(1982), 89–98.

16. P. Crewson, 'Public Service Motivation: Building Empirical Evidence of the Incidence and Effect', *Journal of Public Administration Research and Theory*, 7(1997): 499–518.

17. J. Coyle Shapiro and I. Kessler, *Beyond Exchange* (Paper presented to the Academy of Management, New Orleans, 2004).

18. T. Clark and A. Dilnot, *Long Term Trends in British Taxation and Spending* (Briefing Note, 25; London: Institute of Fiscal Studies, 2002).

19. I. Kirkpatrick, S. Ackroyd, and R. Walker, *The New Managerialism and Public Service Professions* (Basingstoke, UK: Palgrave Macmillan, 2005).

20. P. Du Gay, 'Entrepreneurial Governance and Public Management: The Anti-Bureaucrats', in J. Clarke, S. Gewirtz, and E. McLaughlin (eds.), *New Managerialism. New Welfare?* (London: Sage, 2000).

21. P. Beaumont, *Public Sector Industrial Relations* (London: Routledge, 1992).

22. R. Klein, *The Politics of the NHS* (2nd edn.; Harlow, UK: Longman, 1989), 20–1.

23. K. MacDonald, *The Sociology of the Professions* (London: Sage, 1995).

24. M. Larson, *The Rise of Professionals: A Sociological Analysis* (London: University of California Press, 1977).

25. A. Abbott, *The System of the Professions* (Chicago: University of Chicago Press, 1988).

26. A. Etzioni, *The Semi Professionals and Their Organization* (New York: Free Press, 1969).
27. T. Johnson, *Professions and Power* (London: Macmillan, 1972).
28. S. Ackroyd, J. Hughes, and K. Soothill, 'Public Sector Services and Their Management', *Journal of Management Studies*, 26/6(1989): 603–19.
29. M. Haron, *British Labour Government and the 1976 IMF Crisis* (Basingstoke, UK: Palgrave, 1997).
30. K. Meier and G. Hill, 'Bureaucracy in the Twenty-First Century', in E. Ferlie, L. Lynne, and C. Pollitt (eds.), *Oxford Handbook of Public Management* (Oxford: Oxford University Press, 2005).
31. C. Foster and F. Plowden, *The State Under Stress* (Buckingham, UK: Open University Press, 1996).
32. C. Hood, 'A Public Management for all Seasons', *Public Administration*, 69/1(1991): 3–19.
33. S. Kessler and F. Bayliss, *Contemporary British Industrial Relations* (Basingstoke, UK: Macmillan, 1992), 133.
34. K. Escott and D. Whitfield, *The Gender Impact of CCT in Local Government* (London: HMSO, 1995).
35. C. Skelcher, 'Changed Images of the State: Overloaded, Hollowed Out, Congested', *Public Policy and Administration*, 15/3(2000): 3–19.
36. M. Power, *The Audit Society* (Oxford: Oxford University Press, 1997).
37. E. Ferlie, 'Quasi Strategy: Strategic Management in the Contemporary Public Sector', in A. Pettigrew, H. Thomas, and R. Whittington (eds.), *Handbook of Strategy and Management* (London: Sage, 2002).
38. M. Culley, *Britain at Work* (London: Routledge, 1999).
39. TOPSS, *London Workforce Survey and Partnership Mapping Analysis* (London: TOPSS, 2003).
40. K. McLaughlin, S. Obsorne, and E. Ferlie (eds.), *New Public Management: Current Trends and Future Prospects* (London: Routledge, 2002).
41. OECD, *Policy Brief: Paying for Performance: Policies for Government Employees* (Paris: OECD, 2005).
42. D. Marsden and R. Richardson, 'Performance Pay: The Effects of Merit Pay on Motivation in the Public Services', *British Journal of Industrial Relations*, 32/2(1994): 243–61.
43. C. Hood and G. Peters, 'The Middle Ageing of New Public Management: Into the Age of Paradox', *Journal of Public Administration Research and Theory*, 14/3(2004): 267–82.
44. OECD, *Policy Brief: Public Sector Modernization* (Paris: OECD, 2003), 4–5.
45. Department of Health, *Our Health, Our Care, Our Say* (London: HMSO, 2006) 1.
46. I. Kessler and S. Bach, *Skills for Care. New Types of Worker Project: Evaluation Report* (Leeds: Skills for Care, 2007).
47. G. Drewry, 'Citizen's Charters: Service Quality Chameleons', *Public Management Review*, 7/3(2005): 321–40.

48. Lord Laming, *The Victoria Climbié Inquiry* (London: HMSO, 2003).
49. S. Banks, 'Professional Ethics in Social Work—What Future?', *British Journal of Social Work*, 28(1998): 213–31.
50. J. Harris, 'State Social Work and Social Citizenship in Britain', *British Journal of Social Work*, 29/9(1999): 915–37.
51. Department of Health, *More Staff Working Differently* (London: HMSO, 2002).
52. S. Bach, I. Kessler, and P. Heron, 'Changing Job Boundaries and Workforce Reform: The Case of the Teaching Assistant', *Industrial Relations Journal*, 37/1(2006): 2–21.
53. V. Bogdanor, *Joined-Up Government* (Oxford: British Academy Press, 2005).
54. National Audit Office, *PFI Construction Performance Report* (London: National Audit Office, 2003).
55. H. Sullivan and C. Skelcher, *Working Across Boundaries* (Basingstoke, UK: Palgrave, 2002).
56. S. Snape and P. Taylor, *Partnerships between Health and Local Government* (London: CASS, 2004).
57. J. Newman, 'Beyond the New Public Management? Modernizing Public Services', in J. Clarke et al. (eds.), *New Managerialism. New Welfare?* (London: Sage, 2000).
58. D. Guest and N. Conway, *The State of the Psychological Contract* (London: CIPD, 2002).
59. M. Saks and J. Allsop, 'Social Policy, Professional Regulation and Health Support Work in the UK', *Social Policy and Society*, 6/2(2007): 165–77.
60. I. Kessler, S. Bach, and P. Heron, 'Understanding Assistant Roles in Social Care', *Work, Employment and Society*, 20/4(2006): 667–85.
61. I. Kessler, S. Bach, and P. Heron, 'Comparing Assistants' Roles in Education and Social Care', *International Journal of Human Resource Management*, 18/9(forthcoming).
62. J. Clarke et al., *Creating Citizen-Consumers: Changing Identities in the Remaking of Public Services* (London: Sage, 2007).

7

Professional Service Firms: The Challenges of Innovation

Tim Morris

Over the last two decades professional service firms (PSFs) have come to the forefront of economic activity, growing rapidly on the back of the global liberalization of markets. The largest of them now generate billions of dollars in annual revenues and are geographically more widely spread than most multinational corporations. They are also politically as well as economically influential. PSFs play a crucial role in virtually all areas of business activity, brokering commercial transactions; facilitating the restructuring of industries, new modes of capital formation, and new ownership forms such as the privatization of public sector assets; and transferring models of capitalism. They influence the nature of regulatory as well as statutory frameworks through which commerce is carried out. As Sharma has put it: 'Without PSFs, business as we know it, would come to a grinding halt.'[1] In a world in which knowledge or expertise has become an important resource and base of competitive advantage for firms (and for nations),[2] these firms are held up as models of wider changes to the economy and leading indicators of the ways in which management structures and processes will evolve.[3,4]

Ironically, PSFs have also been among the biggest beneficiaries of legislative controls triggered by concern with their own activities. Post-Enron, the Sarbanes-Oxley Act actually prompted a rapid period of growth in activity for the audit practices of the accounting firms. They built new practices and lucrative revenue streams to provide advice on how to meet the regulatory requirements arising from that legislation. Not surprisingly, these firms have influenced the regulation of their own activities as well by working with law makers and regulators. There is therefore little doubt that PSFs have become among the most significant players in the global economic system and active participants in the political processes by which this system evolves. And as their significance has grown, so has their notoriety: the demise of Arthur Andersen is the best known example of the sort of publicity that they attract, but other sorts of PSFs, notably the consulting giants and lawyers, have also come in for criticism for their roles, methods, fees, and consequences.[5] Such is the price of success.

No account of how management and business has changed over the last five decades would be complete without attention to PSFs. They have not, however, all pursued the same strategies: some have stuck with their own core expertise, such as law firms; others, such as the accounting giants, have diversified their activities relentlessly into related areas of expertise so that there are now questions as to whether we can think of them either as unified organizations rather than as loose networks under a single brand or as any different from the major corporations for whom they work. That is important because what has driven much of the research interest in these organizations has been the notion that they are distinctive in form and in terms of their goals. I explain more about this below.

In a single chapter it would be impossible to do justice to all of the themes mentioned above and in what follows I have a more modest agenda: to outline how the study of PSFs has evolved particularly with reference to their management models and forms. I argue that research has largely been concerned with their internal workings rather than their external influence, even though what has driven policy and public interest has been their growing size, scale, and influence. I explain how I became involved in the study of these organizations and the areas where I have contributed to what has become a rather wide research area and finally I offer some ideas about where research will go in the future—suggesting that it should focus more on the links between the nature of change in these organizations and their role in society and in the global economic system.

Background

The generic term PSF now embraces a wide variety of organizations, as work in this area has expanded and the firms themselves have become more common and more complex. Early studies (see below) focused on accounting and law firms where formally accredited professionals worked and a proportion of the producers, namely the partners, typically owned the firm. Thus, PSFs had two core characteristics in their purest form: a partnership form of ownership and producers who had a formal professional accreditation. These characteristics contributed to the distinctive nature of these firms. In management terms, an important way in which a PSF differed from a corporation was in the relative decentralization of power and control, which is dispersed among partners responsible for various clients and practices. This dispersion limits the ability of the central management of a PSF to exercise strong control over strategic initiatives.[6,7]

Gradually, the distinctiveness of the PSF has become blurred. First, the nature of ownership and governance has changed. Partnership in its ideal form implied co-ownership and carried with it several rights, notably to information about the firm and its activities and performance, plus governance or decision rights in the conduct of the firm. In other words, the partner was a producer, owner, and manager of resource decision. In smaller firms, this sort of pure peer control system was clearly possible, even if in practice there were variations around the ideal. As firms have grown, however, partner rights have become attenuated. Partners' shares of the total equity not only may be so limited as to make their economic power minimal, but they may well have given up many rights to information and control over the day-to-day running of the firm or have little individual influence over its broad direction, even if a formal partnership meeting still exists to discuss and ratify a strategy. In addition, there has been a trend to some form of incorporation, notably by use of the limited liability partnership form of ownership in recent years; principally it seems as a defensive device against the risk of litigation. What effect that has had on governance processes remains unclear, but it may be that it has accelerated the move to a more corporate style of governance.

Some former partnerships have undertaken public flotations, notably Accenture and the investment banks, in the latter instance to generate capital for the business. Others have long been in public ownership, such as the advertising firms. Still others have been acquired by publicly owned corporations, such as IBM's purchase of PwC's consulting arm. Again, while theory suggests that the move to public ownership would have important effects on the governance and management of a PSF, for example, by enforcing shorter-term financial goals consistent with the quarterly reporting requirements of a public corporation, the evidence here on any differences stemming from public ownership as opposed to a partnership of some form is so far unclear.

Second, the notion of which occupations qualify as professions has become blurred. As will be clear already, we no longer simply discuss the formal professions, but now include a range of occupations with quasi-professional status or with no desire to pursue the traditional traits of the professions. This reflects a wider sociological recognition that the term professional is itself so contested. Narrow definitions of expertise based on formal accreditation, membership of a professional body, and adherence to a set of ethical standards have long been challenged.[8] More contemporary theories have seen the concept of profession not in terms of a set of traits but as a strategy by an occupational group to assert status and material rights.[9] Thus, theories focus on professionalizing processes: the ways occupations seek to monopolize particular areas of work by claims to expertise that clients find persuasive, while being open to challenge by other occupations when such professional jurisdictions are seen to be attractive in status and material terms. Perhaps the arena of medicine is the best example of this process, but in the business professions it is also an important feature. Importantly, not all groups seek to assert the privileged position of the profession by accreditation. Some may simply rely on market power and knowledge: the occupations that have emerged around the computing and communications industries or some of the media-based occupations would be exemplars.[10]

Generally, this change in the way we think about professions has also influenced definitions of the boundaries of the PSF field. In addition, there has been an expansion in what is called the knowledge economy, namely the set of economic activities that are based on the exchange of information or expertise, and this has fuelled the growth of new groups of PSFs and new practices within existing firms. Consequently, use of the term knowledge-based (or knowledge-intensive) firms has become widespread, including software and other types of media-related firms.[11,12] This group clearly overlaps the PSF footprint.

Getting some order back into this definitional confusion is difficult. It is evident that the boundary of this field is unclear and becoming more so. Routinely, when we use the term PSF we are grouping together the largest accounting/business service firms such as PwC with the smallest architectural practice. There are similarities, notably around the notion that they compete on the basis of supplying some intangible, expertise-based, and quite complex service, which is likely to have both product (an audit or an architect's drawing) and process (delivering an audit; developing the plans for a building) in which the client plays some role, or 'co-produces'. There are also important differences. These include, as well as size and scale of firm, the nature of the expertise (creative or more formally accredited); the extent to which the firm relies on non-human capital as well as human capital to compete (investment banks clearly need not only good quality human capital but also access to financial capital to compete; other PSFs say they do not formally own their assets who 'go down the elevator each night'); type of client and therefore the extent to which the product or service is relatively routine and standardized (mortgage contracts for private house buyers) or highly customized and complex (innovative tax advice for large corporations); the formal professional status of the producers; and the role of the client in the production process.[13]

One way to address the definitional quagmire is by funnelling the PSFs field from the broadest definition to the most parsimonious. Thus, at one extreme we have all firms that trade on their know-how including software, advertising or executive search firms, whether incorporated or not; at the other we have the unincorporated partnerships of formally accredited professions such as law providing the most customized products to corporate clients.[13] These differences make the job of producing generalizable theories or even propositions that might provide the foundations for theory difficult. They also make comparative analysis between professions and between sectors (or even within them) complicated— how do we speak meaningfully of the accounting sector for instance? Nonetheless, more qualified theorizing about particular issues, themes, and problems that affect all or part of this field does still seem possible and appropriate. I illustrate this in reference to my own work below.

Before discussing the management of these firms, it is worth noting that there has also developed a stream of work that expresses concern about their role and influence. Such work reflects the sheer growth and success of PSFs over the last five decades. Here, I simply summarize some of this work as it is beyond the scope of this chapter. First, there has been concern about the risks for clients that occur because their professional advisers have an expertise advantage. Of course, such expertise is the reason the adviser is hired in the first place, but it may open the door to poor advice or unscrupulous behaviour such as 'mis-selling'. While this is meant to be mitigated by the requirement that professionals adhere to professional standards and codes of ethics, the critical view is that these standards have either never really existed or have not been policed properly by the professions themselves. A variation on this sort of argument is that commercial pressures on individual professionals or professional firms have increased through the opening up of many professional activities to marketized relationships and through the adoption by firms themselves of more aggressive 'corporatized' modes of managing. These modes involve the introduction or extension of performance management methods that require individual professionals to pursue stretching targets and, in the process, risk putting short-term commercial gain over professional standards. Or, professionals decline to offer advice that the client finds unpalatable because of the risk that the relationship will finish; thus, the professional becomes 'captured' by the client with concomitant risks for owners and other stakeholders that the executives employing these advisers may stifle proper outside evaluation. Where there is an asymmetric knowledge relationship between professional and client it becomes difficult for the latter to know if the advice the latter is receiving is the most appropriate or is delivered in the most cost effective way.

Second—and relatedly—there have been critiques of the basic effectiveness of professional work, particularly in the arena of consulting advice. One line of criticism here suggests much of what passes as expert advice is either little more than common sense or standardized 'cookie-cutter' work, rehashed from client to client with little appreciation of the different contexts in which clients operate. This sort of critique raises questions about why clients employ professional advisers and it has to be recognized that the consultant–client relationship is complex: corporations may genuinely seek outside advice to solve a pressing problem, which is the textbook explanation for using a professional adviser. But the client may also hire outside expertise for other reasons, including simply the need for an extra pair of hands. Clients may have a clear idea of the sort of solution they expect from the consultant *ex ante*. They may employ consultants to rubber stamp a decision or as reinforcements in an internal political battle where they expect a particular point of view to be expressed.

Third, a different sort of research has critically analysed the roles that some of the largest professional firms play in the political arena through lobbying, seeking to influence the structure and operations of regulatory regimes and elected representatives (e.g. Roberts). All of this research reflects an assumption that professionals and professional firms have considerable power based on their expertise and do not consistently operate as trusted advisers.

Research on the Organization and Management of PSFs

Early studies of professional organizations were prompted by interest among sociologists in the role and organization of professions as areas of institutionalized expertise, increasingly colonized by different occupations.[9,14,15,16] At the same time, a growing trend towards the employment of professionals within organizational settings, rather than as independent practitioners, raised questions about the relationship between occupational and organizational forms of control.[17,18] Research interest focused on ways that professional values, emphasizing task autonomy and external regulation of professionals' activities, could coexist with the use of bureaucratic forms, particularly as professional firms grew in size and scale.

In the 1960s, a number of empirical studies addressed the question of how a professional–bureaucratic conflict was managed in practice. These detailed how large professional firms blended professional authority that lay outside the organization with an internal administrative component that designed and implemented bureaucratic control. Litwak and Smigel coined the term *professional bureaucracy* to describe this organizational form.[19,20] Montagna's study of accounting firms found that large firms used centralized managerial decision-making, combined with a sharing of other administrative tasks among partners.[18] Partners typically remained active in professional work undertaken by small teams using informal working methods. By comparison, the centralization of decision-making in a sample of smaller firms was relatively low. Montagna concluded that the dysfunctional aspects of bureaucratization were offset both by the support provided by external rule-making bodies, such as professional associations, and by the high level of personal autonomy in executing professional tasks. The results suggested that professionals were tolerant of complementary forms of organization, combining professional forms of control with processes reminiscent of bureaucratic organizations.

While this appeared to be a benign structural solution, the idea of an inherent conflict between professional and bureaucratic forms of organizing persisted. Montagna argued presciently that as professions such as accounting colonized 'new areas of uncertainty',[18] the professional bureaucracy would come under strain because of the lack of an extant external professional regulatory framework; knowledge colonization, in other words, would outrun professional regulation. Hall also concluded that there was no inherent conflict between professionalization and bureaucratization.[17] Hastings and Hinings argued that the nature of accounting work in producing rule systems made accountants 'comfortable' with bureaucratic systems.[21] Thereafter, debate on the professional–bureaucratic conflict thesis continued but the research focus shifted to problems of de-professionalization,[22] the nature of professionals' work commitments,[23] and the nature of professional power and its consequences.[24,8] Interest in the structure of professional organizations diminished.

Organizational Form and Archetype Ideas

Interest in the structure of professional *firms* re-emerged in the late 1980s for two reasons: First, an interest in the 'knowledge-based' organization, of which PSFs were seen as prime examples.[25,26] Second, increased competition over professional jurisdictions and the continuous expansion of professional services.[27] Organization theorists examining professional service organizations built on earlier intellectual foundations, but their work had a more dynamic and managerial flavour. Research questions were framed around a detailed examination of the archetypal organizational form dominating PSFs.[28] An archetype is a configuration of structures and systems that are consistent with an underlying interpretive scheme.[29]

Greenwood et al. identified the 'P^2' archetype as the dominant form traditionally used by PSFs.[6] This form can be characterized in terms of structures, systems, and underlying values embedded in notions of *partnership* and *professionalism*. Partnership as a governance form embodies three beliefs: the fusion of ownership and control, a form of representative democracy for purposes of strategic and operational decision-making, and the non-separation of professional and managerial tasks because the professionally and partnership-focused organization discourages any emphasis on management.[30,6] Management positions are seen as part-time responsibilities with a managing partner retaining clients; being a managing partner is an addition to being a lawyer. There is minimal investment in formal systems of management as it is assumed that partners manage their work demands and client relations themselves. The notion of professionalism encompasses five key beliefs: professional knowledge is central, control and evaluation is exercised by peers, authority is widely distributed across partners as well as other senior professionals, consensus in decision-making is critical, work responsibility is indivisible, and there are strong individual links with clients.[31] Structurally, the P^2 archetype is characterized by a low degree of differentiation as specialities are built around individuals rather than formal departments. Use of integrative devices is low and the application of rules and procedures is minimal. Overall, the P^2 archetype has minimal hierarchy and emphasizes collegial structures.

In terms of human resource systems, the P^2 form emphasizes an up-or-out promotion 'tournament' towards the goal of partnership.[32] Those who fail to make a partner are expected to leave the firm relatively soon after.[33] In the USA, the up-or-out practice was first formalized by Paul Cravath in his New York law firm and was thereafter adopted by other elite law firms[34–37] and across other professions, including, for example, the consulting firm McKinsey and Co.[38] Up-or-out provides a solution to the problem of monitoring work levels, where outputs are difficult to measure, by providing a motivating mechanism wherein junior professionals exert great effort and handle cases with greater responsibility in return for the chance of getting the prize of partnership.[39,40,41] Another important institutionalized human resource practice of the P^2 archetype is the use of a 'lockstep', that is seniority-based form of partner compensation. By rewarding on this basis rather on the basis of an individual's contribution to the firm's earnings, lockstep assumes a sense of shared commitment to the partnership, encouraging cooperation between partners and limiting the transaction costs of monitoring partners' efforts.[39,42] Decision systems in the P^2 model entail weak emphasis on strategic planning, particularly long-term planning, and there is little analysis of market trends and opportunities. Strategic management is a matter of guiding, nudging, and persuading. There is little specification of targets for portfolio expansion, market share, or industry penetration and there is a high degree of tolerance if revenue targets are not met.[6]

As changes in the external environment started to affect PSFs there was a shift in research enquiry to understand changes occurring in these firms. Environmental factors such as changing client demands, forces of globalization, and changing regulations governing professional services precipitated changes in how these firms were governed and managed. An emphasis on efficiency, productivity, marketing, and growth strategies became increasingly important.[31,43] In the interest of efficiency, there was pressure to separate professional and management roles, challenging the strongly held value of professional autonomy underpinning the P^2 archetype. More formal managerial structures and systems resembling larger corporations developed. Hierarchies developed, performance targets became more explicit, and day-to-day decision-making devolved to management teams from the partnership at large.

These changes in structures, systems, and underlying values suggested a new emerging archetype: the managed professional business (MPB).[31] This research was mainly grounded in accounting and law firms.[31,44] Cooper et al., in an in-depth analysis of two Canadian law firms, demonstrated that structures, systems, and values characteristic of the P^2 archetype were being superimposed or layered by the more business-like and managerial structures, systems, and values of the MPB, producing sedimented structures.[31] The study suggested that the new archetype (i.e. the MPB) was still emergent since it retained attributes of the P^2 archetype. Studies of Canadian accounting firms have also shown movement from the P^2 to the MPB form and toward more complex forms of the MPB, including multidisciplinary practices (MDPs) and global differentiated network (GDN) structures.[45–47]

Subsequently, several studies emerged that supported the emergence of an alternative to the P^2 archetype. Morris and Pinnington examined whether changes to internal labour markets and the introduction of 'business-like' methods of management had prompted a decline in the use of the traditional up-or-out system of promotion to partner in UK-based law firms.[48] They found the traditional up-or-out system in less than a third of the firms. Morris and Pinnington also examined the shift from the lockstep system of profit sharing to one based on individual performance.[49] They assessed whether this was a response to the adoption of 'business-like' methods of managing among UK-based firms but could not conclude that there was any clear linkage. Furthermore, in a survey of change in UK law firms, Morris and Pinnington found evidence of the adoption of more business-like methods, including formal marketing and strategic planning methods, coexisting with traditional features of the partnership form, including the persistence of partner control over client selection and relations.[49,50] Research expanded beyond law and accounting to include health care and architecture. Kitchener observed that publicly funded hospitals in the UK were moving from the professional bureaucracy form to a quasi-market form, which shares key characteristics with an MPB form.[51] Pinnington and Morris examined architectural practices and found that those that had moved from the partnership form of governance were more likely to have adopted 'business-like' methods of management than those continuing to operate as partnerships.[52] However, they also found that architecture practices were highly influenced by the value of professional creativity, which could cut across the pursuit of profits.

All these studies confirmed that a combination of various institutional and market forces was undermining the legitimacy of the prevailing P^2 archetype.[43] It is important to note, however, that while supporting a departure from the P^2 archetype these studies did *not* confirm that the emerging archetype replacing the traditional P^2 archetype was necessarily the MPB form. Flood,[53] in a comparison of British and American law firms, found that the former adhered somewhat to the P^2 archetype while the latter was more corporate-like and managerial. This difference may reflect contextual differences but leads to the same conclusion that there is likely more than one archetype emerging in the field of PSFs. Kitchener found that although changing environmental pressures aimed to reform the UK hospitals from a traditional professional bureaucracy (akin to P^2) to a quasi-market archetype (akin to MPB), what appeared to be emerging is some form of hybrid that embodied characteristics of both.[51] These sedimented structures evident in several studies suggest that as professional service organizations deviate from the institutionally prescribed P^2 archetype they are not necessarily adopting the complete MPB form. Further, the cumulative results of these different studies in different contexts and sectors suggest that these sedimented forms or hybrids may not be mere transition points or a stage leading up to an MPB, but emergent archetypes in themselves.[54]

My Work and Contribution

My interest in PSFs was triggered from two directions: one practitioner based and the other theoretical. The theoretical motivation related to my long-standing interest in professions and professionalism and to the question of how organizations and institutions reconciled the (sometimes very different) interests of management and producers. The practitioner angle arose from teaching a group of managing partners from different firms: while they could see the value of much of what they were learning, they pointed out that no one seemed to take into account the distinctiveness of the PSF setting. As one of them told me, having being elected as managing partner, he had asked his partners, the co-owners of his firm, what their personal objectives were and their objectives for the firm. While some sought to maximize profits and therefore earnings, others sought the challenge of interesting work or to *satisfice* by maintaining earnings at a particular level. The fact that they were the partners and active producers in the firm meant that this managing partner had to work to an agenda in which different objectives coexisted and influenced his strategic proposals. Indeed, he was conscious that he had been elected by his peers and answered to them via the partnership meeting. His difficulty was how to make sense of and reconcile the range of different goals into a coherent management policy. Ideas of a coherent strategy to which all partners could adhere in their day-to-day work were a million miles away. Such problems piqued my interest.

Another problem to which all of the partners I taught referred was what is known in the economics literature as shirking. In practice, this seemed to be more an issue of partners electing to cruise in terms of effort at some point in their career or to turn their attention to work that was of interest but of little economic value to the firm as a whole. How did a firm that offered tenure to its partners deal with this when the economic lever of an incentive was limited by the use of a lockstep/tenure-based profit sharing system? Such problems intrigued me sufficiently to explore the literature and to find that, at the time, little empirical or theoretical work existed on the management of these firms and how their distinctive structure and owners' values might influence activities and decisions. My aim was to try and produce work that would be theoretically interesting while providing insights for the sort of practitioners who had got me interested.

I took up the challenge by seeking research funding for a survey of firms in different professions, believing that there was a need to map the terrain and find out more about existing practices and the patterns of change. I was fortunate to receive funding from the Leverhulme Trust and to work with a research colleague, Dr. (now Professor) Ashly Pinnington, who proved to be an able fieldworker and excellent co-researcher. We worked closely together in all stages of the research adopting a strategy of deploying both quantitative and qualitative methods in our enquiry. Qualitative methods were vital to develop close understanding of the field and to persuade firms that we were worth taking seriously: at that time we were the first management researchers most had ever met and the sheer problem of obtaining data from professionals with little interest or understanding of what management meant was a considerable task. Quantitative techniques allowed us to build a broad picture of firms in the professions for we had noted that extant research generalized from small samples and often across professions. We therefore conducted surveys of firms in three established professions: architecture, law, and accounting.

Our first publications were empirical tests of theories, incentives, and motivation inside the PSF: we explored promotion and profit sharing policies focusing on law firms where our data were particularly rich.[48,42,55] For example, there is something of a puzzle in the profit sharing model of lockstep wherein partners are rewarded for tenure rather than performance and which, at the time, predominated in PSFs. Ideally, we would like to have known whether non-lockstep firms outperformed lockstep firms, as theory would predict. While we could not do that conclusively, we were able to examine how practitioners dealt with the shirking risk that lockstep (theoretically) carries, showing that firms formally ran lockstep systems but mitigated them effectively either by manipulating the system to reward stars or punish offenders. We also found that firms preferred lockstep over the economically rational model of performance-based rewards because performance management was too difficult to run and therefore could fall foul of strong feelings of equity of treatment among partners and because performance-based systems, focused around an individual's billing or economic earnings, had the undesirable consequence of inhibiting cooperation between partners, thereby undermining the synergistic profit potential of a firm of co-producers. Thus, we produced work that was both theoretically interesting and practically relevant.

Subsequently, we addressed debates about theories of change in professional firms in a number of papers and chapters.[49,52,50] Again, our strategy was to draw on survey data supplemented with qualitative research to provide extra insight to the statistical results and to ask to what extent theories stood up across large samples of firms. For example, we argued that the notion of a radical, archetype change in the management of professional firms was overstated. We found evidence of important dimensions of continuity alongside changed modes of managing that suggested a more sedimented model of change and one in which while managerial techniques had been embraced along with a commitment to the ideology of managerialism, there were still distinctive dimensions of a professional model of organization where partners made key decisions for themselves rather than working to a centrally conceived plan. Further, in looking at architect firms, we were to argue that cross-profession generalizations had to proceed with caution as there were clear differences in the values that architects operated with relative to other professions. This we explained in terms of the historic development of the profession of architecture and the preoccupation with a set of aesthetic values in work alongside commercial ones.[52] I returned to this theme of differences between professions in their trajectory of change and in the values underlying their preferred forms of organizing in a chapter with colleagues that compared and contrasted the development of law and accounting firms.[56]

My more recent work has again tried to tackle the problem of understanding the process of knowledge-based innovation. I started to think about this some years ago while trying to theorize the role of knowledge in PSFs.[57] Clearly, innovation is of profound interest to practitioners and policy makers but also theoretically very important. Specifically, our concern has been with the organization of innovation, so that we are concerned not just with the innovative services or products but also how firms organize to develop and deliver these. We started with a simple but difficult question: How do firms deal with a problem they have never seen before? In knowledge-based environments, this must surely be a real problem and potentially a tricky one. This problem actually led us to focus on the process of innovation via the creation and formalization of new practice areas, for new practices are the form that is created to harness, develop, and exploit knowledge that is new to a firm. While other researchers had built exogenous models of innovation in professional firms and focused at the level of profession or field in their analytic frameworks, ours focused on the internal processes of firms and we conceptualized the firm in a novel way as a federation of practices rather than as a unified organization. We undertook fieldwork in consulting and law firms to create comparative analyses of the innovation process and its attendant organizational problems.

At a theoretical level, we produced work that contributed to the literature on the nature of communities of practice in the context of knowledge-based innovation and on the politics of legitimizing new practice formation.[58,59] Our work had clear practical applications: for example, we developed and rigorously tested with practitioners a pathway model of new practice creation. This proposes that there are four ingredients to successful practice creation: creating a differentiated knowledge domain, obtaining central support and sponsorship, creating the turf in which a practice can exist by political support internally and externally, and the existence of partner agency or a 'champion' who will drive the creation in conjunction with the other ingredients. These ingredients can combine in different ways or proceed down three different pathways, which we termed consultant push, client led, and centre led, but all ingredients must be present for success to occur. In our work on the politics of knowledge-based innovation, we explore the differences between radical and incremental innovations in professional firms. Using a sample of law and consulting firms, we show that the legitimating strategies of successful innovations differ from failed ones and that the legitimating strategies of successful radical innovations differ from successful incremental ones.

Directions for Research and Policy and Practitioner Interests

In this concluding section I will outline a number of directions for research and policy. First, it is clear that large- and medium-sized firms in many professional sectors, including law, accounting, and strategic and IT consulting are internationalizing their operations and their client activities. This raises interesting questions about what forms of organization they adopt and how the international firm is to be managed. In policy terms, an important area of interest is what form of international organization seems to work best. Professional firms are different from other types of organization to the extent that they do not have to invest heavily in plant or factory to produce or deliver their products. Indeed, one can argue that professional firms do not need to go abroad to service their foreign clients successfully: many international transactions are run from the home base of the firm, often in conjunction with a local supplier.

Thus, we have several models of international organization: at one extreme we can observe firms that have very few overseas offices (if any) and seek to do work only on their home base (for foreign or domestic clients); at the other are those that have built their own international office networks and pursue what looks like a true global firm strategy with a seamless integration of service standards, transfers of work across offices, and unified human capital management with a single profit pot shared across the globe. In between are firms that have built alliances or relationships with other firms to deliver international services. Further, firms may have an international office network but actually be little more than brand-sharing; profits may not be shared internationally, human capital standards may vary, and there may be few flows of people across international boundaries, limited knowledge sharing, no common IT platform or service standards. Such firms can actually be less integrated than those in 'best friends' arrangements with other firms who do not share ownership. Each strategy has different sorts of cost structures, operational requirements, and potential pitfalls as well as paybacks; studies are starting to compare these, but there is scope for more work here on both the management and organizational implications of different models and on the outcomes of each.

Second, there are a number of human resource issues that have affected firms strongly in recent years and are grouped around the phrase 'the war for talent'. Indeed, as I write this, I would argue that the attraction and retention of staff in sufficient quality and quantity is the most pressing problem facing PSFs, outweighing concerns on the client side of the market: in a context of high and growing demand for their services, the biggest limiter on performance and competitive advantage is the relative shortage of expertise. Such a pressure is forcing many firms to adapt longstanding policies on hiring, promotion, and full-time working. In particular, the traditional up-or-out promotion system is under great pressure because of the implied wastage of so many good quality staff, in whom the firm is likely to have invested substantially. Indeed, in the traditional model of the up-or-out 'tournament' where the critical stay/go decision was taken at the point of partnership entry the firm deliberately shed staff when many are at their most productive relative to cost.[60] Yet the up-or-out model has been highly institutionalized among leading professional firms and it is by no means inevitable that they will change, notwithstanding labour market pressures.

A number of related areas of enquiry are likely to prompt interest among scholars and practitioners. These include gender differences in careers, the implications of a perceived disinterest in partnership as an incentive, and work/life balance; one can plausibly argue that these are related, of course. Consider the matter of career trajectories of female professionals. These have generally been markedly inferior (in terms of earnings and promotion chances) to their male peers. Traditionally, this has been explained either by reference to the career break females took at a critical time in the promotion system or by reference to bias in promotion decisions among senior professionals or by virtue of the career choices females made to enter less lucrative areas of activity. In a world of labour shortages and greater sensitivity to the need for equal opportunity among employers, it will be interesting to examine the consequences for career outcomes and, from a policy perspective, what sorts of strategies firms are using and with what consequences.

The other pressing issue for practitioners is that many young professionals express relative disinterest in the traditional incentive of partnership. They will stay and gain some credentials and experience but do not plan to remain for their whole career and are more concerned about the personal costs of the long hours expected of them, regardless of the attractive pay packages on offer. Is this part of a wider change in attitudes to the prospect of a career as employment with a single organization, or are other factors at play? For example, in many PSFs partnership itself is no longer what it was: gone is the permanent tenure and relative autonomy of the traditional partner role, to be replaced by a contract that promises high rewards in return for high performance and long hours, closer management control of activities, and relatively greater insecurity of tenure, so that the partner looks now more like a senior employee than an owner and controller of the business. There may be other reasons for the decline in attractiveness of partnership and this may be a cyclical issue rather than a structural change: if labour markets loosen, younger professionals may once more become inclined to express interest in career commitment to one organization and permanent employment. For researchers interested in applied research, the implications of these challenges to the traditional human capital model used by professional firms present a great opportunity.

Finally, I believe that the issue of innovation remains of great importance and under-researched. As I have indicated above, these are firms that trade on their expertise, but as this expertise ages it inevitably commodifies. This is one factor driving innovation. The other is that new problems are thrown up by clients and unless firms can address them they risk being stuck with outdated solutions that fail to solve new problems. We are starting to understand how innovation occurs and what explains the success or failure of innovation efforts within the firm, but more needs to be done to understand the innovation process in different national contexts and across different professional sectors. Thus, are there particular reasons why professional firms in India or Brazil might outperform their rivals in other economies? Or, what are the effects of large-scale 'jolts' to the system of professions and professional firms of innovations such as venture capital funding? And do professional boundaries and institutions encourage or discourage particular types of innovation? Work on this problem in the British public sector provides some interesting pointers,[61] but much more research needs to be done at the level of the profession, the firm, and the practice group on the processes by which innovation is encouraged or stifled, for this is at the heart of competitive success for PSFs.

References

1. A. Sharma, 'Professional as Agent: Knowledge Asymmetry in Agency Exchange', *Academy of Management Review*, 22/3(1997): 758–98.
2. P. S. Adler, 'Market, Hierarchy and Trust: The Knowledge Economy and the Future of Capitalism', *Organization Science*, 12/2(2001): 215–34.
3. B. Lowendahl, *Strategic Management of Professional Service Firms* (Copenhagen: Handelshojskolens Forlag, 2000).
4. D. J. Teece, 'Expert Talent and the Design of [Professional Services] Firms', *Industrial and Corporate Change*, 12/4(2003): 895–916.
5. J. O'Shea and C. Madigan, *Dangerous Company: The Consulting Powerhouses and the Businesses They Save and Ruin* (London: Nicholas Brearley, 1997).
6. R. Greenwood, C. Hinings, and J. Brown, ' "P²-Form" Strategic Management: Corporate Practices in Professional Partnerships', *Academy of Management Journal*, 33(1990): 725–55.
7. H. K. Gardner, N. Anand and T. Morris, 'Chartering Innovative Territory: Diversification, Legitimacy and Practice Area Creation in Professional Service Firms, *Journal of Organizational Behavior*, (forthcoming Mar. 2008).
8. M. S. Larson, *The Rise of Professionalism: A Sociological Analysis* (Berkeley, CA: University of California Press, 1977).
9. A. Abbott, *The System of Professions* (Chicago: University of Chicago Press, 1988).
10. M. Reed, 'Expert Power and Control in Late Modernity: An Empirical Review and Theoretical Synthesis', *Organisation Studies*, 17/4(1996): 573–98.
11. M. Alvesson, 'Knowledge Work: Ambiguity, Image and Identity', *Human Relations*, 54/7(2001): 863–86.
12. L. Empson, 'Fear of Exploitation and Fear of Contamination: Impediments to Knowledge Transfer in Mergers between Professional Services Firms', *Human Relations*, 54/7(2001): 839–62.
13. A. von Nordenflycht, 'What Is a Professional Service Firm and Why Does It Matter?' (Paper presented at the Clifford Chance Conference on Professional Service Firms, IESE, Barcelona, 2006).
14. A. W. Gouldner, 'Cosmopolitans and Locals', *Administrative Science Quarterly*, 2(1957): 281–306.

15. H. Volmer and D. Mills, *Professionalization* (Englewood Cliffs, NJ: Prentice-Hall, 1966).
16. H. Wilensky, 'The Professionalization of Everyone?', *American Journal of Sociology*, 70/2(1964): 137–58.
17. R. Hall, 'Professionalization and Bureaucratization', *American Sociological Review*, 33(1968): 725–55.
18. P. Montagna, 'Professionalization and Bureaucratization in Large Professional Organizations', *American Journal of Sociology*, 74(1968): 138–45.
19. E. Litwak, 'Models of Bureacracy Which Permit Conflict', *American Journal of Sociology*, 67(1961): 177–84.
20. E. Smigel, *The Wall Street Lawyer* (New York: Free Press, 1964).
21. A. Hastings and C. R. Hinings, 'Role Relations and Value Adaptation: A Study of the Professional Accountant in History', *Sociology*, 4(1970): 353–66.
22. M. Haug, 'De-Professionalization: An Alternative Hypothesis for the Future', *Sociological Review Monograph*, 20(1973): 195–211.
23. S. Bacharach, P. Bamberger, and S. C. Conley, 'Negotiating the "See-Saw" of Managerial Strategy: A Resurrection of the Study of Professionals in Organizational Theory', *Research in the Sociology of Organizations*, 8(1991): 217–38.
24. T. Johnson, *Professions and Power* (London: Macmillan, 1972).
25. T. J. Peters and R. H. Waterman, *In Search of Excellence* (New York: Harper and Row, 1982).
26. M. Alvesson, *Management of Knowledge-Intensive Companies* (New York: De Gruyter, 1995).
27. R. Greenwood et al., 'The Global Management of Professional Services: The Example of Accounting', in S. Clegg, E. Ibarra, and L. Bueno (eds.), *Theories of Management Process: Making Sense Through Difference* (Thousand Oaks, CA: Sage, 1998).
28. C. R. Hinings, J. L. Brown, and R. Greenwood, 'Change in an Autonomous Professional Service Firm', *Journal of Management Studies*, 24(1991): 373–95.
29. R. Greenwood and C. R. Hinings, 'Understanding Strategic Change: The Contribution of Archetypes', *Academy of Management Journal*, 36/5(1993): 1052–81.
30. R. Nelson, *Partners with Power: The Social Transformation of the Large Law Firms* (Berkeley: University of California Press, 1988).
31. D. J. Cooper et al., 'Sedimentation and Transformation in Organizational Change: The Case of Canadian Law Firms', *Organization Studies*, 17/4(1996): 623–47.
32. M. Galanter and T. Palay, *Tournament of Lawyers: The Transformation of the Big Law Firm* (Chicago: University of Chicago Press, 1991).
33. D. Maister, *Managing the Professional Service Firm* (New York: Free Press, 1993).
34. R. T. Swaine, *The Cravath Firm and Its Predecessors: 1819–1948* (New York: privately printed, 1948).
35. R. J. Gilson and R. H. Mnookin, 'Coming of Age in a Corporate Law Firm: The Economics of Associate Career Patterns', *Stanford Law Review*, 41/3(1989): 567–95.

36. W. Hobson, *The American Legal Profession and the Organizational Society, 1890–1930* (New York: Garland, 1986).
37. P. D. Sherer and K. M. Lee, 'Institutional Change in Large Law Firms: A Resource Dependency and Institutional Perspective', *Academy of Management Journal*, 45(2002): 102–19.
38. C. M. McKenna, *The World's Newest Profession* (New York: Cambridge University Press, 2006).
39. R. Gilson and R. H. Mnookin, 'Sharing Among the Human Capitalists: An Economic Inquiry into the Corporate Law Firm and How Partners Split Profits', *Stanford Law Review*, 37(1985): 313–92.
40. S. B. Malos and M. A. Campion, 'An Options-Based Model of Career Mobility in Professional Service Firms', *Academy of Management Review*, 20/3(1995): 611–44.
41. A. Siow, 'Hierarchical Careers', *Industrial Relations*, 33(1994): 83–105.
42. T. Morris and A. Pinnington, 'Patterns of Profit Sharing in Professional Firms', *British Journal of Management*, 1(1998): 1–15.
43. D. M. Brock, M. J. Powell, and C. R. Hinings, *Restructuring the Professional Organization* (London: Routledge, 1999).
44. C. R. Hinings, R. Greenwood, and D. Cooper, 'The Dynamics of Change in Large Accounting Firms', in D. M. Brock, M. J. Powell, and C. R. Hinings (eds.), *Restructuring the Professional Organization: Accounting, Health Care and Law* (London: Routledge, 1999).
45. R. Greenwood, R. Suddaby, and C. R. Hinings, 'Theorizing Change: The Role of Professional Associations in the Transformation of Institutional Fields', *Academy of Management Journal*, 45/1(2002): 58.
46. R. Greenwood and R. Suddaby, 'Institutional Entrepreneurship in Mature Fields: The Big Five Accounting Firms', *Academy of Management Journal*, 49(2006): 27–48.
47. T. Rose and C. Hinings, 'Global Clients' Demands Driving Changes in Global Business Advisory Firms', in D. Brock, M. Powell, and C. Hinings (eds.), *Restructuring the Professional Organisation* (London: Routledge, 1999).
48. T. Morris and A. Pinnington, 'Promotion to Partner in Professional Service Firms', *Human Relations*, 51/1(1998): 3–24.
49. T. Morris and A. Pinnington, 'Continuity and Change in Professional Organizations: Evidence from British Law Firms', in D. M. Brock, M. J. Powell, and C. R. Hinings (eds.), *Restructuring the Professional Organization: Accounting, Health Care and Law* (London: Routledge, 1999): 200–14.
50. A. Pinnington and T. Morris, 'Archetype Change in Professional Organizations: Survey Evidence from Large Law Firms', *British Journal of Management*, 14(2003): 85–99.
51. M. Kitchener, ' "All Fur Coat and No Knickers": Contemporary Organizational Change in United Kingdom Law Practice', in D. M. Brock, M. J. Powell, and C. R. Hinings (eds.), *Restructuring the Professional Organization: Accounting, Health Care and Law* (London: Routledge, 1999).

52. A. Pinnington and T. Morris, 'Transforming the Architect: Ownership Form and Archetype Change', *Organization Studies*, 23(2002): 189–210.

53. J. Flood, 'Professionals Organizing Professionals: Comparing the Logic of United States and United Kingdom Law Practice', in D. M. Brock, M. J. Powell, and C. R. Hinings (eds.), *Restructuring the Professional Organization: Accounting, Health Care and Law* (London: Routledge, 1999).

54. D. Brock, 'The Changing Professional Organization: A Review of Competing Archetypes', *International Journal of Management Reviews*, 8/3(2006): 157–74.

55. T. Morris and A. Pinnington, 'Strategic Fit in Professional Service Firms', *Human Resource Management Journal*, 8/4(1998): 76–87.

56. N. Malhotra, T. Morris, and C. R. Hinings, 'Variation in Organizational Form among Professional Service Organisations', *Research in the Sociology of Organizations*, 24(2006): 171–202.

57. T. Morris and L. Empson, 'Organizations and Expertise: An Exploration of Knowledge Bases and the Management of Accounting and Consulting Firms', *Accounting, Organizations and Society*, 23(1998): 609–24.

58. N. Anand, H. Gardner, and T. Morris, 'Knowledge-Based Innovation: Emergence and Embedding of New Practice Areas in Management Consulting Firms', *Academy of Management Journal*, 50/2(2007): 406–28.

59. H. Gardner, T. Morris, and N. Anand, 'Developing New Practices: Recipes for Success', in L. Empson (ed.), *Managing the Modern Law Firm: New Challenges, New Perspectives* (Oxford: Oxford University Press, 2007).

60. R. Landers, J. B. Rebitzer, and L. J. Taylor, 'Rat Race Redux: Adverse Selection in the Determination of Work Hours in Law Firms', *American Economic Review*, 86/3(1996): 329–48.

61. E. Ferlie, L. Fitzgerald, M. Wood, and C. Hawkins, 'The Non-Spread of Innovations: The Mediating Role of Professionals', *Academy of Management Journal*, 48/1(2005): 117–34.

8

Insights into the Management of Major Projects

Peter Morris

In 1980, a small group of business executives, financiers, and civil servants met, under the baton of the newly appointed President of Templeton College, Uwe Kitzinger, to propose the formation of an association that would seek to better understand the promotion, financing, and direction of major projects. Since then, this unlikely group has flourished, holding seminars and conferences approximately a dozen times a year and running a highly successful management course annually. Even more important, perhaps beyond these more parochial successes, has been its influence on the way the discipline, if such there is, of managing projects is now perceived, both by scholars and by practitioners.

Uwe Kitzinger's vision of work in the area of major projects led not into the macro-engineering world of Frank Davidson[1,2] but instead into shaping a broader conceptualization of the discipline of managing projects— one that has had the intellectual strength to move project management away from the dominant closed system, execution-oriented, overly limited perspective with which it had saddled itself. The management of projects remains today a very live practical management discipline and field of academic endeavour, and much of today's debate was framed by the work done at Templeton College in the 1980s and 1990s through the leadership of this group.

Provenance

Major projects—defined by the Major Projects Association (MPA), the group in question, as those 'requiring the knowledge, skills or resources that exceed what is readily or conventionally available to the key participants'[3]—have a heady provenance. Macro-engineering projects[1,2] provided a pure, if sometimes suspect, intellectual vision: their implementation has often been more questionable: Soviet-style social and civil engineering is excoriated; many World Bank projects such as dams have fared little better; NASA's projects and programmes too, while perennially fascinating, are often flawed in conception (as with Apollo) and execution (as with Challenger). Some large-scale projects appear to offer revolutionary hope, but these too often presage trouble. The Channel Tunnel was for many years a veritable icon of the MPA, although difficulties were always suspected. Overruns were foreseen, but who foresaw the decline in traffic with the rise in cheap air flights?

Meanwhile, major projects remain beacons for business: major sources of revenue for contractors, equipment suppliers, consultants, lawyers, and bankers. The MPA was a marvellously real source of networking in a domain that was simultaneously both important and almost invisible!

From 1981 onwards, the MPA held a series of seminars at which some of the best and most directly informed people spoke on major projects and issues in their 'initiation, acquisition, finance, and execution'. Seminars, which were for members only, were nearly all held in Templeton College, beginning with dinner followed by a seminar presentation, then after overnight rest and breakfast, a final half day of more presentation and discussion. The discussion was based on Chatham House rules—full, frank, and unattributable—although a verbatim transcript of the event was published in confidence to members.

By late 1983, the transcripts were building up and with them the belief that some work was needed to make sense of the undoubted rich vein of knowledge that they surely represented. Accordingly, the post of Research Fellow in Major Projects at Templeton College was advertised in the spring of 1984, and I took up the fellowship in September of that year.

The Initial Research Programme: 'The Preconditions of Success and Failure of Major Projects'

'Where to start, what to focus on?' was the initial challenge. I began by reviewing and summarizing the seminar transcripts published to date (nineteen in all). I meanwhile interviewed the MPA board—the chairman and a project economist of a mineral extraction and processing company, the finance director of another mining company, an insurance expert, a senior civil servant, two bankers, a distinguished consulting engineer, a contractor, and an academic. The only suggestion they all had in common was the need to investigate why so many major projects fail. As Alan Sykes, a director of Consolidated Goldfields said, 'this is an industry characterised by failure. Couldn't you develop some kind of template—a cookie cutter—to enable us to tell when projects are going out of control?' Why not? But there are multiple issues even in formulating that question, although I was too innocent to perceive that then.

So, a consultant retained by the MPA—George Hough, until recently a director of British Aerospace—and I began an eighteen-month research programme into 'the preconditions of project success and failure'. The work began with an extensive literature review—all the studies we could find. We recognized that there may be different definitions of success, which may vary with role and change with time. Nevertheless, we were able to identify a number of distinguishing features of major projects via the literature; we used these as guides in the creation of eight case studies of major project success and failure:

- *The Channel Tunnel, 1960–75*: a failure. 'Born of political will, it died of political indifference'[4] and was sabotaged ultimately by the British Rail Board who did not wish to spend £330 million, in 1974 money, on a high-speed rail link that the British Government had unnecessarily mandated in the Channel Tunnel Treaty (1972) should be an integral— though not necessary—part of the scheme.

- *Concorde*: another failure. Again, this was a political project, representing enormous leaps in (unproven) technology, with no project management. (The Tornado Multi-Role Combat Aircraft was contemporaneously managed on sophisticated project management principles.)[5]

- *The Advanced Passenger Train*: another failure, again using unproven technology, tested (foolishly) under the full glare of the media on a trial run, with no support from its real sponsors, British Rail.

- *The Thames Barrier*: a huge civil engineering project; cost and schedule overrun. Long in the planning, it was characterized by a hands-off client and no will on the part of the construction team (initially of second-order quality) to pull together and succeed—at least until the contractual regime had been renegotiated to permit this, after which things went well.

- *Heysham 2 Nuclear Power Station*: a long story, ultimately of failure. Britain tried through the 1960s and 1970s to promote its own distinctive nuclear power technology: the Advanced Gas Cooled Reactor (AGR) programme. The first phase was a project management nightmare with technical problems arising in design when construction was well underway (leading to problems of 'concurrency': simultaneously trying to manufacture or build before the design is settled—a practice common in high-tech industries at the time and causing havoc, for example, in weapons system acquisition).[5] Lessons were learnt, however, and more time was allowed for technology proving. Nevertheless, control systems problems escaped this regime and ultimately caused the target completion date to be missed.

- *The Fulmar North Sea Oil Project*: a failure. Great care went into the development stage of this project but then a relatively inexperienced project manager was chosen. Lacking sufficient experience, and possibly strength of character, he failed to delay the letting of contracts per the initial schedule, even though the design was late and still evolving, and getting later. The result was severe contractual difficulties ('concurrency' once again) leading to some bankruptcies and several missed delivery targets, with, in the end, the summer weather window for installation being missed.
- *The computerization of PAYE*: almost a success. In contrast to Fulmar, the project manager risked the wrath of the Chancellor of the Exchequer by holding off letting contracts and writing code until he was sure that the design and the underlying technology were stable. He also exhibited superb personal leadership and team management. The only problem was that responsibility for the computer buildings lay with another government department, and this held up cut-over.
- *Giotto, the spacecraft that intercepted Halley's Comet*: a success! The schedule was immutable, everyone focused on it, and leadership and team work were outstanding. It also helped in that the contract was 'reimbursable'.

The implications of this research—both in the literature and the case studies—were startling:

- Project failure is—or was then—very common. (It is still too frequent.)
- Few of the things normally emphasized in project management textbooks had any bearing on the factors really causing projects to fail. This was quite remarkable: What kind of discipline is it if it does not address the things that cause it to fail?
- Many of the factors causing failure arise in the project 'front-end'— before project execution, as traditionally conceived, begins. Technological uncertainty is an example.

The research was published as *The Anatomy of Major Projects*,[4] a book that soon became a classic in the specialized world of project management academia and of the more reflective practitioner. Crucially, however, for many practitioners in the field, the emphasis on major projects was beyond their experience. For them, there was little opportunity to influence front-end factors or to address project externalities. The impact of the new model, described below, was therefore slow in being felt, and was distinctly at odds with standard project management—a challenge that has since come to occupy centre stage in the world of the management of projects.

The Management of Projects Framework

From the 'preconditions' research, some eighty-eight factors affecting project success were identified. These were grouped under ten headings: project definition; planning, design and technology management; political and social factors; schedule duration; schedule urgency; finance; legal; contracting; project implementation; and human factors. Ultimately, after several presentations and discussions of the findings, the following diagram (see Figure 8.1) was created to represent what has become, in the project management world, the basis of the new paradigm of 'the management of projects'.

The logic of the diagram is as follows. First, the project needs to be defined (a front-end activity). This definition springs in the first instance from the objectives of the project sponsor. These lead to the formulation of the project strategy, which should be aligned with the objectives, goals, and strategies of the sponsor and principal stakeholders.[6] These all then translate into technical design or product definition via briefing requirements, specifications and the design itself.

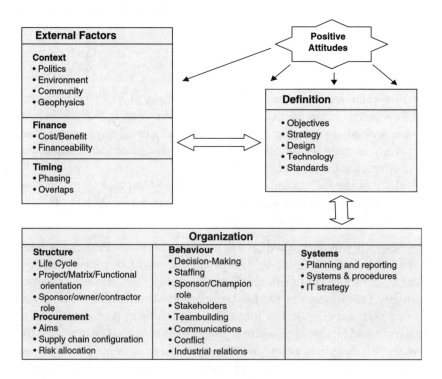

FIG. 8.1 The anatomy of major projects 'management of projects' model

This definition affects—and is affected by—the socio-economic environment, the ecological and geophysical environment, funding and financeability, and the urgency with which the project is required. The important point—typically completely ignored by most texts on project management—is that the interaction between the evolving project definition and its environment can, and should, be managed.

This emerging definition of the project is then managed by an organization that reflects not just the project structure but also the contracting and supply chain relationships, assisted by project control systems: planning and monitoring (perhaps these days we would call these governance and control). And, of course, all this is done by people: personal skills and behaviours are critical. In fact, positive attitudes at the top—and in truth, all along the management ladder—are essential to making the project a success.

The crucial insights of this model are that

- Many of the reasons for the success (or failure) of the project lie in its definitional stages: commercial, technical, socio-economic.
- To be successful, the project needs to be managed within its context.
- People and their behaviour exert a huge influence on the outcome.

The quest to better understand the real elements of the discipline of managing projects was then further developed through a historical account of modern projects and the attempt to manage them in an systematic and professional manner. *The Management of Projects*,[5] written largely while I was executive director of the Major Projects Association at Templeton College, sought to provide

- A record of the seminal events and documents in the development of the modern practice of managing projects
- A detailed picture of how project management is and has been practiced in different industries, countries, and cultures
- A sense of the drama and excitement of the real world of projects
- A model of best practice
- A vision of how the discipline will evolve.

It used as its guide evidence of modern project management terminology—for example, the Gantt chart (1917), the project engineer (Exxon, 1920s), the project office (USAAF, 1930s), the matrix organization (Gulick, 1937), the programme manager (Polaris, 1956), PERT (1957), the Critical Path Method (1957), and a whole slew of techniques brought in with the arrival of Robert MacNamara in the US Department of Defense in 1960 and elaborated by DOD and NASA with the Apollo programme.

The Management of Projects[5] traced the evolution of concepts and terms of this new discipline, documented the key literature decade by decade, and illustrated changing practice with extensive case examples. These included the US missile programmes of the 1950s, Apollo, Challenger, the International Space Station, Bloodhound, TSR-2, FX, Tornado, the Trans-Alaskan Pipeline, the nuclear power programme, North Sea oil, the IT sector, the automobile industry, Third World development projects, the Channel Tunnel, and BOOT (privately funded Build–Own–Operate–Transfer infrastructure) projects.

But in recounting the evolution of this management discipline, one thing became very clear. The emerging project management professional associations in the late 1960s and early 1970s took a radically diminished view of the subject, focusing predominantly on planning and monitoring tools and techniques, and only to a lesser extent on teamwork and leadership issues. This, in a way, was very understandable. Those attending the then typical seminars and conferences were middle managers, nearly all charged with execution implementation. They were downstream from the front-end development work. Typically, their challenge was achieving 'on time, in budget, to scope' completion. The issue of who had established those budget, schedule, and scope targets was not within their purview. The result was in any case a highly unfortunate move, encouraging practitioners to see project management as being focused on downstream execution: a perspective aligning almost totally with the prevailing academic view of the subject as a sub-set of Operations Management—missing totally the lessons of *The Anatomy of Major Projects* and *The Management of Projects*.

The Bodies of Knowledge

This diminished perspective was hardened in the mid-1980s when the largest of the project management professional societies, the US-headquartered Project Management Institute (PMI), issued its *Guide to the Project Management Body of Knowledge*.[7] This grand sounding document essentially elaborates nine (initially there were eight) key topic areas (see Figure 8.2) that PMI members believed represent the bones of what one needs to know in order to manage, that is, to implement the execution of projects.

The formulation of this document was driven by PMI's decision to introduce a programme of certification—a programme of questionable validity but of commercial brilliance. It was of questionable validity because (a) the certification process primarily tests only knowledge rather than broader measures of competence such as knowledge plus skills plus

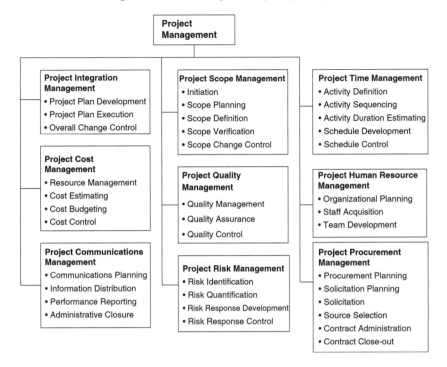

FIG. 8.2 PMBOK Guide (2004)

behaviours plus experience and (b) while there is belief, there is little or no evidence of any relationship between knowledge and successful project delivery performance. It was commercially brilliant because the certification programme has undoubtedly been the driving motor behind PMI's outstanding growth. (It now has more than 210,000 members, 180,000 of whom are certified 'Project Management Professionals'.)

In the late 1980s, I was asked by the UK's professional project management body, the Association for Project Management (APM), to draft their Body of Knowledge, which APM would use for its own certification programme. Given the research evidence developed at Templeton College, I was unhappy to follow PMI in its execution-oriented view of the discipline. Instead, a small team and I used the 'management of projects' insights to emphasize the need, *inter alia*, to ensure

- An effective linkage with the sponsoring organizations' strategies; proper management of technology (requirements, design, verification, and validation)
- Effective management of commercial issues, procurement, and supply chain integration

- Efficient information and configuration management
- Full and effective leverage, and management, of people-related skills and issues; in addition to the core control topics that essentially constitute the PMI Body of Knowledge Guide.

APM explicitly acknowledged the 'management of projects' philosophy (if such it be) in the Foreword to the APM Body of Knowledge. Subsequent questionnaire and interview-based research that I carried out on behalf of the APM while Professor of Engineering Project Management at the University of Manchester Institute of Science and Technology and later as Professor of Construction and Project Management at University College London confirmed that the majority of professionals in the area (more than 85 per cent of the 600 APM members who responded) agreed that the topics included in the APM Body of Knowledge were indeed ones that they considered that professionals in project management ought to be knowledgeable in.[8,9] (Figure 8.3 shows the latest version of the APM Body of Knowledge.)

This conception of the domain spread internationally. The International Project Management Association (IPMA) is a federation of some fifty national project management associations from around the world, many

Project Management in context				
Project Management Programme Management Portfolio Management		Project Context Project Sponsorship Project Office		
Planning the strategy				
Project Success Criteria and Benefits Management Stakeholder Management Value Management		Project Management Plan Risk Management Quality Management Health, Safety & Environment		
Executing the strategy	**Techniques**	**Business and Commercial**	**Organization & Governance**	**People & the Profession**

Scope
  Management
Scheduling
Resource
  Management
Budgeting & Cost
  Management
Change Control
Earned Value
  Management
Information
  Management
  and Reporting
Issue
  Management
	Requirements
	  Management
	Development
	  Management
	Estimating
	Technology
	  Management
	Value Engineering
	Modelling & Testing
	Configuration
	  Management
		Business Case
		Marketing & Sales
		Financial
		  Management
		Procurement
		Legal Awareness
			Project Life Cycles
			Concept
			Definition
			Implementation
			Hand-over and
			  Close-out
			Project Reviews
			Organization Structure
			Organizational Roles
			Methods and
			  Procedures
			Governance
				Communication
				Teamwork
				Leadership
				Conflict Management
				Negotiation
				Human Resource
				  Management
				Behavioural
				  Characteristics
				Learning &
				  Development
				Professionalism &
				  Ethics

FIG. 8.3 APM BOK (2005)

from European countries, the Middle East, India, and several Far Eastern countries including China, but excluding PMI. IPMA too felt the need to be facilitating certification practices among its member associations. Hence, in 1996, it issued its *International Competency Baseline*[10] in which the APM's 'management of projects'-based Body of Knowledge structure became the common template. Subsequently, the French, German, Swiss, Dutch, and Czech associations adopted the APM Body of Knowledge without significant conceptual modification.

Nevertheless, in most people's minds, it is probably true to say, the dominant model of project management was that of PMI's Body of Knowledge Guide—that is, one of an execution-oriented delivery activity. Research, however, has continued increasingly to argue for the broader conception of the domain.

Research and Practical Developments Supporting the Management of Projects Perspective

Two important research programmes published their findings in the early years of the twenty-first century, both explicitly acknowledging the earlier work of *The Anatomy of Major Projects*. Miller and Lessard published *The Strategic Management of Large Engineering Projects*,[11] the findings of the huge International Program in the Management of Engineering and Construction (IMEC) study in 2000. The IMEC team looked at more than sixty engineering projects of more than $1 billion each from around the world. They differentiated their findings between efficiency ('completion on time, in budget, to scope') and effectiveness ('did the project meet the sponsors' goals?'). In terms of the former, 82 per cent met their cost targets and 72 per cent their schedule ones. In terms of the latter, 45 per cent met their objectives, 18 per cent performed alright without crises, 17 per cent had to be restructured after crises, while 20 per cent were abandoned or taken over.[11]

The key issue, they concluded, is the competence of the sponsor, especially the sponsor's ability to deal with (1) exogenous turbulence (political, economic, social) and (2) endogenous issues, particularly supply chain 'partnership' and contractual issues. Three of their major findings seem particularly apposite. First, they recommend a stage-gated approach. The front-end was seen to be key: 3–35 per cent of total project expenditure could be in the front end. Second, they called for a more sophisticated approach to risk management (e.g. using an options approach). Technical, market, social, and institutional risks need identifying and managing. Third, they queried whether there really is such a thing as project management 'best practice', given the variety of configurations of sponsor–supplier relationships that are possible. Each of these issues resonates in today's evolving discourse on the domain.

Three years later, Flyvbjerg et al. published *Megaprojects and Risk: An Anatomy of Ambition.*[12] Working largely on the record of large transportation projects, they found overruns of 50–100 per cent in real terms to be common and above 100 per cent not uncommon. Demand forecasts were often wrong by 20–70 per cent. The key issue, they concluded, was accountability (or rather, lack of it) within the sponsoring organization, not a lack of technical skills or data. In particular, they attacked the tendency to 'low ball' the estimates. Again, the problems were seen to be in the front-end, with the sponsor, and in dealing with externalities.

The issue of estimating schedules, budgets, and benefits is crucial and in general receives far too little attention in the execution view of project management. There are two points. First, is the setting of the estimate part of project management or not? Logically it would seem that, as part of planning, it ought to be, not least because of the project management know-how upon which the estimate and its underlying plans are built. But then if one accepts this argument, surely the shaping of the front-end development is part of project management, for the same reason. This is of course precisely the 'management of projects' thesis. Second, it is widely accepted in the better run projects-based companies, for example the energy companies, that the accuracy of the estimates increases as the development progresses. This is expressed in probabilities—P50 indicating a 50 per cent probability that the budget will be achieved, P90 90 per cent, and so on. Rules vary between companies, but a P50 at the time of sanction is not unusual (remembering that this refers to the spread, not the absolute size, of potential overrun). Hence, overruns should be less shocking than many lay commentators imagine. The issue, however, always is the extent to which decision makers and analysts understand, internalize, and act on the implications of such probabilistic estimating.

Flyvbjerg's work proved to be particularly influential, stimulating, *inter alia*, the UK Treasury to commission in 2002 a study of 'optimism bias' in estimates of proposed projects, *A Review of Large Public Procurement in the UK.*[13] This study identified the areas of risk that impact on the management of projects as, in descending order: inadequate business case, environmental impact, disputes and claims, economic factors, late contractor input into design, contractual complexity, legislation, inadequate innovation, and so on. It then made recommendations on 'project management' actions that should be taken to address these risk areas: optioneering, benefits management, strategy, risk management, change management, stakeholder management, and so on. Although general and high level, the recommendations are clearly biased towards the front-end. Benchmarking data in the process engineering industries similarly reinforces the importance of the front-end. It clearly demonstrates that greater emphasis and more time spent on front-end issues are correlated with better out-turn performance.[14,15]

The UK Treasury in fact proved influential to the development of the management of projects in other ways too, not least as its Office of Government Commerce agency was an early proponent of programme management (see its document *Managing Successful Programmes*[16]). Programme management offers an interesting addition to the modest conceptual confusion regarding just what is the discipline required for managing projects effectively.

Programmes are projects related to a shared objective. They generally have a strategic intent, and in modern programme management there is emphasis on the achievement of outcomes and benefits. For many, programme management has less of a project's tactical and bottom-up character, but is more clearly approached from a general business and top-down perspective. For some people, including OGC, projects are output-oriented; programmes are outcome-oriented. If interpreted too literally, this is surely wrong: all projects are undertaken to achieve a benefit. The error is in seeing project management as execution management. Even if one accepts this view, who manages the front-end definition (design, planning, estimating, financing, stakeholder management, commercial arrangements, finance, etc.)? Certainly not just programme managers—possibly development managers or managers of projects.

In reality what one probably has is a family of roles all clustered within the overall 'management of projects' definition.[17] The Engineering and Physical Sciences Research Council's Network Rethinking Project Management, which is discussed below, even implied some elision between programmes ('programmification') and the model developed in *The Anatomy of Major Projects*: 'at one level, multiple projects or programmes can be considered as "big projects"'.[18] Is a major capital investment project—Sakhalin, Crossrail, the Olympics—a big project or a programme? Frankly, they probably are programmes, but in common terminology would still be called projects. As in many social sciences—and pre-eminently in management—language follows practice rather than theory.

Current Resonances

All this perhaps gives the impression of a domain in some slight confusion. While the popular end of the market is being serviced by purveyors of commodity solutions—methodologies such as PRINCE2, software systems solutions, and 'training solutions providers' (increasingly 'accredited' by the project management professional associations, for a fee, as competent to deliver training to their standards)—the professional associations are themselves in conflict as to the subject's scope. Meanwhile, the academic community is becoming increasingly interested in projects and their management, taking a much more reflective, if not to say sophisticated, perspective. Somewhere in between, more and more companies are looking at their 'project management maturity' at an enterprise development scale.

A good snapshot of the more intellectual debate is the Engineering and Physical Sciences Research Council's Network: Rethinking Project Management, which describes the origins of the network as follows:

One of the most important organisational developments in recent years has been the significant growth in project work across different sectors and industries.... Recent industry reports highlight the growing adoption of project management standards and practices across large numbers of organisations, including the creation of project management centres of excellence within UK government departments. No longer just a sub-discipline of engineering, the management of projects—including programme management and portfolio management—is now the dominant model in many organisations for strategy implementation, business transformation, continuous improvement and new product development. Similarly, in areas such as infrastructure renewal, urban regeneration and community development, project management practices are becoming increasingly important, as more and more work is organised through projects and programmes. Despite these developments in practice however, the current conceptual base of project management continues to attract criticism for its lack of relevance to practice and, consequently, to improved performance of projects across different industrial sectors.... The main argument [is] not that the extant project management body of thought with its concepts, methodologies, and tools is worthless and should be abandoned, but rather that a new research network [is] needed to enrich and extend the field beyond its current intellectual foundations, and connect it more closely to the challenges of contemporary project management practice.

The Network recognized two dominant bases to the discipline among others:

1. The deterministic, 'hard' systems model, emphasizing the planning and control dimensions of project management (e.g. Checkland,[19] Morris,[20] Yeo,[21] and Winch[22])
2. The 'management of projects' perspective growing out of the MPA research, but reflected in the writings of several scholars since

(e.g. Stinchcombe and Heimer,[23] Whipp and Clark,[24] Clark and Fujimoto,[25] Midler,[26] Miller and Lessard,[11] Flyvbjerg,[12] and Davies and Hobday[27]), offering a more rounded view of projects and recognizing the importance of managing the front-end development and exogenous factors in addition to the more traditional 'execution-focused' endogenous ones. (*The Wiley Guide to Managing Projects*[28] gives in 1500 pages a synoptic view of the thinking in this broader, more catholic view of the discipline.)

Many people working in project management, either as practitioners or academics, would however find these paradigms either too limited or too broad. Many academics, meanwhile, might prefer a purer theoretical underlay. The Network identified at least four approaches:

- The oldest (going back to the 1960s) focuses on organizational structure as means of achieving integration and task accomplishment (e.g. Lawrence and Lorsch,[29] Galbraith,[30] Mintzberg,[31] Lundin and Soderholm,[32] DeFillippi and Arthur,[33] Grabher,[34] and Engwall[35])
- The other three are more recent. One builds on the interaction between business strategy and projects as vehicles for strategy implementation (Davies and Hobday,[27] and Morris and Jamieson[36]) emphasizing context and how experience and 'contingent' capabilities are crucial to project performance (Engwall,[35] and Flowers[37])
- Another sees projects as information-processing systems that address the uncertainty that is an over-riding characteristic of projects (Winch[22,38])
- The most recent approach explores projects and project management from relationship, and critical management, perspectives (Hodgson and Cicmil,[39] and Pryke and Smyth[40]).

Such diversity of approaches is not necessarily a sign of immaturity. Competing paradigms can be healthy in a practice-based profession such as management.[41] Management, and project management, deal with a huge range of socio-technical contexts.

The Network's conclusion was clear, however: that a broadening out from the simpler, linear tools and methodologies-based approaches is required—one much more aligned to the paradigm shift that occurred with *The Anatomy of Major Projects*, where, to quote from the Network[42]:

- The complexity and diversity of projects is better represented
- More emphasis is given to contingent perspectives and social interactions between people

- There is less emphasis on product creation, with progress controlled against specification (quality), cost and time, and more on value creation
- Greater recognition is given to approaches which facilitate broader and ongoing conceptualizations of projects
- Training and development moves from teaching people to follow detailed procedures and techniques, towards helping reflective practitioners learn, operate, and adapt effectively in complex environments.

Much in this obviously resonates with a perspective driven by the requirements of managing major projects, and hence of the MPA. Where there does, to me, seem a difference from *The Anatomy of Major Projects* is the greater awareness that there now is of the socially constructed nature of projects ('projects are invented not found'), and the greater insights we have in understanding the people issues involved in the management of projects, compared with the more engineering-oriented, positivistic, normative character flavouring *The Anatomy of Major Projects*: projects are built by people for people; and views on the proper management of projects are similarly formulated and held by people—a view particularly developed by the Relationship School.[39,40]

An important consequence of the recognition of the different perspectives or paradigms underlying the management of projects as a discipline is that we are now concomitantly much more aware of the different epistemological approaches that underlie the different project management world views available in the field. The positivistic approach, which has been that most commonly used for much project management research, is often inappropriate. Positivist and empiricist traditions explain events based on the Humean view of causality: inductive linear thinking. This creates a preference for closed cause–effect models, but social systems are open. Context is extremely important. Popper's well-known theory of falsification in science,[43] developed to address the trap of closed system inductive thinking, is essentially deductive. However, many positivist project management researchers do not work deductively. And there is frequently an implicit normative agenda of what ought to happen. Hence, positivist claims for objectivity are compromised. Indeed, my colleagues and I at University College London have argued that, in consequence, the time is now right for a return to looking at critical realism as a more appropriate epistemology and methodology for work in this area.[44]

Meanwhile, as I write this, there comes news that Oxford is again taking up the challenge of research in the management of projects and programmes. The Saïd Business School has just announced (March 2007) the establishment of 'the world's first research centre for major programme management....Major programmes, such as the Olympics, which are characterised by being complex, high value, long-term projects, have proliferated in recent years. Typically their outcome impacts millions of people. Yet there is a shortage of rigorous, empirically grounded and intellectually robust support for this discipline.'[45] Heard this before?

References and Notes

1. F. P. Davidson and J. S. Cox, *Macro* (New York: Morrow, 1983).
2. F. P. Davidson, E. Frankel, and L. P. Meador, *Macro-Engineering* (MIT Lectures on Global Infrastructure; Cambridge, MA: MIT Press, 1997).
3. Major Projects Association, *Constitution* (Oxford: Templeton College, 1981).
4. P. W. G. Morris and G. H. Hough, *The Anatomy of Major Projects* (Chichester: Wiley, 1987).
5. P. W. G. Morris, *The Management of Projects* (London: Thomas Telford, 1994).
6. Proctor & Gamble developed a methodology, OGSM (Objectives, Goals, Strategies, Measures), that operationalized this extremely well. It is written up in Morris and Jamieson; see 36 below.
7. Project Management Institute (PMI), *A Guide to the Project Management Body of Knowledge* (1st–4th edns.; Newtown Square: Project Management Institute, 1987–2004).
8. P. W. G. Morris, 'Updating the Project Management Bodies of Knowledge', *Project Management Journal*, 32/3(2001): 21–30.
9. P. W. G. Morris, A. Jamieson, and M. M. Shepherd, 'Research Updating the APM Body of Knowledge' (4th edn.), *International Journal of Project Management*, 24/6(2006): 461–73.
10. G. Caupin, H. Knöpfel, P. Morris, E. Motzel, and O. Pannenbäcker, *ICB: IPMA Competence Baseline* (Versions 1 and 2; Zurich: International Project Management Association, 1996; 1999).
11. R. Miller and D. Lessard, *The Strategic Management of Large Engineering Projects* (Cambridge, MA: MIT Press, 2000).
12. B. Flyvbjerg, N. Bruzelius, and W. Rothengatter, *Megaprojects and Risk: An Anatomy of Ambition* (Cambridge: Cambridge University Press, 2003).
13. See http://www.hm-treasury.gov.uk
14. See http://www.cii-benchmarking.org
15. See http://www.ipaglobal.com
16. Office of Government Commerce, *Managing Successful Programmes* (Norwich: HMSO, 2003).
17. P. W. G. Morris, L. Crawford, D. Hodgson, M. M. Shepherd, and J. Thomas, 'Exploring the Role of Formal Bodies of Knowledge in Defining a Profession: The Case of Project Management', *International Journal of Project Management*, 24/8(2006): 710–21.

18. H. Maylor, T. Brady, T. Cooke-Davies, and D. Hodgson, 'From Projectification to Programmification', *International Journal of Project Management*, 24/8(2006): 663–74.

19. P. Checkland, 'Soft Systems Methodology', in Johnnathan Rosenhead (ed.), *Rational Analysis for a Problematic World: Problem Structuring Methods for Complexity, Uncertainty and Conflict* (Hoboken: Wiley, 1989).

20. P. W. G. Morris, 'Science, Objective Knowledge and the Theory of Project Management', *Civil Engineering: Proceedings of the Institution of Civil Engineers*, 150(2002): 82–90.

21. K. T. Yeo, 'Systems Thinking and Project Management: Time to Reunite', *International Journal of Project Management*, 11/2(1993): 111–17.

22. G. Winch, *Rethinking Project Management: Project Organizations as Information Processing Systems?* (Proceedings of the PMI Research Conference July 2004; Newtown Square: Project Management Institute, 2004).

23. A. Stinchcombe and C. Heimer, *Organization Theory and Project Management: Administering Uncertainty in Norwegian Offshore Oil* (Oslo: Norwegian University Press, 1985).

24. R. Whipp and P. Clark, *Innovation and the Auto Industry: Product, Process and Work Organization* (London: Francis Pinter, 1986).

25. K. Clark and T. Fujimoto, *Product Development Performance: Strategy, Organization and Management in the World Auto Industry* (Cambridge, MA: Harvard Business School Press, 1991).

26. C. Midler, *L'Auto qui n'existait pas, Management des Projects et Transformation de l' Enterprise* (Paris: InterEdition, 1993).

27. A. Davies and M. Hobday, *The Business of Projects* (Cambridge: Cambridge University Press, 2005).

28. P. W. G. Morris and J. Pinto, *The Wiley Guide to Managing Projects* (Hoboken: Wiley, 2004).

29. P. Lawrence and J. Lorsch, *Organization and Environment: Managing Integration and Differentiation* (Cambridge: Harvard University Press, 1967).

30. J. Galbraith, *Designing Complex Organizations* (Reading, MA: Addison-Wesley, 1973).

31. H. Mintzberg, *Structure in Fives: Designing Effective Organisations* (Englewood Cliffs: Prentice-Hall, 1983).

32. R. Lundin and A. Soderholm, 'A Theory of the Temporary Organization', *Scandinavian Journal of Management*, 11/4(1995): 437–55.

33. R. DeFillippi and M. Arthur, 'Paradox in Project-Based Enterprise: The Case of Film Making', *California Management Review*, 40/2(1998): 1–15.

34. G. Grabher, 'Cool Projects, Boring Institutions: Temporary Collaboration in Social Context', *Regional Studies*, 36/3(2002): 205–14.

35. M. Engwall, 'No Project Is an Island: Linking Projects to History and Context', *Research Policy*, 32/5(2003): 789–809.

36. P. W. G. Morris and A. Jamieson, *Translating Corporate Strategy into Project Strategy* (Newtown Square: Project Management Institute, 2004).

37. S. Flowers, 'Contingent Capabilities and the Procurement of Complex Product', *International Journal of Innovation Management*, 8/1(2004): 1–20.

38. G. Winch, 'Managing Construction Projects', *International Journal of Innovation Management*, 8/1(2002): 1–20.

39. D. Hodgson and S. Cicmil, *Making Projects Critical* (London: Palgrave Macmillan, 2006).

40. S. Pryke and H. J. Smyth, *Managing Complex Projects: A Relationship Approach* (Oxford: Blackwell, 2006).

41. D. A. Schön, *The Reflective Turn: Case Studies in and on Educational Practice* (New York: Teacher's College Press, 1991).

42. M. Winter et al., 'Directions for Future Research in Project Management: The Main Findings of a UK Government-Funded Research Network', *International Journal of Project Management*, 24/8(2006): 638–49.

43. K. Popper, *The Logic of Scientific Discovery* (London: Routledge, 1968).

44. H. J. Smyth and P. W. G. Morris, 'An Epistemological Evaluation of Research into Projects and Their Management: Methodological Issues', *International Journal of Project Management*, 25/4(2007): 423–36.

45. See http://www.sbs.ox.ac.uk

9

The Retailing Sector: Barrow Boys, Big Business, and New Technology

Jonathan Reynolds

Marketers and economists used to think of retailers as passive agents within distribution channels. Their role was simply that of intermediation—easing the flow of goods and services between suppliers and consumers. Suppliers then drove the retailing process. Over the last forty years, however, retailers have become much more active in their own right within the value chain. Large, professionalized, organizations now run most of the retailing in Western economies and are now seeking to do so in emerging economies. In addition to being substantial commercial enterprises, they have also become trusted brands with, in some cases, retailers' own label brands being regarded as of similar or higher quality than those of branded manufacturers. Now retailing is the legitimate focus of business strategy, marketing, operations management, and other conventional business disciplines. With a number of the largest retail companies worldwide currently generating levels of retail sales larger than that of some countries, and one larger than all but six, the ways in which such companies manage their business, their brand image, and the reality that lies behind it become ever more important. Market share reflects retailers' influence over consumers, competitors, and suppliers. And whilst scale is associated with brand power, it also brings responsibility.

How has this transformation been brought about? This chapter examines the retailer's journey to market power within developed economies to date and explores the nature of the retail business model and of retail change. It singles out two likely (but not wholly risk-free) drivers of growth in the efficiency and effectiveness of the sector into the future: the particular contribution of information and communications technology, and the prospects held out by it for international growth. It concludes by examining retailers' own agenda for change.

The Oxford Institute of Retail Management was founded in Templeton College in 1985—in the middle of this initial period of transformation.[1] Its work, seeking to relate sound scholarship to the practical needs of retailers and other consumer-facing organizations, has involved it in activities ranging from building awareness and insight into the sector within Oxford's management degree programmes to applied research projects as well as to executive education. It has developed a particular interest in the intersection between retailing, marketing, and technology in order to bring about a better understanding of retail change, formats, and strategy. The research conducted by the Institute over the past twenty years forms the basis of some the insights offered in this chapter.

The Retail Journey

Examining the role of the 'middleman', as early as 1960, McVey questioned the correctness of certain alignments in the value chain, which had been presented by others as being somehow 'right' or 'customary', with manufacturers being regarded as pre-eminent.[2] Very little value was added, it was suggested, save perhaps through additional convenience to the end consumer.

Known pejoratively in the UK as 'barrow boys' or costermongers, the earliest retailers were simply itinerant traders.[3] One of the characteristics of retail modernization is the transformation of the sector from one of traders, to family firms with typically only one or two shop units, to a sector that is dominated in many product areas by large businesses controlling several retail outlets. As a result, McVey argued, the power position of manufacturers was—frankly—speculative and, when properly organized, the retailer ought to be capable of exercising economic power in its own right:

the middleman is not a hired link in a chain forged by manufacturers, but rather an independent market, the focus of a large group of customers from whom s/he buys.[2]

Since then, retailers have been assiduous in growing larger and faster than their competitors, whilst seeking either to be different from these competitors or to undercut them on price—either way, attracting and keeping customers, and gaining efficiencies in systems and procedures. Bell has described the way this has happened for food retailing, for example, as being a kind of 'inexorable logic'.[4] The process, he suggests, had four stages and, in general terms, happened earlier in the USA than in other developed markets. It involved:

- The initial development of multiple retail chains, as retailers sought to increase their buying power. The early exponents of this process in Europe were consumer co-operatives and during this stage most chains, including the co-ops, were organized on a regional basis within a country. This was followed by the emergence of national retail chains with large market shares.

- The second stage development of large-scale retail formats. The emergence of these formats across Europe coincided with a period of relaxation in planning regimes, initially in Belgium, followed by France, Spain, Portugal, and then the UK. Although planning regimes have since become more restrictive, the growth of large-scale outlets resulted in a reduction in the number of small corner stores and the decline of town centre and downtown supermarkets.

- The third stage development of dedicated distribution systems by the large-integrated retailers. The development and application of scanning systems and associated technology provided the necessary information for the supply chain to be reversed from 'producer push' to 'consumer pull'. A consequence of this process was the decline of traditional wholesalers and cash and carries, which had the effect of further disadvantaging small retailers.

- Finally, the emergence of retail chains as national brands in their own right. The consequence was a shift from head-to-head price competition to a differentiation strategy based on factors such as range, service, store format, and location. In the process, retailers themselves became branded formats, as well as the suppliers of own-branded products, and in some cases these own-branded products were regarded as of similar or higher quality than those of branded manufacturers.[5]

The Growth of Multiple Retail Chains

Whilst as recently as 1990 there were no retailers in the US Fortune 500, over the intervening period retailers within developed markets have become much more active in their own right within a 'buyer-driven' value chain. By 2006, Fortune reported that nearly one-fifth of their ranking was now made up of general merchandisers, food and drug stores, and speciality retailers alone.[6] The UK Department of Trade & Industry's 2006 Value Added Scoreboard showed that general retailing was the fifth largest sector in the UK by value added, with UK food retailers growing their value added by 8 per cent in the previous year alone.[7] European retailers amongst the top 700 firms across Europe generated some £90 billion in value added during 2005–6. The world's largest retailer, Wal-Mart, employs 1.8 million associates worldwide and operates nearly 6,500 stores across 14 countries.

The implications of size become significant when retailers affect consumer choice, obtain a relative competitive advantage, and/or influence supplier profitability. Market share reflects retailers' influence over consumers, competitors, and suppliers. Absolute size is also important vis-à-vis suppliers. The potential impact of retailer size can be measured by their ability to extract non-cost related discounts from suppliers. Size becomes important here when the potential lost volume to a supplier has a significant effect on profit. Businesses whose profit is highly sensitive to changes in sales volume are more likely to offer non-cost-related discounts and are more vulnerable. Thus the exact level of size at which a retailer exercises power varies with the financial structure of each supplier. These issues have brought retailing increasingly to the attention of the regulatory authorities.

Nevertheless, the ability of domestic retail firms to both stimulate and provide for an upsurge in consumer demand has proved an important contributor to the economic well-being of a number of countries. The UK economy alone was sustained over a ten-year period (1995–2005) by means of buoyant consumer spending. The volume of retail sales increased by 23 per cent over the 2000–4 period alone.

The retail sector has traditionally been characterized statistically in terms of kinds of business (food, non-food, and mixed retail businesses). This differentiation has become more difficult to sustain as some of the larger food retail businesses have extended their activities into non-food and consumer services, becoming in effect general merchandisers. But it is important to get beyond the aggregate characteristics of particular kinds of business. There is as much diversity amongst individual retail firms in respect to their efficiency and effectiveness as between retail sectors overall in some countries and this is masked at the aggregate level. The UK Department of Trade and Industry's 2006 Value Creation Scorecard examined, amongst other things, the wealth creation efficiency of European retail firms. Figure 9.1 shows this for general retailing. The analysis demonstrates real leaders and laggards within the sector.

Branding and the Development of Retail Brands

The use of branding has been a major historical source of supplier power but has now become one of the most important elements of retail strategy. The expression of the retailer as a brand serves as a means of articulating its strategic positioning choices. The traditional dominance of simplistic

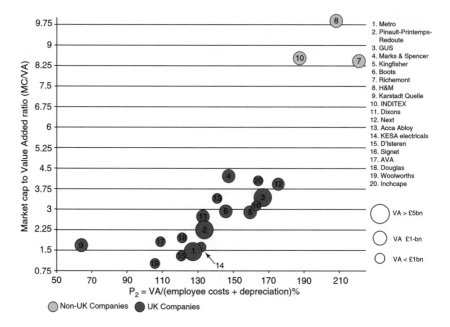

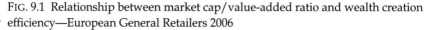

FIG. 9.1 Relationship between market cap/value-added ratio and wealth creation
efficiency—European General Retailers 2006

'product-price' announcements once reinforced commentators' views that
the sector was a relatively unprofessional proponent of marketing principles:

Each store sings the same song ... 'here tomatoes are cheaper'. The result is a poor
attribution of advertising claims and some lack of credibility.[8]

Whilst there are still examples of isolated product-price claims, as retailers
have come to control more of the supply chain, to be larger and more
corporate enterprises, and to face more competition in maturing markets,
they have come to develop increasingly coherent and professional marketing functions and expertise, made manifest in the brand. Some retailers
have even been able to project an image of 'good price' through 'every
day low price' positioning, as well as to professionally package other,
often intangible, 'non-price' factors. Branding serves to protect or increase
product and price differentiation and thereby customer loyalty.

Retail brands are defined much more than by the products retailers
sell: they are 'identifiable clusters of functional and emotional values'
according to DeChernatony and McDonald.[9] Whale proposes that retail
brands are distinctive from product brands in their ability to

- simplify our lives (as in the case of catalogue retailer Argos)
- edit our lives (as in the cases of Zara and Selfridges) or
- provide increased personalization (as in the cases of Amazon or Tesco.com).[10]

In one sense, retail brands can now truly be said to be postmodern brands in that they can seek to assist individual consumers manage their life goals. The marketing director of French hypermarket chain Auchan suggests that the company wants to be 'the creator of solutions that improve the standard of living for the majority of people'. Strong brands create strong differentiation in consumers' minds but can only be created over time. The strength of the UK Marks and Spencer brand for instance, despite its recent difficulties, lies in a long history of familiarity for the British shopper. Whilst price can still be a part of the brand offer and positioning, it is not everything. For example, German discount retailer Aldi offers the customer the chance to be a 'clever' consumer, with a carefully selected low price range (which now includes fresh foods and organics).

The Retail Business Model

The business model defines how a retailer selects its market and customers, defines and differentiates its products and range, promotes itself, acquires and keeps its customers, uses its resources, defines key processes, and captures profit or return on investment. Variety stores, for example, are clearly based on a different business model than are specialist hardware stores. At the same time, it overlaps to an extent with the business model for department stores.

There is no one 'correct' business model for retailing. However, it is not unreasonable to expect organizations with similar objectives, markets, and customers to be found clustered together. By way of example, Figure 9.2 shows, grouped by colour, the respective 'envelopes' within which particular types of retailers trade given their relative levels of labour productivity and efficiency in wealth creation. All clothing retailers, for example, trade at a much lower level of labour productivity compared to furniture retailers.

Although a variety of key performance indicators (KPIs) of this kind are used by the UK retail firms, interviews with senior retail managers by the Oxford Institute of Retail Management in 2004 identified twenty-one indicators in the areas of space, labour, and capital use commonly

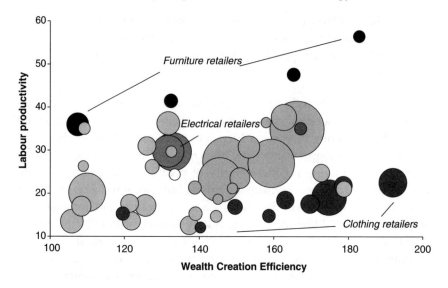

FIG. 9.2 'Horses for courses'

Note: The size of each circle represents the total value-added by each company; a company's position in respect of labour productivity represents the value-added created per employee and, in respect of wealth creation efficiency, the output produced for each pound of input during the year. The analysis demonstrates real leaders and laggards within sectors, but also shows there is considerable variety by subsector, which determines the different potential ranges within which wealth creation efficiency can occur. (*Source*: OXIRM analysis of the Department of Trade & Industry data 2006)

employed by retailers, though with some variations and modifications according to the particular needs of their businesses (Box 9.1).[11]

Retailers often use the KPIs listed above to measure performance according to the various components of their business models, but we need some way of organizing these rather disparate lists. The major elements of retail business models can be divided into those on the supply side—the costs—and those on the demand side—the sales. Put in simple terms, a retail firm has to use its property, people, and technology to provide the right product in the right place at the right time. From these models it is possible to devise a generic retail business model, as shown in Figure 9.3.

The six elements identified here—size, location, number of customers, range, frequency of purchase, and access—are the key components of any retail business model. All additional elements can be interpreted as a function of one or more of these elements.

A measure of the usefulness of such a model is in whether it reveals the differences between retail formats that look similar or, alternatively,

Box 9.1 Key performance indicators identified by OXIRM

Space key performance indicators (KPIs)

The efficient use of space, given its cost, provided the basis for the five most frequently cited KPIs in this area:

- Sales/profit density (sometimes in units per square foot)
- Stock availability (closely relates to and determines space productivity)
- Ratio of selling vs. non-selling space
- Linear density (in an experimental stage for many)
- Trading intensity, or balance of customer traffic, and physical limitations of stores

Labour KPIs

- Labour cost budgets (weekly/monthly) for each store
- Overall labour costs (including as percentage of sales)
- Sales/profit per employee
- Sales/profit per hour worked
- Gross margin return on labour (GMOL)
- Units sold per hour worked
- Till throughput (items per hour going through the checkout till)
- Efficiency ratio (the ratio of hours required to run the store efficiently according to the model, compared to the actual hours used)
- Staff turnover
- Customer satisfaction measures of various kinds

Capital KPIs

- Return on capital employed (ROCE) and its variations
- Economic profit or economic value added (EVA)
- Payback period
- DCF-based (discounted cash flow) metrics
- Cost of maintaining the capital base (store base)
- Depreciation as percentage of sales

detects the similarities in retail formats that look very different but actually share the same underlying structural elements in their business models. This can be done by plotting the various elements on a 'spider web chart'. Figure 9.4 provides a spider web chart for an out-of-town discount clothing format and Figure 9.5 for a jewellery retailer with a chain of shopping centre outlets.

Figure 9.6 differentiates between convenience stores, and Figure 9.7 shows the similarities between two very different businesses.

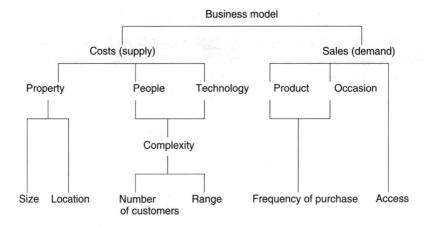

FIG. 9.3 The major elements of retail business models

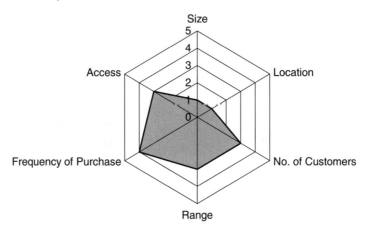

FIG. 9.4 Generic spider web chart for out-of-town discount clothing

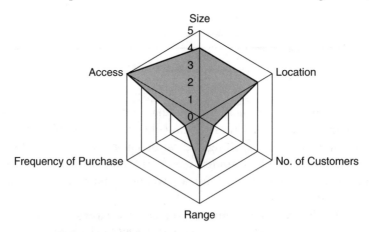

FIG. 9.5 Generic spider web chart for a shopping centre jeweller

FIG. 9.6 The differences between particular types of convenience store

In addition, KPIs can be used to provide a more specific description and quantitative assessment of a business model, as shown in Table 9.1. For example, under 'access', actual footfall figures and number of transactions can be used, and under 'range', the precise number of SKUs carried.

Retail Innovation and Format Change

Retailing does not stand still. Innovation is the lifeblood of the sector, but it is important to recognize that even what retailers call 'strategic innovation' is often continuous rather than of a step-change nature, which can make it more difficult to identify fixed points of stability for analysis.[12] The CEO of one UK retailer pointed out that 'there's no typical process. Companies often create great strategic plans—but opportunities often derail them. More often, they are drawing on a "gut feel" that something will work, rather than anything deeply planned or developed.'

Retail innovation also exhibits hybrid characteristics of product and service innovation and tends to have relatively short cycles, being easy to imitate, and making speed to market essential. Tesco's Sir Terry Leahy

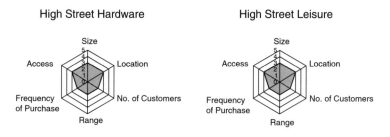

FIG. 9.7 High street stores' similarities

TABLE 9.1 Measuring the elements of a business model

Axis	Example measures
Size	Square metres
Location	Rental, rates
Number of customers	Footfall in the store, number of transactions
Range	Number of product groups, lines and suppliers
Frequency of purchase	Stock availability
Access	Footfall past the store

has suggested that strategic innovation in retailing is akin to 'changing the engine while in the middle of a race'.

Retail brands and formats are not static, however. Here we define a retail format as the physical embodiment of a retail business model, the framework that relates the firm's activities to its business context and strategy. Models of format change were first developed in the USA, where large-scale retailing has been around longer.[13] The apparently cyclical nature of the sector in the USA ('what goes around comes around') led initially to the development of McNair's 'wheel of retailing' concept in 1958 (Figure 9.8), which sought to account for the rise and fall of particular formats. The current weakness of US department stores might be said to exemplify the wheel's 'vulnerable phase'.

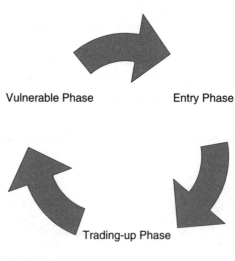

Vulnerable Phase   Entry Phase

Trading-up Phase

FIG. 9.8 The 'wheel of retailing'
Source: Ref. 14.

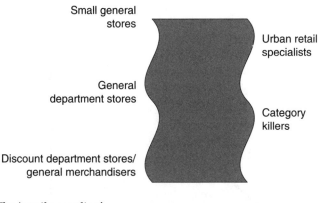

FIG. 9.9 The 'retail accordion'
Source: Ref. 15.

But analysts found the 'wheel' concept difficult to apply to all retail sectors. The concept of the 'retail accordion' (Figure 9.9) was subsequently developed. It replaced the 'wheel of retailing' with the idea of continuing fluctuation between dominance by general merchandisers and specialists, which again seemed to be a clear feature of US retailing.

Arguably, the 'retail accordion' has also been seen at work in the UK, when the weaker firms in the general department and variety stores sector gave way to clothing specialists such as Burton Group and Next, and to category killers such as Toys 'r' Us and IKEA. The contemporary growth of Tesco and Asda—Wal-Mart's non-food activities—might in turn be seen as the resurgence of general merchandisers.

Recently, commentators have come up with the concept of the 'big middle'. This relates the retail life cycle to a framework of relative price and non-price factors (Figure 9.10).

Achieving economies of scale allows innovative and low-price retailers to move into the 'big middle'. Thereafter, complacency, or an inability to sustain the right balance between price and non-price factors for customers, can result in retailers losing the essential centre ground. Under this view companies like Wal-Mart and Target have successfully maintained their dominance within the 'big middle', whereas conventional department store retailers such as K-Mart and Sears find themselves 'in trouble'.

The Contribution of Technology

The application of technology has driven much of the growth and success of modern retailing and is likely to play as critical a role in the future.

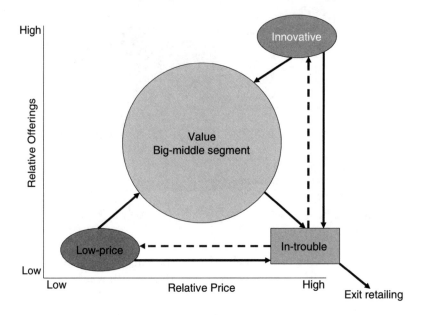

FIG. 9.10 The concept of the 'big middle'
Source: Ref. 13.

Perhaps the biggest contribution to the efficiency and effectiveness of the retail sector over the past ten years from the introduction of technology has come from

- the sector's investment in article numbering and electronic point of sale and
- the increasingly extensive use of information systems to track goods and understand and track customers.

The technologies that have the potential to determine the sector's future efficiency and effectiveness can be thought of in a number of ways. We can think in terms of the characteristics of the technology itself, differentiating between core or foundation technologies such as local area network (LAN) or wireless networking, enabling technologies such as item repositories or databases, and application technologies such as point of sale or item management solutions.[16] On the other hand, we can think in terms of the business impact of the technology on the value chain itself. Some technologies have leveraged—or have the potential to leverage—the whole value chain (such as radio frequency identification technology [RFID]); some address operational efficiencies in either upstream activities (such

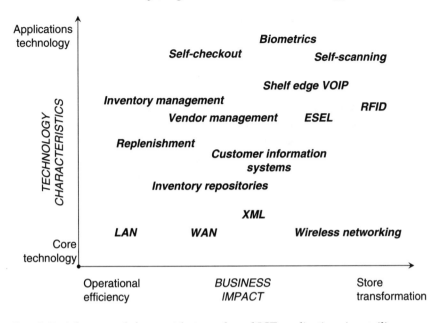

FIG. 9.11 A framework for considering selected ICT applications in retailing
Source: OXIRM (2006).

as automated storage and retrieval) or downstream activities (such as self-scanning or in-store TV).[17]

Figure 9.11 brings these two dimensions together. It is of course by no means clear whether a particular technology offers purely efficiency gains or has the capability of transforming the store. This will depend on a number of factors, not least the ability of the firm to realize the strategic potential of the technology. Similarly, the extent to which particular technologies are simply pre-requisites to compete or have the potential to offer genuine competitive advantage is also open to debate and changes over time. For example, self-checkout—once considered to be a competitive innovation—is seen by a number of retail subsectors in the USA as now being essential to compete.

It has been suggested that RFID will provide the future enterprise-wide, cross-chain technology of the future. RFID is being used upstream even if consumer privacy issues have slowed developments downstream. A study published by the influential Advanced Practices Council (APC) of the Society for Information Management concluded that RFID and its associated applications provided both process and product improvements, as well as some potentially innovative marketing applications.[18]

By making goods easier to trace, RFID could also cut waste, out-of-stocks, and shrinkage. Procter and Gamble estimated in 2004 that between 10 and 16 per cent of its products were out-of-stock at any one time. But there are also several barriers to be overcome. The APC report cautioned that RFID systems would need to operate across the regulatory boundaries of countries and regions to be effective. Costs have also proved to be a significant barrier to extending RFID beyond such applications as animal-tracking and road-toll collection. Nor is the technology, as ever, proving completely foolproof. Palette read-rates of 80 per cent or less have been reported because of electromagnetic interference.

The Limits of Technology

However, there are several sets of constraints affecting the retail sector's ability to undertake successful investment in technology. Constraints of five main kinds can be identified:

1. *Scale, Cost, and Complexity of Transformational Technology Projects*: As ICT has become cheaper and the cost of physical assets has increased, the economics would now seem to favour ICT investment. However, with many operational efficiency gains achieved from existing systems, the increasingly transformational nature of these projects can make them extraordinarily difficult to undertake. The bigger projects essentially and increasingly carry with them the need for cultural transformation, as much as technical. And there are often a great many to choose between. One UK mixed goods retailer suggested to us that 'at any one time we may be actively considering between 75–150 technology-related projects across the business'.[11] For some companies, there is also a legacy of underinvestment, which makes the job even more challenging.

2. *Organization of ICT Investment*: Part of the challenge of ICT investment lies in effective project management and organization. Analysis in Oxford showed that in 2003–4, some 75 per cent of IT projects in the UK (irrespective of industry) were 'challenged' in terms of cost or schedule overrun.[19] Whilst only 9 per cent were abandoned, just 16 per cent were considered successful by companies. The news here is rather better for retailing: fully 23 per cent of IT projects we surveyed were classed as successful according to the externally benchmarked Standish definition.[20] Nevertheless, the challenges of schedule and budget were shared by retailers, where incremental change in projects underway was also an issue. We calculated that for each change in the project specification, 6 per cent was added to the time schedule and 3 per cent to the budget.

3. *Difficulties of Measuring Effectiveness of IT Spend*: A further difficulty comes from the need to measure IT spend effectiveness. Quantifying the link between technology investment, return on that investment, and eventual company performance is a tortuous process at best. In a generally deflationary environment, but with some fixed costs rising and constant pressure to demonstrate the ability IT has to achieve efficiencies within the retail value chain, it becomes even more problematic. This is far from straightforward for three reasons, as a recent study for the DTI established: software costs, ICT investment intangibility, and the time taken for the benefits of ICT investment to emerge.[11] These barriers also affect others within the supply chain, notably smaller suppliers to larger retail firms, who may be too small to bear the costs of introducing required IT systems.

4. *Lack of Products Delivering Real Customer Benefits*: Whilst upstream supply chain ICT investments have an impact on shoppers in terms, for example, of availability, shoppers have to deal with an increasing amount of customer-facing technology in store. For example, according to the Point of Purchase Association International (POPAI), there are some 22,000 screens being used for promotional purposes by retailers in the UK alone, excluding those in electrical and audio-visual retail stores.[21] If we ask what consumers want for their retail technology, then the answer has to be context specific: a contribution to value for money in their transaction or a demonstration that the cost of technology is not funded through higher prices, or is providing benefits for the consumer and not just the retailer.

5. *Customer Privacy Concerns*: Finally, however, what some customers apparently increasingly want is reassurance that the introduction of new information technology will not breach their personal or information privacy. The extent of hardening consumer attitudes to the introduction of RFID is often evidenced to demonstrate this. Paradoxically, however, the technology where consumers feel increasingly in control is just that where they are, in principle, at greater risk of breaches in personal or information privacy: online, at home or at work. In the online marketplace, consumers see themselves as willing adopters of retail technology, through e-commerce, rather than being in the position of having it perhaps unwillingly thrust on them in store.

Technology and Consumers

As a service industry, satisfying the consumer lies at the heart of the retail enterprise. Some regard the customer as the ultimate driver of change for the retail sector. Others suggest that the retailer can play a role in driving innovation and development in the market, addressing consumers' latent needs.[22] Broader demographic and lifestyle changes will also affect the ways in which consumers regard the retail proposition and the extent to which technological solutions will be considered acceptable. But we should also take account of the very different biological, social, and psychological processes associated with ageing. The think-tank Demos has commented:

After having transformed every single life-stage they have passed through, baby boomers are set to change the perception and meaning of older age. [They are] savvy and demanding consumers with clear ideas about the kinds of services and products they want. Boomers are happy to 'shop around' to find the best service and expect flexibility from providers to suit their needs.[23]

Such consumers expect an increasingly wide range of basic requirements to be met in their retail experience. They are technologically literate. The so-called order-qualifying criteria include reliable product availability in store or online, together with a well-priced product based on clear value for money principles.[24,25] This sounds (and is) simple, but it is not easy. 'Basic retail requirements' can be met (but are not always) using the technologies already in place for point-of-sale and inventory management including sales-based ordering and replenishment systems.[26] Underlying technologies for these retail firms 'behind the curve' will be those technologies already in use by the leading players to collect and synchronize data on goods and customers.

However, this may not be sufficient to develop and sustain a competitive advantage. Order-qualifying criteria are proliferating: queue management systems are increasingly necessary in the high-trading intensities of UK retailing; in the USA self-checkout is becoming increasingly the norm not just in grocery retailing but in home improvement retailing and other mass (rather than speciality) retailing sectors. Furthermore, according to some commentators, an emerging generation of consumers are exhibiting much more independent, 'non-linear' requirements: seeking to pick what they want when they want it, without being exposed to traditional branding messages.

Sometimes, this may mean that some consumers will neither appreciate nor respond to in-store technology as presently implemented. For example, despite extensive experimentation, retail digital signage has not yet met its objectives. Underlying technologies to assist with determining customer appeal and return on investment in this in-store area comprise customer insight analytics (including loyalty marketing databases) and promotional effectiveness tools. However, newer technologies catering to consumers' increasing concerns over ID theft and speeding checkout operations may also be of interest here, including biometrics.

Technology and the Retail Value Chain

At heart, retailers do two apparently simple things: (*a*) provide readily identifiable locations (through stores, at home via mail order or Internet or by means of a mixture of channels) where final consumers enter into the transactions by which they acquire goods and services sourced by the retailer; and (*b*) facilitate and encourage such transactions by providing support services of various kinds, including displays, stocks, cash, and credit facilities. Retail logistics comprise a key building block in this process of intermediation.

Leading retailers have increasingly sought to better exploit the sector's conventional value chain. For some elements, this has involved outsourcing to third parties. For some retailers outsourcing has been driven by efficiency issues, but for others it enables them to keep up with the latest developments that work (i.e. have been tried and tested by the third-party logistics providers).

With the recent growth of non-store channels, retailers have had to think rather differently about the conventional value chain and conceive of a chain or network that is not exclusively store-based, but that involves direct-to-home marketing and distribution. Since a simple increase in routes to market does not necessarily increase overall levels of demand, those making extensive online commitments have had to wrestle with new business models. In particular, convergent multichannel value chains at the very minimum require tighter control of costs and creative integration solutions.

We suggested earlier that the retail value chain has been made somewhat more complex by significant growth in non-store retailing channels. Whilst direct mail order channels have accounted for some 5–7 per cent of retail sales in most developed markets, the arrival of the Internet has clearly led to new market channel opportunities for the retailer and additional channel choice for the consumer.[27] Indeed, evidence suggests that e-commerce penetration of total retail sales is higher in the UK than in the USA. Other things being equal, however, additional channels add costs to the retail business. The firms that have chosen market development via channel diversification will face the need to develop effective multichannel strategies.[28]

Underlying technologies include harmonization of standards and business processes and potential integration of store- and non-store-based supply chains. There are specific technologies of relevance to the electronic non-store channel for physical goods, which includes order management, picking and packing systems (in store or in a dedicated distribution centre), and software and systems associated with the design and development of a website or a mobile portal. The future opportunity of a genuinely multichannel solution is the ability to gain cross-channel customer insight, cross-sell, or up-sell between channels.

Technology has been used to leverage particular elements of the retail value chain with varying degrees of success. Indeed, it has been argued that retailers would have found it difficult to expand command and control systems beyond relatively constrained branch networks without the assistance of ICT. Retailers have not always been enthusiastic about technology, however. According to a European Commission study in the early 1990s, the sector in Europe at least was somewhat conservative.[29] Firms were adapters rather than innovators, using information technology to support existing operations. As a result, investment in ICT conferred little lasting competitive advantage even if it managed to raise rudimentary barriers to entry. Indeed, 'successful' retail ICT for many at that time, said the study, comprised projects that did not involve long-term research and development, provided a visible financial benefit, came without extensive capital commitment, and provided for low risk, staged implementation.

There have been exceptions to the rule, both in terms of ubiquitous technologies and in terms of firms. A few leading companies in the early 1990s were using ICT to deal with large strategic issues or to seek integration. Such companies were comfortable undertaking their own R&D and, as a result, had the potential to use ICT to enable a 'new strategic mission'. Such missions have inevitably involved significant organizational change for retail businesses.

Technology Concerns

CIOs in a number of European retail firms were interviewed in 2003. A number felt that they had already achieved many of the individual functional benefits that ICT had to offer and their prime operational concerns were about maintaining existing systems. Their top six strategic priorities looking forward were either to do with incremental improvement and consolidation or with integration:

1. Integrating IT systems and information
2. Expanding the use of IT across the business
3. Improving customer service
4. Increasing supply chain efficiency

5. Using IT to enhance corporate governance
6. Consolidating and driving out business benefits.[30]

Just two years later, however, European CIOs expressed a much higher number of strategic goals:

1. Improving business processes
2. Gaining competitive advantage
3. Demonstrating value of IT projects that help drive business growth
4. Cost control
5. Faster innovation

Commentators report that some (but by no means all) retailers are now looking much further ahead, in terms perhaps of seven to eight years rather than two or three, 'in the wake of many of the visions of the stores of the future, like Metro'.[31] Metro, Germany's largest retailer and the world's third largest retail firm, made the deliberate choice to set out its vision of the store of the future by building one in Rheinberg.[32] The company suggested that 'the application and acceptance of new technologies in retailing will be tested under real conditions. The objective is to find benefit-oriented solutions entailing real advantages for both the retail industry and the consumers.' Vendor partners included SAP, Intel, IBM, and T-Systems as well as multinational consumer goods firms. Strictly speaking, this was a showcase of relevant leading edge technologies brought together in one place rather than a 'store of the future' as such. Nevertheless, they allowed the retailer and German customers to form a view of the attractiveness of particular customer technologies. Metro's approach has precedents: Ahold's Store 2000 and Tesco's Shopping and Information Service (a precursor of e-commerce) in 1980, to name but two.

By comparison, there are no current 'stores of the future' in the UK. Most UK retailers tend to prefer a 'sprinkler' to a 'waterfall' strategy, with isolated technological innovations trialled less obtrusively in individual or small groups of stores or warehouses. Further, for some UK firms, there can be the perception that there is a 'first-mover disadvantage', with each firm waiting for another to make the first move, as well as the inevitable mistakes, from which followers can learn.

Technology and Regulation

Retailers' strategies and the attractiveness of particular technologies are also fundamentally driven by the regulatory environment in which they operate. For example, the combined effects of restrictive planning policy towards out- and edge-of-town retail development in the UK and of wide-spread adoption of congestion charging or road pricing in the absence of concomitant investment in public transport are likely to further reinforce the attractiveness of e-commerce technologies amongst consumers and retailers. Already, e-commerce market shares in the UK are running broadly twice as high as in the USA. Commentators point to lack of satisfaction with the existing offline offer (notably its lack of accessibility—compared to, say, that in the USA—and more general congestion effects).

A second, significant emerging driver is that around future environmental regulation. Firms with extensive property portfolios, such as retailers, are substantial energy users. Further, increased responsibilities for recycling will add complexity to the logistics function. Technologies—such as design simulation and modelling applications—are likely to be important in producing more energy-efficient stores. Similarly, improved materials handling and vehicle utilization systems will materially assist retailers seeking to meet their recycling responsibilities cost-effectively.

Competition in New and International Markets

Curiously, whilst the most successful retailers are clearly focused on branding their offer and are becoming more international as businesses, they have yet truly to make their impression on the global branding stage. In 2000 Interbrand's survey found only three conventional retail brands in the top 100 worldwide by value: Gap, Benetton, and IKEA.[33] A number of vertically integrated luxury goods manufacturers (Gucci, Louis Vuitton, and Armani) were also represented. By 2006, there were still only three conventional retailers in the top 100, but Benetton had been replaced by Zara and these three joined by online retailer Amazon.com.[34]

From a geographical perspective, in a number of subsectors, opportunities for further domestic growth through merger or acquisition are limited by regulation or size of opportunity. The UK Institute of Grocery Distribution[35] has sought to prioritize the size and significance of the market opportunity for retailers, using both hard and soft factors, from one to five:

- *Priority 1 Markets*: Markets that should receive immediate consideration for increased investment and are of strategic importance in the short-term.
- *Priority 2 Markets*: Markets that should be actively researched, with a view to short- or medium-term investment.

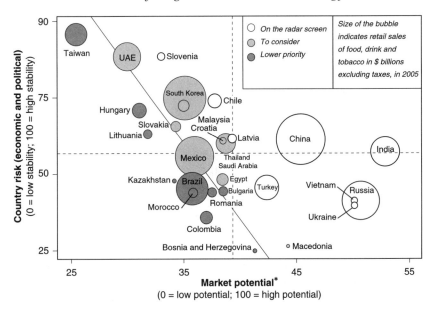

FIG. 9.12 Risks and opportunities in international retail development
Source: Ref. 36.

- *Priority 3 Markets*: Markets that should be considered for medium-term investment.
- *Priority 4 Markets*: Markets that should be considered, although not of immediate importance. These could also be markets that are viewed as 'in-fill' opportunities and that help reinforce an existing regional presence.
- *Priority 5 Markets*: A watching brief should be kept until further development occurs in the long term. These markets may also constitute additional 'in-fill' opportunities.

AT Kearney conducts an annual assessment of international retail market prospects, formally evaluating the risk as well as the market opportunity of particular markets for retail firms. Figure 9.12 illustrates the most recent trade-offs perceived by the consultancy (Table 9.2).

The key challenge from internationalization is the potential for transferability of value chain capabilities honed in the domestic market into a new setting. Some, but by no means all, large retailers have been successful in their attempts to internationalize. The adoption of standardized technology can help with this, but the business environment and the legacy systems (in the case of acquired business) may slow down productivity and profitability growth. For example, Tesco's growth in the Thai market

TABLE 9.2 The IGD global market index

Country	Rank	% Score	Status
China	1	65.2	Priority 1 Markets
Russia	2	63.9	
India	3	60.0	
USA	4	55.7	Priority 2 Markets
Ireland	5	52.2	
Turkey	6	51.3	
Ukraine	7	50.9	
South Korea	8	50.4	

Abbreviation: Institute of Grocery Distribution: IGD.

Source: IGD Research 2005.

was initially hindered by a poor underlying geo-demographic and store location data environment (which is extraordinarily rich in the UK) and then by the tightening regulatory environment following the military coup in 2006.

Retailers: The Agenda for Change

Today, retailers' concerns about the future in many ways remain as tightly focused as they have ever been. Customer loyalty and retention and correct format and channel choice have been paramount. A useful bell-wether of such concerns has been the annual international 'Top of Mind' survey undertaken by the CIES (Table 9.3). Certain aspects of the CEOs' concerns almost remain unspoken: competition has been such an immediate priority throughout this period that the survey thought to quiz executives on this point only in 2005.

Chief executives within retailing see the future scale and intensity of competition as being their chief concern in that it immediately affects profitable business growth. Inevitably this driver tends to focus attention first on technologies that can deliver efficiency and competitiveness gains. There is a particular interest in investments that can reduce both costs and complexity in the retail business. Much of this complexity can arise from the organic growth of large multiple branch network businesses, with enterprise-wide solutions such as ERP being seen as attractive integrative mechanisms. Such investments nevertheless have to provide a convincing return on investment. There have been a number of high-profile enterprise-wide failures that will lead to companies looking much more carefully at their benefits.

TABLE 9.3 'Top of Mind' issues amongst global food retail CEOs, 2002–6

Issue	2006	2005	2004	2003	2002
Competition	1	1	NA	NA	NA
The retail offer	2	3	3	3	3
Technical standards/supply chain efficiency	3	4	4	4	7
Food safety/security	4	4	1	2	1
Human resources	5	10	8	7	8
Customer loyalty and marketing	6	2	2	1	2
Consumer health & nutrition	6	7	6	NA	NA
Retailer–supplier relations	8	6	5	NA	
Internationalization	9	11	5	6	5
The economy and consumer demand	10	12	9	5	
Corporate responsibility	11	9	12	11	NA
Regulations	12	13	10	—	—

Source: CIES 2006,[37] 2005,[26] and 2003.[30]

Driving technologies here include the development of information (inventory and customer) repositories, data warehouses, and technologies that assist with the further streamlining of the supply chain. Smaller more incremental technology applications within the context of longer-term goals can, however, deliver competitiveness benefits more clearly and quickly than enterprise-wide ones and are often very attractive.

But there is another side to improving competitiveness that has less to do with cost control. Whilst seeking efficiency gains, retailers also have to provide levels of customer service in stores and online appropriate to the nature of the retail offer and to the changing demands of consumers. This is, and will continue to be, a challenging trade-off.

The successful growth of a retailer can be seen as a consequence of the effectiveness of its strategy: its ability to create long-term superior financial performance through the cultivation of valuable internal resources and their matching to the set of most advantageous external opportunities as it grows. But the environment for strategic decision-making in retailing has become considerably more complex. The ultimate drivers of retail change and the permissible range of external opportunities are generated by the demographic, political, and economic forces in society, alterations in social values and behaviours and in the communications and technological revolutions we are experiencing. Retailers still respond to, but now in many ways, help create or facilitate these changes.

References and Notes

1. R. L. Davies and D. W. Walters, 'Development Programmes for Retail Management: Templeton's New Institute', *Retail & Distribution Management*, 13/6(Nov.–Dec. 1985): 19.
2. P. McVey, 'Are Channels of Distribution What the Textbooks Say?', *Journal of Marketing*, 24/3(Jan. 1960): 61–5.
3. A. Adburgham, *Shops and Shopping, 1800–1914* (London: George Allen & Unwin, 1964).
4. R. Bell, 'Food Retailing in Southern Europe', *European Retail Digest*, 25(2000): 29.
5. H. Laaksonen and J. Reynolds, 'Own Brands in Food Retailing across Europe', *Journal of Brand Management*, 2/1(1994): 37–46.
6. *Fortune*, 'Fortune 500's Ranking of America's Largest Corporations, 2006'; see http://money.cnn.com/magazines/fortune/fortune500/.
7. Department of Trade & Industry, *The Value Added Scoreboard: Commentary & Analysis* (Norwich: HMSO, 2006); see http://www.innovation.gov.uk/value_added/default.asp?page = 62.
8. J.-N. Kapferer, 'Beyond Positioning: Retailer's Identity', in *Retail Strategies for Profit and Growth* (Amsterdam: ESOMAR, 1986).
9. L. DeChernatony and M. H. B. McDonald, *Creating Powerful Brands in Consumer, Service and Industrial Markets* (3rd edn.; Oxford: Butterworth Heinemann, 2004).
10. M. Whale, 'Same Thing, Only Different: the Retail Pursuit of Differentiation', *European Retail Digest*, 29(Mar. 2001): 7.
11. Department of Trade & Industry, *Assessing the Productivity of the UK Retail Sector* (Oxford Institute of Retail Management, 2004); see www.berr.gov.uk/files/file10996.pdf
12. L. Hristov and J. Reynolds, 'Visions of Innovation: a Practitioner's Perspective' (Paper given at the Conference on Contemporary Issues in Retail Marketing, Nov. 2005, Manchester Metropolitan University Business School).
13. M. Levy, D. Grewal, and R. A. Peterson, 'The Concept of the "Big Middle"', *Journal of Retailing*, 81/2(2005): 83–8.
14. M. P. McNair, 'Significant Trends and Developments in the Postwar Period', in A. B. Smith (ed.), *Competitive Distribution in a Free, High Level Economy and Its Implication for the University of Pittsburgh* (Pittsburgh: University of Pittsburgh Press, 1958).
15. S. Hollander, 'Notes on the Retail Accordion', *Journal of Retailing*, 42(Summer 1966): 29–40.
16. CISCO Systems Inc., *2010: The Retail Roadmap for Chief Executives* (2003).
17. J. F. Rayport and J. J. Sviokla, 'Exploiting the Virtual Value Chain', *Harvard Business Review* 76/6(1995): 75–85.
18. J. Henderson and N. Ventrakaman, *Disruptive Technologies* (Advanced Practitioner Council (APC), Society for Information Management, 2003).

19. C. Cuthbertson and C. Sauer, 'The State of IT Project Management in the UK, 2002–2003', *Computer Weekly*, 2003; see http://www.cw360ms.com/pmsurveyresults/surveryresults.pdf

20. The Standish definition of a successful project is one 'completed on time, on budget and with all the features/functions originally specified'; see http://www.standishgroup.com

21. According to a recent survey by Point of Purchase Association International (POPAI) and Samsung; see http://www.popaidigital.com/research.html

22. U. Elg, 'Retail Market Orientation: A Preliminary Framework', *International Journal of Retail & Distribution Management*, 31/2(2003): 107–17.

23. J. Huber, quoted in BBC News, 'Viewpoints: Britain's Ageing Society' (2004); see http://news.bbc.co.uk/1/hi/uk/4003731.stm

24. Terry Hill (ed.), *Manufacturing Strategy* (3rd edn.; Basingstoke, UK: Palgrave Macmillan, 2000).

25. J. Reynolds and M. Wilson-Jeanselme, 'Competing for the Online Grocery Customer: the UK Experience', in N. Kornum and M. Bjerre (eds.), *Grocery E-Commerce. Consumer Behaviour and Business Strategies* (Cheltenham, UK: Edward Elgar, 2005).

26. CIES, *The CIES IT Conference 2005* (CIES, 2005); see http://www.ciesnet.com/pdf/programme/it/05_IT_Berlin_EXECUTIVE_SUMMARY.pdf

27. J. Reynolds and R. L. Davies, *The Development of Teleshopping and Teleservices* (Harlow, UK: Longman, 1988).

28. J. Reynolds, 'E-tail Marketing', in P. McGoldrick (ed.), *Retail Marketing* (3rd edn.; New York: McGraw-Hill, 2002).

29. Commission of the European Communities, *The Impact of New Technology and New Payment Systems on Commercial Distribution in the European Community* (Brussels: Commission of the European Communities, 1991).

30. CIES, *Fourth Study on the Use of IT in Food Retailing* (London: KMPG, 2003); see http://www.ciesnet.com/pdf/programme/it/cies_penfold.pdf

31. Stuart Harker, reported in G. Flood, 'Tomorrow's Retail World', *Retail Week*, June, 2005.

32. See http://www.future-store.org

33. Interbrand, *The Best Global Brands 2000 Report* (London: Interbrand, 2000).

34. Interbrand, *The Best Global Brands 2006 Report* (London: Interbrand, 2006); see http://www.interbrand.com/best_brands_2006.asp

35. Institute of Grocery Distribution (IGD), 'Global Retailing' (IGD Factsheets, 9th March, 2005); see http://www.igd.com/CIR.asp?menuid=51&cirid=848.

36. A. T. Kearney, *Building the Optimal Global Footprint* (AT Kearney, 2006); see http://www.atkearney.com/shared_res/pdf/GSLI-2006_S.pdf

37. CIES, *Top of Mind 2006* (CIES Food Business Forum, 2006).

Part III

Management Functions: Towards a New Synthesis

10

Information Management:
A New Age, A New Subject

Michael J. Earl

It would be difficult to contest that in the last sixty years one of the most significant forces for change in our lives has been information technology (IT). One probably could also assert that it was not until the mid-1960s that, other than in a relatively few avant-garde companies, computing or data processing (DP) was regarded as a rather strange, if not optional, business activity. It was at this time that Templeton College, formerly the Oxford Centre for Management Studies (OCMS), was founded. Remarkably, in an initial faculty of five founding fellows, two were interested in what was variously labelled data processing, information systems (IS), and management information systems (MIS).

Bob Tricker was a Research Fellow in Accounting and Control but with a substantive foot in information systems. He was soon to become the first professor of Management Information Systems at Warwick University. Tony Rands was a Fellow in Management Science and was interested in systems analysis and computer applications. Furthermore, Rosemary Stewart, Fellow in Organizational Behaviour, was soon to conduct an early and rigorous study of how computers affect management.[1] It was remarkable that OCMS, whether by design or emergence, identified the importance of what we now call IT and saw it as a significant issue on management agendas *and* for management education and development. I can say 'remarkable' from at least two objective perspectives: I was not at Oxford at the time and so assume no credit; and such an initiative was well ahead not only of most business and management schools in the UK but also worldwide.

Of course, IT then was not as we know it today. IT was computers, information systems were mainly administrative in nature, and IT specialists learnt mainly by doing and with the aid of local, firm-specific standards. This was what we might call the Mainframe or Data Processing Era,[2] where a mainframe computer was centrally located in a computer room; data communication was slow, chunky, and rare; batch processing of data was the norm; and specialists were able to assume control of most operations and decisions about computing applications and architecture.

It was in this era, forty years ago, that I started work as a trainee systems analyst at United Steel, probably the doyen of steel companies in the UK, an industry leader in data processing, and possibly *the* leader in operations research driven successively by Stafford Beer[3] and Keith Tocher.[4] The computer we had at head office was an ICT 1201 with storage of 8 K words (bits). Today's average laptop computer has storage of 2 Gb. Data input was done by means of eighty-column punched cards or paper tape. Most data communication was by voice over the telephone. And although there was a data preparation department of perhaps twenty or more punched card operators, there was also a typing pool of similar size.

Yet data processing was not trivial. Such configurations, and more, were repeated in the company's major plants or divisions, a DP management cadre was in place, and graduates with a diversity of degrees were joining the DP department as programmers and systems analysts.

United Steel, then, was avant-garde but this picture would be repeated in other large manufacturing and commercial companies in the developed world and in one or two service sectors. A particularly graphic account of the sudden transition from a punched card operation to a computer department at British Airways in 1958 captures the dawn of this period.[5]

By the mid-1970s at OCMS, Tricker (who had returned from Warwick to be Director of OCMS) had started to engage with the leaders of the DP and MIS function in business. In 1976, I joined Tricker as a fellow (as had Anthony Hopwood one year earlier), and one of my first executive development experiences was to be a member of a series of 'Top Management Briefings' with these leaders. Looking back, the agendas were cutting edge. I recall the Director of Computing Services at British Aerospace presenting on how computers and telecommunications were being harnessed to enable the four participating companies across Europe to design and manufacture the then new Airbus. His equivalent at Grand Metropolitan would describe the challenges and early principles of running a corporate data centre in a multi-divisional group. The head of MIS at General Motors described the development of global systems and a global MIS function. As participants we all debated such topics that in years to come would become labelled strategic alignment and IT governance.

Soon, another era was dawning, what Applegate, McFarlan, and McKenney label the Microcomputer Era.[2] Computing would become more decentralized, that is to say in the hands of departments and end-users. Although data communication allowed some networking, islands of automation were emerging in organizations, and the technical specialists had to adjust to balancing control over standards and large application development with allowing local, smaller-scale computing-based innovation and adoption of personal software tools such as spreadsheets and word processing. They had to juggle guardianship alongside mentoring and support—plus a willingness to collaborate more with end-users and line managers. At the beginning of this era we ran in Oxford executive development programmes on the promise and implications of microcomputers—and posited significant changes in information use and distribution, management decision-making, and organizational design.

Meanwhile, what was happening in the IS domain in the academic world beyond Oxford? New refereed journals were appearing, such as *MIS Quarterly* and *Information and Management*, but probably the most influential articles appeared in already established journals such as the *Harvard Business Review, Management Science,* and *Sloan Management Review.* There were, of course, practitioner journals, but only a few (including *Datamation* and *EDP Analyzer*) carried managerial and organizational articles as well as technical ones. The *Communications of the ACM* first published in 1958 also had this mix. The International Conference on Information Systems was founded in 1980 at the University of California, Los Angeles (UCLA) to bring together information systems, academics, and research-oriented practitioners.

The Harvard Business School had begun to invest seriously through Warren McFarlan and others in an Information Systems Management curriculum, producing teaching case studies, research colloquia, and textbooks that we all could use. In 1974, Jack Rockart had created the Center for Information Systems Research at the Sloan School of Management at the Massachusetts Institute of Technology and led the way for other business schools to spawn business and management-oriented research units devoted to information systems and what by 1982 we were calling IT. Notable in years to follow were such units at UCLA, the Stern School at New York University, and in 1984 in Oxford at OCMS, which by then was Templeton College.

The Oxford Institute of Information Management (OXIIM) was perhaps a product of several initiatives from 1976 to 1984. First 'Management Information Systems' became a course on the University's M.Phil. in Management Studies. 'Information Management' was an elective on the new undergraduate Engineering/Metallurgy, Economics and Management programme, which started in 1980. And in the same year, I ran a company-specific executive education programme on Managing Information Systems for the UK multinational Reckitt and Colman. This was followed by a twice-yearly executive programme for senior IT managers, jointly with Nolan, Norton & Co (a boutique IT management consulting firm set up by two former professors from Harvard Business School). The pedagogy of 'information management' was fast being developed. What was missing was sustained research. So I founded the OXIIM in 1984, initially with seed corn funding from the College's recent benefaction from Sir John Templeton.

At this time the Distributed Era of IT architecture[2] was dawning where telecommunications and computing were converging and we talked of IT or information technologies. The new-found abilities to connect, collaborate, and coordinate transactions and information, both intra-organizationally and inter-organizationally, expanded the boundaries of our thinking and led the IT industry, consultants, and academics to argue that IT was a real and substantial force for competitive advantage. As a result, both the impact and the promise of IT put IT questions on top management agendas and more business-driven approaches to decisions about information processing were advocated.

The Oxford Institute of Information Management

But why the title Information Management? There were three influences. First, Hopwood and I had written an influential article titled 'From Management Information to Information Management'.[6] This essentially comprised two frameworks for understanding the organizational use of information and information systems—with implications for managers and systems designers alike. It was not necessarily a *managerial* article. Nevertheless, as a former group systems manager in a large telecommunications company, I was convinced that IT, information systems, and information had to be formally managed like other resources. If there were financial management, production management, human resource management, and so on, then why not information management? After all, the DP/IS/MIS/IT function was becoming one of the largest in some corporations. In major airlines by the end of the 1980s, there would be well over 2,000 employees in IT and in a few years the world's larger banks would have 12,000 or so.

Finally, there was the mission of OXIIM, which was to focus on management policy questions, conducting research that rightly should take place in a business school. There were three riders to this mission. The first was

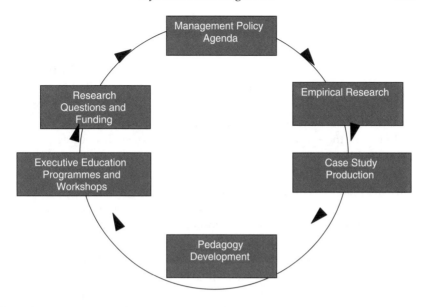

FIG. 10.1 A virtuous circle

to seek research funding from both research agencies and the business sector. The second was a deliberate orientation to field-based, empirical investigation. Third was to seek synergies with executive education. In this regard, a real demand was soon discovered as the Institute provided senior executive development programmes for firms such as Ford, Boots, Philips, Beecham, Courtaulds, Marks and Spencer, ICI, British Aerospace, and Coopers and Lybrand.

Indeed, a virtuous circle was pursued (see Figure 10.1), linking research and education and academe with practice. The latter theme was exemplified by our annual Oxford PA Conference for IT directors sharing research and real-world experiences and by encouraging secondees from industry to join our research team.

An explicit management policy agenda both suggested the need for empirical research and opened up access to organizations. Fieldwork would generate case study production (e.g., Lockett[7] and Earl and Vitale[8]). Together these would influence pedagogy, particularly grounding teaching in contemporary questions and emergent answers. Opportunities would arise for executive education, which would allow us to disseminate research findings and receive feedback as well as to test out learning tools such as case studies. Out of these, further research questions would be derived and occasionally financing opportunities.

The Research Agenda

OXIIM's purpose was 'to improve the body of knowledge on how to manage information resources so that information technology in particular and information processing in general can be fully exploited in business, government and other large organisations to the advantage of the host organisation, its members and society at large'. Inevitably, there was some flexibility in the scope of research projects but over time three principal themes evolved:

1. The planning, organization, and control of IT activities.
2. How and whether IT can be a source of competitive advantage.
3. Managing information as a resource.

Interestingly, or fortunately, these themes have not lost their currency over time. Indeed, they remain as sharp, albeit continuously evolving both theoretically and practically, over twenty years after OXIIM was founded, in what Applegate, McFarlan, and McKenney describe as the Ubiquitous Era of IT and Architecture. Here, portable and mobile intelligence is networked where everyone can access information and knowledge everywhere and where businesses and information age entrepreneurs look to IT and information as a source of value creation.

The first of the three themes has been dominant and the third theme has been most challenging. However, the research productivity has been high over twenty-two years and the business impact substantial. A regular flow of articles to top journals such as *MIS Quarterly* and the *Journal of Management Information Systems* is one test. A substantial flow of articles in the two top impact journals, the *Harvard Business Review* and *Sloan Management Review*—twelve to date—has secured an executive audience as well as academic readership. But what has been 'discovered' and said?

Organization, Sourcing, and Leadership

In the first theme, how to organize and govern IT activities has been one contribution. A series of studies here concluded that the recurring question of whether to centralize or decentralize the IT function was answered on the one hand by established principles of organization theory and on the other hand by analysing the components of IT activity and the performance of an organization's IT function.[9] The question of organizing for *new* technologies was a matter of delineating specialist responsibilities and user responsibilities—relating in part to theories of the management of innovation and of technological diffusion.[10]

For example, I and others established that host organization characteristics mostly should determine configuration of the IT function.[9] As the balance of organizational centralization and decentralization was often a function of the heterogeneity and predictability of a firm's external environment, particularly markets,[11,12] *effective* alignment of IT resources to serve business needs was likely to follow the same logic.

However, the *efficiency* of IT resources might be determined differently. The same study suggested that IT operations could benefit from economies of scale and enterprise-wide IT architecture. Centralization of operations and technical policymaking could be beneficial. Most decisions regarding the choice of IT applications in which to invest and application development and support would benefit from being decentralized to business units to facilitate alignment with business need.

Logically, of course, these recommendations can lead to creation of a federal IT organization and the question is: just how federal? Hodgkinson showed that the choice rested on fit with the corporation's strategic management style.[13] Pragmatically, it was observed that major configuration questions often arose when there was a performance crisis in IT or when a new set of technologies emerged. In the former case, our research advocated evolution and adaptation not revolution and 180-degree turns—these were costly in time, money, and morale. In the latter case, the appropriate solution was to learn from research on technological innovation—push responsibilities initially towards line users and local experimentation[6] and create new breakaway IT groups and practices.[14]

One particular IT management question that emerged in the late 1980s and has prevailed since is IT outsourcing. The risks of outsourcing were identified early on from field studies by Willcocks and Fitzgerald,[15] Lacity, Hirschheim, and Willcocks,[16] and others. They were variously a function of inevitable illogicalities in analysing what should be left to markets and what to hierarchies—to use Williamson's transaction cost economics terminology,[17] of naive management decision-making and of opportunistic or equally naive behaviour by vendors. While I concluded[18] that so much 'management' was required to minimize these risks that firms should proceed with great caution, Lacity, Willcocks, and Feeny,[19] Lacity and Willcocks,[20] and Lacity, Willcocks, and Feeny[21] conducted studies on how to make sourcing decisions and manage such risks. Key decision criteria include how critical IT is to both business operations and competitive positioning, the twin economic considerations of available in-house scale economies and the IT management track record, and the degree of technological maturity (experience) the organization has together with the degree of integration of an IT activity with other business processes. The outcome of such analyses permits decision-makers to adopt selective IT sourcing.

In the 1990s, the IT industry was prone to adopt the language of 'core' and 'non-core' in debating whether IT activities should be outsourced. This often was an over-interpretation of the concept of the core competence of the corporation developed by Hamel and Prahalad.[22] Feeny and Willcocks[23] argued that in this debate the question was more 'which IS capabilities are core to the business's future capacity to exploit IT successfully?' Based on three related research studies, they suggested that there were nine core capabilities in the three domains of business and IT vision, design of IT architecture, and delivery of IS services that should be analysed in any IT function in working out the degree of ownership or control required.

Overseeing IT activities and decisions in large organizations today, there will be a Chief Information Officer or CIO. David Feeny and I[24] examined how CIOs add value to their organizations, using data collected by Feeny in 1992 for a study of the CIO–CEO relationship and data collected later by Vivian and me for an exploration of CIO survival.[25] They concluded that seven factors differentiated effective CIOs from others. It could be argued that what is required is a combination of being a specialist manager and a general manager, as three factors relate to IT and the IT function but four factors are much more about engaging with the business and its senior executives.

This stream of work has continued for several years[26–28] and was accompanied by a study of CEO behaviours in the realm of information management.[29] Here, David Feeny and I hinted that many CEOs found provision of leadership in the information age difficult. The few who were effective focused on ten key areas of attention or intervention, all very much driven by a belief that IT was required not only to support competitive strategies today but was a potential enabler of new competitive strategies as well—indeed both a strategic threat and a strategic opportunity.

This link between IT and business strategy, often called the strategic alignment question, raises the question: How do and should organizations plan their IT investments? In short, how should they identify IT applications that both support the current competitive strategy and create new strategic options? This question has been on CIO agendas for many years.

I examined this planning process in UK companies and identified five approaches in use.[30] Each approach had a distinct emphasis and was influenced by a distinct set of stakeholders. The most effective approach in achieving alignment with current strategies, identifying new strategic alignment, and overall executive satisfaction was an 'organizational' approach. This embodied teamwork focused on key business operational problems out of which one or two themes for improving business positioning and performance emerged. Very similar to emergent and incremental models of business strategy-making proposed by Mintzberg[31] and Quinn,[32] respectively, this approach certainly was neither technocratic nor bureaucratic. It once again suggested that information management was as much a challenge of organizational behaviour and general management as of technological know-how and specialist management.

A later field study[33] of Business Process Re-engineering also revealed alternative strategies in use reflecting not only quite different concepts of process but also different beliefs of how to launch and then sustain business process re-engineering initiatives. Although robust data on the relative effectiveness of these strategies were limited, the field study evidence suggested that alignment across the domains of process, strategy, information systems, and change management and control—what we called a Process Alignment Model—could make a difference.

At a higher level of analysis, Periasamy and Feeny[34] suggested from a study of information architecture practices that while information architecture methodologies can help in creating a blueprint for IT infrastructure, which complements a business plan, a holistic approach comprising both business strategic planning and IS planning is more likely to achieve strategic alignment as a plan and as an outcome. Sauer and Willcocks[35] argued likewise and in particular that IT architecture should be placed within the larger issue of organizational architecture. Given the need for flexibility and adaptability as well as robustness and efficiency in architecture, they emphasize that there must be a recognition of how IT and organization interact to produce degrees of freedom or constraints. Importantly, therefore, Sauer and Willcocks advocate the need for a senior executive—an organizational architect—who promotes this thinking and brokers the inevitable tensions that arise.

One could conclude that in the studies summarized here the message is quite simply that information management is really just general management. In that, on the one hand, technocentric, functionally isolated, and naive models of the relative contribution of markets and hierarchies are shown to be dysfunctional this is an important conclusion. On the other hand, unreconstructed models of general management—of planning, organization, and control—which do not recognize the value-creating potential of IT, the complexity of IT operations, and the considerable impact to IT will be deficient. The central question perhaps is therefore what is different about IT—a question addressed in the last section of this chapter.

IT and Competitive Advantage

Much of the hype that comes with IT, information systems, and, today, information itself arises from the promise and claims the IT industry and profession make. Strategists ask: Can investment in IT create competitive advantage? Opinions can differ.[36] Economists ask whether investment in IT shows in improved productivity,[37] and answers seem to depend on how the relationship is measured and when the data are gathered. Micro-level evidence may be more reliable than macro-level data,[38] and it seems plausible that there are lags in returns to IT investment.

If we were to try and answer the question drawing on grand theories from business strategy, we might expect competitive advantage to be derived from IT where market positioning was enhanced, where competencies and capabilities (or firm-specific resources) were enhanced, or where new businesses or business scope were created. Feeny and Ives[39] posited three pillars of sustainable IT-based competitive advantage: generic lead time, or the time it takes for competitors to respond to a competitive initiative; competitive asymmetry, or the positioning, structural, and capability potentials of competitors to respond; and pre-emption quality, or the built-up advantages that a prime mover has to pre-empt retaliation. This framework neatly combined theories of competitive strategy and industrial economics with what makes IT different to provide both a practical framework for business and IT strategies and a research agenda.

Some years later, David Feeny[40] adopted a similar approach to revisit the question as e-commerce was taking shape. Here, the three pillars of sustainability were combined with an information analysis of the product, supply chain and value chain in business operations, a buyer behaviour and product differentiation analysis of a firm's market, and an activity and information analysis of the customer life cycle in the services domain. As an antidote to hype, this framework brought analytical rigour to help strategists discern those e-commerce applications that are more likely to enhance competitiveness—whether of competitive necessity to stay in business or competitive advantage to move ahead.

Perhaps a bigger question is: Do we have to radically rethink our models of competitive strategy given the oft-claimed power of IT and information? Jeff Sampler has argued that the strategic characteristics of information should lead to a redefining of industry structure in terms of the real boundaries of competition, industry concentration, related diversification, and innovation.[41] He sees two characteristics of information as critical: information specificity, or the extent to which the acquisition or use of information is limited to certain individuals; and information separability, or the extent to which information can be meaningfully separated from the transaction generating the information and captured in digital form. Analysis of industries and their players on these two dimensions may suggest a very different set of competitors from those identified through more industrial age examination. Indeed, this information age analysis may suggest IT applications that break the rules of established competition or introduce new rules.

Much early work on whether or how IT can yield competitive advantage rested on case study research in North America and this slowly migrated to Europe and Asia. However, whether national culture and local industry structure was a mediating variable was rarely asked. In a study of IT management practices in Japan, M. Bensaou and I found a much more 'middle ground' approach to the question.[42] Here, continuous improvement of current performance in daily business operations was likely to drive IT investment.

To Western eyes, this philosophy may seem tactical rather than strategic, but long-term commitment to IT support of how a firm was competing, particularly in manufacturing operations and sales and service, appeared to pay off. We also speculated that Japanese firms might create new product markets based on their industrial prowess in consumer electronics, particularly miniaturization and entertainment. In other words, there is a research and policy agenda on national competitiveness and IT.

Equally, given the power of IT to reduce the costs of coordination, we might expect new sources of competitive advantage to be sought as corporations increase their global reach.[43] While certain industries such as the airlines and banking depend on global information systems and other sectors have shown how in a network economy a firm can reach customers worldwide (e.g., Amazon or eBay) or configure their supply chain flexibly exploiting local comparative advantages (e.g., Dell), David Feeny and I found that often the planning and organization of IT resources was at best a residual policy question addressed by companies pursuing global strategies.[44] One suspects or hopes that such remiss thinking is now obsolete, but it does remind us that a business strategy or strategic management is incomplete if the opportunities presented by IT are forgotten and the implications for IT governance ignored. To repeat, general management has to incorporate information management.

Managing Information as a Resource

In 1984 when OXIIM was founded, this theme perhaps was somewhat ahead of its time. A UK government report had been published on *Making a Business of Information*,[45] but perhaps it was too macro and policy-oriented to make an impact on traditional industrial corporations. Of course, information itself had attracted over time the theoretical interest of philosophers, psychologists, political scientists, economists, sociologists, and computer scientists but not really as a resource to be managed in a corporate setting.

It possibly has taken the more recent developments of the digital economy or information age to help us see the value creation opportunities offered by information in traditional industries as much as in the information sector. Sampler's observation[41] that digitization has enabled the separation of information from the transaction has been one driver of this learning, as has the concept of information specificity.

Indeed, drawing on case study research in two firms, I made a number of propositions about the strategic value of information, if transactions at the heart of a company's distinctive operations could be stored, analysed, and modelled to pursue a competitive strategy of differentiation or niche positioning.[46] Actually, the core proposition was that knowledge could be a strategic asset or weapon, and distinctions were drawn from the case study data between data, information, and knowledge.

Looking back, the new and emergent concept and practice of knowledge management in the 1990s provided a set of research questions that could fit the theme of managing information as a resource. I proposed a taxonomy of knowledge management strategies derived from a variety of sources and studies.[47] Again, this research suggested that organizational (or behavioural) and strategic knowledge management initiatives were at least as likely to succeed as technocratic and bureaucratic ones. But each of the seven strategies identified required certain specific success factors to be in place first—both information management factors and general management factors.

Often propelling such initiatives and strategies was a Chief Knowledge Officer (CKO), and Ian Scott and I in a study of twenty such CKOs identified the personal attributes they required and what they should do.[48] In a subsequent paper we suggested that the CKO was primarily a change agent and, importantly, was likely to be quite different from the typical CIO.[49]

Whether we distinguish between information and knowledge or not, the theme of managing information as a resource scores highly on business relevance and connects with several referent disciplines. It could be *the* central challenge not only for those companies and organizations that would classify themselves as information businesses but also for those who have conceptualized themselves as transactional or traditional enterprises. New entrants to the information space demonstrate policy questions almost daily, for example Google or Wikipedia,[50] and more familiar business models such as Capital One, Tesco, or Amazon[51] show us the wisdom of collecting, storing, and analysing transactions as content.

IT, Ambiguity, and Information Management

It is not uncommon when Information Systems, MIS, or Information Management academics come together for them to begin agonizing whether their subject is going to survive. They debate what is their core or heartland. Is it computer science-oriented, concerned with the workings of IT, with databases, systems analysis, and project management? Is it economics-oriented, concerned with electronic markets, the impact of IT on firms' productivity, positioning, and configuration, and the impact on resource allocation and distribution? Is it a subset of decision science, technology management, or operations management, concerned with how better information, new technologies, or ambitious information systems are transforming decision-making, supply chains, manufacturing processes, products, service management, and the like? Or can it be seen as part of strategic and general management, where the models, rules, and practice of the industrial age are being rewritten for the information age?

Such debates have some value but do not seem to produce an answer to the survival question. An alternative question that I hear from academics, senior executives, and policymakers alike is 'What is different about information technology or IT?' If, as has been suggested in the above description and analysis of Oxford's particular contribution to information management, much of what is required in practice is general management, albeit reconstructed, is this alternative question helpful? Indeed, is there a heartland or core somewhere in Information Management as a subject?

I have proposed that what is different about IT is that it is an *ambiguous* technology.[52] While some technologies are very specific in

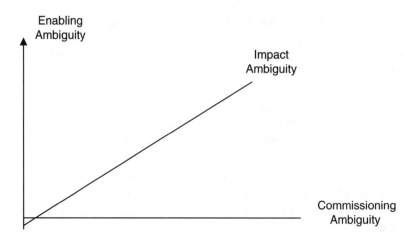

FIG. 10.2 IT as 'ambiguous technology'

their application and relatively predictable in their impact, information technologies are either general purpose or more general in their
application and relatively unpredictable in their impact. To be sure,
the internal combustion engine or the jet engine has transformed how
we live, but the essential functions they have fulfilled stabilized quite
quickly: they are specific. Equally, certain advances in technologies can
lead to product obsolescence and the innovator's dilemma posed by
their disruptive product market impact, as described by Christenson.[53]
But information technologies are 'of uncertain issue', one definition that
the Oxford English dictionary suggests for 'ambiguity'. For example,
who predicted that the SMS text traffic generated by mobile phones
would exceed e-mail traffic, or who is making confident predictions
about the trajectory, use, and impact of portable, mobile technologies
as information media converge? Indeed, who made any reliable predictions about the uses, impact, and sustainability of the Internet and World
Wide Web?

There are three important ambiguities about IT (see Figure 10.2):
enabling, commissioning, and impact. These ambiguities or uncertainties
may be stronger in the case of new or emerging information technologies:
'new' or 'emerging' may be assessed relative to a technology's adopting
context as much to its arrival in the marketplace.

Enabling ambiguity is about scope. What can a particular IT do? This
question is often asked in practice and receives frustrating replies, namely,
'It can do what you want it to do', or 'Its use is only limited by our
imagination', or 'It will change the way we do business', etc. Alternatively,

inventors and developers of an IT may have a clear view, vision, or theory about its application, but the history of IT shows that it is quite normal for IT forecasters to be short on prescience about the killer application or the timing of the predicted revolutionary impact. Indeed, business history analyses of the evolution and impact of pervasive IT applications tend to show that today's scope was never envisaged or planned; there is often a heuristic path of discovery as the capabilities of a technology are learned or developed, as the economic context evolves, as organizational and human acceptance grows, and as imagination or vision unfolds. The evolution of computerized reservation systems in the airline industry is a paradigm case.[54]

Commissioning ambiguity is about the most obvious and commonly emphasized anxiety of IT: will a particular technology work? Put more graphically, is this latest technology another example of 'vapourware' or 'snake oil'? Or more managerially, is this IT at the risky end of 'bleeding edge' where examples of successful adoption so far are rare. Or when might I adopt a particular new technology? I use the personal pronoun here deliberately, having just chosen to replace home ISDN telecommunications with broadband—a decision that weighed up the installation and usage costs, the application benefits, the risks of being at the outer geographical limits of broadband connection, the bet on which supplier to choose, and the probability of an annoying period of commissioning unreliability. Commissioning ambiguity at the business level is more significant; it is unlikely to be tolerated if the technology in question is underpinning an operation that needs to be running 24 hours a day, 7 days a week.

Impact ambiguity is about both impact and implementation. One obvious question is whether users—employees, customers, citizens, other businesses—will adopt and use a new IT or system. Another is whether a system will work in its intended context. A vital one is the effect on user behaviour, work practices, organizational decision-making, and so on. An IT application that creates unintended, dysfunctional consequences is not only unwanted and a failure, it obviously negates the anticipated scope, or put another way, the enabling vision originally held. Implementation failures have the same effect or, if rectified, are likely to increase the investment cost and reduce the benefit flow. This combination of implementation and impact ambiguity (or risk) is sometimes expressed today in terms of technological, organizational, or social 'readiness'.

Readiness, however, implies a single state point of ambiguity. To be sure, ambiguity is likely to be highest when a particular IT is new to the world. We are not certain of its scope and probably cannot envision all its applications. We do not know whether it will work in all conditions and may not know how to make it work. And we are unlikely to be able to predict all its impacts or even be sure of all the implementation challenges. If this were all that lay behind the concept of ambiguous technology, we could just say the problem or challenge is one of new technology.

What is no longer new to the world, however, may be new to the particular organization or user, and although some borrowed or vicarious learning from earlier adopters is possible, it does seem that experiential learning matters in this field.[55,56] Furthermore, any one organization or user may reveal new scopes or impacts, and so ambiguity exists for new adopters as well as for new technologies.

It also exists for adopted technologies and those who have adopted. As argued earlier, scopes and benefits of IT applications can be learned or discovered through use and by surprise over time; enabling ambiguity is continuous. Commissioning ambiguity can be encountered as scopes are enhanced, technology add-ons made, new releases of hardware and software embraced, or a technology is pushed to its limits. Impact ambiguity is possibly the most continuous of all. Contexts change, users become inventive, unforeseen problems and counter-implementation tactics arise, and experiential learning happens.

Thus, while it is tempting and probably insightful to explain ambiguous technology, and to develop the managerial implications, by comparing conditions of high ambiguity and low ambiguity, the essential argument is that *all* information technologies are *always* ambiguous.

So how might the concept relate to the research themes of information management described earlier in theory and in practice, particularly the planning, organization, and control of IT activities?

In strategy-making, ambiguity of all three types suggests that experimentation is required alongside more business goal-led or business strategy analysis-inspired IS planning. Indeed, this was proposed as organizations addressed how to respond to the threats and opportunities posed by e-business.[57] It also suggests that business and IT strategies should be reviewed quite frequently as learning occurs through rolling plans, as proposed by B. Khan and me in our study of e-business.[14] Finally, enabling ambiguity and the learning of extended scope that arises through impact ambiguity suggest that continuously investing in a favourable IT application over time—one of the few themes of my organizational approach to IS strategy-making[30]—is a wise practice.

Ambiguity also has implications for IT sourcing decisions. The risks identified by several researchers and experienced by many organizations arise as much from ambiguity as from poor management. Lacity, Willcocks, and Feeny[21] argue that one important factor in making sourcing decisions is technological maturity, defined as 'when the technology itself is new and unstable, when the business has little experience with a technology that may be better established elsewhere, and/or when the business is embarking on a radically new use of a familiar technology'. This captures all three types of ambiguity, albeit implying that they are a single point in time condition. Lacity, Willcocks, and Feeny suggest that a state of low technological maturity leads to either insourcing IT activities or selecting a preferred supplier with whom to develop a relationship to help mediate risk.

In short, where ambiguity exists, the policy advice would be to avoid tight performance-based sourcing contracts because learning, adaptation, or even exiting might be negated or costly. If outsourcing makes sense due to other factors in the Lacity, Willcocks, and Feeny frameworks, then a partnership rather than transactional or contractual relationship with a vendor would be recommended, especially because ambiguity is continuous. One recalls the frustrated anguish of some IT vendors in the mid-1990s who said, 'We thought the deal was about cost and reliability—nobody mentioned innovation and flexibility.' Such statements provide an epitaph for IT executives and suppliers who believe that IT is essentially predictable, reliable, and only ever a victim of its context—that is to say unambiguous.

In contrast, recognition of the essential ambiguity of IT may be why Feeny and Willcocks placed 'informed buying' alongside leadership at the centre of their model of nine core IS capabilities.[23] It can also be seen why Lockett's research on IT-based innovation indicated that experimental application developments at local level led by line managers close to business operations paid off.[58]

What then might the concept of 'ambiguous technology' imply for the roles of the CIO and CEO? First, it might help explain why the role of CIO is so challenging. On the one hand, the CIO and IT function are commonly expected to deliver reliable, cost-efficient IT operations, craft a set of IS plans that are grounded in business realities and will be implemented, and oversee a governance structure that imposes few demands on other executives. On the other hand, ambiguity does imply some operational risks, the need to incorporate surprise learning and flexibility in IS planning, and a governance structure that allows, indeed encourages, line management involvement in IT decisions and the freedom to champion local experiments. In short, the CIO has to be a leader who is not only tolerant of ambiguity but can manage it as well.

This characteristic often causes anxieties in CEOs who wish that IT was more like many other technologies: unambiguous in scope, proven in reliability, relatively straightforward in impact, and, above all, easier to delegate as a responsibility to others. Unfortunately for such CEOs, the ten attention areas that David Feeny and I argue are required for CEOs in the Information Age are not optional.[29] Understanding and internalizing the essential ambiguity of IT—and its implications— may well come from the 'believing, living, and practising' that we advocate.

The message of 'ambiguous technology' for the other two research themes of whether IT can be a source of competitive advantage and how to manage information as a resource are perhaps more indirect.

The argument that IT of itself provides no sustainable competitive advantage is based on various grounds: that its impact depends on the strategic rationale or context, or on the time it takes for others to replicate an IT application, or for advantages to be competed away, or depends on how it is implemented, integrated with business processes, and used. All these constraints are, of course, aspects of enabling, commissioning, and impact ambiguity. From this perspective, the concept of 'ambiguous technology' shows that achievement of competitive advantage comprises both uncertainty and complexity. This is an important message to those who seek 'silver bullet' transformations from IT or think the goal is just a specialist technical one. It also could be a message to strategists: the very complexity and uncertainty mean that any success will present benefits of inimitability. Ambiguity from this perspective is a provider of sustainability.

The concept of 'ambiguous technology' impacts managing information as a resource the more that technological convergence makes information processing more IT-based. The separability of information is made possible by digitization and so the three types of ambiguity become influential. Sampler's argument[41] that our conceptualization of industry boundaries and dynamics has to change is one of enabling ambiguity. It might be further argued that more disappointments have come from information technologies and their applications that are information-oriented than transaction-oriented. Examples such as expert systems, artificial intelligence, data warehouses, knowledge networks, and so on require not only quite complex technologies (commissioning ambiguity) but also, in particular, robust assumptions about what information we use in different situations, how we use or abuse it, and the impact on power and influence (impact ambiguity). Here, key questions of social science are added to computer science.

This is perhaps why CKOs were found to have broader backgrounds than CIOs and why their skills and personalities were seemingly different.[48] Indeed, the more that information management embraces information and knowledge as resources—as well as data—the more ambiguities arise.

Conclusion

Information Management has been positioned here as a new subject in a new age. Academics both inside and outside the 'field' do ask what it is and is it a sustainable subject. Senior executives can ask either why this activity is so difficult or what is different about it. Forty years ago a new institution, the OCMS, recognized that IT (before we coined the label) was likely to become an important challenge for business and managers. When this institution became Templeton College, it invested in a research institute, the OXIIM.

OXIIM's agenda was driven by the issues faced by large organizations and their managers. It therefore sought to engage in both research and teaching, the one informing the other. Forty years on, managerial questions prompted by IT, information systems, and information have not gone away. They mostly require perspectives from both general management and what we have called information management in seeking robust answers.

A retrospective and prospective paper like this allows an attempt at 'grand theory-building'. In responding to the challenging and fundamental question of what is different about IT, the proposition has been that it is and must be seen as an ambiguous technology. This concept has not explicitly driven the research described here, nor is it likely to be the organizing framework for the research programme ahead. However, it may offer a framework for the analysis of information management challenges and deliver an important message to IT executives and practitioners by providing an answer to the question of what makes IT different from other technologies—and thus what is needed to understand information management's ability to complement or modify our models of general management.

References

1. R. Stewart, *How Computers Affect Management* (London: Macmillan, 1971).
2. L. M. Applegate, F. W. McFarlan, and J. L. McKenney, *Corporate Information Systems Management: Text and Cases* (4th edn.; Chicago: Irwin, 1996).
3. S. Beer, *Cybernetics and Management* (London: English Universities Press, 1967).
4. K. D. Tocher, *The Art of Simulation* (London: Hodder and Stoughton, 1969).
5. B. Harris, *BABS, BEACON and BOADICEA* (Basingstoke: Speedwing Press, 1993).
6. M. J. Earl and A. G. Hopwood, 'From Management Information to Information Management', in H. Lucas (ed.), *The Information Systems Environment* (Amsterdam: North-Holland, 1979).
7. M. Lockett, *The Manufacturing Integrated Control System* (Harvard Business School Case Study; Boston: Harvard Business School, 1988).
8. M. J. Earl and M. Vitale, *British Home Stores PLC* (Harvard Business School Case Study; Boston: Harvard Business School, 1988).
9. M. J. Earl, B. Edwards, and D. F. Feeny, 'Configuring the IS Function in Complex Organizations', in M. J. Earl (ed.), *Information Management: The Organizational Dimension* (Oxford: Oxford University Press, 1996).
10. D. F. Feeny, M. J. Earl, and B. Edwards, 'Organizational Arrangements for IS: Roles of Users and Specialists', in M. J. Earl (ed.), *Information Management: The Organizational Dimension* (Oxford: Oxford University Press, 1996).
11. P. R. Lawrence and J. W. Lorsch, *Organization and Environment: Managing Differentiation and Integration* (Boston: Harvard University Graduate School of Business Administration, Division of Research, 1967).
12. T. Burns and G. V. Stalker, *The Management of Innovation* (London: Tavistock, 1961).
13. S. L. Hodgkinson, 'The Role of the Corporate IT Function in the Federal IT Organization', in M. J. Earl (ed.), *Information Management: The Organizational Dimension* (Oxford: Oxford University Press, 1996).
14. M. J. Earl and B. Khan, 'E-Commerce Is Changing the Face of IT', *Sloan Management Review*, 43/1(2001): 64–72.
15. L. Willcocks and G. Fitzgerald, *A Business Guide to IT Outsourcing: A Study of European Best Practice in the Selection, Management and Use of External IT Services* (London: Business Intelligence, 1994).
16. M. Lacity, R. Hirschheim, and L. Willcocks, 'Realizing Outsourcing Expectations: Incredible Expectations, Credible Outcomes', *Journal of Information Systems Management*, 11/4(1994): 7–18.
17. O. E. Williamson, *Markets and Hierarchies* (New York: Free Press, 1975).
18. M. J. Earl, 'The Risks of IT Outsourcing', *Sloan Management Review*, 37/3(Spring 1996): 26–32.
19. M. Lacity, L. Willcocks, and D. F. Feeny, 'IT Outsourcing—Maximize Flexibility and Control', *Harvard Business Review*, 73/3(May–June 1995): 85–93.

20. M. Lacity and L. Willcocks, *Best Practices in Information Technology Outsourcing* (Oxford Executive Research Briefings, 2; Oxford: Templeton College, 1996).

21. M. Lacity, L. Willcocks, and D. F. Feeny, 'The Value of Selective IT Sourcing', *Sloan Management Review*, 37/3(Spring 1996): 13–25.

22. G. Hamel and C. K. Prahalad, 'The Core Competence of the Corporation', *Harvard Business Review* (May–June 1990).

23. D. F. Feeny and L. P. Willcocks, 'Core IS Capabilities for Exploiting Information Technology', *Sloan Management Review*, 39/3(Spring 1998): 9–21.

24. M. J. Earl and D. F. Feeny, 'Is Your CIO Adding Value?', *Sloan Management Review* (Spring 1994): 11–20.

25. M. J. Earl and P. Vivian, *The Role of the Chief Information Officer* (London: London Business School and Egon Zehnder International, 1993).

26. D. F. Feeny, 'The Five-Year Learning of Ten IT Directors', in L. P. Willcocks, D. F. Feeny, and G. Islei (eds.), *Managing IT as a Strategic Resource* (London: McGraw Hill, 1997).

27. M. J. Earl and P. Vivian, *The New CIO: A Study of the Changing Role of the IT Director* (London: London Business School and Egon Zehnder, 1999).

28. M. J. Earl, 'Are CIOs Obsolete?', *Harvard Business Review* (Mar.–Apr. 2000): 60.

29. M. J. Earl and D. F. Feeny, 'How to be a CEO for the Information Age', *Sloan Management Review*, 41/2(Winter 2000): 11–23.

30. M. J. Earl, 'Experiences in Strategic Information Systems Planning', *MIS Quarterly*, 17/1(1993): 1–24.

31. H. Mintzberg, 'Crafting Strategy', *Harvard Business Review*, 66/4(July–Aug. 1987): 66–75.

32. J. B. Quinn, 'Strategic Goals, Plans and Policies', *Sloan Management Review*, 19/1(Fall 1977): 21–37.

33. M. J. Earl, J. L. Sampler, and J. E. Short, 'Strategies for Business Process Reengineering: Evidence from Field Studies', *Journal of Management Information Systems*, 12/1(Summer 1995): 31–56.

34. K. P. Periasamy and D. F. Feeny, 'Information Architecture Practice: Research-Based Recommendations for the Practitioner', *Journal of Information Technology*, 12/3(Sept. 1997): 197–205.

35. C. Sauer and L. P. Willcocks, 'The Evolution of the Organizational Architect', *Sloan Management Review*, 43/3(Spring 2002): 41–9.

36. M. E. Porter, 'Strategy and the Internet', *Harvard Business Review* (Mar. 2001): 663–78.

37. E. Brynjolfsson, 'The Productivity Paradox of Information Technology', *Communications of the ACM*, 36/12(1993): 66–77.

38. E. Brynjolfsson and L. M. Hitt, 'Beyond the Productivity Paradox', *Communications of the ACM*, 41/8(1998): 49–55.

39. D. F. Feeny and B. Ives, 'In Search of Sustainability: Reaping Long-Term Advantage from Investments in Information Technology', *Journal of Management Information Systems*, 7/1(Summer 1990): 27–46.

40. D. F. Feeny, 'Making Business Sense of the E-Opportunity', *Sloan Management Review*, 42/2(Winter 2001): 41–51.
41. J. L. Sampler, 'Redefining Industry Structure for the Information Age', *Strategic Management Journal*, 19(1998): 343–55.
42. M. Bensaou and M. J. Earl, 'The Right Mindset for Managing Information Technology', *Harvard Business Review* (Sept.–Oct. 1998): 119–28.
43. M. E. Porter, 'Competition in Global Industries: A Conceptual Framework', in M. E. Porter (ed.), *Competition in Global Industries* (Boston: Harvard Business School Press, 1986).
44. M. J. Earl and D. F. Feeny, 'IS in Global Business: Evidence from European Multinationals', in H. Thomas, D. O'Neal, and J. Kelly (eds.), *Strategic Renaissance and Business Transformation* (Chichester: Wiley, 1995).
45. Cabinet Office, Information Technology Panel, *Making a Business of Information: A Survey of New Opportunities* (London: HMSO, 1983).
46. M. J. Earl, 'Knowledge as Strategy', in C. Ciborra and T. Jelassi (eds.), *Strategic Information Systems: A European Perspective* (Chichester: Wiley, 1994).
47. M. J. Earl, 'Knowledge Management Strategies: Toward A Taxonomy', *Journal of Management Information Systems*, 18/1(Summer 2001): 215–33.
48. M. J. Earl and I. A. Scott, 'What Is a Chief Knowledge Officer?', *Sloan Management Review*, 40/2(Winter 1999): 29–38.
49. M. J. Earl and I. A. Scott, 'What Do We Know About CKOs?', in C. Depres and D. Chauvel (eds.), *Knowledge Horizons* (Oxford: Butterworth Heinemann, 2000).
50. M. J. Earl, 'Wikipedia's Struggle to Govern a Knowledge Democracy', *Financial Times*, 19 Dec. 2005.
51. M. J. Earl and J. Anderson, *Amazon.com* (London Business School Case Study, LBS-CS97-001-00; London: London Business School, 1999).
52. M. J. Earl, 'IT: An Ambiguous Technology?', in B. Sundgren, P. Martensson, M. Matring, and K. Nilsson (eds.), *Exploring Patterns in Information Management* (Stockholm: Stockholm School of Economics, 2003).
53. C. M. Christenson, *The Innovator's Dilemma: When New Technologies Cause Great Firms to Fail* (Boston: Harvard Business School Press, 1997).
54. J. L. McKenney, D. C. Copeland, and R. O. Mason, *Waves of Technology: Business Evolution Through Information Technology* (Boston: Harvard Business School Press, 1995).
55. R. L. Nolan, 'Managing the Computer Resource: A Stage Hypothesis', *Communications of the ACM*, 16/7(1973): 399–405.
56. R. L. Nolan and D. C. Croson, *Creative Destruction: A Six-Stage Process for Transforming the Organisation* (Boston: Harvard Business School Press, 1995).
57. N. Venkatraman, 'Five Steps to a Dot-Com Strategy: How to Find Your Footing on the Web', *Sloan Management Review*, 41/3(Spring 2000): 15–28.
58. M. Lockett, 'Innovating with Information Technology', in M. J. Earl (ed.), *Information Management: The Organizational Dimension* (Oxford: Oxford University Press, 1996).

11

Corporate Strategy and Structure: The Rise and ?Fall of the Conglomerate

John McGee and Paul Simmonds[1]

Templeton College (né the Oxford Centre for Management Studies) has celebrated its 40th anniversary. So have a number of other business schools, not to mention many of us now approaching retirement, who joined these fledgling schools as young new-minted academics.

The business school took off as an idea, then a movement, in the USA in the late 1950s as a result of the Howell and Gordon reports. In the mid-1960s, a similar groundswell developed in the UK. But at this time business itself was also changing rapidly. The period of post-war restrictions had given way to economic expansion, albeit often fitful and unreliable. Both in the USA and in the UK, the way in which businesses saw their product markets and organized themselves began to change. In particular, the diversified corporation and its sibling, the conglomerate, were beginning to emerge.[2] Since then conglomerates have had a che-quered history, exhibiting growth, crisis, and reinvention but eventually becoming unfashionable and unwanted.

This seems an appropriate moment, therefore, to take stock of the conglomerate phenomenon that has so closely paralleled the business school movement over the past forty years. Unlike conglomerates, busi-ness schools have expanded in number and size and are here to stay. But all of us who have been involved at Templeton and other centres of executive education remember the many diversified or conglomer-ate companies that we served as clients. We remember the debates we had about the logic of the diversified corporation and the struggles these companies had in establishing new managerial logics in order to conduct their business effectively. We remember the acquisitions, the rush to restructure and turnaround, the repeated reorganizations, the cost-cutting, the turnover of management teams. Although memory is distorted by recent biting critiques of the conglomerate, we also remem-ber the many clients who fought seemingly against the odds to create

Corporate Strategy and Structure

viable businesses and in doing so created a new breed—the conglomerate manager.

A Brief History of the Conglomerate

The growth in conglomerate companies can be traced back to the 1960s. Before then companies expanded either organically or by acquiring companies in the same or similar industry segments and becoming 'related diversifiers'. These horizontal (acquisition of businesses in the same industry) or vertical (acquisition of supplier or consumer businesses) acquisitions, frequently justified in terms of economies of scale or scope, created several well-known large focused groups including Ford and General Motors. The core activity of both these companies remains the same: the design and manufacture of motor vehicles, although both have added related activities including the provision of finance or loans to vehicle purchasers (trade and retail) and component manufacturing. A prime UK example is ICI, which became a related diversifier on its creation in 1927 through the merger of several UK chemical companies.

The 1960s saw conglomeration gain acceptance as another valid corporate strategy. The third twentieth-century US merger wave—between 1965 and 1969—is often known as the conglomerate merger period. The FTC reported that 80 per cent of the mergers that took place in the 10-year period between 1965 and 1975 were conglomerate mergers. In the major European economies—UK, France, and Germany—there was a similar increase in related diversification and conglomeration, as Figure 11.1 shows.

However, in the USA—and, to a lesser degree, Europe—the diversification strategies of the largest non-service companies did not stand still. In the USA, by 1970 single business companies had become a minority, with related and unrelated (conglomerate) diversified companies increasingly pre-eminent; 20 per cent of Fortune 500 companies were conglomerates.[7] But by the 1980s the tide turned, and US companies began to refocus their activities, retreating from conglomeration back towards related diversified and dominant business strategies.

Research by Franko has shown that—as with adoption of diversification strategies—US companies led Europe and Japan in the move back to greater focus and away from conglomeration. Globally, the percentage of conglomerates amongst the same group of large companies (177 companies in 15 industries in 1980 and 201 companies in 17 industries in 1990 and 2000) remained broadly constant between 1980 (19%) and 1990 (18%) but fell to only 5 per cent by 2000 (Figure 11.2).

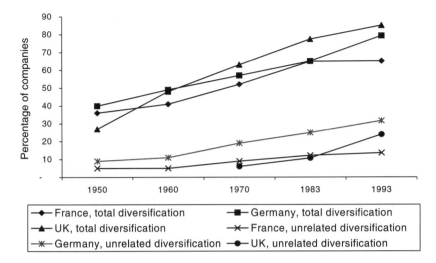

FIG. 11.1 Diversification in post-war France, Germany, and the UK
Source: UK 1950–70, Channon[3]; France 1950–70, Dyas[4]; Germany 1950–70, Thanheiser[5]; All 1983–93, Whittington & Mayer.[6]

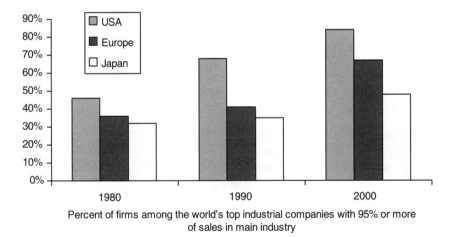

Percent of firms among the world's top industrial companies with 95% or more of sales in main industry

FIG. 11.2 The rise of focused firms
Source: Franko.[8]

In the UK, growth in conglomerate strategies amongst non-service companies took place some ten to fifteen years later than in the USA. The most recent research suggests that through the 1980s and early 1990s, rather than declining as in the USA, conglomeration in the UK continued to grow. By 1993, 24 per cent of the UK's largest manufacturing companies by sales were conglomerates compared to only 11 per cent in 1983[6] and 6 per cent in 1970.[3] The refocusing strategies prevailing in the USA had yet to be adopted by UK conglomerates.

However, by the mid-1990s many hitherto highly successful UK conglomerates had changed their strategies from serial acquisition to serial divestment, with many shrinking rapidly to a fraction of their peak size and some experiencing severe financial problems. BTR, for example, declined from a position of pre-eminence amongst the top ten London Stock Exchange listed companies by market capitalization in the early 1990s to ejection from the FTSE100 in 2003. This happened despite its merger with Seibe (another major FTSE100 company) in 1999, forming Invensys and aggressively addressing its problems, many of which were rooted in the scale and complexity of activities.

M&As and Diversification

In the USA and UK, M&A activity was volatile through the twentieth century, displaying four clearly identifiable peaks of activity, each larger—both in volume and in constant value terms—than its predecessor. Each of the first three peaks can be attributed to a different phenomenon:

- 1895–1900: consolidation
- 1920s: utility consolidation, manufacturing (vertical integration)
- 1960s: diversification[9,10]

The final peak at the end of the 1990s (which saw global activity reach $3.7 trillion in 2000)[11] has been attributed to acquirers' growth aspirations and to rising opportunism, especially amongst the increasingly active private equity houses. Considered in value terms, M&A activity in the late twentieth century was undertaken by a relatively small number of highly acquisitive companies. Between 1983 and late 1987, only eight companies accounted for more than 50 per cent, by value, of UK acquisitions.[12] These companies were Guinness, Hanson, BAT, BTR, Vantona Viyella, Habitat, Burton, and P&O. But by 2006, only Hanson and BAT remained independent quoted companies, albeit significantly smaller and more focused.

An illustration of the frequency and effect of UK acquisitions is provided by the extent of the changes in membership of the major *Financial*

TABLE 11.1 FTSE100 survivors 1984–2004

Barclays
BOC Group
Boots Group
British Petroleum
Cadbury Schweppes
Aviva (Commercial Union Assurance)
GUS
Imperial Chemical Industries
Hilton Group (Ladbroke)
Land Securities Group
Legal & General Group
Lloyds TSB (Lloyds)
Marks & Spencer Group
Pearson
Prudential
Reckitt Benckiser (Reckitt & Colman)
Reed Elsevier (Reed International)
Rio Tinto (Rio Tinto-Zinc Corporation)
Royal Bank of Scotland
J Sainsbury
Shell
Tesco
Unilever

Source: Klinger, Bolger, and Waller.[13]

Times share indices. Many of the constituents in 1970, 1980, and 1990 have disappeared through acquisitions. Prime examples include Midland Bank, Dunlop Holdings, and Distillers—acquired by HSBC, BTR, and Guinness, respectively. The changes in the FTSE100 over the twenty years since it began life on 13 February 1984 are testament to acquisitions activity amongst the UK's leading companies. Only 23 of the original 100 survived the index's first 20 years as Table 11.1 shows.

The high level of M&A activity in the USA and UK has not been matched in France, Germany, and Italy, where M&As remain a relatively rare phenomenon. During the 2000 hostile takeover bid for Germany's Mannesmann AG by Vodafone of the UK, the German media were as interested in the moral and ethical issues of the proposed transaction as in the economic issues. Vodafone eventually won control of Mannesmann, with many commentators attributing victory to Mannesmann's unusually high level of foreign ownership. German shareholders, who traditionally include a significant proportion of 'conservative' banks either directly or by proxy, would have rejected Vodafone's hostile bid. Similarly, M&A activity is also rare in the leading Asian economies of Japan and South Korea, where outright acquisition is uncommon and companies prefer to develop alliances through complex cross-shareholdings (commonly known as Keiretsu in Japan and Chaebol in South Korea).

The majority of M&A activity, therefore, occurs in the USA and UK where stock markets are seen as most developed. In both countries the 'market for corporate control' is well developed, and acquisitions are accepted as part and parcel of corporate life, albeit with some regulatory safeguards.

However, given the widely acknowledged high rates of M&A failure, the drivers for diversification and conglomeration even in these markets must be strong for companies and managers to take the risk. Using data from the *Annual Reports* of the Director-General of Fair Trading,[14] it is possible to see how the popularity of diversification waned in UK in the 1990s. Table 11.2 shows that through the 1970s and 1980s between a quarter and a third of all proposed acquisitions were diversifying transactions and that in the 1990s activity in this category fell dramatically, accounting for less than a tenth of proposed acquisitions. Vertical acquisitions fell from approximately 10 per cent to only 1–2 per cent of total activity, while horizontal transactions gained in popularity in the 1990s. This data, although covering proposed rather than consummated transactions and without any distinction between related and unrelated diversification, strongly supports the contention that in the UK diversification has lost much of its charm.

The Logic Behind Conglomeration

Many factors drove the adoption of conglomerate strategies in the 1960s, 1970s, and 1980s, including

- Leveraging management skills
- Regulatory limits to growth
- Declining industries
- Geographic expansion
- A shift in the balance of power from shareholders to management
- Opportunism
- Asset stripping or asset mining
- Availability of financing
- The achievement of critical mass
- Spreading risk

TABLE 11.2 Percentage of proposed mergers classified by type of integration

Year	Horizontal	Vertical	Diversifying	
1970–74	73	5	23	⎫
1975	71	5	24	
1976	70	8	22	1970s
1977	64	11	25	
1978	53	13	34	
1979	51	7	42	⎭
1980	65	4	31	⎫
1981	62	6	32	
1982	65	5	30	
1983	71	4	25	
1984	63	4	33	1980s
1985	58	4	38	
1986	69	2	29	
1987	67	3	30	
1988	58	1	41	
1989	60	2	37	⎭
1990	75	5	20	⎫
1991	88	5	7	
1992	93	1	6	
1993	90	3	7	1990s
1994	88	5	7	
1995	91	1	8	
1996	93	2	5	⎭

Source: Annual Reports of the Director-General of Fair Trading.[14]

Issues of risk are certainly a significant factor in conglomeration decisions. There is a commonly held view that while neither can reduce the systematic risk of their investment portfolio—that is, the level of risk inherent in the economy—investors can be as successful as conglomerates in reducing their unsystematic risk. They can construct a portfolio of investments containing the same businesses a conglomerate could acquire (and probably more cheaply given that investors would not have to pay acquisition premiums).

Nevertheless, it may be possible for companies to produce superior returns from their portfolio of businesses than investors could from the same individually held portfolio. Investors, despite recent increases in investor power, are effectively passive, that is they have little or no effect on the day-to-day running or strategy of 'their' company, whereas by bringing its superior management skills to bear an acquirer may be able to increase the profitability of a business.

Furthermore, conglomerates may be better placed to undertake high-risk high-return projects: their financial resources are greater and they would not be 'putting all their eggs in one basket'. The Boston Consulting Group (BCG) used a gambling analogy to highlight the risks to companies of focusing, although the same risks are faced by individual investors: 'this is the dilemma of focusing: putting all your chips on one number has the potential to generate higher rewards than spreading your bets, as conglomerates do, but the potential losses are also greater if your number doesn't come up.'[15]

So, diversification and the key issue of 'risk and return' are closely linked. Companies aim to reduce the risk and variability of returns by investing in a range of businesses with differing economic or business cycles. The principles behind the creation of lower risk investment portfolios by companies through efficient diversification were first propounded by Markowitz.[16] Theoretically, by constructing a portfolio containing investments with perfectly negative correlation coefficients, cyclicality will be minimized. Increasing the stability of returns may also result in lower borrowing costs as investors will view the company as being more stable and offering a safer investment. The availability of low-cost finance may provide additional funds for further expansion and constitute an advantage over competitors. Diversified companies may also cross-subsidize activities, with strong businesses helping investment in new activities or providing support to underperforming businesses, for example those facing difficult trading environments.

There exists a 'conglomerate effect' wherein economic activities are unrelated and the pure conglomerate profits remain static but are stabilized only by bringing together businesses with zero or negative correlations.[17] The theory is logical although in practice flawed by the difficulty of identifying businesses with the required cyclicality. Of course, diversification would in general be expected to produce negative correlations as the investments would be, by definition, unrelated, and would therefore reduce variations in performance.

However, many observers are dismissive of the ability of conglomerates to stabilize earnings in practice and do not see risk reduction on its own as a valid rationale for selecting unrelated diversification instead of related diversification. Salter and Weinhold agree, proposing that two of the common misconceptions about diversification are that a related strategy is always safer than an unrelated strategy and that adding countercyclical businesses to a company's portfolio leads to a stabilized earning stream.

The Contribution of Strategic Theory

The late twentieth century saw an explosion of management theories and models designed to help managers to develop or refine their strategy and decide on the mix of companies or business activities that should comprise their portfolio. Consultants and researchers developed and fostered a mania for matrices to guide managers in making decisions regarding the strategic direction of their company. The most popular of these models included Porter's Five Forces and Value Chain,[18,19] BCG's Growth-Share Matrix (Boston Box),[20] and Ansoff's Product/Market Matrix.[21] Salter and Weinhold developed a matrix based on industry attractiveness and business positioning to assess whether a company should diversify.[10] They also considered diversification in relation to three other well-known models:

- The Strategy Model. Companies should diversify where there is potential for skills, know-how, or technology transfer between merging company's businesses.
- The Product/Market Portfolio Model (a form of BCG's market share and growth matrix). Companies should diversify to build a presence in key areas of the matrix, for example as 'question marks' or 'cash cows', where they can either dominate markets or use excess cash to develop opportunities: 'A company with a balanced portfolio of cash cows feeding question marks and stars is in a position both to reap the current benefit of its high market share and advantageous cost position and to develop sources of future cash flow.'
- The Risk-Return Model [developed from the capital asset pricing model (CAPM)]. Companies can use diversification to reduce unsystematic risk—the risk inherent in investing in particular industries or businesses. However, investors can diversify for themselves with similar results: 'various studies have shown that as few as eight to ten unrelated investments are sufficient to eliminate over 80% of a portfolio's unsystematic risk.'

While each approach has its merits, it may be argued that none reflects the complexities of major strategic decision-making.

The Role of Management

Conglomeration also brought with it significant new management challenges, not least the need to manage a diverse and complex portfolio of businesses effectively. It is now generally accepted that portfolio management is 'based primarily on diversification through acquisition',[22] with shareholder value being created through the acquirers' superior abilities (compared to individual shareholders) to

- Identify acquisition or investment targets
- Provide funding at the lowest rates through access to capital markets
- Supply professional management, especially expertise in areas such as taxation
- Apply business planning and review disciplines to target areas of weakness for remedial action, for example BTR's annual profit planning process and monthly detailed reporting package.

Management structures have become more convoluted, reflecting the greater complexity of the businesses they control, and this has become fertile territory for researchers. Organization structures have been classified as Unitary (U-form), Holding Company (H-form), Multidivisional (M-form), Transitional Multidivisional (M^1-form), Corrupted Multidivisional (*M*-form), and Mixed (X-form).[23] There is a substantial body of research showing that the overwhelming majority of conglomerates adopt the multidivisional M-form. According to Whittington and Mayer, seven of the eight companies identified as conglomerates in 1983 had divisional structures; the corresponding figures for 1993 were fifteen of sixteen. The non-divisional companies—Rank Organization in 1983 and Metal Box/Caradon in 1993—adopted holding company structures. The primary advantage of divisional structures is that they attempt to group similar businesses together in often largely autonomous divisions—for instance, automotive, chemical, retail—each being overseen by a management team with appropriate skills and knowledge.

The choice of structure is important, but so are the quality, skill, and experience of the management team. Finally, luck also plays a part in success or failure. An extreme (some may say realistic) view of management success or failure comes from Alfred P. Sloan who commented: 'It is not to say why one management is successful and another is not. The causes of success or failure are deep and complex, and chance plays a part.'[24]

Conglomerate Performance in Practice

One of the major goals of conglomeration is to achieve superior levels of profitable growth compared to other categories of company. However, there is no clear evidence that conglomerates do consistently outperform other categories or that their record of success in making acquisitions is any better. There have been many methodological criticisms of these studies but each successive refinement of approach leads to broadly the same conclusion. Table 11.3 is a typical example of the kind of results that have been obtained.

Salter and Weinhold found that in each year both the average return on equity and the average price earnings ratio of conglomerates were substantially below that of the all-industry composite. The authors also quoted statistics of relative economic performance between 1965 and 1978, showing the S&P index of ten conglomerates underperformed the S&P 400 index of industrial companies and the S&P index of major companies by a substantial margin.[10]

TABLE 11.3 *Business Week* Survey of Business Profits[a]

Year	Conglomerates[b]		All industry composite	
	Average return on equity	Average price–earnings ratio[c]	Average return on equity (%)	Average price–earnings ratio[c]
1973	11.3	6	14.0	11
1974	11.8	5	14.0	9
1975	11.3	8	11.8	12
1976	13.2	8	14.0	10
1977	12.9	7	14.1	9
1978	13.5	6	15.1	8

Notes:
[a] Based on *Business Week's* Quarterly Survey of Business Profits.
[b] The composition of *Business Week's* conglomerate category is Teledyne, Northwest Industries, Textron, Avco, Studebaker-Worthington, Southdown, Martin Marietta, Signal, Colt Industries, Whittaker, Bliss & Laughlin Industries, Tenneco, Chromalloy American, Gulf + Western Industries, Fuqua Industries, Kidde (Walter), City Investing, IU International, U.S. Industries, IC Industries, Litton Industries, LTV.
[c] Based on price–earnings ratio in effect on evaluation date.
Source: Salter and Weinhold.[10]

When assessing performance it is important to recognize that the reliability of financial performance data in recent years has been increasingly called into question. The lack of transparency of financial information adds to a general mistrust of conglomerates. In the UK, Smith wrote a best seller in which he claimed to be 'stripping the camouflage from company accounts' to highlight how financial performance may be manipulated.[25] While he did not confine his analyses and criticism to conglomerates, they were well represented in his book, which drew attention to a number of the 'creative' accounting practices then in widespread use and looked at how many leading public companies adopted them—inferring that by doing so they were manipulating their accounts and to some degree misleading the investing public as to their financial performance. Companies he examined included Trafalgar House, BAE, Grandmet and Lonrho.

It is important to note that these practices were, at the time, all legal and within the range of accounting treatments acceptable under accounting standards. However, several have since been restricted or eliminated by new or revised standards issued by the Accounting Standards Committee and its successors. But, while the ASB and FRC have undoubtedly closed loopholes, many still remain.

In the second edition of his book Smith defends his record, noting that several of the companies he originally criticized for questionable accounting practices had by 1996 experienced difficulties.[26] Table 11.4 lists the criticized companies and their subsequent problems and notes in parentheses the number of dubious practices adopted by each company.

A company singled out by Smith is BTR, one of the largest UK conglomerates of the 1980s and 1990s. He points to the 'misuse'—aggressive but not illegal—of provisions during the company's acquisition of Hawker Siddeley in 1990. According to Smith, BTR acquired Hawker Siddeley, which had net assets of £748 million, for £1,513 million and then created provisions, primarily to adjust book asset values to fair values, of £445 million (£285 million in 1991 and £160 million in 1992). These 'fair value' adjustments made under the revised rules of SSAP22 and ED35 represented 59.5 per cent of the net asset value and 29.4 per cent of the purchase consideration.

Smith's point is that the judicious reversal of these provisions and of others relating to other acquisitions and activities, helped BTR maintain its historically high margins in subsequent years, confusing the markets into believing that it was continuing to trade very profitably. BTR released provisions totalling £305 million in 1992 (28.1% of the reported profit of £1,085 million) and £81 million in the first half of 1993 (13.5% of the reported profit of £602 million). With its provisions largely exhausted by mid-1993, BTR's true underlying profitability became apparent. City confidence in the company was shaken, and the share price fell in 1994. The second half of the 1990s saw a series of disposals as the company attempted unsuccessfully to restore its profitability through focusing its operations. Therefore, it could be that the underlying profitability of some conglomerates was declining long before they undertook strategic reviews that led to the adoption of divestment strategies and refocusing.

The Decline of the Conglomerate?

Conglomeration began to falter in the USA in the 1980s and the UK in the early 1990s as the underlying ambiguity of some of the drivers became apparent. Investors, especially the increasingly influential and dominant institutional shareholders, began to realize that they could diversify their investment portfolios to spread unsystematic risk as easily as and more cheaply than companies that had to pay a control premium to gain control of another company. In addition, the financial performance of conglomerates was becoming less transparent: where they could be compared against 'pure play' companies, they were seen to perform poorly. Finally, conglomerates were not seen as efficient allocators of capital: cross-subsidization of underperformers by strong businesses reduced overall returns.

Furthermore, many business writers and academics had started to advocate 'sticking to the knitting'—concentrating on core activities. It was around this time (the early to mid-1990s) that several conglomerates, most notably BTR and Hanson Trust, decided to break themselves up through a series of trade sales, floats, MBO/MBIs, and share splits. These companies had put into practice the advice of Whittington and Mayer: 'Corporates need to know when to be practitioners of corporate euthanasia.'[27]

As a result of those perceived problems with conglomerates there has been a significant reduction in the proportion of acquisitions classified as diversifying. Very few companies embarked on or continued diversification after 1989. Nevertheless, the phases in the conglomerate life cycle can vary greatly. In some cases, notably Williams Holdings, companies moved through the cycle in a relatively short period. These companies developed and grew in the 1980s and divested in the 1990s, effectively ceasing to exist in the new millennium. They could be described as 'shooting stars'. Interestingly, these companies frequently appear to have enjoyed success in each phase; that is they were not forced into decline but chose to break themselves up in a controlled and, for shareholders, profitable way.

Releasing Value Through Divestment

With the decline in financial performance of conglomerates in the early 1990s, an extensive literature emerged on the strategic reactions of those companies and the pay-offs from divestment and other forms of spin-off. It started from the view that, in broad terms and regardless of the category of the acquiring company, acquisition is not a successful activity and that acquisitions are frequently divested. For example, Porter undertook a study of the acquisition and diversification activity of thirty-three of the largest US corporations, several of them conglomerates, between 1950 and 1986 and found that 'most of them has divested many more acquisitions than they had kept... these firms divested 53% of the acquisitions that brought the acquiring companies into new industries.'[22]

A poor M&A record is only one of a number of drivers behind a company's decision to pursue a 'break-up' or divestment strategy. Other drivers include

- Concentration on a core activity, for example focusing management and resources to maximum effect
- Business trends, for example identifying growing problems within specific business segments
- Failure to achieve critical mass in specific markets or industries
- Poor performance/results, for example profitability, cash flow, EPS, share price
- Pressure from investors, primarily institutional for quoted companies
- Pressure from debt financiers, for example unwillingness to increase facilities, thereby restricting development or the ability to adequately support all businesses
- Capital rationing, for example when investment opportunities exceed available funds.

However, there is an alternative view of the causes of divestment that does not attribute as much blame to poor acquisitions. Divestments may reflect changed circumstances since the original acquisition.[28] There are many reasons for divestment, as listed in Table 11.4.

The significant increase in divestment activity amongst UK companies in the late 1980s and early 1990s is shown in Table 11.5. The desire of many divestors to get back to the core activities represented 'a rebound from the poor performance of conglomeration which happened on a large

TABLE 11.4 Reasons for divestitures

Reason	No. of divestitures
Change of focus or corporate strategy	43
Unit unprofitable or mistake	22
Sale to finance acquisition or leverage restructuring	29
Antitrust	2
Need cash	3
To defend against takeover	1
Good price	3
Divestitures with reasons	103

Source: Kaplan and Weisbach.[29]

scale in the 1960s and 1970s'.[30] Evidence suggests that when companies split, the post-split value of the two new companies is greater than that of the original single company. One of the reasons is the increase in information available to the stock market; the stock market 'places a premium on corporate transparency'; diversified companies could have 'suffered a conglomerate discount' because of lack of transparency.

There is also growing evidence that, in breaking up, companies gain greater analyst coverage—which, in turn, leads to increased value for the newly spun-off company and for the former parent. Gilson, Healy, Noe, and Palepu considered 103 focus-enhancing spin-offs, equity carve-outs, and targeted stock offerings between 1990 and 1995 and found a '30–50% increase in analyst forecast accuracy for parent and subsidiary firms'. The same authors reported that companies show an increase in financial performance after break-ups:

TABLE 11.5 Acquisitions and divestments in the UK, 1988–93

Year	Acquisitions		Divestments		Total	
	No.	£m	No.	£m	No.	£m
1993	745	8,720	503	8,640	1,248	17,360
1992	684	14,428	468	5,319	1,152	19,747
1991	747	12,180	442	6,001	1,189	18,181
1990	912	17,457	612	10,221	1,524	27,678
1989	1,363	35,318	665	10,206	2,028	45,524
1988	1,633	24,369	608	13,254	2,241	37,623

Note: Acquisitions include both private and public company targets.
Source: *Acquisitions Monthly Annual Reviews*.[11]

The median accounting return on equity (ROE) for the pre-break-up firm in fiscal year -1 is 10%. After the break-up, median ROEs are 12–13% for the parent firms and 10–12% for the subsidiaries. A similar pattern is observed for accounting return on assets (ROA), indicating that the ROE improvements are not due to a change in leverage for the parent and/or subsidiary firms after the break-up.[31]

Several large companies have been forced into break-ups, the most frequently cited reasons being financial problems often connected with a poor acquisition record, that is expensive acquisitions that have failed to perform as expected. Typical amongst these groups are the media groups that expanded rapidly through the 1990s, including Saatchi & Saatchi and, more recently, Vivendi of France and KirchMedia of Germany. The ill-starred Daimler-Chrysler automotive venture also failed to meet expectations.

Active Acquirers

Some conglomerates take an enlightened view of their portfolio of businesses, constantly reviewing the rationale supporting each company's retention. In many ways BTR and Hanson differed in their attitudes towards managing their portfolios. BTR very rarely divested unwanted parts of acquisitions, preferring to try and make them work despite their adding to group complexity. In consequence, BTR ended up with businesses as diverse as heavy engineering and women's hosiery.

Conversely, Hanson was known for selling off parts of acquisitions it did not believe fitted its strategy. Lublin, discussing Hanson's 1989 acquisition of Consolidated Gold Fields, noted that between 1973 and April 1989 'Hanson's US arm spent more than $3.6 billion on acquisitions and recouped nearly $2.7 billion, according to analysis by London brokers Hoare Govett.' He further noted that 'Hanson paid $930 million for SCM, Smith Corona's parent; so far, it has reaped more than $1.5 billion from SCM asset sales.'[32]

Hanson exemplified a 'restructuring' company—an acquirer that looks for businesses with unrealized potential and, post-acquisition, intervenes by

- Frequently changing management
- Changing strategy
- Adding new technology
- Building critical mass
- Divesting unneeded or unconnected parts

Ultimately, the restructured unit is sold off as soon as recovery is evidenced by financial performance. Porter believed BTR could be placed in the same category, but the evidence seems to suggest otherwise; BTR held on to units long after their recovery plans had been completed and their turnaround was evidenced in profit performance. As Porter says, 'companies find it very hard to dispose of business units once they are restructured and performing well. Human nature fights economic reality.'[22] Companies that fail to dispose of businesses after turnaround effectively become portfolio managers, a strategy found to be flawed.

However, turnarounds themselves are not always successful, and failure is often followed by divestment. In 1988, British Aerospace (BAe), an aviation and technology company, bought the Rover Group, a volume car manufacturer, from the British government. The acquisition was intended to give BAe a more diversified portfolio of businesses and an opportunity to turn a company long seen as in terminal decline into a successful business. The experiment was not successful, and BAe divested Rover in 1994 to BMW of Germany, a focused automotive group looking to broaden its product range to include lower priced vehicles and 4×4s. In 2001, BMW, despite devoting substantial financial and management resources to Rover, also divested the business, retaining only the Mini and effectively giving the volume Rover business to a consortium. Ultimately, Rover went into receivership in 2005.

Although it is accepted that a conglomerate can be successful if it thinks of itself as a trader, few of the old-style conglomerates chose to operate in this way. Maybe the 'old-style' conglomerates had been replaced by new-style venture capitalist conglomerates, that is venture capitalists whose portfolios of businesses span several industries (see below). Well-known examples include Nomura, whose investments include public houses, betting shops, and housing estates, Cinven, Electra, Kholberg Kravis Roberts.[33]

Is There an Optimal Level of Diversification?

Investors—professional and amateur—like to have clarity, to be able to see and understand how a company has performed. Diverse conglomerates are anathema to many investors: their complex management, accounting, and tax structures do not help foster greater understanding of underlying performance. A clear and deliverable strategy is what investors want to see—a difficult task for a company with diverse business activities.

If conglomeration is at one end of the spectrum of business strategies and focus at the other, is there a middle way: moderate diversification? There is a body of literature providing evidence that conglomerates do not produce superior returns, but is poor performance linked to the size or complexity of the conglomerate? It has been suggested that moderate diversification provides the best of both worlds, whereby the company is able to grow through diversification and avoid over-reliance on one industry but does not spread itself and its management team too thinly.[34] If there is evidence that the incidence of conglomeration has fallen, is there also evidence of a similar reduction in the incidence of focused companies and of an increase in moderately diversified companies?

It is interesting to look at underlying growth in serial acquirers to try and isolate their organic and acquisitive growth rates. Unfortunately, with few periods of stability and with multiple changes to structures, it is impossible to isolate these two figures through analysis of published accounts. Some companies do provide growth data but usually only to support a 'success story' in the context of annual report or trading update presentations to City investors. Given the purpose for which they are prepared, the reliability of such data must be questioned. However, the importance of this information is significant; if an acquisition or series of acquisitions contributes more than 100 per cent of a period's growth, organic growth must be negative, that is businesses once owned actually shrink (this could be deliberate as loss-making activities are closed down or discontinued).

However, in a recent research report into diversified, slightly diversified, and focused companies in the USA, Europe, and Asia, the BCG concluded that conglomerates do have a future and that their poor status with analysts and investors, especially in Europe where they found evidence of a conglomerate discount in valuation, is largely unfounded. BCG argued that, while on average over the period 1996–2005 the relative total shareholder return (RTSR) of focused companies (2.19%) exceeded that of diversified companies (1.34%), the average performance of focused companies was distorted by a few outstanding performers. BCG failed to be convinced of the benefits of divestment and refocusing, concluding that such strategies were often ill-conceived, poorly executed, and diminished shareholder value:

There is no evidence that diversified companies would necessarily produce higher returns if they focused on a smaller number of businesses. In some cases, notably break-ups, there is a strong probability that focusing will destroy shareholder value.[15]

Towards a New Conglomerate?

As the 'traditional' conglomerate declined in popularity in the 1990s, a new form of conglomerate emerged. In the UK and USA private equity houses, by backing MBO/MBI transactions, have become the new conglomerates with controlling interests in a wide variety of businesses. In a *Sunday Times* article Durran quoted data from Nottingham University's Centre of Management Buy Out Research that in the UK in 2002 there were 620 private equity deals (468 buyouts and 152 buy-ins) worth £15.3 billion, compared to only 20 deals worth £23.9 million in 1979.[35]

These 'second generation' conglomerates do not attempt to obtain synergies across the often wide spread of businesses they control: they merely back the management to improve value with a view to subsequent divestment. They are excellent examples of Porter's turnaround specialists.[22] Private equity companies such as Blackstone, Apax, Cinven, and CVC have become conglomerates by default but this time with little or no daily management input and with exit strategies. Unlike many of the traditional conglomerates these second-generation companies have no intention of retaining businesses. Instead, they appear to have heeded Porter's advice and buy with a view to divestment within 3–5 years. In effect, the businesses acquired are their stock-in-trade, held for sale at a profit.

There are, however, signs that the profitability of this strategy may be in decline. As its popularity increases and more companies bid for control of available targets, the acquisition price rises and the margin for profit on resale declines.

The Debate Goes On

British and American experience suggests that the corporate strategy of conglomeration has a conventional life cycle of development, growth, maturity, and decline. In the UK, as illustrated in Figure 11.3, it involved development and growth through the mid-twentieth century, maturity in the 1980s, and decline in the 1990s—the decline being characterized by the unbundling of the portfolio of relatively unconnected business activities accumulated. Clearly, understanding the life cycle and its phases and their characteristics has significant implications for investors and managers, both of whom seek to optimize their investment strategies.

Is decline, whether triggered by size or complexity, inevitable, or can management sustain or reinvigorate their companies through changes in management control and style? Is the conglomerate no more than a

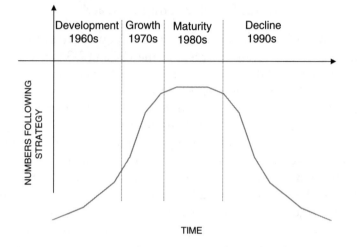

FIG. 11.3 Life cycle of conglomerate corporate strategy

transitory corporate form? Writers have tried to link the evolutionary theories of Charles Darwin to economic and business development. The broad Darwinian concept of the 'survival of the fittest' may be applicable, albeit simplistically, to different corporate strategies and conglomerates in particular. One important difference, however, stands out: Darwinism in nature is shaped by the environment; in business, it is not only the environment but also the collective decisions of business managers that shape companies.

The life cycle of the conglomerate raises a number of issues for further investigation:

- In the 1980s the widespread popularity and success—real or perceived—of conglomerates waned dramatically in the USA. Similarly, several leading conglomerates in the UK reported sharp declines in their financial performance in the 1990s. In the face of investor criticism and pressure, conglomerates that had taken twenty or thirty years to grow and develop changed strategy and embarked on extensive divestment and break-up programmes, seeking to focus on activities where they had or could achieve profitable and dominant market positions. Were these actions driven by unavoidable problems in specific industries, or had conglomerates become too large and complex to be managed effectively? Had the decline in conglomerate performance translated into a decline in adoption and continued pursuit of conglomerate strategies? The most recent UK study showed increasing conglomeration up to 1993.[6] Has the trend really reversed?

- Recognizing a trend towards greater focus, have conglomerates really reduced the breadth of their activities to bring a greater level of focus to their operations.
- The success conglomerates enjoyed prior to the 1990s appears to contradict (the predominantly US-based) research, which consistently shows that conglomerates with notable exceptions do not outperform either the market in general or 'pure play' comparative companies in the long run; the greater the diversification, the worse the relative performance. Using financial return and profit data, how well have conglomerates actually performed and how do they compare to the performance of other categories and the market in general? What were the key drivers of conglomeration strategies and are they likely to reappear?
- Is there an optimal level of conglomerate diversification, as measured by a Herfindahl or Product Diversification Index (PDI), that could provide a guide to companies seeking to grow through unrelated diversification?
- Is conglomerate survival related to the existence of a substantial core activity that effectively underpins overall financial performance allowing other activities to be pursued. Similarly, does the length of tenure of the CEO or chairman have a positive or negative correlation with the continued pursuit of conglomeration?
- Given that in most developed economies, competition regulation has become an accepted and expected part of business life, how will companies be able to sustain growth in single or dominant businesses?

Organic growth will always be possible, but growth by acquisition will be limited by regulators where competition is in danger of being compromised. Effectively, therefore, competition regulators will restrict the non-organic growth of focused companies. Therefore, it could be argued that the current fashion for divestment and focusing on core business activities is a transitory phase to be superseded by a reinvention of diversification strategies as companies seek paths to growth. Shareholders demand growth in their dividends as well as capital value and a stagnant company is not attractive. Building on the life cycle concept, the conglomerate strategy may currently be in the decline phase but a new growth phase could be imminent. This may involve 'new' conglomerates created by providers of private equity building portfolios of unrelated businesses through their acquisition of unwanted or undervalued companies and their support of MBO and MBI transactions.

In short, is conglomeration a fundamentally unstable corporate strategy or is it capable of reinvention? It may be that the strategy will survive because it increasingly represents the only way in which large focused companies can grow and maintain returns in the face of the regulatory pressures and interventions limiting growth in core business sectors.

Notes and References

1. This chapter is based on doctoral research being carried out at Warwick Business School by the second author, which has as its centrepiece a database on the largest by market capitalization UK non-service FTSE-listed companies, 1993–2003. It not only examines the history of the conglomerate from a British perspective but also acknowledges experience in the USA.

2. 'Diversification' and 'conglomeration' are both frequently used to mean a company with several different business activities. However, it is essential that each is defined accurately. Gribbin[36] defines a diversified firm as one that 'instead of operating in one market the firm operates in a number, and each separate market is different in important ways, implying significant changes in products, production and marketing, with vertical integration being excluded'. In other words, a diversified company is one that produces a number of different products or services and/or operates in a variety of markets. Gribbin continues by saying that conglomeration is 'joining together disparate products or activities which have virtually no common characteristics'. Considering both definitions together, the overall group of diversified companies may be split into two subgroups; related diversifiers where there are links between activities and unrelated diversifiers or conglomerates where no such links exist. In addition to the two categories of diversified company, there are two further key types of business—single business and dominant business companies—which complete the spectrum of corporate activity. The former category consists of companies that effectively operate in only one business, e.g. utility companies including Severn Trent plc and PowerGen plc, and the latter category comprises companies that have more than one business activity but are still dominated by one primary activity, e.g. British Petroleum.

3. D. F. Channon, *The Strategy and Structure of British Enterprise* (London: Macmillan, 1973).

4. G. P. Dyas and H. T. Thanheiser, *The Emerging European Enterprise: Strategy and Structure in French and German Industry* (London: Macmillan, 1976).

5. G. P. Dyas and H. T. Thanheiser, *The Emerging European Enterprise: Strategy and Structure in French and German Industry* (London: Macmillan, 1976).

6. R. Whittington and M. C. Mayer, *The European Corporation: Strategy, Structure, and Social Science* (Oxford: Oxford University Press, 2000).

7. R. P. Rumelt, *Strategy, Structure and Economic Performance* (Boston: Division of Research, Harvard Business School, 1974).

8. L. G. Franko, 'The Death of Diversification? The Focusing of the World's Industrial Firms, 1980–2000', *Business Horizons*, 47/4(July–Aug. 2004): 41–50.

9. B. Lev, 'Observations on the Merger Phenomenon and a Review of the Evidence', in J. M. Stern and D. H. Chew (eds.), *The Revolution in Corporate Finance* (2nd edn.; Oxford: Blackwell, 1982).

10. M. S. Salter and W. A. Weinhold, *Diversification through Acquisition: Strategies for Creating Economic Value* (New York: Free Press, 1979).

11. *Acquisitions Monthly*, 1988–2002 (Tudor House/Thomson).

12. J. Scoullar, 'The United Kingdom Merger Boom in Perspective', *National Westminster Bank Quarterly Review* (May 1987): 15–30.

13. P. Klinger, J. Bolger, and M. Waller, 'Doubts that Almost Gave Us the Bland SE100 Instead of the Dynamic Footsie', *The Times*, 14 Feb. 2004.

14. Office of Fair Trading, *Annual Reports of the Director-General of Fair Trading* (HMSO, London).

15. Boston Consulting Group (BCG), *Managing for Value: How the World's Top Diversified Companies Produce Superior Shareholder Returns* (BCG Report, Nov. 2006).

16. H. M. Markowitz, 'Portfolio Selection', *Journal of Finance*, 7(1952): 77–91.

17. H. Levy and M. Sarnat, 'Diversification, Portfolio Analysis and the Uneasy Case for Conglomerate Mergers', *Journal of Finance*, 25/4(Sept. 1970): 795–802.

18. M. E. Porter, *Competitive Strategy* (New York: Free Press, 1980).

19. M. E. Porter, *Competitive Advantage* (New York: Free Press, 1985).

20. For 'BCG 'Box' see B. D. Henderson, *Henderson on Corporate Strategy* (Cambridge, MA: Abt Books, 1979).

21. I. Ansoff, *Corporate Strategy: An Analytic Approach to Business Policy for Growth and Expansion* (New York: McGraw-Hill, 1965).

22. M. E. Porter, 'From Competitive Advantage to Corporate Strategy', *Harvard Business Review*, 65/3(May–June, 1987): 43–59.

23. O. E. Williamson and N. Bhargava, 'Assessing and Classifying the Internal Structure and Control Apparatus of the Modern Corporation', in O. E. Williamson (ed.), *Economic Organization: Firms, Markets and Policy Control.* (Brighton: Wheatsheaf Books, 1986), 54–80.

24. A. P. Sloan, *My Years with General Motors* (Harmondsworth: Penguin, 1963).

25. T. Smith, *Accounting for Growth* (1st edn.; London: Random House, 1992).

26. T. Smith, *Accounting for Growth* (2nd edn.; London: Random House, 1996).

27. R. Whittington and M. C. Mayer, *The European Corporation: Strategy, Structure, and Social Science* (Oxford: Oxford University Press, 2000), 217.

28. J. F. Weston, 'Divestitures: Mistakes or Learnings', *Journal of Applied Corporate Finance*, 2/2(Summer 1989): 68–76.

29. S. N. Kaplan and M. N. Weisbach, 'The Success of Acquisitions: Evidence from Divestitures', *Journal of Finance*, 1(Mar. 1992): 107–38.

30. P. S. Sudarsanam, *The Essence of Mergers and Acquisitions* (Englewood Cliffs: Prentice Hall, 1995).

31. S. C. Gilson, P M. Healy, C F. Noe, and K G. Palepu, 'Analyst Specialization and Conglomerate Stock Break-Ups', *Journal of Accounting Research*, 39/3(Dec. 2001): 565–82.

32. J. S. Lublin, 'Hanson Seeks Consolidated Gold Fields', *Wall Street Journal*, 23 June 1989.

33. T. Jackson, 'Too Much Focus: The Difference between Old-Style and Modern Conglomerates Is Less Obvious than It Looks', *Financial Times*, 17 Mar. 1998.

34. N. W. C. Harper and S. P. Vegurie, 'Are You Too Focused?', *McKinsey Quarterly* (special edition), 2(2002): 28–39.

35. P. Durran, 'Private-Equity Firms Are New Conglomerates', *Sunday Times*, 2 Nov. 2003.

36. J. D. Gribbin, 'The Conglomerate Merger', *Applied Economics*, 8(1976): 19–35.

12

Employment Relations: From Industrial Relations to Human Resource Management

Roger Undy

Much has changed in the study and practice of employment relations over the past forty years. In the 1960s, the 'Oxford School' represented the pre-eminent national, if not international, academic approach to the study of industrial relations. It tended to the view that 'one ounce of fact was worth one pound of theory'. The research was primarily empirical, inductive in method, and strongly policy-oriented. It aimed to shed light on, or help solve, some of the critical industrial relations problems of the day. At the same time it had sympathy with, and noted, the important and positive contributions of trade unions and collective bargaining to industrial relationships and social justice. In the 1960s, this was not politically controversial: such research was supported directly and indirectly by government funding—under both Labour and Conservative governments.

The term 'industrial relations' in the 1960s and 1970s covered both the practice and the study of the 'relationships within and between workers, working groups and their organisations'.[1] It was 'an all-inclusive term covering all aspects of the employment relationship'. The focal point was the 'effort–reward bargain' and associated substantive and procedural rules. The process and context that helped determine the outcome of the effort–reward bargain were also of central interest to researchers. Practitioners who attended industrial relations courses at the Oxford Centre for Management Studies (the forerunner of Templeton College) reflected on such issues and related the lessons that they learnt to their own work experiences. British Rail, BHS, United Biscuits, and the London Fire Brigade were amongst the organizations participating in such programmes.

But by 2006, the term 'human resource management' (HRM) had displaced 'industrial relations' as the dominant focus in employment relations practice. It had also gained popularity in the academic world as posts, departments, and courses in HRM mushroomed, while those in industrial relations declined. Oxford was not exempt from such developments. The Oxford M.Sc. in Industrial Relations and Human Resource

Management (introduced in 1983) was suspended in 2004–5 and replaced by a human resources stream in the M.Sc. in Management Research. As noted by Sisson,[2] university courses in 'industrial relations' had become difficult to sell to managers. A survey of practitioners in 2005 reported that 'industrial relations' was a term 'no longer widely used by employers'.[3] Moreover, its replacement, HRM, was more than just another name for personnel management. It brought with it from the USA 'a radically different philosophy and approach to the management of people at work'.[4]

HRM in this wider sense was initially recognized as antipathetic to industrial relations. As the 'new orthodoxy',[5] it offered a different lens through which to view the employment relationship, starting from the premise that employees were a resource in the same way that capital was a resource. Further differences were identified distinguishing HRM from industrial relations. Indeed, Storey identified twenty-five such points of difference.[6] Guest, drawing on empirical evidence, noted that the driving force behind HRM had little to do with industrial relations: rather it was driven by the pursuit of competitive advantage.[7]

Critically, the assumption that industrial relations were inherently pluralist was replaced by HRM's unitarist frame of reference. Hence, conflict—institutionalized in industrial relations—was de-emphasized (or considered deviant) in HRM: it focused on the individual worker and not the collective. Trade unions, which had been central to industrial relations, were thus marginalized in the pursuit of an HR strategy. In addition, while the management of industrial relations had frequently been a specialist's job, HRM was seen as the responsibility of line managers. Managements' authority over employment relations was therefore largely seen as unproblematic. In both its hard form, emphasizing the use of the worker as a resource, and its soft form, emphasizing the human potential for commitment, HRM was thus well suited to the new 'enterprise culture' of the 1980s.[8]

This chapter considers what produced such a transformation in the employment relationship in Britain over forty years. The demise of industrial relations and the rise of HRM fall into three phases, each characterized by a changing political perspective on how to regulate management–union relations. The post-Second World War consensus around 'collective *laissez-faire*'[9] collapsed between 1966 and 1979 and was replaced in the late 1970s by an emergent corporatism or 'tripartism'. However, corporatism had a very short 'shelf life' as the regulation of trade union behaviour, and the denigration of collectivism, became a prime political aim between 1979 and 1997. Finally, a new consensus or 'Third Way' began to emerge between 1997 and 2006. This combined an attenuated form of collectivism with extended individual employment rights and thus encouraged the exercise of the managerial prerogative as reflected in HRM.

1966–79: Dismantling Collective Laissez-Faire

There was a broad party-political consensus after the Second World War that the leading actors in industrial relations—employers, management, and trade unions—should largely be left to determine voluntarily the outcomes of the effort–reward bargain. Otto Khan-Freund termed this 'collective laissez-faire'.[10] Government regulation of industrial relations in Britain was negligible compared with that in the rest of Europe. For this reason the overt use of bargaining power by managers and trade unions was central to the determination of labour negotiations, which had failed to reach a more amicable or win–win solution. However, following the Donovan Report (1968)—much influenced by the Oxford School, and Hugh Clegg and Bill McCarthy in particular—both Conservative and Labour governments began to question more seriously the efficiency of collective laissez-faire and their own industrial relations neutrality.[11]

Critically, as argued by Martin, in the 1970s and early 1980s, the central issue in political economy became the balance of power between management and unions.[12] A major contributory factor was a remarkable surge in union membership. Between 1948 and 1968, union membership had stagnated around 9–10 million or a density of 43 per cent.[13] But by 1979, union membership had reached 13 million or a density of 54 per cent.[14] This rapid growth was caused by a mixture of structural and interventionist factors.[15] Structurally, hyperinflation drove employees to unionize to protect their earnings against rapidly rising prices. The 'credit and threat effect' that trade unions generated by bargaining hard to protect existing members' standards of living impelled non-members to seek similar protection.[16] At the same time, unions organized themselves to exploit this favourable environment. Recruitment drives, successful strikes, active local representatives, and their high political profile gave trade unions both the appearance of 'delivering the goods' and a new legitimacy as the 'representatives of labour'.[17]

Inflationary pressures and unions' claims for matching wage increases emerged as leading economic questions for both the Labour government of 1964–70 and the Conservative government of 1970–4, and both adopted similar policies. First, they opted for voluntary and then statutory incomes policies, while initiating schemes to increase productivity via the National Economic Development Office (NEDO). This initiative represented a form of corporatism, drawing employers and unions into consultation with government over economic issues. Second, Labour and Conservative governments alike looked to produce a new legislative framework for industrial relations, including the reform of trade unions. The Labour government in 1969 contemplated introducing legislation based on its White Paper *In Place of Strife*, and in 1971 the Conservatives actually introduced the Industrial Relations Act. At this point trade unions were insisting on 'free collective bargaining' and bent on resisting both the Conservative's Industrial Relations Act and its incomes policies. The miners, organized by the National Union of Mineworkers (NUM), led the action against Heath's statutory incomes policy. It did not augur well, either for collective laissez-faire or for future incomes policies, that Heath's Conservative government lost the 1974 election on the question of 'Who runs the country—the government or the unions?'

The Labour government elected in 1974, therefore, faced a trade union movement confident in its power to resist both legislative reform and restraints on free collective bargaining. But the inherited high rate of inflation, further fuelled by the quadrupling of oil prices in 1973–4, led to hyperinflation. This, together with concerns over the balance of payments and unemployment, rapidly restored incomes policy to the Labour government's agenda. After gaining union cooperation, not least by repealing the Industrial Relations Act, the Labour government of 1974–9 launched the last corporatist attempt at solving the problem of inflation. This was the 'social contract', which sought to engage both unions and employers between 1975 and 1977 in the management of the economy by means of wage and price restraints.

Initially, the social contract had the desired effect on wage and price inflation. Also, between 1975 and 1977 strikes, which had been running at historically high levels, subsided. However, in helping the government control wage increases and thus inflation trade union leaders encountered problems in persuading their own rank-and-file to comply with the policy. Most notably, Jack Jones, General Secretary of Britain's largest union (the Transport and General Workers Union), lost a pro-social contract motion at his union's biennial national conference in 1977.

This effectively spelt the end of voluntary incomes policies and bargained corporatism. In response, the government introduced a statutory incomes policy, which, in turn, resulted in major industrial unrest. The so-called 'Winter of Discontent' saw a post-war record of 4,608,000 workers on strike and 29,474,000 lost working days.[18] This was for the Labour government and the trade unions the most politically damaging strike action since 1945. In particular, the unions' public image was scarred by public sector strikes in hospitals and mortuaries: the people could not bury their dead. Furthermore, it destroyed the electorate's belief that a Labour government rather than a Conservative government could best protect them from the downside of trade union power. The political outcome was the Conservative's 1979 general election victory.

Thus, the political consensus surrounding collective laissez-faire and its potential successor, bargained corporatism, was unintentionally destroyed by trade union power. The struggle to contain inflation exposed the limits of voluntarism. In particular, it showed that centrally agreed incomes policies made between government and union leaders were not sustainable in the economic and institutional context of the period.

1979–97: The Demise of Collectivism

The Conservatives, led by Mrs Thatcher, won the 1979 election and were also to win three further elections in 1983, 1987, and 1992. In 1979, they inherited an economy in deep difficulties over inflation and rising unemployment. Union membership was at its peak, even if the unions were chastened by their role in bringing down the Labour government. The Conservative's new leadership, recognizing that statutory incomes policies and trade union power had helped unseat two previous governments, were driven by circumstances, as well as their growing neoliberal tendencies, to search for alternatives to collective laissez-faire and corporatism for dealing with industrial relations. Broadly, economic objectives took priority, and monetary policy was adopted as the chosen means of eliminating inflation. Hence, other macroeconomic policies, such as maintaining a high level of employment, were subordinated to this goal.[19] The freeing of market forces, including the deregulation of the labour market and the regulation of trade unions, became key elements of Conservative's policy.

As regards union reform there was, initially, some continuity. Mrs Thatcher's first Secretary of State for Employment, Jim Prior, was personally committed to the voluntary tradition in industrial relations.[20] Thus, the Conservative's first piece of trade union legislation (1980 Employment Act) pressed unions to adopt voluntarily secret ballots for the calling of industrial action and the election of key national officials. (For a full discussion of the six major pieces of Conservative legislation on trade unions between 1984 and 1993, see Undy et al.[21]) Indeed, Prior consulted widely with the trade union leaders over the 1980 Act, taking care to keep the moderates onside and urging his colleagues not to aggravate the situation by attacking the trade union movement. This period of constructive consultation between government and unions, however, was short-lived. In 1981, Mrs Thatcher signalled her determination to impose her neoliberal agenda on the Department of Employment by replacing Prior with Norman Tebbit who had promised to '... protect people against the mis-use of union power'.[22]

Such statements resonated strongly with, and were influenced by, the work of two academics, Friedrich Hayek and Patrick Minford. Working from classical economic premises, they had argued that unions' legal privileges, or immunities (protection against the common law 'in restraint of trade'), damaged the economy. Such 'privileges' led unions to interfere with market forces, restrain the living standards of the working man, and increase unemployment (see McCarthy[23] for extracts from Hayek and Minford's commentary on the failings of trade unions and collectivism). Just as the Oxford School had provided the intellectual underpinning for voluntarism and collectivism, so Hayek, in a different context, was used to justify the legal regulation of trade unions in the interests of a more efficient economy and greater individual choice.

Subsequent union legislation after 1983 had a more aggressive edge to it. It sought to move the balance of power from union to management and, via secret postal ballots, to give individual union members a greater say in key union decisions. Acting incrementally over a lengthy period in order to avoid the kind of union resistance that had sunk the ill-fated 1971 Industrial Relations Act, the Conservatives between 1983 and 1997 introduced legislation that affected the internal affairs of unions (including the election of officials and their period of office), the closed shop, the collection of members' subscriptions, unions' affiliations to political parties (in effect the Labour Party), unions' powers to discipline union members, and the right to union recognition for bargaining purposes.

Most important, several restrictions were placed directly on the exercise of bargaining power. Secondary action was excluded from protection under common law (workers could take industrial action only against their own employer). Detailed rules were prescribed for the calling of industrial action, which also required majority support in a secret postal ballot. Picketing was also regulated and restricted. Unofficial strikers were denied claims for unfair dismissal. Critically, unions were also made liable to employers for industrial action that did not comply with the complex process required by law. In the event of such 'unofficial' action, unions had to repudiate, and therefore disown their members, if they were to avoid potentially costly consequences. By 1997, therefore, British unions were amongst the most heavily regulated and restricted in the Western world.[24]

Union power was further diminished by other structural factors. Its membership plummeted 40 per cent, from 13 million in 1979 to 7 million in 1994. Economically, the tight monetary policy adopted by the Conservatives, as they jettisoned incomes policy, contributed to the 'worst recession of the post-war years'[25] between 1979 and 1981. In 1982, unemployment peaked at 3.1 million. As well as damping down union militancy, the recession together with other structural changes also disproportionately reduced employment in manufacturing, mining, construction, energy, and water—all traditionally male-dominated and heavily unionized industries. Employment shifted towards the private service sector, which was female-dominated and largely non-unionized. By 1990 male union membership had fallen to 36 per cent compared to 63 per cent in 1978 (by contrast, female union membership was 38% in 1978 and 30% in 1990).

The Conservatives also took steps to reduce the role and standing of the unions in general and to expose the limits of union militancy by vigorously contesting the mineworkers' union's attempt to resist pit closures. In summary, the Conservatives had by 1993 dismantled virtually all the institutional arrangements previously built to support corporatism, including the symbolic closure of the NEDO in 1992.

As for the public sector, far from following the traditional government position and acting as a model or good employer setting the standard for the private sector, the government tried to emulate the private sector. Privatization, contracting out, and similar policies were meant to expose public sector unions and their members to private sector values and management. In the Civil Service, employees were no longer encouraged to join unions, and in some parts of the public sector unions were derecognized. Finally, with regard to the mineworkers, seen as the vanguard of the union movement when it came to successful strike action, the Conservatives succeeded where other governments had failed, defeating the NUM after a very bitter year-long (1984–5) strike. It was at this time that Mrs Thatcher referred to trade unions as the 'enemy within'.

A complex mixture of political, economic, and social factors therefore created an environment very detrimental to trade unions and collectivism between 1978 and 1997. Moreover, unions could not find ways to combat such changes effectively. As a result, union membership was radically reduced and collectivism followed suit. For example, in 1984, 64 per cent of establishments (with twenty-five or more employees) recognized a union for collective bargaining. By 1998, the proportion was 42 per cent and falling. The proportion of workplaces with a trade union representative fell from 54 per cent in 1984 to 33 per cent in 1998. The number of strikes also fell sharply. Between 1974 and 1979 there was an average of 2,416 strikes a year. In 1998, there were just 166 strikes.[26] Thus, by the time of the 1997 General Election, the central issue in the political economy of the 1970s and 1980s—the balance of power between management and unions—had been resolved and in management's favour.

1997–2006: A Third Way?

Compared to the previous two periods of radical adjustment in the balance of management–union power, the 1997–2006 period was more of consolidation than of change. New Labour's 1997 election victory, unlike the elections of 1974–9 that were influenced greatly by governments' approaches to employment relations, was not overly concerned with management–union relations. Moreover, New Labour had, in opposition, distanced itself from the trade unions: the trade unions' constitutional role within the Party had been reduced, and the Party actively sought alternative sources of funding and membership to lessen its dependence on the trade unions. In 1997, and in subsequent Labour victories in 2001 and 2005, there was thus little, if any, electoral advantage to be gained by publicizing Labour's historical links with the trade unions. Indeed, New Labour's 1997 rhetoric was one of 'fairness not favours': it looked to treat trade unions and employers with an 'even-handed' approach. This was summarized by Prime Minister Tony Blair in his foreword to the 1998 White Paper *Fairness at Work*, as a replacement for the notion of conflict between employers and employees with partnership, while not re-regulating the labour market.[27]

In facing the question of how to deal with employment relations in a new economic and political context, New Labour had its own favoured legitimating strategy. In this case it was Anthony Giddens and the 'Third Way'.[28] Originating in the USA, the Third Way accepted that globalization was a fact of life and that a flexible labour market was an essential part of the nation state's response to such international pressures. Individual employees therefore had to be empowered to develop their own skills and expertise to survive in a dynamic economy.[29] Having abandoned collectivism, Third Way politics looked for a new relationship between the individual and the community: a redefinition of rights and obligations.[30] However, in looking to protect individual workers' rights New Labour could call on the cooperation of other nation states to limit the worst excesses of globalization. By cooperation on social policy in the EU and regulating some aspects of the labour market, the member states could avoid adopting competitive 'beggar your neighbour' economic policies that might otherwise have been used to attract global capitalism's investments.

New Labour's Third Way, as applied to employment relations, was therefore something of a hybrid. On the one hand, New Labour in practice supported a deregulated labour market, did not reverse the main privatizations, and retained most of the restrictive union legislation, including that directly restricting union bargaining power, such as the ban on secondary action. While New Labour urged unions and management to work in partnership, it did very little itself to 'partner' with trade unions in the area of economic or social policy: tripartism was still off the government's agenda. On the other hand, individuals gained a raft of new employment rights, in particular, through the EU's Social Chapter signed in 1997, and the Working Time Directive applied to Britain in 1998. The European Works Council Directive was also introduced in 1999. Perhaps most important, the National Minimum Wage was introduced in 1999. As for other individual rights, improvements were made in the following areas: maternity and paternity rights, childcare, requests for more flexible working, fixed term contracts, right to be accompanied at grievance/disciplinary meetings, and equal opportunities was given a higher priority.

Even though trade unions remained disappointed at the rate and degree of changes made in collective rights, New Labour did make some improvements of value to the trade unions. Most noticeably, unions regained the legal right to claim recognition for the purpose of collective bargaining in New Labour's 1999 Employment Relations Act. Protection against dismissal of union members pursuing lawful industrial action was also extended. Trade unions further stood to gain influence over managerial decisions under the EU's Information and Consultation Directive, transposed to Britain in 2005.

As part of the government's supply-side economic policies aimed at improving human capital, the TUC in 2000 also benefited from government grants to support its 'Learning Services Project', while individual unions drew on the government-sponsored 'Union Learning Fund'. More controversially, in 2004 a trade union modernization fund was proposed, which in 2006 supported a number of projects aimed at improving union effectiveness. Finally, New Labour's industrial relations reforms, initially introduced in the public sector, were broadly welcomed by the unions themselves. So, although unions were no longer at the centre of government's employment relations policies, they did make a number of gains under Labour governments between 1997 and 2006.

These changes initiated by New Labour were, however, in the wider context of the period of little consequence for the management–union balance of power. Other structural factors, including changes in the labour market, economic conditions (particularly low inflation), and trade unions' continued exclusion from anything resembling high-level tripartism or corporatism, all militated against a trade union recovery.

Importantly, the role and employment policies of management also remained largely unchanged from the earlier 1990s. In line with HRM orthodoxy, private sector management tended to resist unionization and collective bargaining from the 1980s onwards. Even in such traditional union strongholds as engineering, union recognition declined from 65 per cent of this workforce in 1980 to only 19 per cent in 1998.[31] Perhaps most revealingly there was a 'dramatic shift from union to non-union representatives' (in the private sector) between 1980 and 1998.[32] Clearly, managements were promoting an alternative to trade unionism, which, lacking independent organization, was more open to managerial influence. Also, management preferred to communicate directly with employees as individuals rather than use union channels. In the period of New Labour governments, management increased its use of face-to-face 'meetings with the entire workforce or teams of employees, and greater use of systematic communication through the management chain'.[33]

In this environment, trade unions generally adopted a more conciliatory and partnership approach towards employers (see Undy[34]). As recognized by the TUC in 1999, 'the rhetoric of struggle, strikes and strife...has little resonance in today's world of work...Embracing partnership is therefore the right strategic choice for the trade union movement.'[35] Cooperation rather than conflict with management was therefore the preferred model of union behaviour. Industrial action continued at a very low level, and the number of strikes reached a new post-war low of just 133 strikes in 2003.

However, the effect of attenuated collectivism and expanded individual employment rights was not encouraging for the trade unions. Union membership under New Labour governments stagnated around 6.4 to 6.7 million (30% or so density). The distribution of union membership between the public sector (60% density) and the private sector (18% density) also remained reasonably constant. Collective bargaining coverage similarly remained static, below 50 per cent between 1997 and 2005.[36] Trade unions failed to penetrate new job territories: membership in private services remained abysmally low in 2005 at 11 per cent in wholesale and retail trades and around 5 per cent in hotels and restaurants.

Management had used the power it had accrued during the Conservative period in office between 1979 and 1997 to create in 2006 a reasonably stable employment relationship resistant to the advance of a new moderated trade unionism. Not surprisingly, therefore, the most remarkable change in a largely unchanging employment relationship between 1998 and 2004 was the 'striking...continued decline of collective labour organisation'.[37]

Conclusions

There were then between 1966 and 2006 very radical changes in the practice of employment relations. Most important, the power balance between management and unions moved strongly in management's favour. Structurally, changes in the British economy and labour market initially helped trade unions grow in membership and bargaining power. But, ultimately, the use of that power in a period of high inflation became self-defeating as it exposed the political frailties of governments wedded to industrial relations voluntarism as expressed in collective laissez-faire and their experiments with corporatism. In 1997, the New Labour government, haunted by the ghost of the Winter of Discontent, most obviously had no wish to return to the 1970s. New Labour's synthesis, the Third Way, tended more towards the continued regulation of trade unions and the development of individual, rather than collective, rights. A casualty of this forty-year process was the term industrial relations. Associated in the practitioner's mind with industrial disputes and trade unions it had by 2006 become largely passé.

The new dominant term in the practice and study of employment relations was by 2006 HRM. Seen as the new orthodoxy in the early 1990s it was nevertheless subject to different academic uses and interpretations in the period leading into the new millennium. For example, much discussion focused on its normative nature as arguments developed over the relative merits of its hard or soft models: in the hard model, employees to be treated as a resource and managed in a calculative and rational manner; in the soft, managers to focus on employees' development potential and their organizational commitment (see Storey and Sisson[38]). Others examined the evidence for HRM in practice and debated whether it differed significantly from personnel management.[39] Moving 'upmarket', other academics switched attention to strategic HRM, suggesting that such a change in the level of analysis offered a more theoretically satisfactory approach to the subject.[40]

In contrast—and somewhat more sceptically—the problems posed if HRM became the new 'lingua franca' in employment relations, given the 'conceptual weaknesses and dearth of empirical support for the practice of HRM', were discussed.[41] Yet by 2003, it was reasonably claimed by Purcell and Boxall that the term HRM could be taken as equivalent to employee relations and labour management, albeit with an emphasis on the management of employment relations.[42] Moreover, in 2005 Bach considered the controversy surrounding the meaning of HRM had 'largely dissipated', although he limited its scope to 'all aspects of personnel practice'.[43]

Such a marked movement over forty years in the study of employment relations from the language and values of industrial relations to that of HRM is best understood by reference to the contextual changes described above. Just as bargaining power between management and unions moved in management's favour, so the language used to describe academics studying employment relations and the related degrees and courses followed suit. As unions were no longer 'the problem', it may be argued that in true Oxford School tradition, it made sense to focus research and teaching on the new priority—the effective management of employee relations. However, may it also be the case that the hegemony achieved by HRM and its values was so successful because the associated political agenda made the term industrial relations an academic liability, whereas that of HRM became an academic advantage?

References

1. A. Marsh, *Concise Encyclopaedia of Industrial Relations* (Aldershot, UK: Gower Press, 1979), 150.
2. K. Sisson, *What 'Industrial Relations' Suggests Should Be at the Heart of Employee Relations*; see http://www.buira.org.uk
3. M. Emmott, *Change Agenda: What Is Employee Relations?* (London: CIPD, 2006), 5.
4. J. Storey 'Introduction: From Personal Management to Human Resource Management,' in J. Storey (ed.), *New Perspectives on Human Resource Management* (London: Routledge, 1989), 4.
5. K. Legge, 'HRM: Rhetoric, Reality and Hidden Agendas', in J. Storey (ed.), *Human Resource Management: A Critical Text* (London: Routledge, 1995), 33.
6. J. Storey and K. Sisson, *Managing Human Resources and Industrial Relations* (Buckingham: Open University Press, 1993), 16.
7. D. Guest, 'Human Resource Management: Its Implications for Industrial Relations and Trade Unions', in J. Storey (ed.), *New Perspectives on Human Resource Management* (London: Routledge, 1989), 43.

8. K. Legge, 'Human Resource Management: A Critical Analysis', in J. Storey (ed.), *New Perspectives on Human Resource Management* (London: Routledge, 1989), 40.

9. W. McCarthy, 'The Rise and Fall of Collective Laissez Faire', in W. McCarthy (ed.), *Legal Interventions in Industrial Relations: Gains and Losses* (Oxford: Blackwell, 1992), 1–71.

10. Ibid. 4.

11. *The Royal Commission on Trade Unions and Employers' Associations 1965–1968: Report* (Cmnd 36231968; London: HMSO, 1968).

12. R. Martin, *Bargaining Power* (Oxford: Oxford University Press, 1992), 1.

13. H. Clegg, *The Changing System of Industrial Relations in Britain* (Oxford: Blackwell, 1979), 177.

14. G. S. Bain and R. Price, 'Union Growth: Dimensions, Determinants and Density', in G. S. Bain (ed.), *Industrial Relations in Britain* (Oxford: Blackwell, 1983), 7.

15. B. Mason and P. Bain, 'The Determinants of Trade Union Membership in Britain: A Survey of the Literature', *Industrial and Labour Relations Review*, 46/2(1993): 332.

16. G. S. Bain and R. Price, op. cit. 16.

17. R. Undy et al., *Change in Trade Unions* (London: Hutchinson, 1981).

18. C. Wrigley, *British Trade Unions Since 1933* (Cambridge: Cambridge University Press, 2002), 43.

19. J. MacInnes, *Thatcherism at Work* (Stony Stratford: Open University Press, 1987), 50–1.

20. D. Marsh, *The New Politics of British Trade Unionism* (London: Macmillan, 1992), 66.

21. R. Undy et al., *Managing the Unions* (Oxford: OUP, 1996), 69–149.

22. D. Marsh, op. cit. 71.

23. W. E. J. McCarthy, *Trade Unions* (Harmondsworth: Penguin Books, 1985), 357–75.

24. R. Undy et al., op. cit. 263–83.

25. S. Kessler and F. Bayliss, *Contemporary British Industrial Relations* (London: Macmillan, 1998), 39.

26. R. Undy, 'Trade Unions and the Employment Relationship', in B. Towers (ed.), *The Handbook of Employment Relations* (London: Kogan Page, 2003), 278–9.

27. R. Undy, 'New Labour's Industrial Relations Settlement: The Third Way', *British Journal of Industrial Relations*, 37/2(1999): 315.

28. A. Giddens, *The Third Way* (Cambridge: Polity Press, 1998).

29. G. Corea, 'More by Default than Design: Some Clinton Experiences of the Third Way', *Renewal*, 6/2(1998): 14.

30. A. Giddens, op. cit. 65.

31. N. Millward, A. Bryson, and J. Forth, *All Change at Work* (London: Routledge, 2000), 98.

32. Ibid. 114.

33. B. Kersley, C. Alpin, J. Forth, A. Bryson, H. Bewley, G. Dix, and S. Oxenbridge, *Inside the Workplace* (WERS First Findings, 2005), 36.
34. R. Undy, in B. Towers (ed.), op. cit. 274–5.
35. Trades Union Congress, *Partners for Progress* (London: TUC, 1999), 8.
36. Department of Trade and Industry, *Trade Union Membership 2005* (DTI Employment Market Analysis and Research; London: DTI, Mar. 2006).
37. B. Kersley et al., op. cit. 35.
38. J. Storey and K. Sisson, op. cit. 17.
39. K. Legge, in J. Storey (ed.) (1989), op. cit.
40. P. F. Boxall, 'Strategic Human Resources Management: Beginnings of a New Theoretical Sophistication', *Human Resource Management Journal*, 2/3(1992): 60–79.
41. P. Blyton and P. Turnbull (eds), *Reassessing Human Resources Management* (London: Sage, 1992), 256.
42. J. Purcell and P. F. Boxall, *Strategy and Human Resource Management* (Basingstoke: Palgrave Macmillan, 2003), 1.
43. S. Bach (ed.), *Managing Human Resources* (Oxford: Blackwell, 2005), 15.

13

Operations Management: Realizing Its Strategic Role

Alex Hill and Terry Hill

The area of Operations Management (OM) is often misunderstood by both students of business and managers within firms. This misunderstanding is generated partly by the way the subject is presented and taught, and partly by the way the function is perceived and explained by operations managers to their fellow executives.

However, part of the problem also lies in the changing field of study. Originally, the conceptual orientation and emphasis within OM was towards the management of the area. Later, specialist developments introduced techniques that made useful, sometimes fundamental, contributions to help manage operations. From this developed a strong, often overriding, impetus to teach and develop OM as a body of techniques involving detailed analysis and tactical considerations, but often not discriminating between the usefulness and relevance of one approach or technique to another. Furthermore, this emphasis towards the quantitative perspective as a way to resolve and present OM issues also increasingly included explanations and mathematical derivations of the formulae and solutions proposed.

Some of the technique-oriented approaches include manufacturing resource planning (MRP), lean operations, total quality management (TQM), total production management (TPM), and several IT-based developments such as enterprise resource planning (ERP), while the mathematical approach championed by operations research (OR) continues to have a sizeable following in academic teaching and research communities.

The outcomes were significant. In the academic world, OM became uninteresting and apparently lacked business relevance. Demand fell, and growth in faculty resources, research, and teaching did not match the general expansion experienced in business education at the undergraduate, postgraduate, and post-experience levels during the last three decades of the twentieth century through to the present day.

The Development of OM in Practice

Within the manufacturing and service sectors of the economy the role of OM became devalued. Consequently, the critical perspectives of this large and substantial function were not clearly recognized and were often inadequately presented. Typical results were unbalanced corporate arguments, inappropriate allocation of key management resources to operations, and a failure to attract the necessary management talent into the area by matching task, responsibilities, and contribution with appropriate status, influence, and reward.

However, from the increasingly competitive nature of markets in the last fifteen to twenty years of the old millennium the key role of operations in bringing about the growth and profitability of organizations has re-emerged. Fast and on-time delivery, providing products and services right first time, being able to respond to increasing variety, and the need to cut costs were increasingly important factors in most markets. How well operations were managed to bring these about became a key corporate issue. As a function responsible for 60–70 per cent of costs, assets, and people (while also typically contributing much to the way organizations compete), the emphasis swung in terms of what was key in operations from a bias towards techniques and solutions to one that stressed and highlighted the effective management of this large business function.

Manufacturing versus Services: An Irrelevant Debate

Looking at the overall mix of sectors in most Organization for Economic Cooperation and Development (OECD) countries from 1980 shows a similar pattern: the service sector continues to grow in itself and also as a proportion of Gross Domestic Product (GDP). However, the OM role, no matter what the sector, is similar in terms of task and significance. Growing foodstuffs, extracting minerals, making products, or providing services are parts of the basic task of any business and central to its continuing success. Consequently, it is essential to understand the concepts and approaches that are involved, the interfaces this function has within a business, and its key role in helping to grow sales and to meet an organization's short- and long-term financial goals.

Although it is useful to separate activities into primary (agriculture, mining, and quarrying), secondary (manufacturing and construction), and tertiary (utilities, retail, transport, and services) in order to help identify, understand, and discuss the whole, in reality they form part of a total economy. The mutual interdependence between the sectors is acknowledged and addressed in developed countries at both the national and corporate levels. Arguments suggesting that developed nations can rely on the service sector as a way of sustaining standards of living or as a means of improving below-average trade performance are without foundation. Each sector is not only an integral part of the same whole but performance in one sector will often have an impact on another. For example, a large part of many service sales comprises a product provided by activities in the primary or secondary sectors (e.g. foodstuffs and equipment). Equally, the economic success of countries like Japan and Germany and the rapid emergence of countries like China, India, and South Korea highlight the critical nature of a sound manufacturing base. On reflection, it is also not surprising that in the 1990s, several of the largest asset banks in the world were in Japan.

To sustain or improve corporate prosperity, it is essential to achieve the level of effectiveness required to compete successfully in chosen markets. To do this, those activities responsible for the provision of goods and services have to be well managed. These tasks are critical to the success of an organization, and operations managers oversee these tasks. They control the inputs and processes that together produce the goods or provide the services that a business sells. But, as with other functional executives, operations managers have a strategic as well as operational dimension to their responsibilities. They have to develop a functional strategy as part of the corporate debate that identifies and agrees the strategic direction that an organization needs to follow. Determining the emphasis of what is taught, researched, and written in the OM field needs to be set within the context of a business and reflect its overall contribution to an organization's ongoing success.

Operations Management's Strategic Role Has Been Undervalued

As with all the major functions within a business, the role of the operations executive comprises three distinct but related parts. The first concerns the day-to-day or operational aspect of the task. Typically being responsible for managing 60–70 per cent of both assets and costs results in a sizeable day-to-day role for operations and one which appropriately demands and receives much time and attention. And rightly so. Without due management and control of these major elements of expenditure, the essential cost base would be eroded and the margins underpinning an organization's financial projections would not be realized.

The second element comprises the strategic task. For each function this concerns providing those competitive factors for which it is solely or jointly responsible. The final element of the task concerns the style of management adopted. People are a key resource in an organization and central to meeting both the operational (day-to-day) and strategic tasks. Managing some 60–70 per cent of those employed and the relationship-building that comes from the ongoing need to interface with other functions, together with the outsourcing of work, constitute a significant part of the operations executive's job. This challenging task competes for attention with other operational priorities as the sound and responsive management of human resources underpins the long-term success of all organizations.

Traditionally, operations executives have always recognized the need to fulfil the tasks that comprise their operational role. It is understandably central to a business, and as such commands attention and requires capable management. Consequently, it attracts questions that reflect the fundamental nature of operations' contribution to meeting the sales revenue and profit targets of a business as a whole and duly places appropriate emphasis on the day-to-day task of managing the operations function.

Over the last twenty years, there has been a similar recognition of the key contribution that people at all levels of an organization make to its overall and continued success. Running in parallel to the rethinking of the hierarchical structure that characterized the traditional view of how to best manage organizations, the de-layering that has taken place in the last two decades has required a rethink of the role and contribution of all staff. Operations management has, for the most part, led this review, and the empowerment of staff to handle broader sets of responsibilities has been central to the change in management style within the function.

Regarding its strategic role, however, the outcome has not been the same. The size of the operations executive's day-to-day task has typically squeezed out the time and attention that its strategic contribution requires. Consequently, although a sizeable contributor to retaining and growing market share, operations has typically failed to fulfil its fuller business role. It is too late in the market debate and reactive in its contribution. Yet, as markets become increasingly different rather than increasingly similar, a business needs to understand the nature of these different sets of demands, the strategic role of functions in meeting these differences, how well these needs are being met, and the functional priorities that result in order to ensure appropriate responses that contribute to sustaining growth.

On the whole, operations managers do not have a history of explaining their function clearly and effectively to others within an organization. This is particularly so in terms of the strategy issues that need to be considered and the operations consequences that will arise from the corporate decisions under discussion. Reasons for this failure, however, cannot wholly be placed at the operations manager's door. The knowledge base, concepts, and language so essential to providing explanations and insights have not been adequately developed. Surrogates for strategy in the form of panacea have more often than not taken the place of strategic inputs, and the support given to these approaches by academics and consultants have reinforced this stance. The regular heralding of just-in-time (JIT), lean operations, and TQM-type initiatives have been seen, in part at least, as operations' strategic contribution. In a similar way, calls to become flexible, for instance, point to an apparent state in operations that offers a capability to do most (if not all) things.

Purposefully general, these overtures are without essential definition and direction and, more importantly, purport to offer the rest of the business an ability to support strategic alternatives equally well and with trade-offs to be neither considered nor made. Furthermore, when the superficiality of this state is exposed, the pundits for strategic alternatives merely switch the phrase 'flexible' to becoming 'agile and versatile' in this instance, arguing that the subtle differences in the proposed redefinition remedy the serious misgivings inherent in the discarded phrase. The cycle then resumes.

The Strategy-Making Process

As organizations grow they become more complex and the way they cope with the increased complexity that comes with size is to break the whole into parts that we call functions. The result is that strategy is now at two levels—the level of the business and the level of the function. Then, with further growth, an organization cannot cope with viewing the business as a whole and consequently again breaks the whole into parts, hence creating a third layer of strategy, as shown in Table 13.1.

Having split an organization into parts to cope with the complexity that comes with size and secure the gains of specialisms that result, a business needs to put the parts back together again. The ideal strategy-making process is depicted in Figure 13.1. Businesses are whole and not parts, and the need to embody the perspectives and insights of the functions making up a business is an essential element of the strategy-making

TABLE 13.1 Levels of strategy and their distinctive tasks[1]

Level of strategy	Distinctive tasks
Corporate	Strategic activity at the corporate level concerns the direction of the total business and addresses issues such as where to invest and/or divest, and priorities in terms of sales revenue growth. Implementation concerns the allocation of investment funds in line with these priorities
Business unit	Business units comprise different parts of a total business. For example, corporate banking, retail banking, financial markets, mortgages, pensions, and insurance would be separated into different business units within a bank. For each business unit, strategic direction concerns identifying the markets in which it competes, agreeing where it intends to grow (including new markets), the nature of competition and the relevant competitive criteria in its current and future markets, in terms of maintaining and growing share. Implementation concerns discussing and agreeing how and where to invest, in terms of functional tasks and alternative approaches
Functional	Each business unit will comprise a number of functions such as sales and marketing, operations, and IT that make up the total activities within a business unit. The strategic role of each function is to support those competitive dimensions within a market that comprise the agenda for functional strategies and become the mechanism for determining development and investment priorities. Implementation concerns consistently meeting the competitive norms involved and selecting the alternative approaches to attain the improvement goals laid down

process and a key factor for today's business organizations in the competitive markets in which they compete. Reality, however, is typically far removed from this ideal, being more like the process illustrated in Figure 13.2.

In many firms, corporate strategy is developed as a series of independent statements. Lacking essential integration, the result is a compilation of distinct, functional strategies which sit side by side, layer on layer in the same corporate binder. Integration is not provided if, in fact, it was ever intended. The question then is why this crucial task is so inadequately and inappropriately performed with overtones of being a ritual rather than a core executive task. There are five main reasons.

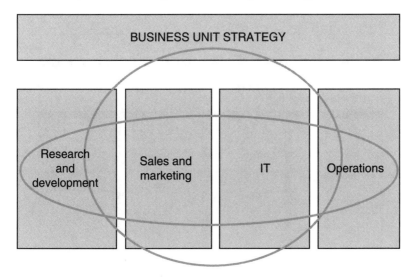

FIG. 13.1 Ideal strategy-making process[2]

1. The Strategy Debate Stops at Each Interface. The essential discussion, understanding, and agreement between corporate and business units, between business units and functions, and between functions themselves typically stop at each interface as illustrated in Figure 13.3. Rather than being an ongoing debate, executives address this critical role infrequently, confuse it with financial planning, and use 'away day-type' approaches as the structure by which to undertake this fundamental task.

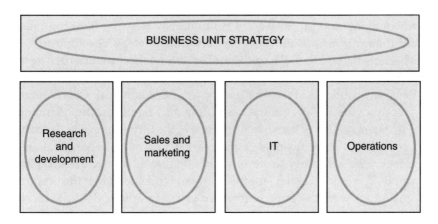

FIG. 13.2 Real-life strategy-making process[3]

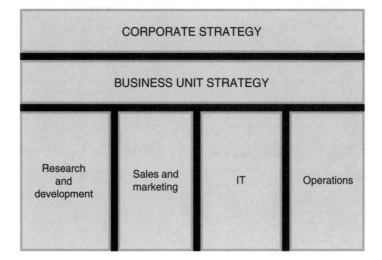

FIG. 13.3 Strategy debate stops at the interface

2. The Pursuit of Generic Strategies. Whereas businesses are increasingly complex rather than increasingly simple, approaches to developing strategies review businesses as whole, thereby overlaying the diversity that exists with generic solutions. Niche, low-cost core competence-type arguments are seductive in their apparent offerings. The promise of uniformity is appealing to those with the task of developing strategies for businesses typified by difference not similarity. Such approaches purport to identify a corporate similarity that, though desirable, is inherently not available and thereby cope with the complexity of their businesses and markets by ignoring it. Instead of continuously working hard to understand their business as the basis for corporate strategy developments, it has become the search for the philosopher's stone that can turn base metal into gold.

Examples abound. Take, for example, the Analytical Coordination Reports provided as part of the Government's Manufacturing, Planning, and Implementation Scheme. In fifty-three of the fifty-four in-depth analyses completed, the outcomes of the market analysis, the key first step in developing a strategy, were unusable. Figure 13.4 provides a typical example. The market review for this company concluded that the needs of all customers were the same in terms of price sensitivity, delivery speed, delivery reliability, and quality conformance. A post-assignment review by the analytical coordination team is given in Figure 13.4 and shows

Aspect	Relative position of the four market segments		
Price sensitivity	Most  Least		
Length of delivery lead time	Short ——————— Long		

FIG. 13.4 Result of post-assignment market review[4]

distinctly different levels of price sensitivity and length of lead times for the top four customers.

3. History of Functional Dominance. A by-product of the approach adopted has led to strategy formulation being seen as functionally rather than business-driven. Reinforced by uncoordinated sets of performance measures, functions have largely developed strategies independently of other parts of the business, the formulation of which have, in turn, been seen to belong to the function itself. Whereas the implementation of agreed strategies belongs to each function, formulation does not. The formulation of, say, marketing strategy does not belong to marketing but belongs to the business. And the same goes for operations and the other functional strategies. The lack of recognition of business ownership of functional strategy formulation has helped fuel functional competition rather than functional cooperation in undertaking this key task.

4. Market versus Marketing. While all functions need to be market-driven or market-driving, none should be marketing-driven or marketing-driving. The similarity of the two words 'market' and 'marketing' has added to the lack of clarity typically associated with the ownership of strategic direction. This task belongs to the business (market) and not to a function (marketing).

5. Operations' Reactive Role. Traditionally, OM has adopted a reactive approach to undertaking its strategic role. In part dominated by the day-to-day part of its overall task, operations is too often too late in the corporate debate and finds itself placed in a position of having to respond to strategic change after the fact. Couple this with a tendency to adopt a 'can't say no' culture, operations fails to appropriately assess strategic fit and also fails to evaluate strategic alternatives ahead of time.

TABLE 13.2 Current problems and retention rates[5]

Sector	Percentage total of customers experiencing problems	Retention rates (percentage total) for customers having	
		No problem	Problem
Consumer goods	22	83	54
Appliance repairs	44	73	40
Car rentals	47	92	75
Branch banking	49	86	76
High-tech (business customers)	60	91	81
Air travel	69	91	77

Linking Operations to Corporate Strategy via Focus on the Market

Visiting a city for the first time and seeking advice on where best to eat will often result in dining at the restaurant recommended. If the food, wine, and service live up to expectations you may well go there again. If they do not, you will be most unlikely to return. While in this example brand name secured the first sale, it would be operations in the form of the product or service offering delivered that secures the second. In this way the operations function is typically responsible for securing repeat business, so providing a significant and essential contribution to retaining and growing market share, as Tables 13.2 and 13.3 illustrate. Furthermore, operations perspectives on markets make a significant contribution to the strategy development process in two ways.

1. It Brings Key Insights into Ascertaining Customers' Needs. Look at a bottle of mineral water and consider that your company provides the label on the outside of the bottle. Now, in which market segment would

TABLE 13.3 Trends in annual profit per customer[5]

Sector	Annual profit per customer				
	1	2	3	4	5
Car servicing	100	140	280	350	350
Credit cards	100	250	283	290	309
Distribution	100	220	270	320	373

Note: Figures indexed on year 1.

your sales and marketing department place the customer … the one who produces and sells the bottle of mineral water? The likelihood is that this customer would be placed in the 'beverage' or 'soft drinks' segment (i.e. the sector in which your customer operates). From an operations point of view, however, on which product a customer attaches the label it provides is of little consequence. The key issues for operations concern factors such as level of price sensitivity, the length of delivery lead times, and the size of demand peaks throughout the year. By segmenting markets, in this instance by the sector in which a company's customers operate, the implication is that the customers in this beverage or soft drinks segment (our example here) are equally price sensitive, require similar delivery lead times, and have similar demand profiles throughout the year. Taking only one function's view will give insufficient insight and lead to unfounded assumptions that result in inappropriate strategic decisions.

2. It Links Implementation to the Strategic Formulation Process. In so doing it ensures the strategic options include a feasibility check both in terms of investment level and lead time to bring it about. Given the size of the operations' contribution to the development and implementation of strategy, it is both necessary and appropriate that operations executives move from a predominantly reactive to a predominantly proactive approach to undertaking this role. Only then will operations realize its full role and make its full contribution to the strategic discussion and decision that ensures the long-term successful growth of an enterprise. In a world where increasing difference as opposed to increasing similarity is the hallmark of today's markets, operations needs to ensure that strategy formulation is business-based by making markets (the neutral arena) the centre of this development. Without appropriate strategic direction, functions do what they think is best for the business. One outcome of this scenario is that currently functions' strategic contributions are solution-led rather than problem-led (Box 13.1).

Developing an Operations Strategy

Functional strategies concern investing and developing in ways that support the needs of markets in terms of being market-driven and market-driving. As Figure 13.5 shows, the role of functional strategies is to contribute to meeting agreed business objectives with markets at the centre of strategy development. The form and size of contribution will vary from market to market, but the strategic development process for all functions is similar:

Box 13.1 Operations development at Benetton

In the mid-1960s Luciano Benetton and his sister Giuliana started designing and making brightly coloured clothes. With cutting-edge designs, the company's sales and profits grew year on year. An integral part of this success story has been the company's operations developments to support the whole supply chain.

Information system and manufacturing process investments
In fashion markets, forecasting which styles and colours would sell best is difficult. An integrated information system to provide feedback on current actual sales at each retail outlet, coupled with a manufacturing process that makes woollen garments and then dyes them in line with actual sales, led to major gains for Benetton. Inventory—and consequently the size of retail outlets—was reduced, and the products that sold well were the ones that manufacturing made. This fast feedback, short manufacturing lead times, and quick deliveries better meet market needs while cutting inventory and asset investments.

Modern manufacturing facilities
The late 1990s saw the opening of Benetton's state-of-the-art manufacturing plants in Castrette, north of Venice. The latest developments were part of a $350 million investment to make tailored apparel, skirts, jeans, and cotton garments. These plants had been integrated with the woollen plant built in 1986 and the automated warehouse handles all the storage, invoicing, pickup, and shipment of garments to the 7,000 points of sale around the world. The aim of the latest investments was to reduce staff and the existing cutting and packaging operations as a way of matching unit costs from alternative suppliers in the Asia Pacific and other low-cost areas of the world, while maintaining Benetton's local subcontractors' bias comprising 200 companies and their 30,000 employees. While many competitors now outsource from countries such as Indonesia and Turkey, Benetton has continued to develop its local supply base while achieving its essential cost reductions through combined investments in operations. In this way it is able to reflect the short lead time requirement of its markets with its in-house and outsourcing policies. High investment in the front and back end of garment making, with local subcontractors providing a short response service—a manufacturing sandwich with advanced technology encasing a more labour-intensive filling—provides low costs and fast response advantages in a competitive, fashion-led market.

- *Phase 1: Understand markets,* ensuring both a market-driven and market-driving approach while maintaining an ongoing rigorous review throughout this first critical step.
- *Phase 2: Translate these reviews into strategic tasks.* For example, if price is a competitive driver, then the task is to reduce costs; similarly if

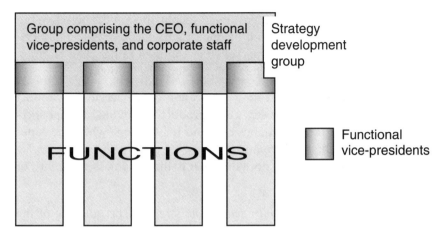

| Group comprising the CEO, functional vice-presidents, and corporate staff | Strategy development group |

FUNCTIONS

Functional vice-presidents

FIG. 13.5 Functional contributions to meeting corporate objectives with markets at the centre of strategic development[6]

on-time delivery is a competitive factor, then improving the reliability of meeting customers' due dates is the task.

- *Phase 3: Check that what is currently provided matches what is required in a market-driven scenario or the new level in a market-driving scenario.*
- *Phase 4: Develop a strategy* (the prioritizing of investments and developments) to close the gap where the level of provision falls short of the requirement or to achieve the new level of performance in a market-driving scenario.
- *Phase 5: Implement the necessary investment and development priorities.*

Returning to an earlier point that has been emphasized throughout, companies need to develop strategies that reflect the range of market needs that characterize their businesses. As explained above, the key first step in developing a functional strategy is to analyse the markets in which a company competes. Clarity about markets is essential. Where companies are in multiple markets then the outcome of the debate on markets should identify and provide a clear understanding of the differences that exist. The steps to secure these insights are as follows:

1. *Avoid general words and phrases. As markets are at the core of strategy development, using general words and phrases needs to be consciously and rigorously avoided.* Each dimension should be expressed on its own and a single definition needs to be associated with each word or phrase used. In this way, each competitive dimension put forward as relevant can be discussed separately and its relevance assessed. Thus, phrases such as 'customer service' or 'delighting the customers' must be avoided, not

because 'customer service' or 'customer delight' are not the objective but because their meaning is not self-evident. Using such phrases to describe the competitive nature of a market thus confuses rather than clarifies. Further examples to illustrate this point include the following:

- 'Quality' embodies both the specification of the service or product as well as how well the service or product is provided to that specification. The former dimension concerns 'design' while the latter concerns 'quality conformance'.
- 'Delivery performance': does this refer to the timeliness, reliability, or speed of delivery?

2. *Do not use long lists, which denote poor strategy.* The outcome of the discussion on how a company competes in its market is typically a long list. The intention seems to be to leave nothing off the list, thereby covering all aspects. Nothing, however, could be further from the truth. This phase of the strategy process concerns distillation and not long lists.

3. *Separate out order-winners and qualifiers.* A further step to improve a company's understanding of its markets is to separate out relevant criteria into order-winners and qualifiers:

- *Qualifiers*
  These criteria get a service or product into a market or onto a customer's short list and keep it there. They do not in themselves win orders but provide the opportunity to compete. Conversely, the failure to provide qualifiers at appropriate levels will lead to a loss of orders. In this way, qualifiers are order-losing in nature, as the opportunity to compete is not in place.
- *Order-winners*
  However, gaining entry to a market is only the first step. The task then is to know how to win orders against competitors who have also qualified to be in the same market or on the same customer list. With qualifiers you need to match customers' requirements, whereas with order-winners you need to provide them at a better level than your competition.

Finally, when applying this concept there are some key points to remember:

- Qualifiers are not less important than order-winners: they are different.
- Order-winners and qualifiers are time-specific and market-specific. They vary between markets and change over time within a market.

- The relevance and importance of order-winners and qualifiers will typically be different to retain market share, grow market share in existing markets, and enter new markets.
- The relative importance of order-winners and qualifiers will change when moving from being market-driven to being market-driving.
- As highlighted earlier, not all criteria will be either a qualifier or an order-winner. Some criteria do not relate to some markets.

4. *Weight qualifiers and order-winners.* To improve clarity still further, it is essential to weight qualifiers and order-winners in the following way:

- *Qualifiers*: It is adequate and appropriate to limit the classification of qualifiers to two categories—qualifiers (denoted by Q) and order-losing sensitive qualifiers (denoted by QQ). The latter is intended to alert a company to the fact that failure to provide criteria that are considered to be 'order-losing sensitive' will lead to a rapid loss of business.
- *Order-winners*: The appropriate step here is to allocate 100 points across all the order-winners within a market. This forces the different levels of relevance to be exposed and provides an essential step in distilling out importance. It is essential, therefore, to avoid procedures where stars (for example) are allocated as a way of indicating relative importance, as this approach avoids confronting and resolving the key step of determining the relative importance of one criterion with another.

5. *Check opinion with data.* Having started the market review by seeking the opinion of executives, it is essential to verify these views with data. The source of many of these checks is contained in the customers' orders received. For example, the degree of price sensitivity is reflected in the contribution of an order by taking the price charged less the actual direct costs incurred. Similarly, the extent of delivery speed required can be measured by calculating the length of time between the date an order was placed and the date of the required delivery. Basing such analyses on a representative number of orders for the customers under review will check whether the opinions put forward reflect reality.

Reflections

Developing an operations strategy involves a number of phases, and the first of these is the most critical but typically the one in which operations does not adequately participate. Being proactively part of—and

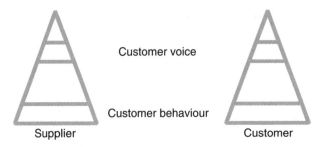

FIG. 13.6 Checking what customers say they want will show how they behave[7]

contributing to—the ongoing debate about markets, agreeing the order-winners and qualifiers in current and future markets, and being party to market-driving opportunities comprise the critical first step. Furthermore, not only can operations provide a significant contribution to this discussion but it is also often the function that experiences at first hand the nature of customer needs. As illustrated in Figure 13.6, while contract discussions are typically conducted towards the top of the supplier and customer organizations (termed here as 'customer voice'), the reality of what customers need (termed here as 'customer behaviour') takes place in operations where customer orders are fulfilled. Analysing customer orders enables operations to help the business check opinion with data and in that way provides a fuller insight into the market.

Decisions about markets need to be made at a business not a functional level. Whatever the strategic mix between being market-driven and market-driving, they lie at the very centre of strategic development, interconnecting corporate objectives with their delivery and interfacing between functional strategies as illustrated in Figure 13.7.

Companies need to continuously seek to align their functional strategies to the needs of markets, and one of the major players in delivering strategy is operations. The critical nature of its role reflects the increasing importance of the order-winners and qualifiers for which it is solely or jointly responsible, especially with regard to customer retention. Getting it right in operations results in sizeable and sustainable advantage. Although not the only strategic player, in most organizations its role will be important, while in many it will be central to the continued success of the overall business.

Operations Now and in the Future

The significance of operations within a business is seldom in question. Its size alone is enough. What needs to be assimilated into the business

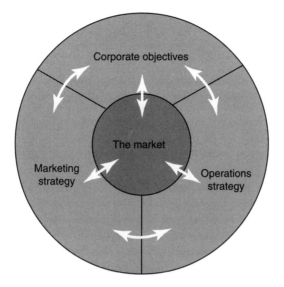

FIG. 13.7 Markets at the centre of strategy development[8]

mindset is to identify where revenue and profits are generated and then reflect these essential contributions in its reward systems and key executive appointments. If essential contributors to the short- and long-term success of a business continue to be recognized but not acknowledged, then the opportunity to create lasting sustainable advantage will continue to be missed. As markets move to increasing difference not increasing similarity, the role of executive functions such as operations will come to the fore and need to be reflected in corporate responses.

Within the academic community, a similar change in emphasis needs to be reflected in teaching, research, and writing. What operations faculty teach should point to the core contribution this function can and needs to provide. Core OM courses need to reflect the function's business role and essential strategic contribution. As most participants will not subsequently be directly involved in the operations function, their takeaway needs to be a clear recognition of the OM role and its essential contribution to the success of a business. Similarly, what OM faculty research and write and the mix of published material within journals need to reflect a similar contribution and emphasis. For this to be put into practice, editors need to acknowledge the lack of business relevance that typifies the leading OM journals and contribute to an essential switch in orientation by making a policy change and reflecting it within the editorial process.

With overcapacity being the hallmark of markets today and tomorrow, business success will increasingly depend on appropriate strategic direction and sound implementation. With operations typically a substantial provider of strategy, changes in the perception of its business contribution and in the orientation of teaching and research programmes need to reflect this.

References

1. T. Hill, *Operations Management: Strategic Content and Managerial Analysis* (2nd edn.; Basingstoke: Palgrave Macmillan, 2005), 33, exhibit 2.2.
2. Ibid. 39, exhibit 2.9.
3. Ibid. 9, exhibit 2.10.
4. Ibid. 42, exhibit 2.12.
5. Based on F. F. Reichheld and W. E. Sasser, Jr., 'Zero Defections: Quality Comes to Services', *Harvard Business Review*, 68 (Sept.–Oct. 1990): 105–11.
6. T. Hill, *Operations Management: Strategic Content and Managerial Analysis* (2nd edn.; Basingstoke: Palgrave Macmillan, 2005): 39, exhibit 2.8.
7. Based on T. Hill, *Manufacturing Strategy: Text and Cases* (2nd edn.; Basingstoke: Palgrave Macmillan, 2000), 42, exhibit 2.10.
8. Ibid. 35, exhibit 2.5.

14

The Brave New World of Business Marketing

Keith Blois

An essential component in Intel's Centrino Mobile Technology was the chip, code named Calexico, that enabled laptops to be connected wirelessly to local area networks. However, the development of the market for this chip in 2002 presented Intel with significant marketing problems and required it to co-operate and work with a large number of organizations, including competitors, suppliers, and customers. In addition, there were a number of organizations that were not potential purchasers of chips but nevertheless influenced the possible success of Calexico, and Intel needed therefore also to interact with them. For example, because Calexico was based on non-proprietary technical standards, Intel had to deal with the Institution of Electrical and Electronic Engineers (IEEE), which sets such standards, and because in the UK the British government issues licences for the use of radio frequencies, Intel also needed to liaise with government bodies.

However, there was also another group of organizations whose behaviour crucially influenced Calexico's success, but with whom Intel normally had no contact at all. Laptops with Centrino Mobile Technology would be in demand only if there were numerous 'Wi-Fi hot spots'—small base stations plugged into a high-speed broadband connection that linked laptops within fifty metres of the base station to the Internet. Intel believed that these hot spots should be in public places such as hotels, airports, cafes, etc. However, owners of such locations would need to purchase appropriate equipment and negotiate agreements with a wireless Internet server provider to provide the network services.

Thus Intel's ability to create value from Calexico depended on a lot of organizations, with some of whom it had direct exchanges—though not necessarily of products—and others with whom it had no exchanges at all. Thus, while in the case of the government and the IEEE Intel appointed senior managers to lobby or act as representatives on committees, it had no natural link with the potential owners of Wi-Fi hot spots. It followed that an essential part of Intel's marketing campaign had to take account of potential hot-spots' owners need to justify the necessary investments.

Detailed examination of the Calexico case lies beyond the scope of this chapter, but Intel's marketing problem can be broken down into the following interrelated issues:

1. Managing the marketing mix
2. Organizational buying behaviour
3. Relationship management
4. Networks
5. Concepts of value creation

Of these five issues only the first two were matters of concern to what forty years ago was know as 'Industrial Marketing'. Thus, the nature of Intel's twenty-first century business marketing challenge was considerably more complex than that faced by businesses in the 1960s—the period when Industrial Marketing first became a distinct field of study. However, the marketing problem that Intel faced with regard to Calexico was not unique. Firms now face much more complex 'market ecosystems' or 'market forms'[1] of the type illustrated by the marketing of Calexico.

Forty Years Ago

From the late 1960s onwards, there was a growing recognition that Industrial Marketing was a topic of interest, less because of academic curiosity, but because a lot of people were engaged in it. A couple of books on Industrial Marketing had been published before the Second World War and the first edition of *Industrial Marketing* by Alexander, Cross, and Cunningham had been published in the USA in 1956.[2] A considerable influence on the development of the study of Industrial Marketing in the USA was that the Marketing Science Institute (MSI), established in 1961 as a bridge between business and academics, funded some research into it. MSI's mission remains to initiate, support, and disseminate academic studies on issues specified by its member companies. It initiated, for example, the influential PIMS study.

So, from its beginnings as a subject of academic study Industrial Marketing has had a strongly applied and practical outlook. Marketing managers wrote sixteen chapters of one of, if not, the first UK book in this field, *The Marketing of Industrial Products*, a paperback whose first edition had three print runs and whose second edition appeared in 1972.[3] Interestingly, since the development of marketing as an academic subject in the UK was still limited (Lancaster University appointed the first UK

Professor of Marketing in 1965), the readership of this excellent book presumably must have mostly been practising managers.

It was noticeable that in the book's preface Wilson commented upon the limited material available on Industrial Marketing, adding that, even in the material that was available, there were big gaps and that there were few studies of pricing, physical distribution, and supporting services. Interestingly, Corey, who in 1957 offered Harvard Business School's first course on Industrial Marketing, made a similar comment in the preface to his book *Industrial Marketing*.[4]

The Development of a Continental Divide

Initially, US and European academics adopted the same approach to Industrial Marketing. The logic of this approach was clear. There was an established body of knowledge and a recognized set of research techniques in the field of consumer marketing, and therefore studies of Industrial Marketing should try to utilize these approaches. What might be called 'the consumer marketing analogy' was pursued and so, because consumer marketing had evolved through the study of consumer buying behaviour, attempts were made to study organizational buying behaviour.

Three American studies (which, incidentally, remain the only recognized models of organizational buying behaviour) exemplified this: *Industrial Buying and Creative Marketing*[5] (based on primary research funded by MSI), *Organisational Buying Behaviour*,[6] and *A Model of Industrial Buyer Behaviour*.[7] Furthermore, consumer marketing had emphasized the development of strategies and tactics aimed at influencing consumers' behaviour through manipulation of the marketing mix. Industrial Marketing followed the same path. Books on Industrial Marketing copied books on consumer marketing by having separate chapters on each of the main elements of the marketing mix.

However by the end of the 1970s, different approaches had developed in Europe and the USA. While the USA pressed on with the consumer marketing analogy, in Europe a different approach that was strongly influenced by the IMP (International Marketing and Purchasing) Group developed. This had been formed in 1976 on the initiative of a group of Swedish researchers as a collaborative research group with the aim of pursuing international research in industrial marketing and purchasing. It was composed of 'academic' marketers in five European countries—France, Germany, Italy, Sweden, and the UK.

The IMP Group of Swedish researchers was fortunate to have exceptionally good access to manufacturers through the Marketing

Technology Centre which had been established in 1973 with the aim of stimulating research in marketing and had been initially supported by eighty Swedish companies. The contrast between US and European approaches was marked, with the Europeans believing that the US approach ignored the realities of Industrial Marketing. Hakansson, writing on behalf of the IMP Group, opened its first book with 'A CHALLENGE' to the US position, stating that the IMP Group would

- emphasize the relationships between buyers and sellers in industrial markets rather than analyse single discrete purchases
- reject the perception of the industrial buyer as passive and instead emphasize the positive interaction between buyers and sellers
- emphasize the relative stability of industrial markets
- reject the idea of studying marketing and purchasing in isolation from each other[8]

These views became known as the 'IMP' or 'interaction approach'. The latter term reflected the fourth assertion that to study industrial marketing and purchasing as separate activities was to ignore the fact that the supplier is not always the initiator of an exchange. Often it is the customer, and in any case to examine the situation solely from either the supplier's or the customer's point of view is to fail to understand the complexity of business marketing exchanges. (In the late 1960s Corey, jointly with Wilbur England—a purchasing specialist—developed a course at Harvard, but the emphasis of the course was for suppliers 'to know the enemy' rather than recognizing the 'dyadic' nature of Industrial Marketing.)

The continuing success of the Annual IMP Conference, whose participants subscribe to these four principles, indicates the strength of this position. The 2007 Annual IMP Conference was its twenty-third; it has spawned an annual conference for Australasian researchers and established an electronic journal.

Since the early 1990s the gap between Europe and the USA has narrowed, with US academics now regularly attending the IMP conferences and US journals also publishing studies that explore 'the interaction approach'. A factor in this development has been three journals, all of whom have American editors, that have taken Industrial Marketing and Business Marketing as their focus. These are *Industrial Marketing Management* (first published in 1971), the *Journal of Business and Industrial Marketing* (first published in 1986), and the *Journal of Business-to-Business Marketing* (first published in 1993).

Another reason for the narrowing of the gap is that it is now recognized by European academics that business marketers do in fact meet some situations that are more similar to consumer marketing than those described by the IMP Group.[9,10] For example, a component manufacturer may have some customers whose relationship with their supplier can be adequately described only by the interaction approach. Yet the same firm may also have large number of customers who each make only very small purchases and necessarily have to be treated as a homogeneous group— much as a consumer goods firm would treat its individual consumers as an undifferentiated group. Furthermore, studies of particular marketing activities such as price setting, sales force organization, which may have been conducted outside the 'interaction approach', are still nevertheless useful to managers in a variety of buyer–seller situations.

Industrial Marketing Becomes Business Marketing

Studies in the 1980s continued to use the term 'Industrial Marketing', thus reflecting the assumption that what distinguished 'Industrial Marketing' from 'Consumer Marketing' was that the products being marketed were technically complex. (At this time academic studies almost ignored services; the *European Journal of Marketing*'s first paper on services was published in 1974.[11]) Indeed, the title of the first edition of Hutt and Speh's very successful US textbook was *Industrial Marketing Management*.[12] As well as text it contained fourteen case studies that dealt with 'Industrial Marketing' problems such as 'A marketing strategy for a plastics manufacturer' and 'Product line decisions for a motor controls manufacturer'. A noticeable feature was also that these cases were concerned with direct buyer–supplier interactions identified with the physical flow of a product. However, the ninth edition (2007) was entitled *Business Marketing Management* and included cases on a number of products, such as wine and airlines, to which the term 'industrial' would not normally be applied.[13]

Underlying the change from 'Industrial Marketing' to 'Business Marketing' was the recognition that the essential issue was not the nature of the product but the difference in the buying procedures and behaviour of organizations compared with those of individual consumers. Although many industrial products are most unlikely to be purchased by an individual consumer (while a really enthusiastic DIY-er might purchase an industrial lathe, it is hard to conceive of circumstances which would lead them to buy a multi-spindle lathe!), there are many products that are purchased both by organizations and by consumers: jam, for example, is bought both by hotel chains and individuals. Therefore defining the field of study as

'Industrial Marketing' limited the range of marketing problems studied. The shift from 'Industrial Marketing' to 'Business Marketing' reflected an acceptance that the challenge of marketing of, say, car components ('industrial' products) to a vehicle manufacturer is fundamentally little different than marketing biscuits ('consumer' products) to a retail chain. In both cases, the supplier is dealing with a customer that is a business that will use professional buying procedures.

Business Marketing Issues in 2006

The Intel example illustrated five issues which are typically of concern to marketing managers:

1. Managing the marketing mix
2. Organizational buying behaviour
3. Relationship management
4. Networks
5. Concepts of value creation

It is therefore appropriate to both review the current state of understanding of these issues and to suggest their likely development.

Managing the Marketing Mix

The marketing mix concept has suffered from Macarthy's representation of it as the '4 P's'.[14] In contrast, both Borden's[15] and van Waterschoot's[16] papers make clear that creating an appropriate marketing mix is a complex activity that requires the ability to combine a number of marketing components (for instance, price, product specification, service levels) into a coherent whole. Indeed, a carefully constructed marketing mix is an essential component of any product's marketing strategy.

Three aspects stand out in marketing literature:

- Textbooks devote chapters to the specific activities which are the individual components of a marketing mix (e.g. pricing, sales management, product line management, advertising), and articles in journals also tend to deal with one component of the marketing mix in isolation.
- Little, if anything, is said about the creation of a marketing mix by combining these individual components, even though this requires judgements about complex interactions between the components and the assessment of intricate financial consequences.

- Certain topics are only thinly covered. Few journal articles deal with them, and the chapters concerned with them in many books lack depth.

There can be little doubt that the marketing mix will continue to be an important concept, and it is also possible that the problem of a product simultaneously requiring two or more marketing mixes will become more common. There are two reasons for this. First, it seems that the trend towards increased concentration in the retail sector, which has now extended beyond the field of food retailing into other markets such as domestic appliances, travel, and clothing, is unstoppable. Thus, many firms now find that they can get effective access to individual consumers only via large intermediaries. This requires them to develop marketing mixes directed at each of these intermediaries as well as mixes directed at the final consumers who are the intermediaries' direct customers. Second, as firms find it increasingly necessary to operate within networks (see below), they need to simultaneously manage multiple but interrelated exchanges, each of which requires its own marketing mix.

Organizational Buying Behaviour

The organizational buying behaviour models that have been developed aim to provide insights into the processes and structures of organizational buying behaviour. However, there are two problems in creating general models that provide managers with useful knowledge or generate non-obvious theoretical insights. The first difficulty is that business purchasing situations are so varied, ranging from the one-off purchase of complex and costly items of capital equipment to the routine purchase of commodity items, sometimes in vast quantities and sometimes in tiny amounts. This means that organizational buying behaviour models struggle to strike a balance between generality and detail. As Pugh et al. commented about their research: 'It is the strength and the weakness of this project that no items were used unless they are applicable to all work organisations, whatever they did;...the result was superficiality and generality in the data.'[17]

The second problem is finding appropriate research methodologies. There is often real difficulty in gaining access to both a supplier and its customers. Firms are worried about keeping their policies confidential, and even if a supplier is prepared to discuss its approach with a researcher, it will seldom agree to them talking to its customers about the same issue. Another problem is that in most business purchasing situations several managers are involved, and it can be difficult to identify precisely who they are. Even when this can be done, there is the difficulty in ascertaining how their individual views combine to determine a particular policy.

As pointed out above, only three models of organizational buying behaviour have much authority, and the most recent of these dates from 1973. That so few studies of organizational buying behaviour have been carried out almost certainly reflects the difficulty of conducting such research. Nevertheless, there is a real need for further research on this topic. This gap is shown, for example, by the poor quality of researchers' predictions of the impact of e-commerce on business marketing. The effect of e-commerce in this context is known to be extensive, but few studies of this significant development have appeared.

Relationship Management

In the 1960s and early 1970s the relationships between suppliers and their customers were typically adversarial.[18,19] This is illustrated by Corey's *Charlestown Chemical Products Case*, which describes the response of a purchasing director to a supplier's unexpected announcement of a substantial price rise.[20] Corey's *Instructor's Manual* neither suggests that the supplier's opportunistic action is unusual nor that the purchaser might have adopted a more conciliatory response than that portrayed in the case.[21] Indeed, Corey, an authority on business marketing, seems to accept this adversarial behaviour by both parties as the norm.

A feature of buyer–supplier relationships in this period was that neither suppliers nor customers readily shared information with each other. Not infrequently, for example, new product development would reach an advanced stage before a firm sought its suppliers' assistance, and firms often ended up needing to redesign some aspects of the product as a result of the suppliers' advice. Furthermore, both suppliers and customers often deliberately distorted the information they did provide to the other party. Indeed, the automobile manufacturers regularly and deliberately overestimated their requirements from their suppliers, apparently believing that this made it more likely that they could be sure of obtaining the smaller volume of supplies actually required.[22]

However, a number of factors came together in the late 1980s that sparked a development of interest in relationship marketing. The work of the IMP Group with its emphasis on 'interaction' was a contributory factor, but the shift from multiple sourcing of many supplies to single sourcing—which in the UK sprang from improvements in the industrial relations environment—also led naturally to closer interactions.

By the late 1990s relationship marketing in business markets had become a hot topic, though there remained some dispute as to what it precisely entailed. However, it is generally agreed that relationship marketing 'concerns itself with long-term value exchanges' between a supplier and some of its customers.[23] A critical element in the concept was the belief that when buyers and suppliers move towards a relational form of interaction, both benefit.

Indeed, it has been claimed that where a relationship exists between two organizations and there is mutual trust and commitment,[24] they will be able to work together to eliminate many costs because of their willingness to share information.[25] Moreover, as Kalwani and Narayandas showed, supplier firms in long-term relationships with customers are more able to maintain or even improve their profitability levels than firms that employ a transactional approach.[26] Both the added value and the reduction in costs are made possible because, as Sheth and Parvatiyar stated, a relationship 'assumes overlap in the plans and processes of the interacting parties and suggests close economic, emotional and structural bonds.... It emphasizes cooperation rather than competition.'[27]

It is argued that where a strong relationship exists between a customer and a supplier, exchanges can proceed without a detailed contract. In this atmosphere, as Blois commented,[28] either party can assume that while it is *theoretically possible*, it is not *realistically probable* that

- the other party will take advantage of circumstances where opportunistic behaviour is possible
- the other party will exploit situations where moral hazard exists
- where, because of bounded rationality, unexpected circumstances arise, the other party will do other than seek a 'win–win' solution.

That said, the enthusiasm for relationship marketing has been dampened by the behaviour of a number of prominent firms. This is demonstrated in Lewis's book *The Connected Corporation: How Leading Companies Win through Customer–Supplier Relationships*.[29] This influential book was primarily based on the behaviour of Marks and Spencer, Chrysler, Motorola, and Philips Consumer Electronics Company. Each of these in the first half of the 1990s was recognized as a leader in the management of customer–supplier relationships. The book, which contains descriptions of these four companies and their relationships with their suppliers, supports the arguments regarding the benefits to both suppliers and business customers of developing relationships. Yet, if Lewis had written his book only a few years later, he would have had to drop three of his four examples because the behaviour of Marks and Spencer, Chrysler, and Motorola in the late 1990s led their suppliers to radically reassess the appropriateness of pursuing relationship marketing policies with them.[30]

The future of relationship marketing is unclear, but it nevertheless seems unlikely that business marketing relationships will fully revert to the adversarial state of the 1960s. As the Calexico case illustrates, to be successful Intel needed to work closely both with its immediate customers and its suppliers, and this required mutual trust in these relationships. That said, it seems likely that firms will become more cautious in the degree to which they commit themselves to relationships. They are now more conscious of the 'burden of relationships'—a topic which has received minimal academic attention. (For an exception to this view see Ref. 31.)

Networks

Business marketing's interest in networks grew out of the IMP Group's work in the early 1980s. At that time, as Mattsson and Johanson admitted (referring to Granovetter[32] and Baker[33]), the IMP Group was 'not aware of the contemporary market-related network research in Sociology'[34] nor was it aware of the existing network research in Economics.[35] Prior to this the focus of the industrial marketing literature of the 1960s and early 1970s had been how a supplier related to its customer. It only took account of other organizations, such as competitors, that might have a direct impact on this behaviour. It was a view of the business world 'as an atomistic structure of single actors that individually performed discrete transactions'[36] and resulted in the marketing literature being written from a 'single company perspective'.[37]

The reason for extending the study of business marketing was the recognition that 'the interaction in one relationship influences the interaction in another, making the interaction processes in different relationships contingent on each other.'[38] In some cases—for example, the development of a genuinely new product or market—a network is created with one firm taking the lead and seeking to manage it. In other cases, though, such as Intel's Centrino Mobile Technology, networks grow up over a period of time and often without an obvious leader. Networks are dynamic, and their membership constantly changes, as does the relative importance of the members. Indeed, an important management skill for firms is to identify and react to changes in the networks of which they are part (a firm might be a member of several networks).

Networks remain an area of study in which much has been promised but relatively little delivered. Indeed, there is no agreement as to how to define the term 'network', nor as to the criteria by which an observer should determine, when seeking to understand the behaviour of a single organization, how many interactions need to be taken into account. Although some writers argue that 'empirically a business network may be identified by starting out from a focal business unit, then mapping the significant business relationships, and thereafter tracing the connections from the firm and its relationships',[39] the weakness in this statement lies in its failure to define what is 'a significant business relationship'. As the discussion of 'relationships' (above) and of 'value' (below) shows, the judgement of whether or not a business relationship is 'significant' remains highly subjective.

   Intel's development of the market for Calexico shows the importance of networks. Firms must be able to recognize the structure and membership of any network which is likely to impinge on their behaviour. Second, they have to understand the behaviour of the individual members of the network and especially how they think they create value (see below). Third, they must constantly monitor the structure of their network to ensure that they identify any significant changes in its membership and the relative strength of the centres of influence within the network. Research into networks will therefore continue not only because it represents an academic challenge but also because it has obvious utility for practitioners.

Value

In the marketing literature of the 1960s and 1970s, the word 'value' appeared relatively infrequently: the objective of marketing was seen to be to help the firm earn profits. Nevertheless, by the 1990s, 'value' cropped up more and more often in management literature, and 'value creation' was increasingly described as the objective of marketing. An illustration of the overriding concern with value creation was the statement in Roberts' influential book *The Modern Firm* that value creation is the purpose of the firm.[40]

   Two major factors led to this change in emphasis. The first was the growing interest in relationship marketing and networks described above. Establishing and maintaining relationships requires that the parties do not take advantage of short-term opportunities to make profit but take a longer-term view of the potential value of the relationship—even though this involves discounting the stream of profits by forgoing 'a reasonably predictable immediate gain in favour of a much more uncertain gain in the future'.[41] Second, in the case of networks there is now a greater understanding that a firm can acquire considerable value through membership of a network. It is not uncommon for competitors to be members of the same network. For example, competitors such as Kodak and Fuji, together with others, collaborated to develop the APS camera film. However, it is clear that membership of the network calls for the avoidance of opportunistic behaviour on the part of its members.

An unresolved issue is how the concept of 'value' should be defined. Indeed the view that 'value has been conceptualized in various ways'[42] indicates that little has changed in this regard since Zeithaml commented on the 'diversity of meanings of value'[43] or since Woodruff observed that delving 'deeper into customer value concept discussions reveals substantive meaning differences. They typically rely on other terms, such as *utility, worth, benefits* and *quality,* that too often are themselves not well defined.'[44] As Roberts stated, when discussing value creation, 'it is not immediately clear what it means'![45]

Opportunities for value creation occur through firms entering into exchanges. Through these exchanges they gain access to resources owned by other individuals or organizations. A firm anticipates that by adding these resources to those that it already owns or controls, it can create additional value for itself. Therefore, an important issue for a supplier is to understand how its customers perceive that they create value and then to adapt its product offering, as represented by the marketing mix, to match those perceptions.

It is essential, though, that suppliers remember that it is the customer's interpretation of 'value' that is important and not what they think it ought to be. As long as the supplier understands how the customer interprets 'value', it does not matter what that interpretation is. However, it is all too easy for suppliers to assume that the customer shares their interpretation of 'value creation', given that suppliers enter into transactions only on the assumption that by doing so they will create value for themselves.

If an exchange is to be made, both parties must expect that they will gain value from it. As Day's concept of the 'customer value equation' illustrates,[46] the sacrifices that a customer believes it will have to suffer by entering into the exchange must be less than the benefits it anticipates the exchange will bring. Both the perceived benefits and sacrifices may be made up of a number of attributes, as Day's example illustrated. Others have proposed that in business-to-business exchanges the supplier will also have a value equation.[47,48] In this both the perceived benefits and sacrifices that arise from dealing with a particular customer are identified. The concept of the supplier's value equation acts as a reminder that— just as the customer will evaluate the supplier's view of the offering—the supplier must also evaluate the customer's view. Indeed, if an exchange is to occur, the supplier's perception must be that it too will gain value. As the interaction approach emphasizes, in business-to-business exchanges it is as likely to be the customer as the supplier which initiates the process of creating an exchange.

Opportunities for new marketing tactics and strategies can be identified by combining the concepts of the customer and the supplier value equation.[48] Indeed, as the Intel case illustrates, understanding how all members of a network perceive they can derive value is critical to the success of an individual member's strategy. Unless the value equation of the owners of potential Wi-Fi hot spots had been understood and steps taken to ensure that they saw the investment in a Wi-Fi transmitter as a potential creator of added value for them, Intel's investment into Calexico would have been wasted.

Conclusion

Business marketing, like all areas of management, is subject to fashion. In the last two decades relationship marketing, networks, and the creation of value have attracted the attention of researchers. It is difficult to believe that these three topics will not remain important in the future. However, two other topics—managing the marketing mix and organizational buying behaviour—have received much less attention than they deserve, and yet there is also nothing to suggest that the need for attention to them will go away.

In the future, some old topics may receive renewed attention and some new topics are likely to arise. Among the former is the topic of power—an issue which received a great deal of attention in the 1980s but seems to have been quietly ignored once the difficulties of understanding the concept and especially operationalizing measures of power became apparent. However, in business marketing the challenges faced by firms supplying customers in markets with a high degree of concentration have in the early part of the twenty-first century once again become issues and have attracted the attention of competition regulators. The concentration in the automobile manufacturing industry, long an issue for suppliers, has recently intensified. In other industries, such as domestic appliances and clothing but especially food retailing, there has also been a rapid increase in the market share controlled by a small number of retailers over the last two decades, and their power, especially over their suppliers, is now frequently discussed in the press and in parliamentary bodies.

As for the new topics which may gain in importance in the next few years, forecasting is always risky. However, given the complex market ecosystem faced by Intel with its Calexico chip, there would seem to be a need for greater understanding of the mechanisms whereby firms— especially when introducing new products—can identify the members of those ecosystems and understand how they perceive value is created for them. For industrialists this is a very real and practical problem, and as such lies firmly in the tradition of industrial and business marketing with its strong roots in practise.

References

1. K. J. Blois, 'The "Market Form" Concept in Business Marketing Markets', in H. Hakansson (ed.), *Rethinking Marketing* (Chichester: Wiley, 2004), 33–54.
2. R. M Alexander, R. S. Cunningham, and J. S. Cross, *Industrial Marketing* (Homewood, IL: Irwin, 1956).
3. A. Wilson, *The Marketing of Industrial Products* (London: Pan, 1965).
4. E. R. Corey, *Industrial Marketing: Cases and Concepts* (Englewood Cliffs, NJ: Prentice-Hall, 1962).
5. P. J. Robinson, C. W. Faris, and Y. Wind, *Industrial Buying and Creative Marketing* (Boston, MA: Allyn and Bacon, 1967).
6. F. E. Webster, Jr. and Y. Wind, *Organizational Buying Behavior* (Englewood Cliffs, NJ: Prentice-Hall, 1972).
7. J. N. Sheth, 'A Model of Industrial Buyer Behavior', *Journal of Marketing*, 37/4(Oct. 1973), 50–6.
8. H. Hakansson (ed.), *International Marketing and Purchasing* (Chichester: Wiley, 1982), 1.
9. K. J. Blois, 'Don't All Firms Have Relationships?' *Journal of Business and Industrial Marketing*, 13/3(1998), 256–70.
10. K. J. Blois, 'Business to Business Exchanges: A Rich Descriptive Apparatus Derived from Macneil and Menger's Analyses', *Journal of Management Studies*, 39/4(2002), 523–51.
11. K. J. Blois, 'The Marketing of Services: An Approach', *European Journal of Marketing*, 8/2(1974), 137–45.
12. M. Hutt and T. W. Speh, *Industrial Marketing Management* (Chicago, IL: Dryden Press, 1981).
13. M. Hutt and T. W. Speh, *Business Marketing Management* (9th edn.; Mason, OH: South-Western Publishers, 2007).
14. E. J. Macarthy, *Basic Marketing* (Homewood, IL: Irwin, 1960).
15. N. H. Borden, 'The Concept of the Marketing Mix', in G. Schwartz (ed.), *Science in Marketing* (New York: Wiley, 1965), 386–98.
16. W. Van Waterschoot, 'The Marketing Mix as a Creator of Differentiation', in K. Blois (ed.), *The Oxford Textbook of Marketing* (Oxford: Oxford University Press, 2000), 183–211.

17. D. S. Pugh, D. J. Hickson, C. R. Hinings, and C. Turner, 'Dimensions of Organization Structure', *Administrative Science Quarterly*, 13/1(1968), 65–105.

18. K. J. Blois, 'The Growing Power of Large Customers', *Journal of the Industrial Marketing Research Association*, 8/1(1972), 2–8.

19. K. J. Blois, 'Large Organizations: How Large Are They?', *The Business Economist*, 4/3(1972), 151–5.

20. E. R. Corey, 'Charlestown Chemical Products Inc.', in E. R. Corey (ed.), *Industrial Marketing: Cases and Concepts* (3rd edn.; Englewood Cliffs, NJ: Prentice-Hall, 1983), 81–7.

21. E. R. Corey, *Industrial Marketing: Cases and Concepts; Instructor's Manual* (3rd edn.; Englewood Cliffs, NJ: Prentice-Hall, 1983).

22. K. J. Blois, 'Supply Contracts in the Galbraithian Planning System', *Journal of Industrial Economics*, 24/1(1975), 29–39.

23. J. N. Sheth and R. H. Shah, 'Till Death Do Us Part...But Not Always: Six Antecedents to a Customer's Relational Preference in Buyer–Seller Exchanges', *Industrial Marketing Management*, 32/8(2003) 628.

24. R. M. Morgan and S. D. Hunt, 'The Commitment–Trust Theory of Relationship Marketing', *Journal of Marketing*, 58/3(July 1994), 20–38.

25. D. Corsten and N. Kumar, 'Do Suppliers Benefit from Collaborative Relationships with Large Retailers? An Empirical Investigation of Efficient Consumer Response Adoption', *Journal of Marketing*, 69(July 2005), 80–94.

26. M. U. Kalwani and N. Narayandas, 'Long-Term Manufacturer–Supplier Relationships: Do They Pay Off for Supplier Firms?' *Journal of Marketing*, 59/1(1995), 1–16.

27. J. N. Sheth and A. Parvatiyar, 'The Evolution of Relationship Marketing', *International Business Review*, 4/4(1995), 399.

28. K. J. Blois, 'Relationship Marketing in Organizational Markets; When Is It Appropriate?', *Journal of Marketing Management*, 12(1996), 161–73.

29. J. D. Lewis, *The Connected Corporation: How Leading Companies Win through Customer–Supplier Relationships* (New York: Free Press, 1995).

30. K. J. Blois, 'Business Customers' Behaviour: A Challenge for the Relationship Marketing Concept?', *Journal of Business Market Management*, 1 (2006), 41–57.

31. H. Hakansson and I. Snehota, 'The Burden of Relationships or Who's Next?', in D. Ford (ed.), *Understanding Business Markets* (London: Thompson Learning, 2002), 88–94.

32. M. Granovetter, 'The Strength of Weak Ties', *American Journal of Sociology*, 78/6(1973), 1360–80.

33. W. Baker, 'Markets as Networks: Multi-Method Study of Trading Networks in Securities Markets', Ph.D. dissertation (Northwestern University, 1981).

34. L.-G. Mattsson and J. Johanson, 'Discovering Market Networks', *European Journal of Marketing*, 40/3–4(2006), 259–74.

35. G. B. Richardson, 'The Organisation of Industry', *Economic Journal*, 82(1972), 883–96.

36. D. Ford and H. Hakansson, 'IMP: Some Things Achieved—Much More To Do', *European Journal of Marketing*, 40/3–4(2006), 249.
37. Ibid. 253.
38. F. Prenkert and L. Hallen, 'Conceptualizing, Delineating and Analysing Business Networks,' *European Journal of Marketing*, 40/3–4(2006), 384.
39. Ibid. 385.
40. J. Roberts, *The Modern Firm* (Oxford: Oxford University Press, 2004).
41. A. M. Okum, *Prices and Quantities: A Macroeconomic Analysis* (Oxford: Blackwell, 1981), 149.
42. W. S. Desarbo, K. Jedidi, and I. Sinha, 'Customer Value Analysis in a Heterogeneous Market', *Strategic Management Journal*, 22/9(2001), 846.
43. V. A. Zeithaml, 'Consumers' Perceptions of Price, Quality and Value', *Journal of Marketing*, 52/3(1988), 13.
44. R. B. Woodruff, 'Customer Value: The Next Source for Competitive Advantage', *Journal of the Academy of Marketing Science*, 25/2(1997), 141.
45. J. Roberts, *The Modern Firm* (Oxford: Oxford University Press, 2004), 20.
46. G. S. Day, *Market Driven Strategy* (New York: Free Press, 1990).
47. R. Ramirez and J. Wallin, *Prime Movers: Define Your Business or Have Someone Define It for You* (Chichester: Wiley, 2000).
48. K. J. Blois, 'Using Value Equations To Analyse Exchanges', *Marketing Intelligence and Planning*, 21/1(2003), 16–22.

Part IV

Mapping the Future

15

Forty Years of Scenarios: Retrospect and Prospect

Rafael Ramírez

This chapter presents an overview of an approach whose development has run in parallel with that of Templeton College over the past forty years: the emergence and use of scenario practices.

Scenarios are stories about how the contexts within which decision makers—individuals and teams, public and private—operate may develop in future. They have been used in companies for over three decades[1] and even longer by military planners and policymakers. In business, Shell's successful use of scenarios to anticipate oil crises gave them prominence.[2-4] Scenarios have now become part of the landscape in business strategy and public policy. The LexisNexis press database[5] identifies over 400 papers annually on the topic, and about 450 academic papers are cited each year on the subject of scenarios in social science journals. Scenarios—and, more generally, futures—have also become a central focus of the College's work during the last few years.

The Roots of Scenario Planning

Scenario planning had multiple origins. However, it is broadly agreed that scenario activity as we know it today originated in both the USA and France. As it partly involved state (and particularly military) activities at the end of and after the Second World War, the actual story of its development remains shrouded in secrecy and may never be fully known. The strategic importance associated with scenario planning has conferred on it an aura of prestige that has lasted to this day. Scenarios may be 'punching above their weight'—and several researchers have tried to debunk them—yet the fact remains that the secrecy associated with scenario practices in both the public and private domains has helped make scenarios difficult to research.

In the English-speaking world, scenario planning is widely believed to have begun with the work of Herman Kahn and his colleagues at the RAND (Research & Development) Corporation financed by the US government.[6] Kahn is particularly famous for his 'thinking the unthinkable' approach to the possibility of nuclear war,[7] an approach further developed at the Hudson Institute, which he established upon leaving RAND in 1961.[8] At about the same time, Stanford Research International, set up by Stanford University in 1947, began work on long-range planning and environmental scanning at least by 1956.[9]

In the francophone world, scenarios are thought to have begun with the work of Gaston Berger and other colleagues at DATAR (the 'Délégation à l'aménagement du territoire et à l'action régionale'—the planning department of the French government), which was created in 1963 and built on earlier urban planning work.[10] In 2005 it was renamed DIACT, 'the interministerial department for territory planning and competitiveness', which like its predecessor reported to the Prime Minister's office. At roughly the same time, Futuribles International, an independent non-profit organization, was launched in 1967.[11] Its roots lay in the Comité International Futuribles (a term combining the words 'futures' and 'possibles') set up in 1960 by Bertrand de Jouvenel and the Centre d'Etudes Prospectives established in 1957 by Gaston Berger.

Whatever the exact origins of scenario planning, the French and the Americans collaborated from early on and, given the secrecy of state and military affairs, may indeed have collaborated from the very beginning. Futuribles' founder, de Jouvenel, visited the RAND Corporation, and in 1965 wrote a RAND report, *Futuribles*, whose 83 essays outlined possible future developments in various areas. De Jouvenel maintained that while there cannot be a science of the future, there are rigorous ways of thinking about it, and the report described methods and some of the complexities involved.[12]

Current Use of Scenarios

Scenarios are currently used for many different purposes, including the following:

- making sense of intractable problems
- reducing complexity or obtaining clarity about something in one's context
- reframing a situation or dissolving a problem
- finishing a problem
- surfacing assumptions to test how valid they are
- testing strategic options
- initiating or sustaining dialogue

- wind tunnelling a given strategy, where a set of scenarios plays the role of a set of wind tunnels within which the robustness of a 'business model' or policy option can be assessed
- team building
- changing organizational culture
- anticipating events (particularly when forecasts are not reliable)
- entertaining
- sensitizing
- engaging stakeholders
- enhancing organizational learning
- mapping and assessing uncertainties and risks
- creating a better world or future
- challenging an official future—breaking away from group think
- increasing the future orientation of a practice, group, or mindset
- story telling on the sources of the future
- facilitating emotional change
- understanding systemic behaviour
- building confidence to act
- developing language to articulate thinking and enhance conversational quality
- rendering disagreements as assets and avoiding them become liabilities
- helping disagreements to become more constructive
- enabling and eliciting innovations and new options
- preparing efforts to move beyond scenarios themselves into simulations/war games (as in a pilot trainer cockpit)[13]

It is probably impossible for any one person to know everything that is now known abut scenarios. By November 2006 Amazon had listed 175,819 books in English with the keyword 'scenarios'. Even if we assume that only 5 per cent (or 8,791) of these books are 'serious' works on the subject, it would still take a scholarly student of scenarios reading a book a day for 24 years to plough through them all! By then, many more thousands of books would have been published.

There are two different types of surveys that try to track scenario use—commercial and academic. A prominent example of the first is the survey produced by the international consulting firm Bain. It reported that 50 per cent of the companies it surveyed in 2004 used scenarios, and that among these there was an 80 per cent satisfaction rating.[14] In their earlier surveys they suggested the use of scenario activities is on the rise, but, interviewed by phone by me a few years ago, they admitted that the

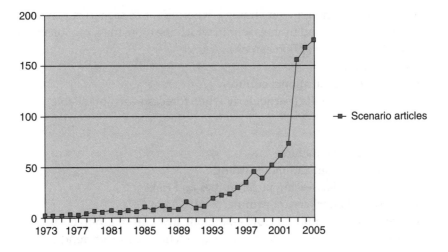

FIG. 15.1 Increased interest in scenarios since 9/11 (*Source*: EBSCO database)

term 'scenarios' had never been precisely defined in their surveys, and that their scope and definition may have shifted from year to year. This makes identifying trends of actual use difficult. The same problem applies to research by the Conference Board in the USA, an industry research organization, which also found that the use of scenarios has been on the rise.[15] Despite the claims by these independent surveys that scenarios are being increasingly used, we still do not know exactly how widely, or by whom, where, or why. The fact that the most effective use of scenarios is often kept secret acts as a further obstacle to the accurate assessment of the extent of scenarios practice.

However a more reliable measure of a growing interest on scenario practices comes from academia, which tracks scholarly publications by year. As Figure 15.1 shows, interest in scenarios has increased dramatically since 9/11, when the importance of knowing that the unpredictable happens was driven home to decision makers.

Templeton College's Contribution

Trying to account for the fact that scenario practices 'fly' well in the face of turbulent conditions has been rather like trying to explaining the flight of bumblebees—for a long time biologists knew they fly effectively but were at a loss to explain exactly how.[16] So in 2004, I got together with Kees van der Heijden, an Associate Fellow of Templeton whom I have worked with on and off since 1986, whose book *Scenarios: The Art of Strategic Conversation*[17] has sold over 60,000 copies, and my old Wharton School colleague and friend John Selsky to see if we could improve our theoretical understanding of scenario practices and thinking. We decided to convene an 'Oxford Futures Forum' the following year, the theme of which would be 'what have we learnt in the last forty years?'[18]

This theme was chosen for two reasons. First, John and I and others who had done our doctorates in the Social Science Systems programme at the Wharton School had been discussing for some time how to commemorate the fact that 1965 was the year that a seminal paper by two of our teachers, Fred Emery and Eric Trist, in which they coined the term 'turbulence', was published.[19]

The second reason was that Pierre Wack (who is credited for having been the individual who institutionalized scenarios in Royal Dutch/Shell) had published his first French scenarios in 1965. Pierre Wack has unfortunately passed away, but everyone who worked with Pierre Wack—including Kees van der Heijden—remembers him as a remarkable individual, and, as with Emery and Trist, we thought it vital to try to keep alive his work and preserve its insights for the future. To this end, with the help of our friends Napier Collyns and Jaap Leemhuis we arranged for Templeton College to accept and take care of Pierre Wack's library and personal papers. With luck and some deft footwork from the College's librarians, the library was ready for opening by the time the first 2005 forum was held.

We invited people we knew might be interested in either turbulence or scenario thinking and practice or both, and open to exploring the links between the two, and were delighted when seventy participants turned up. In the final plenary, we asked participants if they would be willing to contribute chapter-length papers, and thirty-eight people volunteered to do so. As a result, two studies are now in the pipeline: the first on the relationship between scenarios and strategy and the second exploring the link between the take-off in scenarios and increasing environmental turbulence. The aim of this second book is to show how Emery and Trist's theories on causal textures—in particular, turbulent textures—help explain the effectiveness of scenario practices in addressing environmental complexity.

The Theory of Causal Textures

Emery and Trist both trained as psychologists. The achievement of Eric Trist is represented in the remarkable trilogy he edited, *The Social Engagement of Social Science*.[20] Fred Emery was originally his student but quickly became his partner, and they worked very productively together for many years on what is now known as 'social ecology'.

In their 1965 paper, they had suggested that organizations have four different kinds of relationships:

- First, organizations have internal links: links from things within the organization to other things within that organization. They called these links 'L11'.
- Second, as organizations release things—be they products, services, advice, or pollution—from their own internal 'L11' context into their environment, they set up a connection with elements outside and surrounding them. These links they called 'L12': links from internal (1) to external (2).
- The third type of link occurs when organizations buy in elements from their environment, such as supplies. These links they called 'L21': links from external (2) to internal (1).
- These three links were being studied at the time when 'open systems theory' held sway, an approach borrowed from biology, by which organizations are studied as if they were natural organisms. Where Emery and Trist were innovative was to suggest that an organization also needed to take into account the evolution in the ways that the actors and factors in their environment relate to each other, independently of these links to the organization itself. This fourth type of link they termed 'L22' links: links from external (2) to external (2). They pointed out many good reasons for paying attention to 'L22' links. 'L22' links determine how change will occur in the overall context of an organization, and thus have a crucial bearing not only on an organization's 'L12' and 'L21' links but also on the very survival of its 'L11' core.

Emery and Trist defined 'L22' links as the 'causal texture' of an environment. They identified four distinct causal textures, in response to which organizations should ideally pursue individually appropriate strategies. The most complex and unpredictable and—if treated with inappropriate strategies adopted from other, less messy contexts—eventually catastrophic texture they called the 'turbulent environment'.

When an environment takes on the characteristic of 'turbulence', it ceases, they said, to be 'just the aggregated effect of multiple decision-makers'. In turbulent textures, the unintended consequences of the actions of the players proliferate unpredictably and generate new forces that ricochet around the whole field and rebound on the strategy-making of the players themselves.

Recent Work on Turbulence

Like scenario studies, social science articles on turbulence have also increased dramatically, as shown in Figure 15.2.

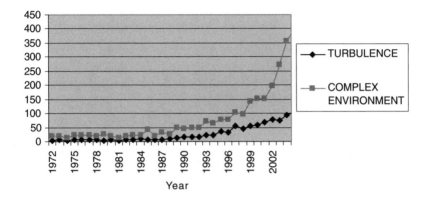

FIG. 15.2 Number of peer reviewed articles since 1972 (*Source*: EBSCO)

Along with this increase there has also been progress in understanding causal textures. Since the original 1965 paper, two students of Emery and Trist—McCann and Selsky—proposed a fifth environmental causal texture based on research they had carried out in health care, which they called 'hyperturbulence'.[21] Another Emery–Trist student, Baburoglu, working in the turbulent context of Turkish society, proposed in 1988 the notion of 'the vortical environment', identifying the 'hyperturbulence' described by McCann and Selsky as a transitional stage in the emergence of this environment.[22] Martin Thomas, who studied at Templeton College the evolution of thinking on turbulence for a master's dissertation on scenarios with reference to Venezuela,[23] analysed these developments and classified them as in Table 15.1.

Thomas summarized the situation as follows:

- Whereas tactics are good enough in type 1 (perfect market) environments, strategy and optimal location are key to success in type 2. In type 3 the strategic challenge requires operational skills, and for type 4 environments values are needed to address the unpredictability of the turbulent field.
- With hyperturbulence, adaptive capabilities are required from a set of organizations, not from one alone.
- In type 5 vortical environments, internal resources are not enough to break out of the enclave formation. 'The way out requires...a collective strategy that includes the outsiders.'

TABLE 15.1 Causal textures: environments and organizations

Type	Environment	Characteristics	Successful strategy	Organizations	Consequences
1	*Placid Randomized*	Economist's classical market. Static	*Tactics* (= Strategy) 'Optimal strategy is just doing one's best on purely local basis'	Decentral	Optimal is learned by trial and error
2	*Placid Clustered* (Emery and Trist)	Economist's imperfect competition. Stable	*Strategy* dominates over tactics Keys are distinctive competencies and 'optimal location'	Central control and coordination grow central hierarchies	Knowledge of the environment becomes critical to success
3	*Disturbed Reactive* (Emery and Trist)	Economist's oligopolistic market. More than one big player seeking same pot of resources. Dynamic	*'Operations'* (campaigns of tactical initiatives) between strategy and tactics. Key is capacity to move more or less at will to make and meet competitive challenge	Flexibility needs decentralization. Premium on quality and speed of decision at peripheral points Interdependence emerges	'One has to know when NOT to fight to the death.' Dynamic stability is obtained by a coming to terms between competitors
4	*Turbulent Fields* (Emery and Trist)	Not just the interaction of organizations; 'The ground is in motion' Autochthony (= momentum from within) literally from ground	*Values* become 'power fields' overriding both strategy and tactics Effective emerging values create ethical codes that enable simplified action to	Individual organizations cannot adapt alone Relationships between dissimilar organizations, 'Organizational Matrix' help to	1. Increase in 'relative uncertainty' 2. Unpredictable results of actions 3. May not fall-off with distance, but be amplified

TRANSITIONAL				
Hyperturbulent (McCann and Selsky)	Increased reliance on R&D	diverging causal strands	attenuate effects of turbulence	4. Emergent forces may attenuate strong action *NB* changes in values take about a generation to develop
	Interdependency between economic and other social factors	'Institutionalization' (embodying society's values) becomes strategic objective	But values must be shared between all parts of the matrix for this to be effective	Dysfunctional vortex relationships
	Partitioned. Enclaves attract scarce resources	*Adaptive capacity* to deal with the 'relevant uncertainty' is the determinant of short-term success (enclave formation).	Social enclaves partitioned by social triage from vortices and with no collaboration between the two	Decoupling of interdependencies
	Vortices are left without resources or skills needed to adapt to the environment	Strategy needs to come from a set of organizations, not one		Entropy emerges
5 *Vortical environments* (Baburoglu)	1. Monothematic dogmatism 2. Stalemate 3. Polarization	*Double-loop learning* to develop new skills and more resources are needed for long-term removal of vortices. Collective and external strategy is needed	Apparently sealed-off from the environment, but not really. Parts effectively immobilize each other	Decline of vortices depends on external forces, as internal adaptive capacity is inadequate

- Strategy therefore progresses from none at all in causal textures
  of type 1, through campaigns of tactical initiatives in type 3
  environments, to developing new common values in type 4 turbulent
  environments, and involving outsiders and coming to rely upon them
  in type 5 vortical environments.[24]

Linking Causal Texture Theory and Scenario Practise

Failing to address turbulent environments effectively is expensive. Such
failures and their destructive, not to say catastrophic, consequences have
been extensively documented. In 2006 the Stern report[25] commissioned
by the UK government examined the real cost of climate change out to
2050 if nothing is done and concluded that it may lead to the biggest ever-
recorded economic meltdown. Another failure has been documented by
Professor Stiglitz, the Nobel Prize winner in Economics. He has calculated
that failures by the Bush administration to comprehend the complexities
of Iraq have resulted in a war that was originally expected to cost some
$60 billion costing over $1 trillion—and possibly double that.[26] Using tools
such as scenarios to avoid such debacles is therefore clearly worthwhile.

The strategy literature has recently highlighted 'high velocity' change
in turbulent environments, driven by the dynamic nature of high-tech
electronic and bioscience businesses. But another aspect of turbulence—
disruptive change across a whole field—received less attention, at least
until 9/11. Scenario practitioners, beginning with Herman Kahn and his
'thinking the unthinkable' approach to the prospect of nuclear war, have
on the whole been better than strategy researchers at addressing disruptive change.

Scenario practices help address turbulence, and it is therefore important
to try to understand just how and why they do so. As environmental
turbulence has increased across all fields, the importance of scenarios
has also grown. First of all, scenarios help address turbulence because
they establish the common ground needed to confront it. Emery and Trist
developed a technique called 'search conferences' to identify and create
the common ground and the related values required when confronting
turbulent environments. Search conferences can be used independently or
in association with scenarios, many of which deliberately set out to create
this common ground. The search for common ground was an approach
that, for example, Thomas explored in his dissertation on Venezuela,
only to conclude that the 'quasi-vortical' conditions there at the time of
his research ruled it out.[23] But there is at least one other way in which
scenarios can help address turbulent environments.

Clarity Is Key

My research suggests that scenarios should be judged in terms of the greater clarity they produce. Clarity is not, however, the same as simplification. Henri Atlan[27] has suggested that while simplification is a good way to address some types of complicated systems, for other types of complexity simplification can be counterproductive. In these cases, clarification is more effective and this in turn may require more complex explanations. My research suggests that turbulent fields represent the second kind of complexity—the kind that cannot be described by means of simplifying models or formulae.

In complex situations like turbulent environments, scenarios can provide additional clarity. How do they achieve this? Scenarios embrace the future of a turbulent field in several different 'packages' that are all equally plausible. When they do this well, they shed light on how the situation might play out in time and how the dark, murky waters of turbulence will flow further downstream.

In a two-day workshop I organized on the relationship between aesthetics and scenarios while at Shell International in 2003, my colleague Hardin Tibbs suggested that clarity, in practice, is 'rendered'—a word that encompasses several meanings ranging from 'transmitting' to 'translating' and 'refining'. What scenarios 'render'—in addition to the common ground described earlier—is aesthetic clarity. Kees van der Heijden, who also participated in the event, suggested that the best presenters of scenarios like Pierre Wack attend to rhythm and tone as they speak. They artfully use silence, repetition, and captivating metaphors and images to bring to life the pattern that they are rendering and by so doing remove the thickness and opacity of turbulence and generate clarity of insight. Scenarios and those that render them, whether in writing, workshops, or presentations, must show how what would otherwise remain fragmented—or, as Emery and Trist put it, 'dissociated'—can come together again in the future in a viable and holistic pattern that has its own sharp aesthetic resonance.

In a paper, 'Organising Aesthetics: The Case of Exhibition in Enterprising—Managing Vision, Will, and Realisation', presented at the Academy of Management conference in 2001, Katja Lind of Stockholm University School of Business proposed that how one appreciates something aesthetically depends on its goal or purpose.[28] This too was the consensus of our 2003 workshop: the purposes of scenario projects have a bearing on how they are experienced aesthetically. I have suggested (1991) that ugliness is experienced when the underlying purposes of something that would otherwise be experienced as beautiful are confounded.[29] Thus, when a doctor is used by the Nazis in a spurious attempt to achieve racial purity or radar to guide nuclear bombs on to cities, we find the beauty of medicine or of the science of radio waves has been rendered ugly.

In the messy, 'wicked',[30] or intractable problems involved in turbulent conditions, the purposes of the system are often rendered obsolete or obscure by the turbulence. So an overriding aim of scenario intervention is to identify clearly a viable and relevant purpose. Examples of these identified in our workshop were enhancing the health of people in Glasgow, making traffic in Mexico City work well, or transforming the Okavango River Basin in Namibia into a peaceful habitat. In all of these cases the deployment of scenarios can create not only new common ground but also new clarity of purpose. The intervention together with the various elements and players in the 'intervened' situation and the overall purpose of that situation are united in a new, holistic, and clear pattern that is instinctively felt to be aesthetically attractive. The extent to which the intervention reconnects previously dissociated elements into this pattern is a measure of its success.

Scenarios—stories about the future contexts that organizations will inhabit—have gained wider recognition over the last four decades in corporate planning and policymaking. However, because the practice has often been shrouded in secrecy, it has been less well researched than one might expect and requires further scholarly attention to improve its robustness and effectiveness. Templeton College Fellows have been addressing this challenge by relating scenario practices to theories of causal textures in the environment and, in particular, by studying how turbulent conditions can be tackled using scenarios. Several students at the College like Martin Thomas have focused their research on this topic, and we expect that more graduate students on masters' and doctoral programmes will follow in his footsteps and help create an extended academic–practitioner community whose work will make an innovative and useful contribution to a wide range of social, commercial, and organizational issues.

References and Notes

1. J. Lesourne and C. Stoffaes (eds.), *La prospective stratégique d'entreprise: De la réflexion à l'action* (Paris: Dunod, 2001).
2. P. Wack, 'Scenarios: The Gentle Art of Re-Perceiving' (Harvard Business School Working Paper 9-785-042; Boston, MA: Harvard Business School, 1984).
3. Peter Schwartz, *The Art of the Long View: Planning for the Future in an Uncertain World* (Garden City, NY: Doubleday, 1996).

4. Kees van der Heijden, *Scenarios: The Art of Strategic Conversation* (Chichester: Wiley, 1996).

5. LexisNexis press database. See http://www.lexisnexis.co.uk/businessandnews

6. http://www.rand.org/

7. H. Kahn, *Thinking about the Unthinkable* (New York: Horizon Press, 1962).

8. www.hudson.org

9. http://www.sri.com

10. http://www.diact.gouv.fr

11. www.futuribles.com

12. B. de Jouvenel, *Futuribles* (Stanford, CA: Rand Corporation, 1965).

13. This list was compiled by participants in a two-day scenarios research workshop I convened while at Shell International in March 2003.

14. http://www.Bain.com

15. http://www.conference-board.org/

16. I am grateful to Adrian Thomas of Oxford's Zoology Department for the information on this issue.

17. Kees van der Heijden, op. cit.

18. www.oxfordfuturesforum.org

19. F. E. Emery and E. L. Trist, 'The Causal Texture of Organizational Environments', *Human Relations*, 18(1965): 21–32.

20. E. L. Trist, F. E. Emery, and H. Murray (eds.), *The Social Engagement of Social Science: A Tavistock Anthology* (3 vols.; Philadelphia: University of Pennsylvania Press, 1997).

21. J. E. McCann and J. Selsky, 'Hyperturbulence and the Emergence of Type 5 Environments', *Academy of Management Review*, 9/3(1984): 460–70.

22. O. Baburoglu, 'The Vortical Environment: The Fifth in the Emery-Trist Levels of Organisational Environments', *Human Relations*, 41/3(1988): 181–210.

23. Master's dissertation completed for the Oxford-HEC programme, *Consulting & Coaching for Change* (2004); 66.

24. M. P. Thomas, personal communication, quoted with permission.

25. Stern review; see http://www.hm-treasury.gov.uk/independent_reviews/stern_review_economics_climate_ change/stern_review_report.cfm

26. http://www2.gsb.columbia.edu/faculty/jstiglitz/index.cfm

27. Henri Atlan, 'L'Intuition du Complexe et Ses Théorisations', in F. Soulié (ed.), *Les Théories de la Complexité* (Paris: Editions du Seuil, 1991).

28. K. Lind, 'Organising Aesthetics: The Case of Exhibition in Enterprising: Managing Vision, Will, and Realisation' (Paper given at the Academy of Management Conference; 2001).

29. R. Ramirez, *The Beauty of Social Organization* (Munich: Accedo, 1991).

30. H. Rittel and M. Webber, 'Dilemmas in a General Theory of Planning', *Policy Sciences*, 4/2(June 1973): 155–69.

16

In Pursuit of Agility: Reflections on One Practitioner's Journey Undertaking, Researching, and Teaching the Leadership of Change

Keith Ruddle

As we are increasingly assailed by prescriptions for 'leading in a world of constant change', the management dictionary has swung into action with a host of new terms: agility, adaptiveness, resilience, ambidexterity, dynamic capabilities, absorptive capacity, and more. But what should the practising leader and manager make of it all? What can, and should, they do differently to deal with change. That is the world I have lived in. In the course of thirty years of management practice, teaching, and research, my own journey has been one of flux, change, and transformation, working with—and learning from—leadership teams as they grappled with a changing world.

Can experience help us frame new practices and ideas for the future? My own research in the 1990s on organizational transformation used the metaphor of a journey to help understand, frame, and explain strategic and organizational change—and then applied it with some success in the classroom for many of Templeton's company executive education clients. My approach in this chapter will be to take the reader through my own journey, reflecting on the way on some changing assumptions about organizational change. There will be a light connection to theory but a stronger one to practising managers who are seeking lessons, tools, insights, and action. Colleagues at Templeton have thrived from this mixture of the academic and practitioner worlds, and I reflect at the end of the chapter on the changing nature of practitioner-based relevant research.

Four Eras of Leading Change

How has the interplay of theory, practice, and teaching evolved in the course of my journey and that of Templeton College? Increasing turbulence and the accelerating pace of change have certainly had an impact on the world of practice. Different mindsets, both theoretical and practical, have conditioned my research, teaching, and actions at different times. I characterize my experience in terms of four eras: first, the era of planned incrementalism in a world of changing industry and functional positions, consisting mainly of low-level, often uncoordinated, change; second, the era of radical transformation, often in response to crisis or the need for radical reform, in which heroic leader-managers wielding heroic programmes of change attempted to make major shifts in resources or capabilities across whole enterprises; third, the era of 'journey orchestration', when the messy interplay of external and internal forces for change itself became an instrument in the hands of the leader as 'journey navigator'; and, finally, the current era of agility and flux, in the course of which leaders have learnt they are merely part of a complex and adaptive world where different perspectives and metaphors of organization can themselves suggest new forms of collective leadership and action.

Table 16.1 uses some of the key influences and examples from my own journey to illustrate how the search for agility evolved during these eras.

The 1970s: Planned Incrementalism—The Leader as Technician

Two years of an MBA at Harvard Business School had lifted me by 1975, after early training as an engineer, into the rarefied world of general management and business policy—then seen as a separate area of thinking and analysis intended to inform 'strategy'. The Harvard mindset, engrained with Chandler-esque thinking,[1] assumed that change was preceded by strategy, which in turn was incrementally implemented through structure and the detail of separate functional plans. To complement this, my post-MBA employer (then the 'administrative services' wing of Arthur Andersen) thrived on the design and implementation of such detailed improvements. My first Andersen training school, after the rarefied atmosphere of Harvard, had me spending three weeks on the systems and processes of Suburban Pump, laboriously working through small improvements in each area. The sequential connection between a chosen strategic position and underlying systems design was cemented in the 1980s when I worked with Michael Porter's research team on connecting his value chain with the use of information for competitive advantage.[2]

In this world, change is planned and designed by the technocrats, with the leader the archetypal technocrat owning the solution. Change of

TABLE 16.1 Leading change—four eras of theory and practice

	1970s Planned incrementalism	1980s Radical transformation	1990s Journey orchestration	2000s Agility and flux
Context	• Bounded stability	• Recession and reinvention	• Organic growth, capability	• Turbulence, uncertainty, intangible assets
Some influences	• Porter and Millar (strategy, position and information technology) • Lewin (Incremental change and OD) • Chandler (structure following strategy)	• Peters (excellence and 7S) • Hamel, Stalk (resources, capabilities) • Hammer (reengineering) • Kotter (transformational leader)	• Collins (Built to last) • Senge (learning) • Pettigrew (processual change) • Stace and Dunphy, Hinings and Greenwood, Tichy and Sherman and others (journeys and change tracks)	• Stacey, Pascale (Complexity and disturbance) • Brown and Eisenhardt (chaos, rules and timepaced evolution) • Hamel (Resilience) • Heifetz (Adaptive leadership) • O'Reilly and Tushman (Ambidexterity)
Leadership focus	• Leader as technocrat	• Leader as programmatic hero	• Leader as navigator	• Complexity and adaptive leadership
Practice teaching and learning	• Planning • Functional change • Projects • Tools and method	• Heroic cases • Programme management • Integration	• Contextual analysis • Journey maps • Scorecards • Change management • Knowledge	• Futurizing • Conversation • Metaphors • Renewal • Trial and error • Action labs & adaptive work
Personal practitioner experience (examples)	• Consultant as plumber (Cummins Engines, Yamaha)	• Consultant as programme enabler (SmithKline Beecham, Ford of Europe)	• Teacher as journey mapper and synthesiser (Thames Water, Standard Chartered, O2)	• Facilitator as reflective challenger/coach (UK public services)
Personal research agenda (examples)		• Positivist and quantitative (EU92 restructuring, Transformation cases—Andersen Consulting)	• Descriptive and constructionist (Journey Management—D. Phil. Oxford; Public service leadership—UK Cabinet Office)	• Reflective and co-created (Strategic Renewal—Oxford; Liberating the Entrepreneurial Spirit—Accenture)

course can be incremental and separated off if the world moves relatively slowly. While the 1970s experienced some instability (e.g. oil shocks), change emerged in a more orderly fashion. Practice involved use of 'professionalized' approaches such as systems analysis and organizational design. Change projects were undertaken in periods during which an organization was successively unfrozen and then re-formed—Lewin's classic model described much later by Rosabeth Kanter as a 'quaintly linear and static conception'.[3]

The task for the practising manager was to learn the new approaches, learn about functional change, and be trained in the tools of the 'plumber'. Management training followed this route in the classroom and the training manual, occasionally using teams and groups to make it happen. My world (the consultant as plumber) followed suit. Many examples of technical solutions emerged—my own major areas being the automating of manufacturing and inventory control through the new MRP (Manufacturing Resource Planning) systems. My experience at Cummins Engines saw considerable developments. There was even some exchange between these new style socio-technical systems and Japanese JIT (Just in Time) practices, which were combined with MRP in places like Cummins and Yamaha with its Synchro-MRP.

The 1980s: Radical Transformation—the Leader as Programmatic Hero

The Japanese systems and ideas (such as JIT and Total Quality Management) in the 1970s and 1980s were perhaps the peak of this planned incremental approach. The late 1980s and early 1990s, however, saw new challenges, particularly in the West. The increasing pace of technology and competitiveness of the Japanese, the long boom of the 1980s and the complacency it bred, left many of the traditional industries in crisis when capital became scarce and global recession hit. At the same time, many industries, previously protected by regulation and monopolies, were opened up to competition. A new agenda arose based on the search for excellence and the demand for radical shifts in capability and resources.

The clamour for significant and radical change saw gurus and pseudo-academics bending the ear of top managers and exhorting them to lead from the top. The purveyors of mantras of excellence (Peters and Waterman at McKinsey[4]), re-engineering (Hammer[5] etc.), and transformation (Kanter[6] and Kotter[7]), all shared an emerging resource-based view of strategy and change. Competences (Hamel[8]) and capabilities (Stalk[9]) would be the focus of re-invention from the top, very often driven by a clear, stretched strategic intent or 'view of the future'. Re-invention had to happen fast to stay in the lead. Sluggish giants like GE, IBM, General Motors, and ABB had to be transformed. The leader, very often newly appointed to the top, was anointed as the programmatic hero.

It was certainly not business as usual. Change, being far from trivial, could not be brought about by a single project or within a single functional silo. Understanding how things needed to connect together across the organization to deliver new and different capabilities and business models was critical. For the practitioner, having an integrative framework such as McKinsey's 7S model was key, as was involving the many parts of the organization in this radical change. Management education saw the classroom discussion of many different 'heroic' cases describing how whole businesses had been transformed through new ways of working and transformational leadership.

The goal was to learn from what others did, and then apply the prescriptions embedded in the specific examples. (Kotter's 'eight steps to transformation' in *Leading Change*[7] springs to mind: was it really always eight steps and in that order?) We might recall Percy Barnevik at ABB, Jack Welch at GE, even Colin Marshall and John King at British Airways. Transformational change was led from the top, often with many special programme enablers in place to help (witness the rise of the integrated consultants such as Gemini, Andersen Consulting, EDS, CSC, IBM, and others). This era saw academic interest shift from single professions, such as the OD movement, to a more integrated change management approach (see Ref. 10).

My own experience as a consultant working at the top as 'programme enabler' with two companies was instructive. Harry Groome, Chairman at SmithKline Beecham's (SKB) consumer business, led a major journey of strategic, organizational, and operational change for three years in order to align the company with SKB CEO Bob Bauman's vision of a global health care business. The key to progress was hard work on cross-team working and cultural routines—as well as an integrated programme management approach owned by the executive team. Messianically, Bob Bauman and colleagues championed the 'Simply Better Way' approach, loosely based on Japanese *Kaizen* continuous breakthrough techniques, and applied a cultural and process approach to leading change.

Similarly, Bill Hayden at Ford of Europe, faced with the need to reduce Ford's time-to-market from six years to three, set in motion a Europe-wide change programme to create new ways of working between engineering, manufacturing, and procurement. It involved major structural, behavioural, and process changes across boundaries and borders. I recall with some awe how Bill got thirty of the top managers from each function to pack their bags and immerse themselves for several weeks in the project room in the heart of Ford's art deco Dagenham home to crack the problem. Some lessons were learned, but of course many of the failures (reportedly, over 70% of major change efforts) never made it to the classroom. The heroes did not always deliver sustainable change. The reversions at ABB and British Airways come to mind. SKB, faced with merger again with Glaxo, started another cultural journey. Ford continues to face problems with what it calls 'chimneys' between functions.

The 1990s: 'Journey Orchestration'—the Leader as Navigator

Some of these stories of radical shift—often generously termed 'transformation'—were reeled out as simplistic recipes for action. My experience as a practitioner, working alongside some of the senior teams, uncovered a more frustrating picture. On closer examination, changes and leadership styles were problematic, full of false starts and often disconnected from the realities at the coal face. Leadership teams often experienced disruption, changes in direction, and unintended consequences. Linear prescriptions did not work because each situation was different. Meanwhile, as an antidote to the top-down revolutionary formulae of re-engineering, Senge's *Fifth Discipline* [11] and Collins and Porras's *Built to Last*[12] became the take-home books for the C-Suite. They proposed that long-lasting organizations change and survive through in-built learning routines and cultural habits—a kind of DNA that allowed them to find new solutions in new worlds without the top-down revolution. Interestingly, an updated edition of *Built to Last* was reissued successfully in 2005—bearing out perhaps in a minor way its central message.

The rationale for the next stage of my own journey—research at Oxford after twenty years as a senior consultant and practitioner—had become clear. I wanted to explore and better understand the world of leadership teams caught in the throes of these complex strategic and organizational shifts. The challenge was to try and develop some kind of descriptive framework providing a bird's-eye view of journeys of major change. If this could be done, then perhaps it could also help the leaders and practitioners immersed in the journey. By giving them a perspective, a language, a new set of patterns and maps, it might allow them see where they had come from and where they were going, and how they might best orchestrate the next stages of complex and messy journeys.

A number of researchers had already provided some useful frameworks for looking at the different stages of 'change journeys'. In 1993, Tichy

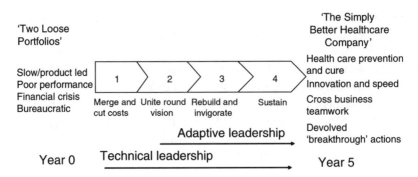

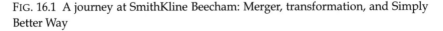

FIG. 16.1 A journey at SmithKline Beecham: Merger, transformation, and Simply Better Way

and Sherman's descriptions of transformational change at GE[13] was one example (using Awakening, Envisioning, Re-architecting, Sustaining—followed perhaps by further Re-awakening!). This mapping was used at the 1992 Strategic Management Society conference to map the SKB journey referred to earlier. My own interpretation of this (building on the richer description by Bauman et al.[14]) is shown in simplified form in Figure 16.1. Another later example (see Figure 16.2) used the journey of British Petroleum (BP) in the 1990s to characterize a shift from being a 'sclerotic bureaucracy' (to quote *Fortune*) to becoming a devolved 'learning organization' by the end of the decade ready for more strenuous global growth (see Ref. 15). Interestingly, the early 2000s have seen BP shift back,

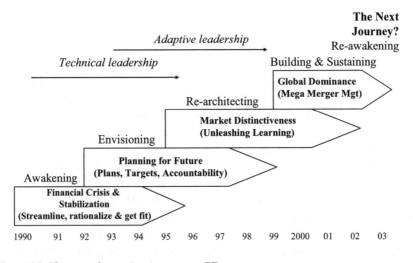

FIG. 16.2 The transformation journey at BP

as downstream profitability, production, and safety issues spurred the management to reassert process and central control.

These journey maps are clearly simplistic. A much richer interpretation of stages, allowing for overlap, different levels, and different tracks of change, had been provided by others, including Hinings and Greenwood,[16] with their archetypes and tracks, and by Stace and Dunphy,[17] who distinguished between *styles* and *levels* of change.

To get a deeper understanding of how such a journey progresses, I turned to the 'processualist' work of Pettigrew and Whipp in the 1980s and early 1990s.[18,19] Pettigrew's *Reawakening Giant* account of ICI's renewal explored the rich interplay of context—external and internal—as the journey progressed over time. Building on this, my research used a framework to trace a longitudinal journey of transformation in terms of the context of change (both internal and external), the content of change, and the journey management process involving the top management team. The interrelationships, dependencies, and mutual configurations of these variables over time provided a lens through which to view an organizational journey. In this processual view, change—even radical transformation—is *emergent*. Key decisions, including those of top managers, evolve over time and are the outcome of cultural and political processes in organizations.

Using this framework, I tracked change over time, from the viewpoint of the top teams and their management process.[20] I carried out a major longitudinal case on Thames Water's journey post-privatization covering seven years (two of which I was observing in 'real time') that provided a rich vein of material on the relationship between context and process. Another twenty-five cases on journeys during the 1990s were used to enrich the framework, drawn from banking, insurance, utilities, consumer products, manufacturing, and healthcare.

A number of common patterns emerged. For example, Figure 16.3 includes examples from a subset of journeys, all of which demonstrated a significant shift in both strategy and organizational capabilities. Within each journey distinct stages were identified, often starting with more technical change to deal with crisis or 'break the old mould' but were followed by more adaptive change requiring much wider engagement.

I developed a simple four-quadrant model for journey management (Leadership, Navigation, Ownership, and Enablement), derived from my work with Andersen Consulting in the early 1990s,[21] and applied it to the elements of the change processes in which senior teams were engaged. This model has top-down and organization-wide dimensions and incorporates notions of the demand and supply of change. A number of styles

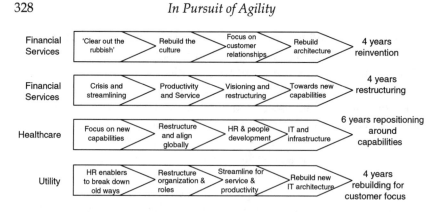

FIG. 16.3 Journey patterns: The redesign/reinvention journeys show how companies moved through distinct stages and sequences

were identifiable. In many journeys top management started with what could be characterized as highly programmatic or technical leadership (with defined and urgent tasks) but then learned—or adopted—a more transformational or adaptive style of leadership in the face of wider uncertainties and longer term challenges. Elements of these two styles are mapped in Figure 16.4.

My research, as well as testing the framework, provided some insights into how senior leadership teams 'navigate' complex and messy change using a mixture of styles, intentional or otherwise. Leaders deployed a

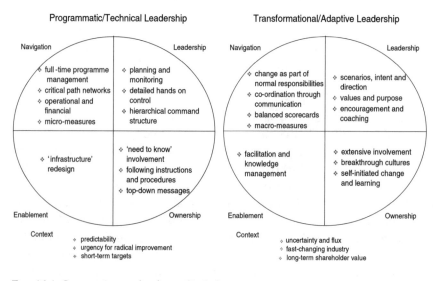

FIG. 16.4 Contrasting styles for radical change

variety of enablers, tools, and resources to help bring about change. In the more complex journeys in the 1990s, the challenge for leadership was how to adopt programmes and styles of change appropriate to both the current situation and capabilities and also to future needs. The notion of *agility* surfaced. I postulated a *meta-style* of navigational leadership style. One of its keys would be the ability to identify when, and how, to switch between styles.

Its elements included the following:

- Sensitive organizational antennae able to monitor and interpret context continuously and switch, as appropriate, to different ways of changing
- A broad range of leadership capabilities among executives and senior management oriented towards experimentation, learning, and adaptation
- A strong sense of purpose and values combined with clear navigational capabilities to set and achieve the targets of the journey
- The ability to adjust to differences in pace, sequence, and timing in different change initiatives and manage the relationships between them
- The ability to coordinate and manage change initiatives, separating them off or integrating them appropriately with the day-to-day line business.

'Navigational' leadership demanded new roles and skills on the part of both the top leadership and the central management of an organization. My research indicated that to achieve sustainable and successful transformation in an environment of continuous flux such capabilities were also needed across senior management. Weaving together the ability to assess contexts, diagnose situations, choose appropriate new directions, set and adjust paths, these capabilities needed to be embedded in new management processes and behaviours.

What was the impact of the 'era of journey orchestration' on teaching and learning in the classroom? I found that the kind of navigational frameworks identified here transferred directly into the classroom where senior leadership teams were grappling with their own 'journey of change'. The opportunity to stand back and reflect on 'where they were on the journey' allowed debate and difference to be put into a context. In particular, the notion of understanding the journey management process and linking it to leadership style was especially powerful.

I used this framework with many organizations at Oxford: Reed-Elsevier transforming its global business and emerging in the late 1990s

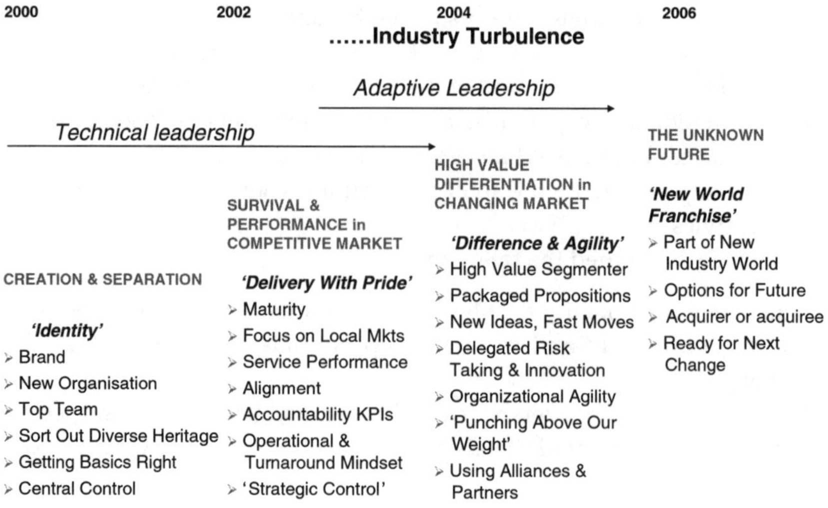

2000	2002	2004	2006

......**Industry Turbulence**

Adaptive Leadership →

Technical leadership →

THE UNKNOWN FUTURE

HIGH VALUE
DIFFERENTIATION in
CHANGING MARKET

SURVIVAL &
PERFORMANCE in
COMPETITIVE MARKET

'New World Franchise'
➤ Part of New Industry World
➤ Options for Future
➤ Acquirer or acquiree
➤ Ready for Next Change

CREATION & SEPARATION

'Delivery With Pride'
➤ Maturity
➤ Focus on Local Mkts
➤ Service Performance
➤ Alignment
➤ Accountability KPIs
➤ Operational & Turnaround Mindset
➤ 'Strategic Control'

'Difference & Agility'
➤ High Value Segmenter
➤ Packaged Propositions
➤ New Ideas, Fast Moves
➤ Delegated Risk Taking & Innovation
➤ Organizational Agility
➤ 'Punching Above Our Weight'
➤ Using Alliances & Partners

'Identity'
➤ Brand
➤ New Organisation
➤ Top Team
➤ Sort Out Diverse Heritage
➤ Getting Basics Right
➤ Central Control

FIG. 16.5 A view of the O2 journey

into a digital world beyond paper; Zurich Insurance coming out of a retrenchment period in the early 2000s and moving to global connection and growth again; Standard Chartered Bank under its new CEO Mervyn Davies seeking to reestablish itself as a leading international bank crucially able to respond to local markets. A final example might be CEO Peter Erskine and his team at O2 embarking as a mobile operator spun out from BT on a journey to achieve new forms of identity, differentiation, and delivery—and then, in the mid-2000s—to adapt agilely to new ownership by Telefonica of Spain.

In the classroom, all of these teams worked with my journey maps and process quadrants to frame their own particular challenges. Figure 16.5 shows an early illustrative version of how O2 might think about its journey of change.

The 2000s: Agility and Flux—Complex and Adaptive Leadership

In many of the change journeys and the associated classroom conversations with executives the notion of a transformational or adaptive change leadership style seemed deceptively appealing. At its extreme, it described not just a style to manage current change, but also an in-built transformational capability that, if sustained, could help an organization to respond to future uncertainties and changes in direction. This capability, however, depended on connecting the top-down processes of decision-making and renewal with organization-wide routines of innovation and entrepreneurial change.

Meanwhile, the 1990s and early 2000s were producing even more turbulence—first the e-revolution that erupted, disrupted, and moved on, and then the aftershocks of 9/11. Open information access and more deregulation were creating even more options for new industries, collaborations, and value constellations predicated on broader cross-boundary behaviour. In this environment was the notion of a journey still relevant or were leaders simply seeking extra elbow room to manoeuvre while delivering success on the ground of current terrain?

In this world of flux, loose connections, and fluidity, both managers and theorists sought not only new theories of change but also new analogies and metaphors with which to describe practice. Richard Pascale, in his *Surfing the Edge of Chaos*,[22] deplored reliance on Newtonian mechanics and machine metaphors as the explanatory and managerial tool for change— perhaps a 100-year legacy from Alfred P. Sloan and the rise of American managerialism. Pascale, probably an 'atheorist' at heart, used basic theories from the life sciences and complex adaptive systems to demonstrate how adaptive leaders work within contexts and disturb systems at the edge. The practical suggestion was that looking at change through a different lens could in fact help the practising manager find alternative approaches to leading change.

In fact, there was already a rich vein of work linking theory with practice in this area. Ralph Stacey, in his 1991 book *The Chaos Frontier*[23] and afterwards with his colleagues at the Complexity and Management Centre at the University of Hertfordshire, was one of the first to link complexity theory to organizational change. In the 1990s, some practitioners had been drawn to the Santa Fe Institute with its focus on complexity in nature. The attractiveness of this lens in a world of flux and agility is obvious: complexity theories are concerned with the emergence of order in dynamic, non-linear systems operating at the edge of chaos—in other words systems which are constantly changing and where the laws of cause and effect appear not to apply. Order in such systems is apparently unpredictable, but patterns emerge through self-organization, and order is often governed by a small number of simple rules.

Armed with this theory, and faced with a world of complexity and flux, other management-watchers tried to identify leadership and organization practices that worked on the basis of these principles. Pascale used examples of 'at the edge' change at Shell and in the US Army, with senior leadership consciously disrupting systems and creating a context for change. Shona Brown[24] and Kathy Eisenhardt[25] espoused patching, time pacing, and other simple rules (ironically, with Eisenhardt later quoting Enron as an archetype of the latter!).

For the practitioner seeking ideas on what to do, the key issue became how to connect and engage with these complex systems, particularly on management problems for which the leader has no immediate solution or predictive method. The real power of Ronald Heifetz's ideas of technical and adaptive leadership work[26] (espoused once more in the 1990s) could now be harnessed to an increasingly unpredictable and complex world. Adaptive leadership would need not just to be exercised at the top but to pervade large organizations if these were to become truly adaptive. These leaders, however, had to be able, as nodes of intelligence, to detect and foster self-organizing routes to growth and change involving new ideas and ways of working. Leaders needed to align themselves with a dynamic for change by plugging into the energy, culture, and self-preserving routines of their systems.

Two programmes of research undertaken around 2000 made this notion particularly relevant and helpful to me as a researcher and management-watcher. First, my old firm—now called Accenture—invited me to join its research team looking at 'Liberating the Entrepreneurial Spirit'.[27] Its focus was on corporate entrepreneurial behaviour, particularly in larger enterprises in the public and private sectors. Some 880 interviews were carried out in 22 countries. Central to the findings was that some of the largest organizations—both in the East and West—were adopting entrepreneurial habits and cultures along with adaptive and collective leadership philosophies. Top executives were becoming leaders of entrepreneurs, not entrepreneurial leaders. The key was to connect top-level purpose and vision with bottom-up entrepreneurial routines and create a culture of confidence. Belief systems had to reward 'be big but work small' strategies, and diversity and deviancy had to be nurtured without incurring disaster (Enron and Andersen come to mind again!). New routines involving futurizing and corporate antennae were being fashioned out of the old.

My second experience was salutary. I worked with a research team in the UK Cabinet Office to explore what kind of leadership might be needed to strengthen and improve UK public services. The immediate focus of attention in our brief 'given from the top' was on the elite cadre of senior public sector managers—mandarins and the like—and enshrined the view that inspirational and managerial leadership at the centre was key. The research team—many of us heavily dosed with concepts of complex systems—pointed out that in fact there were over five million people and 20,000 organizations engaged in the public services, many loosely connected and working at local coal-face levels. Much more interesting, we maintained, was how change actually took place out at the edge where local leaders and communities were facing adversity and opportunity.[28]

We got 300 local leaders around tables to tell stories of both failure and success, and a strong view emerged of how connecting with 'the edge' and the emergence of emotionally intelligent but determined leaders 'out there' was the key to creating adaptive and self-sustaining change. Making this shift, however, in a highly politicized system that demands central accountability, remained problematic. I had previously had some perspective on this at Templeton when helping lead a programme on managing change in government for the then Shadow Labour Cabinet in 1996. The other angle, of course, was that the self-styled centre of this system wants to pull the levers at its disposal in the hope that it can change things 'top down'. More on this below.

How has the era of complexity and adaptive leadership influenced teaching and learning in the executive classroom? In many of the company programmes run at Templeton and the Saïd Business School in the early 2000s, the focus has shifted to how a collective cadre of senior and middle management—not just the top Board—can take on the role of steering and leading in a world of change and flux. This means, first, that the skills of strategic thinking, futurizing, and awareness of context must be the province of the many rather than the few. New skills and tool kits, such as scenario building, have to be brought into broader play. Second, the ability to envisage and navigate the journey shifts increasingly calls for the ability to sense, interpret, and connect. Leaders' power traditionally comes when they can get emotionally and confidently 'up on the balcony' (as Heifetz calls it). But leaders also need to connect with each other and use the power of bold and adaptive initiatives—often involving other colleagues—to make progress.

For Oxford's executive education this has involved some significant shifts in the learning it encourages. One major shift has focused on the role of 'facilitating the conversation'—bringing in the art of conversation and story-telling itself. Further, the use of different interventions and metaphors to help leaders change personally has brought about the use of poetry, performance, and theatre as a vehicle for exploration. The runaway success of Richard Olivier's Shakespeare Mythodrama comes to mind here, with teams re-enacting Henry V's personal journey of Jungian dilemmas along the way.[29] By 2007 Richard has also turned his focus, working with Oxford, on the issues of power, politics, and influence underlying the stories of *Macbeth*. Finally, there has been a move to build in more time for executives to work on real adaptive problems, both in the classroom and through action learning and action labs. Recent programmes with O2, Royal and Sun Alliance, Elsevier Science, Deloitte, and others have all incorporated variations on this theme.

New Paradoxes in an Agile World

So, where next on the journey of theory and practice in leading change? Is the search for agility and adaptiveness simply the quest for another philosopher's stone—an ideal construct or one that genuinely leads to self-changing and self-sustainable enterprises? By the mid-2000s there were many major research programmes in place looking at the phenomena of change in practice. At Oxford, I joined colleagues Rafael Ramirez and Marc Thompson to set up the Strategic Renewal Research Programme (SRRP) in 2004 with Shell and the European Patent Office as sponsors and co-researchers. The team in 2007 are continuing to search for new ways to connect strategic renewal, sustainable change, and innovation. Related programmes at INSEAD, London Business School, Erasmus, and elsewhere are also exploring practice in this area.

At Oxford, much of Shell's interest sprang from its own concern to stimulate an 'agile' renewal and innovation capability in circumstances where traditional top-down prescriptions clash with institutional culture and dominant 'exploitation' mindsets. The European cases we looked at in 2005 and 2006 (reported at the Strategic Management Society panel session in Vienna in 2006) demonstrated how some of these tensions and paradoxes play out in practice. Some of these are now being explored in academic debate and journals of management practice. They fall into three main areas.

First, the organizational dichotomy between exploitation and experimentation was classically demonstrated by Burns and Stalker over forty years ago.[30] Our research in the early 2000s suggests that a fusion of these alternatives can, and should, operate. Managers have both to deliver on the basis of past business models and invent and explore new ones. The term 'ambidexterity' has started to come to the fore (see Ref. 31).

Second, the belief that top-down as well as bottom-up are needed for renewal and agility needs to be made more explicit. Our cases suggest that there are some new dynamic capabilities that can make this combination work. Indeed, as Eisenhardt and Martin put it: 'We define dynamic capabilities as the firm's processes that use resources—specifically the processes to integrate, reconfigure, gain and release resources to match and even create market change. Dynamic capabilities thus are the organisational and strategic routines by which firms achieve new resource configurations as markets emerge, collide, split, evolve, and die.'[32] Our cases indicate that such new capabilities involve identifying future domains for competition, introducing deliberate processes to select and nurture innovations, and reorganizing structures to encourage knowledge transfer.

Third, managers must achieve a balance between tolerating and encouraging diversity and even deviancy and maintaining consistency and standards. The value of 'positive deviancy' and its role in bringing about change has come to the fore with Pascale and Sternin's endorsement of the value of 'secret change agents' within a company.[33] Sternin's study of positive deviants in Vietnam and his work with the Peace Corps and Save the Children has had considerable influence. Currently he heads the Ford Foundation's Positive Deviance Initiative at Tufts University.

So, the search for new capabilities goes on, but continues to involve definitional tension. New words appear—flexibility, adaptiveness, responsiveness, nimbleness—but do they really describe the paradox of successful delivery while straddling unceasing disruptive change? Hamel and Valikangas[34] promote 'resilience', proclaiming it as 'the ability to dynamically reinvent business models and strategies as circumstances change... the capacity to change even before the case for change becomes obvious... continually anticipating and adjusting... companies must become as efficient at renewal as they are at producing today's products and services'.

For practising managers and leaders, the search continues for the philosopher's stone of the agile and self-sustaining enterprise. But is there any evidence to suggest such a notion is possible? Collins and Porras in *Built to Last* put forward such a proposition on the evidence of nearly 100 years' experience in eighteen companies; but can such companies and their successful habits provide the basis for a new era of competition and flux? The idea of resilience or adaptive capacity is extremely appealing, but I suspect achieving it will be seriously constrained in individual enterprises by the lure of 'social engineering' and the dominant mindset of human beings who demand and thrive on certainty, command and control.

Nevertheless recent research has thrown up some fascinating evidence of how new value is being created between and among enterprises and of new solutions—networks, nodes, and connections, distributed intelligence not constrained by the hierarchical rules of a controlling body. Such viral-style change can be seen in phenomena such as anti-globalization protests, in Lucas developing games with its thousands of customers, and maybe even in eBay running itself more as a movement. The corollary may be that future managerial practice will have to learn how social structures can act as a form of distributed intelligence, blurring the boundaries between management and employees and between companies, suppliers, and customers.

Interestingly, this paradoxical concept of viral, loose, and complexly interconnected change is relevant to my own professional and academic circumstances. Consider Oxford University and its 'family'—a complex amalgam of academics, students, staff, colleges, departments, institutes, collaborations, and partnerships. Governance is diffuse, often characterized as hopelessly bureaucratic and cumbersome. Any major change or decision involves democratic consensus to an extreme degree. Detractors say we need more top-down management. But in spite of this Oxford achieves change, pursues radically new research, and continues to educate the political, academic, and business leaders of the future. It has survived revolution and religious strife and has done so for nearly 900 years. Maybe we should study more closely how its loose connections work in action.

The other conundrum facing me in 2007 concerns the UK government's continuing endeavours to reform public services. Tony Blair's New Labour followed on from many years of Conservative reform—at various times echoing its rhetoric that state and central control needed to be pruned back. Educators and policy advisors have continued to suggest that delivering responsive twenty-first century public services demands a more devolved and self-organizing system that can find solutions closer to the changes taking place in the community. Many examples, including my own contribution, can be found in the Social Market Foundation's recent set of essays, *Reinventing Government Again*.[35]

The current Gordon Brown reform agenda is similar and is indeed echoed by the embryonic murmurs of David Cameron's New Tories. But at the same time the centralizing, mechanistic, hierarchical tendencies of politically accountable human beings push for ever-greater control and certainty. I detect the continuing temptation to pursue 'social engineering' together with a wider malaise which has to do with trust and capability. So perhaps it is time for Templeton and Oxford to apply the lessons of their own experience to solving wider problems of policy and practice, in research, the classroom, and beyond!

Seeking a New Relationship between Research and Practice

One final personal reflection on my thirty-year journey has to do with the evolution of management research and its relationship with practice. This is not the place for a full account of how management research has changed over this period, but my own journey might be instructive. The 1980s era of 'leader as programmatic hero' was paralleled by a positivist and prescriptive bias in my own early research. Heroic cases all seemed to be based on a simplistic view of cause and effect operating in easily identifiable and quantifiable form in the interplay between managerial action and results. Many cases were written in retrospect from the viewpoint of the successful leader. Loose assertions were made about the impact of new ideas and tools. Meanwhile, deeper work by social scientists on how organizations and people behaved and interacted was invisible to the executive classroom or indeed the boardroom consultant. Academics with views on economics and markets enjoyed much more attention.

The shift to the 1990s and the era of 'journey orchestration', for me, ushered in a much richer time in that it brought together practice and qualitative and integrative processual research. My research approach became more descriptive and constructionist. For me and the practitioners with whom I worked at Templeton, this approach was far more powerful as it provided them with a clearer framework to understand the context of their own roles as leaders of change. For the academic world this decade also saw the increasing legitimacy of Mode 2 applied research (see Ref. 36), pioneered by Pettigrew and others, requiring researchers to work far more in the field alongside companies. In turn, this made the transfer by me of research back into the executive classroom easier, as language, stories, and the views they provided sparked increasingly insightful debate and interaction with executives in the course of their journeys of reflection and learning.

Much of this kind of work uses forms of grounded theory iteration. It also has the merit of working with new ideas and emerging theories in real time in the field. The latest work at Oxford on Strategic Renewal takes this one step further with managers from sponsoring and case companies participating as co-researchers in the enquiry as co-producers of knowledge. Peer-to-peer discussions in the field and careful debriefing provide a valuable forum to develop and debate theory.

This kind of co-production attempts to bridge old dichotomies between theory and practice where practitioners do not see 'results' until they have been disseminated, post-research, much later on. In the early days of management research, practising managers were often left to interpret their own experience or apply the often ill-researched or poorly devised prescriptions of management consultants. To quote Pettigrew, 'dissemination is too late if the wrong questions have been asked. A deeper...engagement between management researchers and practitioners would entail experimentation with the co-funding, co-production and co-dissemination of knowledge.'[37] These sentiments we have tried to emulate in much of the practice-based research at Templeton.

I believe, however, that the quality and impact of this kind of research will be enhanced by applying principles set out by another scholar of process and practice, Andrew Van de Ven. His approach was to identify questions and anomalies arising in management practise; next, to organize the research project as a learning community of disciplinary scholars and management practitioners; then design and conduct research in appropriate and rigorous ways to examine these questions; and, finally, to analyse and translate research findings not only in order to add knowledge to a scientific discipline but also to advance the practice of management.

In pursuing future research on change there is a strong case for maintaining this combined scholar-and-practitioner research team approach, on the grounds that if knowledge can 'be co-produced and combined in some novel ways the results could produce a dazzling synthesis that could profoundly advance management theory, teaching, and practice.'[38] I personally hope to continue that quest with colleagues at Oxford and elsewhere as well as with managers and leaders seeking more knowledge of a world of change.

References

1. A. Chandler, *Strategy and Structure* (Cambridge, MA: MIT Press, 1962).
2. M. E. Porter and V. E. Millar, 'Information Gives you Competitive Advantage', *Harvard Business Review* (July 1985).
3. R. M. Kanter, B. A. Stein, and T. D. Jick, *The Challenge of Organizational Change* (New York: Free Press, 1992).
4. T. Peters and R. H. Waterman, *In Search of Excellence: Lessons from America's Best-Run Companies* (London: Harper & Row, 1982).
5. M. Hammer and J. Champy, *Reengineering the Corporation* (New York: Free Press, 1993).
6. R. M. Kanter, *The Change Masters* (New York: Simon & Schuster, 1983).
7. J. P. Kotter, *Leading Change* (Cambridge, MA: Harvard Business School Press, 1996).
8. G. Hamel and C. K. Prahalad, 'Strategy as Stretch and Leverage', *Harvard Business Review* (March-April 1993): 75–84.

9. G. Stalk, Jr., P. Evans, and L. E. Shulman, 'Competing on Capabilities: the New Rules of Corporate Strategy', *Harvard Business Review* (Mar.-April 1992): 57–69.

10. K. Moore, K. Ruddle, and N. A. M. Worren, 'From Organizational Development to Change Management: the Emergence of a New Profession', *Journal of Applied Behavioral Science*, 35/3(1999).

11. P. M. Senge, *The Fifth Discipline—the Art and Practice of the Learning Organization* (New York: Doubleday, 1990).

12. J. Collins and J. Porras, *Built to Last: Successful Habits of Visionary Companies* (New York: Harper Business, 1994).

13. N. Tichy and S. Sherman, *Control Your Destiny or Someone Else Will* (New York: Bantam Doubleday Dell, 1993).

14. R. Bauman, P. Jackson, and J. Lawrence, *From Promise to Performance: A Journey of Transformation at SmithKline Beecham* (Cambridge, MA: Harvard Business School Press, 1997).

15. S. E. Prokesch, 'Unleashing the Power of Learning: An Interview with British Petroleum's John Browne', *Harvard Business Review* (Sept.–Oct. 1997): 146–68.

16. C. Hinings and R. Greenwood, *The Dynamics of Strategic Change* (Oxford: Blackwell, 1988).

17. D. A. Stace and D. C. Dunphy, *Beyond the Boundaries Leading and Creating the Successful Enterprise* (Sydney: McGraw Hill, 1994).

18. A. M. Pettigrew, *The Awakening Giant: Continuity and Change at Imperial Chemical Industries* (Oxford: Blackwell, 1985).

19. A. M. Pettigrew and R. Whipp, *Managing Change for Competitive Success* (Oxford: Blackwell, 1991).

20. K. Ruddle and D. Feeny, *Transforming the Organization: New Approaches to Management Measurement and Leadership* (Oxford Executive Research Briefing; Oxford, Templeton College, 1997).

21. T. Neill, 'The New Change Navigators', *Outlook Executive Quarterly*, March 1995.

22. R. T. Pascale, M. Millemann, and L. Gioja, *Surfing the Edge of Chaos: The Laws of Nature and the New Laws of Business* (New York: Crown, 2000).

23. R. D. Stacey, *The Chaos Frontier: Creative Strategic Control for Business* (Oxford: Butterworth-Heinemann, 1991).

24. S. L. Brown and K. M. Eisenhardt, *Competing on the Edge: Strategy as Structured Chaos* (Cambridge, MA: Harvard University Press, 1998).

25. K. M. Eisenhardt and D. N. Sull, 'Strategy as Simple Rules', *Harvard Business Review* (Jan. 2001): 106–16.

26. R. A. Heifetz and D. L. Laurie, 'The Work of Leadership', *Harvard Business Review* (Jan. 1997): 71–97.

27. P. Cullum, L. Padmore, and K. Ruddle, 'Rethinking the Role of the Entrepreneurial Leader', *Outlook Point of View*, 2001. www.Accenture.com

28. K. Ruddle, *Strengthening Leadership in the Public Sector* (PIU Research Study; London: HMSO, 2001).

29. R. Olivier, *Inspirational Leadership: Henry V and the Muse of Fire* (London: Spiro Press, 2001).

30. T. Burns and G. Stalker, *The Management of Innovation* (London: Tavistock Press, 1961).

31. C. A. O'Reilly and M. L. Tushman, 'The Ambidextrous Organization', *Harvard Business Review* (April 2004): 74–81.

32. K. M. Eisenhardt and J. A. Martin, 'Dynamic Capabilities: What Are They?', *Strategic Management Journal*, 21/10–11(2000): 1105–21.

33. R. T. Pascale and J. Sternin, 'Your Company's Secret Change Agents', *Harvard Business Review* (May 2005): 72–81.

34. G. Hamel and L. Valikangas, 'The Quest for Resilience', *Harvard Business Review* (Sept. 2003): 52–63.

35. K. Ruddle, 'Reinventing Leadership', in P. Collins and L. Byrne (eds.), *Reinventing Government Again* (London: Social Market Foundation, 2004): 96–108.

36. A. Pettigrew, 'Management Research after Modernism', *British Journal of Management*, 12(2001): S61–S70.

37. D. Tranfield and K. Starkey, 'The Nature, Social Organization and Promotion of Management Research: Towards Policy', *British Journal of Management*, 9(1998): 341–53.

38. A. H. Van de Ven, 'Andrew Pettigrew, the Engaged Scholar', *European Management Journal*, 20/1(2002): 29–31.

ABOUT THE EDITORS

Sue Dopson

Sue Dopson is Vice-Chair and Fellow in Organizational Behaviour at Templeton College and University Reader in Organizational Behaviour and Director of Research Degrees at the Saïd Business School, University of Oxford. Her research interests include management in the public sector, especially the NHS, managing with professionals, the nature of managerial work, career issues for managers and the changing roles of middle managers. Dr Dopson teaches elements of the University's degree programme in Management, is a postgraduate tutor, teaches on management development programmes for various companies and works on the Saïd Business School's Strategic Leadership Programme. As a member of the Oxford Health Care Management Institute (OHCMI), she is involved in the development of courses for the NHS and a number of research projects, the most recent of which considers how developments in genetic science will influence clinical practice and health care policy. Before pursuing a research and academic career, Dopson worked as a personnel manager in the NHS. Her books include *From Knowledge to Action? The Case of Evidence-Based Medicine* (2005), *Leading Health Care Organizations* (2003), *Leadership in the NHS* (2003), and *Managing Ambiguity and Change: The Case of the NHS* (1997).

Michael Earl

Michael Earl is Dean of Templeton College and Professor of Information Management, University of Oxford. An authority on changing competitive strategy in the Information Age, he has published widely in the *Harvard Business Review, Sloan Management Review, MIS Quarterly*, and the *Journal of Management Information Systems*. His books include *Information Management: The Organizational Dimension* (1996) and the best-selling *Management Strategies for Information Technology* (1989). Michael Earl was previously Professor of Information Management at London Business School, where he also held the posts of Deputy Dean and Acting Dean. He consults for several multinational organizations.

Peter Snow

An Associate Fellow of Templeton College, Peter Snow is a writer and editor specializing in business and management. He has worked on publications for Templeton College, the Saïd Business School, Oxford University, the British Council of Shopping Centres, Logica CMG, the UK Office of Science and Technology, the Chartered Institute of Building, and the Major Projects Association. Publications that he has written or edited include *Intellectual Property in a Digital Market: A Forum for Leaders of Business & Government* (1997), *Progress through Partnership: Office of Science & Technology, Technology Foresight Panel, Construction* (1996), *Beyond 2000: A Sourcebook for Major Projects* (1993–4), *Time for Real Improvement: Learning from Best Practice in Japanese Construction R&D* (1994), *Oxford Observed* and *The United States: A Guide to Information Sources* (1982).

INDEX

Boxes, figures, notes and tables are indexed in bold e.g. 37**b**. More than one figure or table is indicated by (**a**) or (**b**).

Abbott, A. 127, 147, 149
Accenture 146, 332
accounting 71, 145, 150
  see also creative accounting
Ackroyd, S. 126, 130
acquisitions, *see* M&A
adaptive leadership 328, 330, 331,
  332, 333
  see also leadership; normative
    leadership
Adburgham, A. 183
Adler, P. S. 95, 144
administrative heritage 29, 42, 82
  MNEs 21–2, 23, 24, 40–1
Africa 29, 39**b**
agility 321, 329, 330, 331, 334, 335
Ailon-Souday, G. 106
Alexander, R. M. 290
Allsop, J. 138
Alpin, C. 266
Alvesson, M. 147, 150
Amazon 70, 74, 202, 223
ambidexterity 334
ambiguous technology 223–4, 224**f**,
  225–6, 227–9
American Airlines 64, 69
American Hospital Supplies 64, 69
Anand, N. 146, 157
Anatomy of Major Projects, The (Morris
  and Hough) 167, 170, 173, 175,
  177, 178
Anderson, J. 223
Ansoff, I. 241
anti-dumping 39**b**
antitrust legislation 39**b**

APC (Advanced Practices
  Council) 195, 196
APM (Association for Project
  Management) 171, 172, 172**f**,
  173
Applegate, L. M. 211, 212, 214, 216
Arthur, M. 177
Arthur Andersen 144–5, 321, 332
Asia 28, 30, 31, 32, 34, 91, 221
Asia-Pacific 22, 29, 30, 31
assets 34, 37, 328
Atlan, Henri 317
Audit Commission (UK) 124, 136
Australia 28
Australian News Corp 34
authority 113–16, 126
automation 64, 66, 68, 69
automobile industry 32–3

Baburoglu, O. 313
Bach, S. 133, 134, 135, 139, 268
Bacharach, S. 150
back-office services 2, 63, 71, 73–4
Bain, G. S. 259
Bain, P. 259
Baker, R. 121
Baker, W. 298
Bamberger, P. 150
Banks, S. 134
Barley, S. R. 106
Barnard, C. I. 85
barrow boys, *see* retail sector
Barsoux, Jean-Louis 59
Bartlett, Christopher A. 28, 29, 30, 47,
  90

Bauman, R. 326
Bayer 29, 136
Bayliss, F. 263
Beer, Stafford 212
Bell, R. 183
Benetton 282**b**
Bensaou, M. 221
Berger, Gaston 308
Berger, P. 109
best practices 67, 74
  project management 169, 173–4
Bewley, H. 266
Bhargava, N. 242
'bi-regional' multinational enterprises
  33–4, 39, 40
big middle 193, 194**f**
Blair, Tony 264, 336
Blake, Robert 106
Blois, K. J. 290, 293, 296, 297, 300,
  301
Blyton, P. 268
Bolger, J. 237**t**
Bolman, L. G. 90
Borden, N. H. 294
Boston Consulting Group 240, 241,
  250–1
Bouckaert, G. 121
bounded rationality 88
boundaries 98–9
Boxall, P. F. 267
BPR (business process re-engineering)
  70, 72, 73, 219
Brady, T. 175
branding 26, 39, 145, 158, 182, 184,
  185–7, 198, 202, 280
Bratton, J. 110
Brazil 31, 159
Britain, *see* UK
Brock, D. 154
Brown, J. 146, 151, 152
Brown, S. L. 332
Bruzelius, N. 174
Brynjolsson, E. 220
Bryson, A. 266

BTR (UK) 244–5, 248, 249
Built to Last (Collins and Porras) 325,
  333–5
Burchell, S. 93
bureaucracies 84–5, 86, 88, 94–5, 97,
  126, 136, 150
Burns, T. 217, 334
Burr, V. 109
Burrell, G. 88
Burt, R. S. 97
business marketing 289, 293–4, 297–8,
  301, 302
Business Marketing Management (Hutt
  and Speh) 293
business models 38**b(2)**, 39**b**
business operations 220, 275
business processes 71, 74
business profits 243**t**
business schools 42, 214–15, 233
business strategies 182, 220, 250, 278

call centre services 73–4
Cameron, David 336
Campbell, Alexandra J. 40
Campion, M. A. 151
Canada 28, 30, 90, 131, 152
capabilities 323–4, 329, 335
capital 189**b**, 242, 245
capitalism 45, 64, 66, 91, 144
care skills 133, 134
Carlson, Sune 49, 51, 55, 56
Carlyle, Thomas 104, 106, 109
Carr, Nicholas 74
Caupin, G. 173
causal textures 311, 313, 314**t**–15**t**
cellphones, *see* mobile phones
central government (UK) 122,
  129–31
Central Europe 29
CEO (Chief Executive Officer) 218,
  227, 228, 253, 330
Champy, J. 107, 323
Chandler, A. 321
Chandler, A. D. 86

change management 73, 82, 130, 140, 145, 155–6, 174, 248, 327–8, 331, 332, 333–4
Channel Tunnel 165, 166
Channon, D. F. 235**f(a)**
Chaos Frontier, The (Stacey) 331
Checkland, P. 176
Cherns, A. 81
Child, John 59
China 23, 31, 58, 59, 65, 273
  offshoring 39**b**–40**b**
Christenson, C. M. 224
Cicmil, S. 177, 178
CIES 204, 205
CIO (Chief Information Officer) 218, 223, 227, 228–9
civil service 42, 123, 126, 129
CKO (Chief Knowledge Officer) 222–3, 229
Clark, K. 177
Clark, P. 177
Clarke, J. 139
Clegg, H. 259
Clubb, C. 93
Coca-Coca 24, 34
Cold War 93
collaboration 95, 112, 138
  with foreign partners, *see* joint ventures
collective bargaining 257, 260, 263, 265, 266
collective *laissez-faire* 258–9, 261, 267
collectivism 258–9, 262–4, 266
Collins, J. 325, 335
Collinson, D. 108
command 111–15
communication technologies 23, 67, 90, 91, 95, 182
communities
  and networks 97–8
  of practice 157
comparative advantage 42, 144, 221
  IT for 69, 214, 220, 221
  reduced by technology 65

competencies 323–4
competition 75, 90, 91, 128, 221, 335
  policy 38**b(2)**
  regulation 253, 301
  retail sector 202–4
competitive advantage 26, 29, 69, 150–1, 158
  chance in 27, 28
  and IT 216, 220–2, 228, 321
  retail sector 185, 195, 198, 201
competitive strategy 90, 220
  and IT 218, 220–1
competitiveness 27, 205, 220
complexity theory 7, 331, 333
computers 87, 89, 90, 211–12, 223
configuration management 172
conglomerates 233, 234, 238, 240, 242, 248, 250
  diversification 234, 235**f(a)**, 236, 240–1, 253–4
    through acquisitions 242, 245–6; moderate 250
  history 234–6, 250
  life cycle 252, 254
  performance 243–5, 247, 253
Conley, S. C. 150
Connected Corporation: How Leading Companies Win through Customer-Supplier Relationships, The (Lewis) 297
Conservative Party (UK) 259, 260–1, 267, 336
  under Margaret Thatcher 128–9, 261, 262, 263
consumers 293
  choice 185, 199
  electronics 30, 39
  marketing 74, 291
  and retail sector 198–9, 205
context 139
  role of 138, 327
contingency theory 106–7, 108–9, 113, 116, 177
convenience stores 191**f(a)**

Conway, N. 136
Cooke-Davies, T. 175
Cooper, D. J. 151, 152
Cooperrider, D. 111
Copeland, D. C. 225
core competence 70, 71, 72, 218
    see also business process
        re-engineering
Corea, G. 264
Corey, E. R. 291, 296
corporate governance 93, 201
corporate strategy 39, 234, 254, 276,
    278
corporations 93, 233
corporatism 258–61, 263, 266, 267
Corsten, D. 297
costermongers, *see* retail sector
costs 74, 99, 104
    control, in retail sector 201, 205
    and operations management 273,
        282–3
countervailing 39b
Covey, S. 107
Cox, J. S. 164
Cravath, Paul 151
Crawford, L. 175
creative accounting 243–4, 247t
    see also accounting
Crewson, P. 125
critical mass 238, 246, 248
Croson, D. C. 226
Cross, J. S. 290
Culley, M. 130
Cunningham, R. S. 290
custodial management 127, 130
customers 197
    annual profit 280t(b)
    behaviour 286, 286f
    loyalty 204
    needs 280–3
    retention 280, 280t(a), 286
    satisfaction 197–8
    services 283–4
    and supplier relationships 297–8,
        300–1

Cuthbertson, C. 196
Czech Republic 29

Darwin, Charles 252
data processing 68, 211–13
Davidson, Frank 164
Davies, A. 177
Davies, R. L. 182, 199
Day, G. S. 300
de Jouvenal, B. 308
Deal, T. E. 90
decentralization 40–1, 69, 145–6
DeChernatony, L. 186
decision-making 66, 90, 108, 109, 111,
    113, 116, 123, 150, 152, 174, 241,
    331
    management 213, 217
    executive 72–3
    and information 68, 89
    and problems 112, 114
decision-support systems 66
DeFillippi, R. 177
déjà vu, see management
demands, constraints and choices
    model 54–5
Denmark 28
Desarbo, W. S. 300
'diamond' models 26–8, 30
digitization 76, 222, 228
diversification, *see* conglomerates,
    diversification
divestment strategy 246–7, 247t(a),
    249, 250–1, 252–3
Dix, G. 266
dot.com collapse 93
downsizing 72, 90
downstream activities, *see* sales
DP (data processing) 211–12
Drewry, G. 133
Drucker, Peter 55, 121, 122
Dubai Ports International 39b
Dunnette, M. D. 51
Dunning, John H. 28
Dunphy, D. R. 327
Durran, P. 251

Dyas, G. P. 235**f(a)**
Dynamics of Taking Charge, The
   (Gabarro) 52

e-bay 70, 74, 336
e-business 69, 70, 73, 76, 226
e-commerce 197, 199, 202, 220, 296
e-retail 73
Earl, Michael 65, 69, 72, 214, 215, 216,
   217, 218, 219, 221, 222, 223, 226,
   228, 229
East Asia 29
economics 80, 88, 105
   development (Asia) 91
   integration 39–40, 45
Edwards, B. 216, 217
Effective Executive, The (Drucker) 55
effort-reward bargain 257, 259
Eisenhardt, K. M. 92, 98, 332, 334, 335
Elg, U. 198
email 57, 67, 76–7, 224
Emery, F. E. 311, 313, 316, 317
Emmott, M. 258
emotional intelligence 105, 107
employees 138–9
   pay 126–7
   and state (UK) 134
   women 124
   see also professionals
employment 259, 263, 266
   policies of management 266
   relations 257–8, 264, 267, 268
    and New Labour 265
Empson, L. 147, 156
Engwall, M. 177
Enron 93, 144, 332
entrepreneurial change 331, 332
environment 42, 107
   complexity 311, 313f
   regulations 202, 204
   see also organizations, and
    environment
equal opportunities 159, 265
equity 243
   private 251, 254

ERP (Enterprise Resource Planning)
   66, 67, 74, 204, 271
Escott, K. 129
Etzioni, A. 112, 127
Europe 24, 26, 29, 33, 87, 91, 184, 221,
   234
   conglomerates 250
   industrial marketing 291, 292
   industrial relations 259
   MNEs 34, 38**b(2)**
   organizations 82, 86, 88, 89, 96
European Commission (EC), and
   Microsoft 38**b(2)**
European Union (EU) 22, 23, 28, 30, 41
   MNEs 32, 42
   regional trade 30, 31
   use of mobile phones 23–4
Evans, P. 323
Executive Behaviour (Carlson) 49
executives 51, 55–6, 57, 215, 333–4
expert systems 66, 69
exports 27, 31

factor conditions 26, 27
Fairness at Work (UK) 264
Fairtlough, G. 95
Faris, C. W. 291
Fayol, Henri 50
FDI (foreign direct investment) 22, 31,
   41
Feeny, David F. 69, 71, 216, 217, 218,
   219, 220, 221, 227, 228, 327
Fenton, E. M. 89
Ferlie, E. 130, 131, 160
Fielder, F. E. 106
Fifth Discipline (Senge) 325
finance 24, 41
Finland 28
Fitzgerald, G. 217
Fitzgerald, Guy 71
Fitzgerald, L. 160
Flood, G. 201
Flood, J. 153
Flowers, S. 177
Flyberg, B. 174, 177

focusing firms 235**f(b)**, 240, 250–1, 253
food retailing 183, 301
Ford, D. 298
Ford, Henry 105, 106
Fordism 104, 105
foreign markets 22, 41
foreignness 39, 40, 41, 46
Forth, J. 266
Fottler, M. D. 123
France 59, 184, 291
  diversification 235**f(a)**
  M&A 234, 237
  scenarios 307–8
Frankel, E. 164
Franko, L. G. 234, 235**f(b)**
free trade 39**b**, 44–5
Freedland, J. 107
FSAs (firm-specific advantages)
  39**b**–40**b**, 39, 40, 41, 46
FTSE 236, 237**t**
Fujimoto, T. 177
functional strategies 275, 276, 276**t**,
  277, 277**f(a)**, 277**f(b)**, 281–3, 283**f**,
  286–7
  market-driven 279, 281, 283, 286
  market-driving 286
Futuribles (de Jouvenal) 308

Gabaroo, John 52
Galanter, M. 151
Galbraith, J. 89, 177
Gardner, H. 146, 157
GDP (gross domestic product) 30, 272
GE (General Electric) 24,
  38**b(2)**–39**b(2)**, 105, 324, 326
General Motors 212, 234, 324
Gergen, K. 109
Gergen, M. 109
Germany 41, 59, 273, 291
  diversification 235**f(a)**
  M&A 234, 237
Ghoshal, Sumantra 28, 29, 30, 47, 90,
  93
Giddens, A. 264, 267

Gilson, R. J. 151, 152
Gilson, S. C. 247
global economy 21, 28–9, 42, 145
global multinational enterprises 33–4,
  36**t(a)**, 39, 47
global strategies 31, 39, 221
global supply chains 32, 34
global warming 93, 94, 107
globalization 22, 32, 65, 74, 90, 95, 264
Google 70, 74
Gouldner, A. W. 85, 89, 149
governance 123
  and IT 212, 221–2, 227–8
  and PSFs 146, 151
governments:
  barriers to entry 31–2
  role of 27, 28
    UK 121–35
  services provided by 122
  use of IT 75
Gowler, Dan 57
Grabher, G. 177
Granovetter, M. 298
Greenwood, R. 83, 96, 146, 151, 152,
  327
Grewal, D. 192, 194**f**
Gribbin, J. D. 233
Grint, K. 105, 108, 109, 110
growth strategies 152
Guest, D. 136, 258
Guide to the Project Management Body of
  Knowledge, The (PMI) 170

Hakansson, H. 298
Hales, Colin 50
Hall, R. 149, 150
Hallen, L. 298
Hamel, G. 218, 335
Hammer, M. 107, 323
Handbook of Organisations (March) 86
Hanson Trust 245, 248–9
Harker, S. 201
Haron, M. 128
Harper, N. W. C. 250

Harris, B. 212
Harris, J. 134
Harvard Business School 86, 213, 214, 291, 321
Hassard, J. 107
Hastings, A. 150
Haug, M. 150
Hawkins, C. 160
Hawthorne Effect 105, 106
Hayek, Friedrich 262
health services (UK) 123, 133, 139
Health, Department of (UK) 133, 134
Healy, P. M. 247
Heckshcher, C. 95
Hedlund, G. 95
Heifetz, R. A. 332
Heimer, C. 176
Henderson, J. 195
Heron, P. 134, 139
Hickson, D. J. 295
hierarchies 121–2, 125, 126, 137, 152, 217, 219
high street stores 191**f(b)**
Hill, Terry 198, 277**f(a)**, 277**f(b)**, 279f, 280**t**, 283f, 286f, 287f
Hinings, C. R. 83, 96, 146, 150, 151, 152, 156, 295, 327
Hirschheim, R. 217
Hitt, L. M. 220
Hobday, M. 177
Hobson, W. 151
Hodgkinson, S. L. 217
Hodgson, D. 175, 177, 178
Hollander, S. 193f
home regions 39–40
'home region-oriented' multinational enterprises 33–4, 35**t**
Honeywell 39**b**
Hood, C. 128
Hopwood, A. G. 93, 214, 217
Hough, G. H. 166, 167, 170, 175
House, R. 107
Hristov, L. 191

HRM (human resources management) 71, 73, 90, 126–7, 151, 158, 257–8, 267–8, 274
Huber, J. 198
Hughes, J. 93
human capital 92, 96, 158, 159, 265
Hungary 29, 59
Hunt, S. D. 297
Hutt, M. 293

IBM 26, 34, 39**b**, 82, 146, 201, 324
ICI 234, 327
In Place of Strife (1969) (UK) 260
incomes policy (UK) 260, 261, 263
India 31, 159, 273
  IT 38**t**
  offshoring 39**b**–40**b**
Industrial Buying and Creative Marketing (Robinson et al.) 291
industrial marketing 290–1, 293–4, 298, 302
Industrial Marketing (Alexander, Cunningham and Cross) 290
Industrial Marketing (Corey) 291
industrial relations 257–9, 268
  UK 259, 260, 261, 265, 267, 296
Industrial Relations Act (UK) 260
industries 27, 221
information 58, 90, 220–2
  management 57, 65, 69, 214, 216, 219, 222, 223, 226, 228, 229
  processing 214, 228
  see also IS; IT
information-processing systems 89
innovations 26, 27, 29, 38**b**, 159, 201, 217, 221, 227, 331, 335
  knowledge-based 156, 157
  organizations 83, 96
  technological 66, 68–9, 74, 217
  value for 64, 65
Institute of Grocery Distribution (UK) 202
  global market index 204**t**
Intel 26, 201, 289–90, 298–9, 301–2

inter-organizational working 134–5, 136
international business 21, 34
  study 24–5, 25t, 26, 27–8
international organizations 157–8
International Competency Baseline (IPMA) 173
International Monetary Fund 128
Internet 23, 64, 67, 73, 75, 82, 91, 224, 289
intra-regional sales 34, 36t(b)
inventory management 67, 198
investments 23, 27, 30, 242, 250
  portfolio of 239–40
IPMA (International Project Management Association) 172–3
Iraq 115
IS (information systems) 69, 211, 213, 214, 218, 219, 220, 223, 226, 227
IT (information technology) 39, 57, 65–6, 69, 74, 83, 95, 211, 217, 218, 224, 226, 228
  and architecture 216, 217, 218, 219
  cost saving 68–9
  investment 64, 73, 220
  and management 211, 215, 216, 217, 223, 228
  offshoring 71, 73, 74, 76
  outsourcing 70–1, 92, 217–18, 227
  transaction costs 71, 217
  retail sector 182, 197, 200
  see also comparative advantage, IT for; competitive advantage, and IT; competitive strategy, and IT; governance, and IT
Italy 237, 291
Ives, Blake 69, 220

Jackson, P. 326
Jackson, T. 249
Jamieson, A. 177
Japan 22, 23, 24, 26, 30, 33, 41, 58, 82, 221, 238, 273, 323
  MNEs 32, 38t

Jedidi, K. 300
Jenkins, W. O. 106
Jick, T. 323
JIT (just-in-time) 275, 323
Johanson, J. 298
Johnson, T. 127, 150
joint ventures 41
  China and Hungary 59
journey mapping 321, 322t, 323–8, 328f(a), 328f(b), 329, 330, 331, 337
  see also mapping

Kahn, Herman 307–8, 316
Kahn-Freund, Otto 259
Kaizen 324
Kalwani, M. U. 297
Kanter, R. M. 323
Kapferer, J.-N. 186
Kaplan, J. F. 247t(a)
Kearney, A. T. 203
Kersley, B. 266
Kessler, I. 125, 133, 134, 135, 139
Kessler, S. 263
Khan, B. 217, 226
King, A. 108
Kirkpatrick, I. 126, 130
Kirkpatrick, S. A. 107
Kitchener, M. 153
Kitzinger, Uwe 164
Klein, R. 127
Klinger, P. 237t
Knöpfel, H. 173
knowledge 46, 84, 96, 109, 144, 337–8
  clusters 29–30
  control of 104–5
  economy 96–8, 147
  management 70, 72, 92, 222, 229
  and relationships 92
  transfer 87, 335
knowledge-based firms 39b–40b, 97, 147, 150
Kodak 34, 300
  IT outsourcing 70–1
Kondratiev, Nikolai 106

Kotter, John 56, 57, 323, 324
KPI (Key Performance Indicators)
    187–9, 189**b**, 191
Kraut, A. I. 51
Kumar, N. 297
Kunda, G. 106

Laaksonen, H. 184
labour:
    division of 84–5, 104
    markets 73, 74, 127, 152–3, 159, 264,
        266
    organized 68, 69, 73
    standards 217
Labour Party (UK) 259, 260–1
    and trade unions 264, 266
    see also New Labour
Lacity, Mary 71, 217, 227
Laming, Herbert, Baron Laming
    133–4
Landers, R. 158
Larson, M. 127, 147, 150
Latin-America 28
Laurie, D. L. 332
Lawrence, Peter R. 59, 177, 217, 326
Le Grand, J. 124
leadership 49–50, 109, 110, 111–15,
    332
    context 115, 321, 324–5, 326**f(a)**,
        327–8, 328**t(a)**, 328**f(b)**, 329, 331,
        332
    development 104–6, 115
    individual 107–8
    IT 69, 227–8
    openness 115–16
    problem solving 110–11, 113–14
    styles 330–1
    typology 109–15
    see also adaptive leadership;
        normative leadership
Leading Change (Kotter) 324
Leahy, Sir Terry 191, 192
lean operations 271, 275
learning 92, 227, 325, 329, 334
Lee, K. M. 151

Legge, K. 258, 267
Lenovo (China) 26, 39**b**
Lesourne, J. 307
Lessard, D. 173, 177
Lev, B. 236
Levy, H. 240
Levy, M. 192, 194**f**
Lewis, J. D. 297
Lind, K. 317
Litwak, E. 150
local government 122–3, 136
Locke, E. A. 107
Lockett, M. 215, 227
lockstep 152, 153, 154
Lorsch, J. 177, 217
Lowe, Kevin 60
Lowendahl, B. 144
Lublin, J. S. 248
Luckman, T. 109
Lundin, R. 177
LVMH 34, 40

M&A (Mergers and Acquisitions) 234,
    236–8, 239**t**, 242, 246, 247–8,
    250
    see also USA, M&A
McCann, J. E. 313
Macarthy, E. J. 294
McCarthy, W. E. J. 258, 262
MacDonald, K. 127
McDonald, M. H. B. 186
McFarlan, F. W. 211, 212, 214, 216
MacInnes, J. 262
McKenna, D. D. 52
McKenney, J. L. 211, 212, 214, 216, 225
McKinsey and Co. 151, 324
McLaughlin, K. 131
McNair, M. P. 192
MacNamara, Robert 169
McVey, P. 183
Madigan, C. 145
MAI (Multilateral Agreement on
    Investment) 42–3
mainframe, *see* DP
Maister, D. 151

Major Projects Association (MPA), *see* MPA

Making a Business of Information (Cabinet Office) 222

Malhotra, N. 156

Malos, S. B. 151

managed professional business, *see* MPB

management 57–8, 82, 90, 99, 109, 110, 111–15, 128, 137, 145
  conglomerates 242
  general 131, 229
  jobs 51–3, 53f, 54–5, 60
    agendas 56–7; time spent on 55–6
  MWB (work and behaviour) 49, 52–3, 58
  policy 214–15, 215f
  research 337–8
  skills 240, 242
  and trade unions 266–78
  see also change management; information, management; operations management; programme management; project management; public management; relationship management; strategic management; task management

Management of Projects, The (P. W. G. Morris) 169, 170

Managerial Grid, The (Blake and Mouton) 106

Managers and their Jobs (Stewart) 50–1, 54, 60–1

manufacturing 22–3, 34, 39, 183
  outsourcing 92
  scheduling 67

mapping 99, 326, 327
  see also journey mapping

March, J. G. 82, 86

market ecosystems 290, 301–2

market review 278–9, 279f

Marketing of Industrial Products, The (Wilson) 290–1

markets 30, 97, 121–2, 125, 137, 178, 183, 282, 284, 286, 287, 335
  campaigns 289–90
  discipline 136, 137
  failures 88, 93, 122
  and IT outsourcing 217
  mix, managing 294–5, 300–1
  retail sector 202–3
  segmentation 281
  share 70, 182, 184, 280

Markoczy, Livia 59

Markowitz, H. M. 240

Marks and Spencer (UK) 187, 297–8

Marsh, A. 257

Marsh, D. 261

Martin, J. A. 334, 335

Martin, R. 259

Mason, B. 259

Mason, R. O. 225

Massini, S. 95, 97

Mattson, L.-G. 298

May, E. R. 107

Mayer, M. C. 235f(a), 236, 242, 245, 254

Maylor, H. 175

MDPs (multidisciplinary practices) 152

Meador, L. P. 164

Megaprojects and Risk: An Anatomy of Ambition (Flyberg et al.) 174

Merger and Acquisitions, *see* M&A

Mexico 30, 39

microcomputers 212–13

Microsoft 91
  dispute with EC 38b(2), 39b

Middle East 29

Midler, C. 177

Millar, V. 321

Miller, R. 173, 177

Mills, C. Wright 109

Mills, D. 149

Millward, N. 266

Minford, Patrick 262

Mintzberg, Henry 49, 51, 55, 57, 59, 177, 219

MIS (management information
systems) 211, 212, 223
Mitroff, I. I. 98
MNEs (multinational enterprises)
21–2, 23, 24, 32, 40–1, 46
and civil society 43f
classification 33t
regions 37, 47
role of 28, 32, 46
see also administrative heritage,
MNEs
Mnookin, R. H. 151, 152
mobilizers 42–3
mobile phones 23–4, 224
Model of Industrial Buyer Behavior, A
(Sheth) 291
Modern Firm, The (Roberts) 299
Montagna, P. 149
Moore, K. 324
More Staff Working Differently
(Department of Health, UK)
134
Morgan, G. 88, 90
Morgan, R. M. 297
Morris, P. W. G. 166, 167, 169, 170,
172, 173, 175, 176, 177, 178
Morris, T. 152, 153, 155, 156, 157
Morrison, Perry 75
Motorola 24, 297–8
Motzel, E. 173
Mouton, Jane 107
MPA (Major Projects Association)
164–6, 176–7, 178
MPB (managed professional
business) 152–4
Murray, H. 311
Murray, M. 123
MWB, *see* management, MWB

Nadler, D. 107
Nahapiet, J. 89, 93, 97
Narayandas, N. 297
NASA 164–5
NASDAQ 41

National Minimum Wage (UK) 265
national responsiveness 29, 39
Nature of Managerial Work, The
(Mintzberg) 49, 51
navigational leadership 327–9
Neill, T. 327
Nelson, D. 110, 151
networks 87, 97, 121–2, 125, 137, 140,
290, 294, 295, 298–301
innovations 83, 98
organizations 90–1
New Labour 264–6, 336
and trade unions 265–7
see also Labour Party
New Zealand 28
Newman, J. 136, 137
NGOs (non-governmental
organizations) 42–4
NHS (National Health Service)
(UK) 122, 126, 129, 130, 131,
134, 136
Niskanen, W. 125
Noe, C. F. 247
Nolan, R. L. 226
Nordenflycht, Andrew von 148
normative leadership 106, 107,
108–9
see also adaptive leadership;
leadership
North America 22, 31, 80, 91, 221
MNEs 32, 33, 34, 42
offshoring 37
organizations 81, 82, 88
regional business 38b
NPM (New Public
Management) 128–9, 131, 133,
135–6, 137

occupations 146, 147, 149
OECD (Organization for Economic
Cooperation and
Development) 124, 272
Office of Fair Trading (UK) 238, 239t
offshore assembly platforms 39b

offshoring 39**b**, 65, 75
  see also IT, offshoring
Ohmae, K. 41
Okum, A. M. 299
Olivier, Richard 333, 334
O'Malley, Frank Ward 115
open sourcing 83, 98
open-systems 86, 87
operations management (OM) 271,
    281, 287–8
  in business 286–7
  and management 272–3
  strategic role 273–5, 279, 281, 284–5
    long lists 284
  see also functional strategies
opportunism 88, 238
order-winners 284–6
O'Reilly, C. A. 89, 334
Organisational Buying Behavior (Webster
    and Wind) 291
organizations 50, 66, 92, 94, 95, 97, 107,
    145, 149, 219, 242, 323, 331
  buying behaviour 290, 291, 294,
    295–6, 301
  change 320, 325, 329, 331
  and environment 87–8, 94, 312
  design 72, 82, 86–7, 89, 91–2, 95–8,
    213
  management 99, 219, 274, 329
  not-for-profit 122, 140
  ownership 91, 122
  studies 80–4, 87–95, 98, 99–100
    systems 85, 94
  see also Europe, organizations
organizing 95, 96, 98–9
  for assets 92
  business 93, 99
  within enterprise 81, 84–5
Osborne, S. 131
O'Shea, J. 145
Ouchi, W. 88
Our Health, Our Care, Our Say
    (Department of Health, UK)
    133

outsourcing 70, 91–2, 199, 274
overcapacity 287–8
Oxenbridge, S. 266

Padmore, L. 332
Palay, T. 151
Palepu, K. G. 247
Pannenbäcker, O. 173
partnerships (UK) 135–6, 150–1,
    152–4, 158
  compensation 152
  between employers and employees
    264, 266
  and IT vendors 227
  and management 151, 156
  and ownership 145
  and professionalism 151
  public sector 138
Parvatiyar, A. 297
Pascale, R. T. 331, 335
Pedigo, P. R. 52
performance:
  individual 153
  management 136, 148, 155
  measures 130
  pay awards 127
  standards 130, 148
  targets 130, 136, 148, 152
Periasamy, K. P. 219
Perry, J. 123, 125
person-centred services 133, 139
personnel management 26, 126–7,
    267–8
  see also human resources
    management
Peters, T. 107, 150, 323
Pettigrew, A. M. 89, 95, 97, 327, 337,
    338
Pfeffer, J. 108
Pinnington, A. 152, 153, 155, 156
Pinto, J. 177
PMI (Project Management Institute)
    170, 171, 171**f**, 173
  Body of Knowledge Guide 172

Poland 29
Pollitt, C. 121
Pondy, L. R. 98
POPAI (Point of Purchase
        International) 197
Popper, K. 178
Porras, J. 325, 335
Porter, L. 125
Porter, Michael 26, 27, 28, 29, 90,
        220, 221, 241, 242, 246, 249,
        251, 321
Portugal 184
postmodernism 96
Powell, W. W. 95
power 96, 99, 112
Power, M. 130
Prahalad, C. K. 218, 323
Prenkert, F. 298
primary sector 272–3
private sectors 123, 131, 136
PRP (performance-related pay)
        131
problems 111–13, 115
    see also tame problems; wicked
        problems
    critical 111, 113–14
    and leadership 110–11
    solving 89, 110
    typology 112, 113, 113f
    see also leadership, problem
        solving
procurement 67, 71, 171
production 105
productivity:
    and IT 220
    paradox 70
    UK 259–60
professional expertise 126, 127, 134,
        137, 147
    public suspicion of 133–4
professional service firms, *see* PSFs
professionals (UK) 124, 127, 130–1,
        133, 134, 137, 138, 146–7, 150
    female 158–9

professions 155, 156, 159
    occupations and 146–51, 154
programme management 175, 178–9,
        324
project management 86, 140, 169, 171,
        174–8
    certification 170–1
    contracting 169, 173
    in context 172f, 177
    expenditure 173
    failures 165, 166, 167, 169
    front-end 173, 174–5, 177
    major works 164, 168, 170, 178–9
        definition 168–9; environment
        169; model 168f; sponsors 173
    see also supply chains, project
        management
Project Management Institute, *see* PMI
Prokesh, S. E. 326
promotion 155, 158–9
Pryke, S. 177, 178
PSFs (professional service firms) 40,
        144–5, 148, 152, 159
    archetypes 152–3
    employees 158
    innovation 159–60
    and professions 146–7
    research on 150–1
    'p2' archetype 151–3
public expenditure (UK) 125–6, 128
public management 121–2, 126–7, 136,
        137
public relations 42, 43
public sector 133, 136, 138
    management 121–2, 124, 126–8,
        136–7
    organizations 121, 123, 125, 134–5,
        136–7, 140
    provision 122, 126, 128
public servants 124–5
    USA 125
public-services 140
    delivery 137, 137f
    employees 138–9

Pugh, D. S. 295
purchasing 295–6
PWC 146, 147

qualifiers (Q) 284–6
  order-losing sensitive 284
quality 284
Quinn, J. B. 219

Radio Frequency Identification
    Technology, *see* RFID
Rainey, H. 123
rational leadership 108, 109
rational systems 85, 89, 104, 106
R&D (Research & Development) 28
Ramirez, R. 300, 317
Rayport, J. F. 195
Reawakening Giant (Pettigrew) 327
Rebitzer, J. B. 158
Reckitt and Colman 214
recycling 202
Reed, M. 147
reengineering 90, 107, 323, 325
Regional Multinationals, The
    (Rugman) 32
regional strategies 29, 39
  decision-making 40–1
regionalism 32, 47
  trading agreements 46, 47
  versus multilateral integration 45–6
regulations 89, 136
regulatory standards 45**b**
Reichheld, F. F. 280**t(a)**, 280**t(b)**
relationship management 83, 84, 85,
    86, 89, 91, 92, 94, 95, 97, 98, 290,
    294, 296–8
  buyer-suppliers 296–7
  and organizations 312
    L11 312; L12 312; L21 312;
    L22 312
  and project management 177, 178
relationship marketing 296–8, 299,
    301
resources 87, 107, 335

Resource-Based View of Firm 70, 71,
    92
retail accordion 193, 193**f**
retail sector 185, 198, 295
  branding 185–7, 192, 199
  businesss models 187–8, 190**f(a)**,
    190**f(b)**, 190**f(c)**, 192**t**, 199
  chains 183–4
  formats 184, 188–9, 192
  international 203**f**
  research 182–3
  strategy 185–6, 191, 192, 205
  size 184–5
  technologies 194, 198–9, 201–2
  see also comparative advantage, IT
      for; competitive advantage,
      retail sector; IT, retail sector;
      supply chains, retail sector; UK,
      retail sector
Review of Large Public Procurement in the
    UK, A (HM Treasury) 174
Reynolds, J. 184, 191, 198, 199
RFID (radio frequency identification
    technology) 194, 195, 196, 197
Richardson, G. B. 298
Riddell, M. 107
Ring, P. 123
risk management 73, 139, 148
  conglomerates 239–41
  and project management 173, 174
  reduction 240
Risk-Return Model 241
Rittell, H. 110
Robert, A. 192, 194**f**
Roberts, J. 299, 300
Robinson, P. J. 291
Role of the Manager: What's Really
    Important in Different
    Management Jobs (Kraut et al.)
    51
Rose, T. 152
Rothengatter, W. 174
Rowlinson, M. 107
Ruddle, K. 324, 327, 332, 333, 336

Rugman, Alan M. 23t, 25t, 31t, 33t, 35t, 36t(a), 42f
Rumelt, R. P. 234
Russia 31

SABRE reservation system 64
Saks, M. 138
Salter, M. S. 236, 240–1, 243, 243t
Sampler, Jeff 71, 219, 221, 222, 228
Santos, F. M. 92, 98
SAP 66, 201
Sarnat, M. 240
Sasser, W. E. 280t
Sauer, Chris 70, 196, 219
Sayles, Leonard 57
scenarios 307–9, 310, 310f, 311–17, 333
  and aesthetics 317–18
Scenarios: The Art of Strategic Conversation 310
Schön, D. A. 177
Schwartz, Peter 307
scientific management 85, 104, 105
Scott, Ian A. 222, 223, 229
Scoullar, J. 236
secondary sector 272–3
self-checkout (USA) 195, 198
Selsky, J. 313
Selznick, P. 85, 90
Senge, P. M. 325
service sector 22–3, 34, 273
  companies 40
  delivery 139
  provision 128
  regulations 123
  users 137, 139
Shah, R. H. 297
Shapiro, J. Coyle 125
shareholders:
  capitalism 44, 64–5
  growth 254
  value 70, 242, 251
Sharma, A. 144
Shell 34, 43, 307, 317, 331–2, 334

Shepherd, M. M. 175
Sherer, P. D. 151
Sherman, S. 326
Sheth, J. N. 291, 297
Short, J. E. 219
Shulman, L. E. 323
Sinha, I. 300
Siow, A. 151
Sisson, K. 253, 258, 267
'Six Sigma' 24
Skelcher, C. 129
Sloan, A. P. 242
Slovakia 29
Smigel, E. 150
Smith, N. 139
Smith, T. 243t, 244–5
Smyth, H. J. 177, 178
Snape, S. 135
Snehota, I. 298
social capital 83, 92, 96
  and organizations 93, 97
Social Construction of Reality, The (Berger and Luckman) 109
society 89, 99
Sociological Paradigms and Organisational Analysis (Burrell and Morgan) 88
Soderholm, A. 177
software firms 147, 148
Solow, Robert
South Asia:
  M&A 238
  management behaviour 58–9
South Korea 273
Soviet Union 91
Spain 184
SPAM 75–6
Speh, T. W. 293
Stace, R. 327
Stacey, Ralph 331
stakeholder management 42–3, 93, 174
Stalk, G. 323
Stalker, G. V. 217, 334
Starbuck, W. H. 82

Starkey, K. 338
Stein, B. A. 323
Steinem, G. 107
Sternin, J. 335
Stewart, Rosemary 21, 50, 60, 61
Stiglitz, Joseph 316
Stinchcombe, A. L. 82, 177
stock markets 41, 247
Stoffaes, C. 307
Stogdill, R. M. 106
Stoker, G. 122
Storey, J. 253, 258, 267
strategic alignment question 212,
    218–19
strategic alliances 91
strategic management 26, 40, 123, 152,
    221, 223, 241
*Strategic Management of Large
    Engineering Projects, The* (Miller
    and Lessard) 173
strategies 86, 111, 177, 321
  change in 320
  debate 278, 278f
  IO theories 96
  and markets 287f
subsidiaries 29, 47
Sudarsanam, P. S. 247
Suddaby, R. 152
Sull, D. N. 332
suppliers, and customers 295, 296
supply chains 73, 76, 91, 220
  project management 169, 171, 173
  retail sector 184, 186, 197, 199–200
Surfing the Edge of Chaos (Pascale) 331
Sutton, R. I. 108
Sviokla, J. J. 195
Swaine, R. D. 151
Sweden 291–2
Sykes, Alan 165

tame problems 110, 112, 113
task management 89, 104, 177
  strategic 274, 282–3

Taylor, F. W. 104, 105, 106
Taylor, L. J. 158
Taylor, S. 135
technologies 23–4, 75, 91, 183
  convergence 67
  diffusion 217
  manufacturing 74
  new 248
  retail sector 193–5, 195f, 196, 205
  see also IT
Teece, D. J. 144
tenure 154, 155, 159
Tesco 191, 193, 201, 203–4, 223
Thailand 203–4
Thanheiser, H. P. 235f(a)
Thatcher, Margaret 68, 128, 130
  see also Conservative Party
Third Way, The (Giddens) 264–5, 267
Thomas, J. 175
Tibbs, Hardin 317
Tichy, N. 326
Tocher, Keith 212
top-down 334, 336
Top of Mind (CIES) 204, 205t
TQM (Total Quality Management) 74,
    271
trade:
  conflicts 23
  environment 21
  macro-level growth 22
  sanctions 23
  wars 31–2
  worldwide 22
trade unions 257, 258, 259, 260–1,
    262–5
  reform of (UK) 260, 261–3, 266
    legislation 261, 265
  membership 263–4, 266
  resistance to 266
trading blocs 30, 48
Tranfield, D. 338
transaction cost theory 217
  of organizations 88, 96

transformational change 324, 325, 327–8, 330
  at BP 326**f(b)**
transnational solutions 28–30, 40, 82
triad 23, 28
  regions 30, 33–4, 40
  intra-regional trade 31, 31**t**, 32
  sales 33–4
Trist, E. L. 311, 313, 316, 317
turbulence 311–13, 313**f**, 316, 317, 330**f** 331
Turnbull, P. 268
Turner, C. 295
Tushman, M. L. 89, 107, 334

UK 59, 66, 193, 258, 259, 291, 336
  conglomerates 236, 243, 245, 251–2, 252**f**, 253
    diversification 235**f(a)**, 238; divestment strategy 247; private equity 251
  economy 67–9, 125, 129
  government, role of 129, 130
  HM Treasury 174–5
  IT 218–19
  law firms 152–3
  leadership 332–3
  M&A 234, 236, 237–8, 247**t(b)**
  PRP (performance-related pay) 131
  public sector organizations 122, 128, 160
    public expenditure 124; public policy 129
  retail sector 184, 185, 197, 198, 201–2
  see also incomes policy; industrial relations, UK; NHS
Undy, R. 259, 261, 262, 264, 266
up-or-out practice 151–3, 158
USA 22, 23, 24, 26, 30, 33, 34, 44, 59, 183, 258, 291
  conglomerates 236, 245, 246, 252
  economic warfare 39**t**
  management 52, 60, 90

M&A 234, 236, 237, 238
offshoring 39**b**–40**b**
organizations 83, 86
retail sector 184, 192, 193, 195, 202
scenarios 307
triad markets 38**b(2)**

Valikangas, L. 335
value chains 40, 182, 183, 194–5, 199, 203, 220, 321
value creation 83–4, 93, 178, 290, 294, 299, 300–2
  and IT 219–20, 222
'values-driven' concept 43, 300
van Waterschoot, W. 294
Vegurie, S. P. 250
Venezuela 313, 316
Venkatraman, N. 195, 226
venture capital funding 159–60, 249
Verbeke, Alain 40
Vidler, E. 139
Vitale, M. 215
Vivian, P. 218
Vodafone 237–8
Volmer, H. 149
voluntarism 261, 262, 267
vu jàdé, see leadership

Wack, P. 307, 311, 317
Wal-Mart 184–5, 193
Walker, R. 126, 130
Waller, M. 237**t**
Wallin, J. 300
Walters, D. W. 182
Waterman, R. 107, 150, 323
Watson, Tony 57
Ways Forward, The (Stewart) 50
wealth creation 186**f**, 188**f**
Webber, M. 110
Weber, Max 82, 84, 109
Webster, F. E. 291
Weick, K. 94, 110
Weinhold, M. A. 240–1, 243, 243**t**

Weisbach, M. N. 247t
welfare state 135
  UK 125, 127–8
Westmarland, L. 139
Weston, J. F. 247
Whale, M. 186
wheel of retailing 192, 192f, 193
Whipp, R. 176, 327
Whitaker, B. 107
Whitfield, D. 129
Whitney, D. 111
Whittington, R. 93, 235f(a), 236, 242,
    245, 253
Whorton, J. 123
wicked problems 110, 112, 113, 114,
    115, 318
Wilensky, H. 149
Wiley Guide to Managing Projects, The
    (Morris and Pinto) 177
Willcocks, Leslie 70, 71, 217, 218, 219,
    227
Williamson, Oliver 88, 217, 242
Wilson, A. 290, 291
Wilson-Jeanselme, M. 198
win-win solutions 297
Winch, G. 176, 177
Wind, Y. 291
Wood, M. 160

Woodruff, R. B. 300
work:
  measurement 105
  new ways of 139
  procedures 135
work/life balance 158
workers 138
  and economic rationalism 105
  as a resource 258
  rewards 105
*Workplace Employment Relations Survey
    1998* (UK) 130
World Bank 164
world trade 23t, 31
World Wide Web 67, 224
WorldCom 93
Worren, N. A. M. 324
Worthley, J. 123
Wrigley, C. 260
WTO (World Trade Organisation) 21,
    23, 41, 43, 45

yen 41
Yeo, K. T. 176
Yukl, G. A. 107

Zaleznik, A. 110
Zeithaml, V. A. 300